D0939014

Mirror up to Shakespeare

Essays in Honour of G.R. Hibbard

George Hibbard has always endorsed T.S. Eliot's idea that 'we must know all of Shakespeare's work in order to know any of it,' and this idea, implicit in the first essay in this volume, informs the whole collection, written in honour of one of Canada's leading Shakespearian editors and scholars.

The two essays which begin the collection present broad overviews of Elizabethan drama and discuss Shakespeare's first great editor, Theobald. Together with the final essay – on publication and performance in early Stuart drama – these form the frame of the mirror held up to Shakespeare in the other eighteen essays, whether they treat of general themes running through some or all of Shakespeare's plays or the plays of his contemporaries, or whether they treat of specific plays. There is an especially rich concentration on *Macbeth* and *Coriolanus.*

J.C. GRAY is a member of the Department of English, University of Waterloo.

Mirror up to Shakespeare

Essays in Honour of G.R. Hibbard

edited by J.C. GRAY

UNIVERSITY OF TORONTO PRESS
Toronto Buffalo London

© University of Toronto Press 1984
Toronto Buffalo London
Printed in Canada
ISBN 0-8020-5639-3

Canadian Cataloguing in Publication Data

Main entry under title:
Mirror up to Shakespeare: essays in honour of
G.R. Hibbard

ISBN 0-8020-5639-3

1. Shakespeare, William, 1564-1616 – Criticism and interpretation – Addresses, essays, lectures.
2. Hibbard, G.R., 1915- I. Gray, J.C. (Jack Cooper), 1928-
II. Hibbard, G.R. 1915-

PR2976.M67 1984 822.3'3 C83-099114-X

Publication of this book has been made possible by grants from the Canadian Federation for the Humanities, using funds provided by the Social Sciences and Humanities Research Council of Canada, from the Department of English, University of Waterloo, and from the Publications Fund of University of Toronto Press.

PR
2976
.M54
1984

Contents

11969570

Preface

Scholar, critic, teacher – G.R. Hibbard has long insisted that Shakespeare is his own best critic. When students ask for readings to help them with a play of Shakespeare, Professor Hibbard has always recommended – first – the other plays of Shakespeare. In this, Professor Hibbard endorses T.S. Eliot's idea (expressed at the beginning of his 1932 essay on John Ford and quoted by Professor Hibbard in his essay '*Henry IV* and *Hamlet*') that 'we must know all of Shakespeare's work in order to know any of it.' Kenneth Muir, appropriately enough, picks up the idea in the essay that leads off this collection, whose general purpose is to illustrate precisely the point that Shakespeare is his own best critic and that one must know the shape of the whole if one is to know the full meaning of the parts. For all his variety and the 100,000 lines that comprise his dramas, Shakespeare is of a piece. 'No other dramatist of the time,' says T.S. Eliot in the John Ford essay, 'approaches anywhere near to this perfection of pattern ...'

In the years that Professor Hibbard has been at Waterloo, he has become widely known for the summer conferences he has mounted on the Elizabethan theatre. Their high reputation is directly attributable to Professor Hibbard, who presides over them with great warmth and a remarkable breadth of scholarship. Professor Hibbard is, as one of his admirers has asserted, 'perhaps the ultimate seminar leader, wonderfully combining rigour with gentleness and good humour.' In addition, his reputation as an editor of Shakespeare is widely acknowledged. Several essays in this volume attest to the influence of his New Penguin edition of *Coriolanus,* to cite just one example. That he has been asked to edit the New Oxford edition of *Hamlet* attests to his learning and good sense.

The essays that begin the collection take broad overviews of the drama of the period and of Shakespeare's first great editor. Together with the final essay, they form the frame of the mirror that is held up to Shakespeare by the other eighteen essays, both those treating general matters that run through many of the plays and those treating specific plays. There is a rich concentration of attention on *Macbeth* and *Coriolanus.*

In every instance, plays that Professor Hibbard has edited are cited in the essays. Otherwise, different editions of Shakespeare are used, a condition that is a consequence of scholars contributing from Canada as well as from the United Kingdom and the United States.

The generosity of the Department of English at the University of Waterloo made it possible to enter these essays into the computer, thereby greatly facilitating the tasks of assembling and editing the text, of communicating with the contributors, and of automatic photo-typesetting. Additional funds from the Vice-President (Academic) helped to complete the project. The photo-typesetting could not have been accomplished were it not for the lucid directions that Mr Bruce Uttley of the Department of Computing Services gave to the editor, who made countless demands on his time. In addition Mrs Grace Logan and Mr Walter McCutchan of the Arts Computing Office were of invaluable assistance in working out several problems in computerizing the text. A grant from the University of Waterloo's Research Grant Subcommittee made possible the editing and preparation of the preliminary manuscript. Mrs Diana Swart cheerfully and enthusiastically assisted the editor in entering the essays into computer files.

The late Professor J.M. Nosworthy was most helpful in suggesting contributors for the volume. Although he died before he could submit his essay, James Bulman, his literary executor, obtained a draft of an essay that Professor Nosworthy was to have delivered in Toronto. Professor Bulman undertook the task of editing the paper and checking references so that it could be presented in this volume. My special thanks to Professor Bulman.

Of immense value was the counsel and advice given by my colleague, Professor C.E. McGee of the University of St Jerome's College. Professor McGee helped in the verifying of innumerable details. Professor Geoffrey Bullough died suddenly before he was able to check the final version of his essay; once again Professor McGee generously offered to assist.

J.C. GRAY
University of Waterloo

MIRROR UP TO SHAKESPEARE

KENNETH MUIR

T.S. Eliot's Criticism of Elizabethan Drama

A great poet's criticism is always valuable, however much of it is designed to defend his own practice. Wordsworth's preface to the *Lyrical Ballads,* for example, although obviously unjust to eighteenth-century poets, was a necessary apologia for his own style of poetry. Eliot, although he never wrote a preface to his own poems, defended them indirectly in much of his criticism. It was necessary for him to establish the superiority of the metaphysicals to the poets of the nineteenth century and to tumble Milton from his pedestal if his own verse was to find acceptance. Eliot, moreover, was interested in reviving poetic drama, while realizing that it was necessary to escape from the influence of Shakespeare, an influence which had frustrated the efforts of so many poets of the previous century. One has only to think of the poets of the Romantic period with their closet dramas – *Remorse, The Borderers, Cain, The Cenci, Otho the Great* – and the plays of Tennyson, Browning, Swinburne, Bridges, and Stephen Philips, to realize the baleful effects of Shakespeare's greatness. It is significant that the only lines quoted in 'Tradition and the Individual Talent' (1917), the earliest of the *Selected Essays,* are the famous ones from *The Revenger's Tragedy,* the cadences of which were echoed in Eliot's own poetry. In the following year he attacked Gilbert Murray's translations of Euripides, not merely because he turned Greek lyric into 'the fluid haze of Swinburne' but also because they served as a bad model for anyone wishing to revive poetic drama.

'A Dialogue on Dramatic Poetry,' which belongs to the same period as *Sweeney Agonistes*, purports to be a conversation among seven men, who are given letters, not names, and who are not properly differentiated, as Dryden's brilliantly are. Indeed, all the seven seem to express Eliot's own views or at least dramatic exaggerations of his actual opinions. It is said that plays should do more than amuse; that the moral attitude of *Mr. Limberham* is impeccable; that ballet is valuable because it concerns itself with permanent form; that the perfect and ideal drama is to be found in the ceremony of the Mass; that if we want to get at the permanent and universal we tend to express ourselves in verse; that the poet in Shaw was stillborn; that Shakespeare's plays are not morally edifying; that we must find a new form of verse which will be as satisfactory a vehicle for us as blank verse was for the Elizabethans; that the unities of place and time will be found highly desirable for the drama of the future; and 'I am a member of the Labour Pary.' Of these ten remarks, spoken by five characters, only the last seems not to be Eliot's; and even this is in the context of praise of Ernie Lotinga and is directly comparable to Eliot's eulogy of Marie Lloyd, written five years before. The ostensible purpose of the dialogue was to discuss the possibility of modern poetic drama. Now in 1928 there were a number of active poetic dramatists – Yeats, Bottomley, Binyon, Masefield – and that Eliot does not mention any one of them is an indication that he regarded their work as largely irrelevant to the future of poetic drama.[1]

It should be mentioned that when Eliot began to write on Elizabethan drama the two most influential books were probably Bradley's *Shakespearean Tragedy* and Dowden's *Shakspere: A Critical Study of his Mind and Art*, in which he attempted to relate Shakespeare's tragic period ('In the depths') to events in his life. Those critics who rebelled against Bradley and Dowden and reacted against the praise by Lamb and Swinburne of Elizabethan drama either treated the poetry of the plays as irrelevant to the dramatic effect (Archer), or exposed the apparent inconsistencies in Shakespeare's characterization (Stoll) or his primitive technique (Schücking), or blamed his defects on his incor-

1 It is significant that the best plays of Masefield and even of Yeats are written in prose and, indeed, that a better 'poetic' dramatist than either, Synge, wrote wholly in prose. In a later essay, 'Poetry and Drama,' Eliot spoke enthusiastically of the verse of *Purgatory*, which, he said, had put all later poets in Yeats's debt.

poration of material from source plays (Robertson).

Eliot's central position on Elizabethan drama is to be found in 'Four Elizabethan Dramatists,' a preface to a book he never wrote. The dramatists are Webster, Tourneur, Middleton, and Chapman, none of them precisely Elizabethan. In this essay he points out that one should not approach these dramatists by way of Lamb's *Specimens,* nor through Archer's *The Old Drama and the New.* Lamb separated the poetry from the theatre – he could hardly have done anything else at the beginning of the nineteenth century; and Archer deplored poetry as irrelevant to drama. Yet Eliot was more under the influence of Lamb and Archer than he was aware. He laments the 'impure art' of the dramatists, including Shakespeare's. He suggests that only in *Everyman* was English drama free from the foolish pursuit of realism. 'The weakness of Elizabethan drama,' he asserts, 'is not its defect of realism, but its attempt at realism, not its conventions, but its lack of conventions.' To this one can only say that all the better dramatists attempted not realism but merely to arouse in the audience the illusion of realism; and that they all used conventions, as Professor M.C. Bradbrook demonstrated in her first two books. When Eliot goes on to say that Henry Arthur Jones and Shakespeare are 'essentially of the same type' and that both are 'to be read rather than seen,' he is surely mistaken: the life of Jones's plays is in the theatre and only in the theatre, and all the Elizabethan dramatists relied on the collaboration of the players to realize their intentions.

The 'general philosophy of life' to be found in Shakespeare and his contemporaries is summarized by Santayana (with Eliot's approval in this essay) in the statement that 'Duncan is in his grave.' As a summary of the philosophical position of any of the seven or eight major dramatists of the period it is as manifestly inept as only a bad epigram can be. Nor can it be said that Webster is 'a great literary and dramatic genius directed toward chaos.' Here, as elsewhere, Eliot confused the views of characters in a play with those of the author. The same confusion is apparent in another essay when he subscribes to Cunliffe's observation on the hopeless fatalism of *King Lear* as evidenced not, as one might suppose, by Kent's 'it is the stars' but by Gloucester's words: 'As flies to wanton boys are we to the gods: / They kill us for their sport.' This is an appropriate exclamation of a superstitious old man who is suffering both mental and physical agony; but we should remember that not popular audience. Daniel, Greville, and the others, however attractive they sometimes are, are essentially undramatic. One has the feeling that Eliot believed that if only the greater Elizabethans had followed Sidney's precepts, they might have created a classical drama as impressive as that of Corneille or Racine instead of the impure art which was all they could achieve. Many readers of this essay, with its enthusiastic praise of the Jasper Heywood translations, have been disappointed (as I myself was when I bought the volumes); and even the passages Eliot quotes are not to some ears as good as he pretends. The charming lines from *Hercules Furens,* described by Eliot as 'perfect' and 'of singular beauty,' are marred by the awkward syntax of the first three lines:

> Goe hurtles soules, whom mischiefe hath opprest
> Even in first porch of life but lately had,
> And fathers fury goe unhappy kind
> O little children, by the way ful sad
> Of journey knowen.
> Goe see the angry kynges.

As for the other essay in which Eliot argues that Shakespearian tragedy was influenced by the Stoicism of Seneca – although Possum-like he admits that he does not believe his own thesis – this is flawed by his reluctance to recognize 'that Shakespeare's ethic is Christian, and Seneca's is not.'[7] G.K. Hunter is right to emphasize the central importance of this distinction.

In Eliot's essay on *Hamlet,* which contains the notorious comment that the play was 'certainly an artistic failure,' Eliot refers to books by J.M. Robertson and Edgar Elmer Stoll. He was plainly influenced by Robertson's disintegrating attempts and by Stoll's attacks on Shakespeare's artistic integrity. It was probably from Robertson that he got the idea that the dialogues between Polonius and Laertes and Polonius and Reynaldo were inexcusable, and certainly from Robertson that he took the idea that 'the essential emotion of the play is the feeling of a son towards a guilty mother.' This is a gratuitous assumption; and even if it were true, Hamlet's emotion is not 'in excess of the facts as they appear.' After all, Gertrude is certainly an adulteress and possibly an accomplice in the murder of her husband. Eliot's

7 Ibid, p 179

criticism of the play is based on the assumption that Shakespeare 'could not drag to light, contemplate, or manipulate into art' some 'stuff' from his own experience. 'Under compulsion of what experience he attempted to express the inexpressibly horrible, we shall never know.' We shall never even know if there is any foundation for this theory; but it fits in with Eliot's belief[8] that Shakespeare

> was occupied with the struggle – which alone constitutes life for a poet – to transmute his personal and private agonies into something rich and strange, something universal and impersonal.

In *Hamlet,* Eliot thought, Shakespeare had failed to achieve this. No doubt Eliot himself had been occupied with such a struggle when he wrote *The Waste Land,* but that poem was designed to express such a struggle, whereas the emotions of *Hamlet* are largely evoked by the tale which Shakespeare inherited. Whether *Ur-Hamlet* was Kyd's or another's, the murder of Hamlet's father and the marriage of his mother to the murderer were the basic materials with which Shakespeare had to deal. Any dramatist would have been bound to concern himself with the reaction of the son to the mother's guilt – and he had no need of Freud to suggest to him how the subject might be treated.

It may be, as G.K. Hunter suggested,[9] that Eliot was trying to create a symbolist Shakespeare and that this fact accounts for his dissatisfaction with *Hamlet.* By 1930, when he wrote a preface to G. Wilson Knight's *The Wheel of Fire,* Eliot had modified his position and he was speaking of the figure in the carpet, 'the sense of a unifying pattern below the level of explicit statement.'[10] In 1950, in his lecture on 'Poetry and Drama' Eliot gave an admirable analysis of the first scene of *Hamlet,* and, chastened perhaps by his own experience of dramatic writing, he no longer regarded that play as an artistic failure. There are two fine unpublished lectures on the plays of the final period, and scattered through his essays there are many perceptive remarks about Shakespeare, including three pages in 'The Music of Poetry.' As Hunter wittily suggests, Eliot 'virtually invented the twentieth-century Shakespeare in a collection of asides.'[11] We

8 Cited by F.O. Matthiessen in *The Achievement of T.S. Eliot* New York 1959, p 102
9 *Dramatic Identities* p 286ff
10 *The Wheel of Fire* introduction
11 *Dramatic Identities* p 299

may instance the preface to *The Wheel of Fire,* five or six remarks in the Dante essay, or a passage in the essay on John Ford, questionable as it is:

> The whole of Shakespeare's work is *one* poem; and it is the poetry of it in this sense, not the poetry of isolated lines and passages or the poetry of single figures which he created, that matter most.

He had come to realize the qualities which a good critic of Shakespeare should possess. He outlined them in his introduction to Henri Fluchère's *Shakespeare* (1933): The ideal Shakespeare critic should be a scholar, with knowledge not of Shakespeare in isolation but of Shakespeare in relation to the Elizabethan theatre ... and of that theatre in relation to the social, political, economic, and religious conditions of its time. He should also be a poet; and he should be a 'man of the theatre.' And he should also have a philosophic mind.

In a later introduction, to S.L. Bethell's *Shakespeare and the Popular Dramatic Tradition* (1944), Eliot recognizes the importance of performance:

> The constant reader of Shakespeare should be also, to the best of his opportunities the constant theatre-goer, for any play of Shakespeare requires to be seen and heard, as well as read, many times; and seen and heard in as many different productions as possible.

He also recognizes more clearly than before the nature of poetic drama:

> A verse play is not a play done into verse, but a different kind of play: in a way more realistic than 'naturalistic drama,' because, instead of clothing nature in poetry, it should remove the surface of things, expose the underneath, or the inside of the natural surface experience. It may allow the characters to behave inconsistently, but only with respect to a deeper consistency. It may use any device to show their real feelings and volitions, instead of just what, in actual life, they would normally profess or be conscious of; it must reveal, underneath the vacillating or infirm character, the indomitable unconscious will; and underneath the resolute purpose of the planning animal, the victim of circumstance and the doomed or sanctified being.

The best of Eliot's essays on Shakespeare's contemporaries contain striking insights and what seem now to be curious faults of emphasis and even misunderstandings. The Marlowe essay, for example, makes the point, original in its time (1918), that *The Jew of Malta* is a farce rather than a tragedy; but he says little about *Doctor Faustus* and nothing at all about *Edward II* and *Hero and Leander*, arguably Marlowe's masterpiece. He seems, moreover, to imply that *Dido* was written at the end of Marlowe's life.

The essay on Middleton is one of the most persuasive. To it we owe the generally accepted view of *The Changeling* that 'in the moral essence of tragedy it is safe to say that ... Middleton is surpassed by one Elizabethan alone.' Nothing could be better than Eliot's account of Beatrice's development:

> she becomes moral only by becoming damned ... But what consititutes the essence of the tragedy is something which has not been sufficiently remarked; it is the *habituation* of Beatrice to her sin; it becomes no longer merely sin but custom ... The tragedy of Beatrice is not that she has lost Alsemero ... it is that she has won De Flores.

Nevertheless we may feel that by concentrating on a single character Eliot ignores the tragedy of De Flores, the whole of the underplot, and Middleton's collaboration with Rowley. The danger of concentrating on a single character is again apparent in Eliot's remarks on *The Roaring Girl*, and it becomes more serious in his perfunctory treatment of *Women Beware Women*, in which his interest is centred on Bianca. He declares that she 'is a type of woman who is purely moved by vanity.' This ignores her original love for her husband, for whom she embraces comparative poverty, and her genuine resistance to the Duke. Even stranger is the fact that Eliot makes no mention of Isabella, and strangest of all that he does not even mention the central character of the play, Livia, who brings about the downfall and damnation of the other two women.

Eliot recognizes that Middleton is 'in flashes' a great poet, a master of versification. He quotes Beatrice's final speech – with the old Mermaid misprint – as an example. He had previously imitated its rhythms in 'Gerontion.'[12] He says little about the city comedies and does not mention *A Chaste Maid in Cheapside* or that masterly study of hypocrisy, *More Dissemblers Besides*

12 *Collected Poems* 1963, p 41

Women. When he declares that Middleton had no message, that he was merely a recorder, it is difficult to agree. From *The Wisdom of Solomon Paraphrased,* written at the age of seventeen, to *A Game at Chess* Middleton was consistently didactic. In his lightest comedies and in his gloomiest tragedies he analyses the corruption of society from a Calvinistic viewpoint. Allwit is funny, but damned; Dampit is damned, and the humour of the scenes in which he appears is black indeed. The Cardinal, who points the moral in *Women Beware Women,* is not an irrelevant intruder, as George Hibbard used to argue. If Middleton's young prodigals and harlots arouse our sympathy and are let off lightly at the end of the plays, it is because they are less wicked than the people they cheat. So Eliot's idea of Middleton's impersonality and facelessness cannot be substantiated; and this opinion is the more surprising when juxtaposed with the statement that 'Chapman has become a breezy British character as firm as Nelson or Wellington.' Was Eliot thinking of the author of *Bussy D'Ambois,* or of the Rival Poet of Sonnets, or of the translator of Homer? Perhaps he was recalling Keats's epithets for Chapman, 'loud and bold.' In any case, 'breezy' is the last epithet to apply to Chapman.

The essays on Heywood, Tourneur, Massinger, and Marston were reviews, but none the worse for that. The Tourneur essay contains Eliot's finest account of the verse of *The Revenger's Tragedy.* The essay on Massinger has some good pages on his indebtedness to Shakespeare (based on Cruickshank's book) and some excellent appreciation of the masterly structure of his blank verse, marred only by a characteristic hit at Milton's. The Marston essay is noteworthy for the curious judgment that *Sophonisba* was his masterpiece.

Eliot was probably right to suggest that *Perkin Warbeck* and *The Broken Heart* were Ford's best plays and that his greatest quality was his ability 'to manipulate sequences of words in blank verse in a manner which is quite his own.' We may feel that his characterization of Giovanni as 'almost a monster of egotism' and of Annabella as 'virtually a moral defective' is less than just. A more serious flaw in the essay is the use of the plays of Shakespeare's last period as a means of condemning *The Lover's Melancholy.* To say that Ford uses the recognition scene 'on a level hardly higher than that of the device of twins in comedy,' that he 'had no conception of what Shakespeare was trying to do' in the recognition scene in *Pericles,* and that Ford's scene is 'poetry and drama of the surface' underestimates Ford's understanding of Shakespeare.

In his early criticism Eliot had been too much influenced by the disintegrators, who now seem aberrant, and by Archer's attack on drama written before Pinero. He had complained that the dramatists were trying to be realistic, yet at the same time he criticized them for departing from colloquial speech. He complained of the lack of recognizable conventions at the very time when Muriel Bradbrook was analysing them. He objected to Lamb's method of anthologizing scenes and speeches while ignoring their contexts; and yet one is bound to remember his own quotations of passages he admired and imitated rather than his discussion of the dramatic qualities of the plays. He treated the plays as literature and preferred reading them to seeing them performed. He did, however, lend his approval to productions at the Old Vic; and he once wrote a letter to *The Times*, commending Charles Laughton's performance as Angelo, even though to some of us this was an object lesson in how not to speak Shakespeare's verse.

By 1930, stimulated by his own ambitions as a dramatist, Eliot came to respond more warmly to Shakespeare's plays. He says less about Shakespeare's failing as a purveyor of philosophical commonplaces and more about the impressiveness of his total *oeuvre*, in which each play illuminates the whole and the whole illuminates each play. In particular – perhaps influenced in this by Knight's *Myth and Miracle* and his unpublished *Marina*, which was going the rounds of publishers[13] – Eliot had arrived at a new appreciation of the final plays. Yet his criticism, stimulating as it often is, is not concerned with the theatre; and in this lack of concern, surprising in a dramatist, he has been followed by the best of the *Scrutiny* critics, Leavis, Knights, and Traversi.[14] That is why, when the history of twentieth-century criticism comes to be written objectively, it will be found that the writings of Muriel Bradbrook have ultimately contributed more than Eliot's to our understanding of Elizabethan drama. She has always been concerned with the poets as play-

13 See Knight's essay in *Neglected Powers* 1971, p 384.

14 See the revealing passage by Knights in 'How Many Children Had Lady Macbeth?' 'How should we read Shakespeare? We start with so many lines of verse on a printed page which we read as we should read any other poem.' In fact we start with an actor on a stage speaking lines to another actor.

wrights, with their relationship with the theatres and the audience – a relationship which may have caused their art to be 'impure' but which was the condition of greatness.

It may be suggested, finally, that the limitations of Eliot's criticism of Elizabethan drama contributed to the comparative weakness of his own plays. His fear of rhetoric was such that he hoped his audiences would not recognize that his plays were written in verse. In the last and weakest of the plays, *The Elder Statesman,* he eliminated after the first performance most of the lines and images which might be recognized as 'poetical.'[15] There are two further ironies. In all Eliot's plays apart from *Sweeney Agonistes* there are many embarrassing moments, and most of these are due to his uncertainty about conventions. When the knights in *Murder in the Cathedral* drop into Shavian pastiche, when the uncles and aunts in *The Family Reunion* start declaiming as a chorus, when the guardians in *The Cocktail Party* sometimes talk like Noel Coward characters, we are hustled from one convention to another. The other irony is that Eliot tried hard to be more and more naturalistic, so that in his last two plays we are not far away from the style of drawing-room comedy and even farce. Eliot's development was similar to the one he deplored in Elizabethan and Jacobean drama.

Liverpool

15 Matthiessen quotes from an unpublished letter of Eliot's (1933): 'to write poetry which should be essentially poetry, with nothing poetic about it ... poetry so transparent that in reading it we are intent on what the poem *points at,* and not on the poetry.' It may be added that Eliot transferred speeches in the last scene of *The Elder Statesman* from a male to a female character and vice-versa. Denis Donoghue, in *The Third Voice* (Princeton 1959), is much kinder to the play.

GEOFFREY BULLOUGH

Theobald on Shakespeare's Sources

Lewis Theobald (1688-1744), the first great editor of Shakespeare, was a good classical scholar who in his twenties had translated Sophocles' *Electra* (1714), *Ajax* (1714), and *Oedipus Rex* (1715) before turning his attention to Shakespeare in four of the papers he contributed as 'The Censor' to *Mist's Journal* in 1715 and 1717. In the first two of these (numbers 7 and 10) he criticized *King Lear,* providing in number 7 'an Abstract of the real Story of this *Tragedy* as it stands in our Old British History' and in number 1 setting out 'to shew how the Poet by natural Incidents has heightened the Distress of the History, wherein he has kept the Tenor of it, and how artfully preserv'd the *Character* and *Manners* of *Lear* throughout his Tragedy.' Shakespeare's debt to the chronicles (unspecified) is described in general terms. But the catastrophe has been changed – with the imprisonment of Lear and Cordelia and the hanging of the latter; and Lear 'breaks his Heart with the Affliction of it.' Theobald saw 'two practical Morals' in the story, 'against Rash and Unwary Bounty' and against the ingratitude of children. To increase the distress the poet introduced Kent and Gloucester, the latter blinded 'by the Command of the two Savage Sisters.' Theobald was greatly moved by the pathos of the storm scenes and by 'the Charms of the Sentiment and Diction' throughout the play. He did not know the old *Leir.*

His close study of Shakespeare's text and its interpretation did not, however, take public form until he was impelled, by the incompetence of Pope's edition, to produce his *SHAKESPEARE RESTORED; OR, A Specimen of the MANY ERRORS,* As well Committed, or Unamended, by *Mr. POPE IN HIS LATE EDITION of this POET. Designed not only to correct the said Edition, but to restore the True READING OF SHAKESPEARE in all the Editions ever yet publish'd* (1726). Theobald was obviously pleased to show, albeit with superficial courtesy, that Pope had done his work badly, had made only perfunctory reference to the older edition, had no principles of textual emendation save caprice, had not used similar passages in other plays to illuminate obscurity, and showed no acquaintance with Elizabethan culture and beliefs. The body of Theobald's book dealt with *Hamlet,* but in an appendix passages from many of the other plays were discussed, with improved readings or interpretations.

As a working dramatist and friend of the theatre manager Rich, Theobald was interested in theatrical history; so, for the visit of the players in *Hamlet,* II.6, he drew on some knowledge of the Children of the Chapel Royal, 'who were in great Estimation at that Time of day, and outrival'd the Gentlemen of the *Profession.*' He was already exploring Elizabethan social life and was able to emend Pope's – and older editions' – 'Headborough' to 'thirdborough' in *Taming of the Shrew,* induction i.12. He brought to bear an alertness to parallel passages in other plays which supported his corrections and conjectures. At this time his knowledge of earlier writers was limited; for example, in 1726 he went to 'the corrected editions' of *Dares Phrygius* for the names of the six gates of Troy in *Troilus and Cressida* (prologue 16-17), suggesting 'Dardania, Thymbria, Ilia, Scaea, Troia, and Antenidores.' By 1728 he knew Wynkyn de Worde's 1503 edition of *The Three Destructions of Troy* (*The recuyles ... of the historyes of Troye*). He noted Shakespeare's love of the Troy story:

> ... there is scarce a Play throughout all his Works, in which it was possible to introduce the Mention of them, where he has not by *Simile, Allusion,* or otherwise, hinted at the *Trojan* affairs; so fond was he of that Story.
>
> (*Shakespeare Restored* pages 72-3)

Shakespeare's knowledge of Plutarch enabled Theobald to correct Pope on many occasions. For example, in 2 *Henry VI,* IV.i.136, he substituted 'Brutus bastard hand' for Pope's 'Brutus dastard hand' and translated what Plutarch wrote about Caesar's 'tenderness to Servilia, the mother of Brutus' (pages 80-1). As yet he did not know North's translation. His reading of Plutarch and Athenaeus helped Theobald to emend Pope's 'From *Peregenia* whom he ravish'd' (*Midsummer Night's Dream* II.i.78) with reference to a 'minute circumstance in the Story of *Theseus*' telling of Perigouna, 'the Name of a famous Lady by whom *Theseus* had his son *Melanippus*.'

He accused Pope of 'the like Carelessness in a Point of English History.' As he says elsewhere, 'Having an Eye to History ... would easily have discover'd an Error in the Copies here.' Shakespeare had read the Chronicles, so he knew that the name of the 'blind' impostor in *2 Henry VI* II.i was Simpcox, not Simon. Other names taken by the dramatist from the Chronicles were Sir Thomas Erpingham in *Henry V* (not Sir John) and Nicholas Hopkins in *Henry VIII*.

Already Theobald was aware of the many anachronisms in Shakespeare's dramas which might support critics who denied the playwright any book-learning. He regarded them with a kindly eye as 'Liberties taken knowingly by the Poet and not Absurdities flowing from his Ignorance,' but he gave many examples, to be repeated in his 1733 edition, such as Hector's reference to Aristotle ('at least 800 Years subsequent in Time to Hector') in *Troilus and Cressida*, II.i.167[1]; Pandarus's allusion to 'Winchester goose' (*Troilus and Cressida* V.x.55); Menenius's to Galen (*Coriolanus* II.i.130); Edgar's to the Curfew (*Lear* III.iv.113); references to cannon in *King John* and to Machiavelli in *1 Henry VI* and *3 Henry VI*. Theobald suggested that Shakespeare 'may be presum'd to sneer at his own Licentiousness in these Points' when the Fool in *Lear* makes a prophecy of which he says, 'This Prophecy Merlin shall make, for I do live before his time' (*Lear* III.ii.95). The most brilliant of Theobald's emendations here was for *Henry V*, II.iii.18ff, Dame Quickly's description of Falstaff's death: 'His Nose was as sharp as a Pen, and a'babled of green Fields.'

Theobald had come to believe that in textual matters 'Shakespeare's Case has in great Measure resembled That of a corrupt Classic; and consequently the Method of Cure was likewise to bear a Resemblance.' He set out, as he declared in *Remarks* (page 193), to apply Bentley's methods with the classics to Shakespeare and to produce 'the first Essay of Literal

1 As Theobald pointed out, Pope 'to shelter our Author from such an Absurdity ... has expung'd the Name of ARISTOTLE and substitued in its place *graver Sages*.'

Criticism upon any Author in the English Tongue.' In order to give a 'True Reading' and to interpret correctly, all kinds of studies must be brought to bear, including a consideration of narrative and dramatic sources, the language of the time, historical facts, fables, mythology, current ideas and superstitions, politics, and religion. The notes would involve

> explaining Passages where the Wit or Satire depends on an obscure Point of History; others where Allusions are to Divinity, Philosophy, or other Branches of Science. Some are added to shew where there is a suspicion of our Author having borrowed from the Antients ...

Accordingly, Theobald embarked on a strenuous course of reading:

> let it suffice to say, that to clear up several Errors in the Historical Plays, I purposely read over *Hall* and *Holingshead*'s Chronicles in the Reigns concern'd; all the Novels in *Italian*, from which our Author had borrow'd any of his Plots, such Parts of *Plutarch* from which he had deriv'd any Parts of his *Greek* or *Roman* Story: *Chaucer* and *Spenser*'s Works; all the Plays of *B. Jonson, Beaumont* and *Fletcher*, and above 800 old *English* Plays to ascertain the obsolete and uncommon Phrases in him ... (preface 1733, I.lxvii-viii)

As we shall see, this list by no means covers the full scope of Theobald's editorial reading; but considering the large number of plays, it is remarkable how few in fact he cited in his notes.

Such was the idea of scholarship and inquiry into Shakespeare's background on which Theobald constructed the edition of Shakespeare, which was not published until 1733 although it was largely ready by 1731. He was always adding to his knowledge and acquiring old books. Through the antiquary Martin Folkes he got a First Folio which rectified the opinion he expressed in *Remarks* that the Second Folio was the best. Coxeter helped him to acquire quartos of early plays. But he could not find Ascham's *Toxophilus*, and he never saw Thomas Lodge's *Rosalind*, which he continued to think was a collection of poems to Lodge's mistress. But he was able to point out, in a letter to *Mist's Journal* (16 March 1728) that the 'dreadful Sagittary' in *Troilus* (V.v.14) came from *The Three Destructions of Troy* (Caxton's *The recuyles ... of the historyes of Troye*), which he had seen in Wynkyn de Worde's edition of 1503.

Theobald's correspondence with his friend William Warburton,[2] then an obscure parish priest near Newark, shows him working steadily through the plays between 1729 and 1731 and exchanging views and interpretations. A powerful mind and a considerable scholar but overbearing and arrogant, Warburton gave unstinted aid to Theobald, who accepted many of his notes and paid frequent tribute to his 'ingenious friend,' incorporating many of his observations in his preface. Warburton returned Theobald's letters to aid him in his final touches, and from them, as printed by John Nichols,[3] it is possible to trace the course of Theobald's work and some of the friend's reading, as well as the excessive deference paid by Theobald to Warburton's often wild conjectures. As a textual critic the former was certainly the superior. He had flashes of insight denied to Warburton, but his greater knowledge of the classics, history, and Elizabethan literature was complemented by the other man's knowledge of philosophy, science, and magic.

By April 1729 they were in mid-career, exchanging letters two or three times a week when most excited. Nichols had only Theobald's letters, but the drift of Warburton's can often be made out, and many of his notes were used in Theobald's edition. In April Warburton promised to lend the latter a book on Popish Impostures. This, Theobald found (2 December 1730), was by Samuel Harsnet (1603). In November, annotating various comedies, Theobald started false trails by suggesting that 'Taunt him with the licence of ink' in *Twelfth Night*, III.ii.42, alluded to Coke's abuse of Raleigh during the latter's trial in 1603, and that Viola's 'Westward Ho!' (III.i.131) came from the play of that title. His long explanation of 'Cataian' (*Merry Wives of Windsor* II.i.130) dragged in Frobisher's voyages in search of a north-west passage to Cathay; but Warburton rightly suggested 'Scoundrel.' Theo-

2 Warburton (1698-1779) was a Newark man who studied law and practised as an attorney for some time before taking holy orders and the living of Brant Broughton. The University of Cambridge gave him the degree of MA in 1728. At that time he was not an admirer of Pope, who attacked him and his friends Matthew Concanen and Theobald as Grub Street. In 1736 he came into notice with his *The Alliance between Church and State*, followed by *The Divine Legation of Moses* (1737), after which he was embroiled in theological controversies. Appointed chaplain to Frederick, Prince of Wales, he soon became known in literary society largely through the friendship of Pope, whose *Essay on Man* he defended in 1739. Pope made him his literary executor. Appointed Dean of Bristol in 1757, he became Bishop of Worcester in 1759.

3 John Nichols *Illustrations of the Literary History of the Eighteenth Century* 9 vols, London 1817, II

bald ignored any narrative source for *All's Well That Ends Well,* but noted that 'Tom Drum,' V.iii.315, probably came from Holinshed ('of whose Books Shakespeare was a most diligent Reader') in the *History of Ireland* and referred to Patrick Scarsefield, mayor of Dublin in 1551, and his hospitality.

On 27 December Theobald was puzzling over the 'Egyptian thief' (*Twelfth Night* V.i.112): 'I do not know whether I was ever acquainted with this story, but I am sure I cannot now recollect it' (Nichols II.358). By 24 February he had found it in Heliodorus (Underdowne translation, 1587, book 1, chapter 3) and related the incident.

When he started on *The Winter's Tale:* 'I must get the old Tale of *Dorastus and Faunia,* to examine what absurdities of his story the Poet has derived from thence, and what others supplied from his own fund' (Nichols II.358). This play 'a little more deserves our employment' than *Twelfth Night,* but will be 'followed by a Play wholly made up of charms [that is, *King Lear*!]' (Nichols II.361). The mixture of condescension towards the comedies and reverence towards the tragedies seems amusing today.

Theobald's notes on *Lear* did not make use of Harsnet's *Declaration.* He would leave them to Warburton, who claimed the long and valuable note on III.4.48ff in the 1733 edition.[4] But Theobald had read the pamphlet and passed it on to 'our friend Concanen' (25 October 1729).

By 3 January 1730 he had 'done with this play and volume. I wish we were as well over the historical sett,' for he was not looking forward to *Richard III,* which he detested, though he owned six quartos of the play, even less to *Henry VI,* which could not all be by Shakespeare. He wished his friend 'A long and happy train of New Years.'

On the histories Theobald agreed with Dryden in his *Dramatick Poesy* about Shakespeare's telescoping of his materials and the showing many times of 'thirty or forty years cramped into a representation of two hours and a half.' He was the first editor to make some attempt to compare the historical sources with what the dramatist made of them. For *Richard II* he went to Hall's Chronicle as well as to Holinshed, while believing that the latter was the main source. 'Honest Hollingshead' cleared up many difficulties, such as the right name of Henry, Lord Scrope of Marsham, in *Henry V* and the existence of 'the true

4 B. Vickers *Shakespeare: The Critical Heritage* London 1974, II.507

historical Sir John Fastolfe in *1 Henry VI* ... not the comic character introduced in the former Plays, who was at first called Oldcastle.' In the edition he explained why the name was changed. Theobald also noted the intrusion of actors' names into *1 Henry VI* (Harvey and Rossill for Bardolph and Peto) as well as in *Much Ado about Nothing* (Kemp and Cowley for Town-clerk and Dogberry, Jack Wilson for Balthazar).

Having been warned by Warburton not to exaggerate Shakespeare's knowledge of the ancients, Theobald agreed that the young dramatist could have had 'but a slender Library of Classical Learning; and considering what a number of Translations, Romances, and Legends started in his time, and a little before, most of which it is very evident he read, [it is likely that he] rather schemed his plot and characters from these more latter Informations' than went back to the originals. Theobald accordingly proposed to cite the classics, not as proofs 'that he imitated these originals, but to shew how happily he has expressed himself upon the same topics.' A resemblance may, however, 'sometimes take its rise from strength of memory, and those impressions which he owed to the school' (Nichols II.564-5).

As he worked his way through 'the dull Fifth Volume' (II.416), he was for some time 'quite at a loss for what Pistol means here by Hiren' ('Have we not Hiren here?' *2 Henry IV* II.v.150), though he had found the exclamation in two old plays, *Law Tricks* and *The Queen, or Excellence of her Sex* (a piece now lost). On 2 March he was able to give a note on famous swords: 'Sir Amadis de Gaul's was called *Hiren*' (from Spanish *hiriendo,* swashing, cutting). Light was thrown on 'pamper'd jades of Asia' in the same scene (line 155) by 'an old play in two parts, called *Tamburlaine's Conquest*.' Other evidence of Theobald's avid exploration of Shakespeare's background and allusions abounds. The Portuguese wine 'Charnoco' (*2 Henry VI* II.iii.63) was new to him: 'I do not know what liquor this might be,' but he found it in *The Discovery of a London Monster, called The Black Dog of Newgate* (1612). He sought in vain for 'Bargulus, the strong Illyrian pirate' (*2 Henry VI* IV.i.108), and it was left to Warburton's edition to trace him in Cicero's *De Officiis* (II.xi) and Theopompus. For a time he could not find 'whence Our Poet has borrowed *Dii faciant laudis* ...' (*3 Henry VI* I.iii.48), but by 1733 he knew that it was in Ovid's *Epistle from Phillis to Demophoon* (II.443).

Nichol Smith attributed to Dr Johnson the discovery that Shakespeare used North's Plutarch for his Roman plays. In fact, although Theobald often used a later translation, he more than once cited 'the old Translator of Plutarch,' as in writing to Warburton about Cleopatra's 'salad days' (*Antony and Cleopatra* I.v.73): 'For Caesar and Pompey knew her when she was but a young thing, and knew not then what the worlde ment ...'[5]

Considering *Macbeth,* Theobald used both Holinshed and Hector Boece's *Scotorum Historiae,* which helped him to correct a mistake of Pope's, who thought that Donalbain took shelter with Malcolm in the English court. 'Hector Boethius and Hollingshead (the latter of whom our Author precisely follows) both inform us, that Donalbaine remained in Ireland till the death of Malcolm, and his Queen; and then, indeed, he came over, invaded Scotland, and wrested the crown from one of his nephews' (II.528). Boece also gave him an 'account of Suenos's army being intoxicated by bread and ale put upon them by their subtle enemy' containing 'solatrum amentiale,' which 'makes the patient fancy he sees apparitions' (II.520-1).

For *Troilus and Cressida* he went back to the 'old Treatise printed by Wynkyn de Worde, anno 1503, called *The recuyles and sieges of Troy.*' 'I find there that among the list of the Warriors that came with Agamemnon before Troy, a Neoptolemus is mentioned. And to this old Treatise it is, (and not to Lollius, or Chaucer, as the Editors imagine) that our Author owes his Subject; for hence only he could derive the name of Hector's horse, *Galathe;* Troilus' being taken by Diomed; and several other circumstances that I could particularize.'[6]

Although he accepted the orthodox view that Shakespeare took the plot of *Romeo and Juliet* from Bandello, he had come to believe that their distresses 'are no fictitious tale.' Besides referring to Giolamo da Cortes's version he tells how Captain J.D. de Breval in his *Travels* (1726) was told the story as historical fact, and how the bodies of the lovers were found.

By this time Theobald was 'drawing so near the end of my task, that, like a boy with a dear sweet morsel, I am afraid of

5 Geoffrey Bullough *Narrative and Dramatic Sources of Shakespeare* 9 vols, London 1957-75, v.273

6 On 25 September 1730 he mentioned the Sagittary, the bastard Margarelon, Cassandra with Hector shortly before his death, and Diomede's getting one of Cassandra's gloves (sleeve in Shakespeare) v.ii.64.

eating it quite up; and am for extending my pleasure in spite of gluttony' (II.557). However, he had yet to go through *Hamlet* and *Othello.* Still convinced that the former was based on *Saxo Grammaticus,* he summarized the latter's account (14 March) and kept the digest in his edition. For *Othello* he had Cinthio's Italian story, which he cited on 28 March, pointing out that it was directed 'against disproportioned marriages.' The allusion to men 'whose heads appeared below their shoulders' elicited a long note on Raleigh's Voyage to Guiana (which had made Theobald fancy that *Othello,* as well as *The Tempest,* was written soon after 1597).

As soon as the annotations were drafted, Theobald began to draft 'Prologomena' in which he would deal with Pope's attacks on him. On 11 April 1730 he asked Warburton to 'throw your eye over the Editor's Preface' (Nichols II.600) and comment on it, when it was written. The latter had already cautioned him against *'inconsistency,* with regard to my opinion of Shakespeare's *knowledge in languages.'* On 1 May Warburton returned a packet of Theobald's letters, no doubt to help him with his notes,[7] and another batch on 18 November 1731. There had recently been a slight rift in the friendship, maybe because Warburton thought that Theobald was making too many demands on him, and Warburton had grumbled to the Reverend Dr William Stukeley of Stamford on 10 November that Theobald was to receive *'eleven hundred guineas'* for the edition from Tonson, 'and your humble servant for his pains one copy of the royal paper books.' However, all was soon well again, and Warburton wrote, 'I absolve him from hard thoughts' (Nichols II.13-14). Theobald was at pains to explain that he 'had not the least glance, or aim, of trespassing on your friendship.' He was determined 'to tamper with the text' as little as possible, but agreed with Warburton that probable conjectures should be given in the notes; no doubt these included many of Warburton's surmises which he was eager to see in print. Theobald had decided (18 November 1731) not to trouble the public too largely with 'my sentiments of my Adversary's usage,' and 'the whole affair of *Prolegomena* [sic] I have determined to soften into *Preface.'* He appealed to Warburton:

> But, dear Sir, will you, at your leisure hours, think over for me upon the contents, topics, orders, &c. of this branch of

7 See Nichols II.607.

> my labour? You have a comprehensive memory, and a happiness of digesting the matter joined to it, which my head is often too much embarrassed to perform; let that be the excuse for my inability. But how unreasonable is it to expect this labour, when it is the only part in which I shall not be able to be just to my friends: for, to confess assistance in a *Preface* will, I am afraid, make me appear too naked.

Theobald ended by offering to improve any 'negligence in expression' found by Warburton 'during his correspondence, literally written *currente calamo*' (Nichols II.621-2).

It may seem surprising that Theobald should make such demands on his friend, and that Warburton should be willing to have his ideas and notes used so extensively. But at this time, and until after Theobald's edition proved successful, Warburton had no intention of producing an edition of his own; he was still unknown and susceptible to Theobald's grateful flattery. So, as D. Nicol Smith and B. Vickers have shown,[8] much of Theobald's preface was a cento of passages from their correspondence, and the notes included some which Theobald attributed to his collaborator.

Enough has been written above about the making of Theobald's edition to render unnecessary any long account of the edition itself; but it is worthwhile to illustrate the variety of his annotations and how well they proved to Augustan readers that Shakespeare's plays drew on much more source-material than had hitherto been recognized. The edition did much to place Shakespeare in his age and suggest the breadth of his interests and knowledge.

Thus an early note on 'the still-vext Bermoothes' in *The Tempest*[9] led Theobald to write usefully on Sir George Somers's expedition of 1609, although he did not show Shakespeare's acquaintance with the printed account. 'Each putter-out of five to one' (III.iii.48) elicited a note on the explorer-'adventurers' of the time, with references to Fynes Moryson's *Itinerary* and Jonson's *Every Man Out of his Humour.* Theobald believed that, here and elsewhere, Shakespeare showed 'great deference' for Sir Walter Raleigh. An allusion to Guiana in *The Merry Wives of*

8 D.N. Smith *Eighteenth Century Essays on Shakespeare* Glasgow 1903, xlvi ff; B. Vickers *Shakespeare: The Critical Heritage* London 1974, II.475-538

9 Theobald thought that this was an error for 'Bermudas.' Warburton corrected him. Warburton and Thirlby helped with III.iii.48.

Windsor (I.iii.70) raised 'a probable Conjecture that it could not appear till after 1598.'

Without being very learned in Elizabethan life and lore, Theobald touched on them at many points to show the dramatist's participation in current notions, such as the practice of duelling (*As You Like It* V.iv) as taught by Louis de Carazzo and Vincentio Saviolo (II.264). 'The Hobby-horse is quite forgot' (*Love's Labour's Lost* III. i.29) was referred to the puritan opposition by which 'Maid Marian, the Fryar, and the poor *Hobby-horse* were turned out of the [Mayday] Games.' He gave an excellent note, citing Jonson's *Bartholomew Fair* (II.115).

He tried to make clear Shakespeare's distinction between affection and passion in *Merchant of Venice,* IV.i.50-1 (II.62n), 'considering the one as the Cause, the other the Effect'; also Shakespeare's knowledge of the triple soul of man: 'the Peripatetick Philosophy (the learning then in Vogue), which very liberally gave to every man three Souls, the *Vegetative,* or the *Animal,* and the *Rational.*' Having read Macrobius, he knew the idea behind *The Merchant of Venice,* V.i.60, that 'the smallest orb ... has an Intelligence or Angel to direct it.' He was acquainted with the medieval background of allusions to witchcraft in the plays and knew Isidore of Seville and Mengus's *Flagellum Daemonorum.*

Both Theobald and Warburton paid some attention to the references to astrology. Thus, annotating 'Mars his true moving' (*1 Henry VI* I.ii.1): 'Our Poet, in an hundred passages of his Works, has shown us his Acquaintance with *judicial* Astrology; he here gives us a glimpse of his Knowledge in Astronomy ... The Revolutions of the Planet *Mars* were not found out till ... Kepler ... in his *Treatise De Mortibus Stella Martis* [1609]' (III.19). Warburton, discussing Edmund on nature (*Lear* I.ii.1-22), wrote: 'The *Bastard's* Character is That of a confirm'd Atheist, and the Poet's making him ridicule *judicial Astrology* was design'd as one Instance of his Character. For that impious Juggle had a religious Reverence paid to it at that Time; and *Shakespeare* makes his best Characters in this very Play own and acknowledge the Force of the Stars' Influence.' Warburton cited Vanini, 'the infamous Neapolitan Atheist,' in his tract *De Admirandi Naturae* [1616], which 'the Diversity of Shakespeare's genius, as it were, foretold' (V.115). But the modern cleric agreed with Edmund about the folly of astrology when the latter mocked at the tendency to blame the stars for 'our disasters.'

Though Theobald added much to contemporary knowledge of and speculation about Shakespeare's literary background, he had no great acquaintance with medieval works and accepted the attributions in Urry's edition of Chaucer (1721). So, 'the characters of Oliver, Jaques, Orlando and Adam and the Episodes of the Wrestler and the *banish'd Train* were borrow'd from the *Legend of Gamelyn* in the *Cook's Tale*'; but he gave no detailed parallels. Accepting the fact that Chaucer wrote (Henryson's) *The Testament of Cresseid,* he attributed 'Cressida was a beggar' (*Twelfth Night* III.1.58) to a memory of that poem. Shakespeare owed much of the tone and story in *Troilus and Cressida* to Caxton and to de Worde. His knowledge of Homer might have come from Chapman's translation. Before writing *The Comedy of Errors* the dramatist might have seen (as Langbaine asserted) a translation of the *Menaechmi,* 'printed in Quarto in the year 1515, half a Century before our Author was born' (an error, for the publication of W. Warner's version was in 1595, as Langbaine knew).

By the time he edited *The Winter's Tale* Theobald had read the long-sought *Dorastus and Fawnia* and found there 'the Isle of Delphos' and Bohemia as 'a maritime Country,' and was able to dispose of one of Warburton's conjectural emendations, though he printed it (III.98-9; compare Vickers II.501). He made good use of the earlier plays he knew. He traced the highway robbery in *1 Henry IV* to *The Famous Victories of Henry the Fifth*: 'From this old imperfect Sketch I have Suspicions, *Shakespeare* might form his two Parts of *Henry the IVth* and his History of *King Henry V,* and consequently 'tis not improbable, that he might *continue* the *mention* of *Sir John Oldcastle,* till some Descendant of that Family mov'd Q. *Elizabeth* to comand him to change the Name.' He also noted the significance of the prologue of the first part of *Sir John Oldcastle* (1600), of which he owned a copy. He had not read the old tragedy *Cambyses King of Persia* but referred to Langbaine's comment on its metre. He found parallels to *2 Henry IV* in Daniel's *Miseries of Civil Wars*: 'I don't know the Date of that Poem being wrote, so cannot say which Poet has copied from the other.' 'Go by, Saint Geronimy!' in *Taming of the Shrew,* induction i.9, evoked a quotation from the 'fustian old Play, call'd *Hieronymo: Or, The Spanish Tragedy,* which I found was the common *But* of Raillery to all the Poets of *Shakespeare's* Time.' Other old plays which helped him to place Shakespeare's language in its setting included *Soliman and Perseda* and John Day's

Law Tricks. He gave some lines from Whetstone's *Promos and Cassandra* to explain 'lac'd mutton' in *Two Gentlemen of Verona*, I. i.94; and in his endnote for *Measure for Measure*, after observing the turns Shakespeare gave to Cinthio's story, including Mariana ('a Creature purely of his own Invention,' as was 'the Duke's remaining *incognito* at home'), he turned briefly to *Promos and Cassandra:*

> I could prove to Demonstration that *Shakespeare* had perus'd these Pieces; but whoever has seen, and knows what execrable mean Stuff they are; I am sure, will acquit him from all Suspicion of Plagiarism. (I.399)

So Shakespeare still needed to be defended against the charge of appropriating other men's materials. Unfortunately Theobald did not enter into any fertile comparisons between *Measure for Measure* and its sources, for he was not interested in *how* the artist dealt with them, except in the most elementary manner. In treating English and Roman histories, however, he was intent on showing that on the whole Shakespeare was faithful to his authorities, despite deviations accidental or deliberate.

One reason why Theobald doubted whether the *Henry VI* plays were entirely by Shakespeare, 'unless they were wrote by him very early,' was the frequency of 'transgressions against History as far as the Order of Time in concerned' (IV.110).

He did not, however, confine himself to minutiae. In *1 Henry VI* Gloucester's invective against Cardinal Beaufort – 'Thou, that giv'st whores indulgencies to sin' – evoked an interesting note on the history of the 'Brothel-houses or *Stews* on the *Bankside ... under* the Jurisdiction of the Bishop of Winchester,' and the laws of Henry VI and Henry VIII against them (IV.122).

Theobald was the first editor to suggest that Richard III's wickedness may have been exaggerated for political reasons, since ''Tis obvious, that the Historians and Poets, in loading his Character, have at the same time been paving their Compliment to that *Line*, which gave them an Elizabeth' (IV.40).

Similarly, in *Macbeth*, the apparation of the eight kings proved 'the Address of the Poet in complimenting K. James I here upon his uniting *Scotland* to *England:* and when we consider too that the Family of the *Stuarts* are said to be the direct Descendants from *Banquo*' (V.443-4).[10] The account of the Confes-

10 Theobald also provided a pedigree showing the 'Siward's Relation to Malcolm, and Macbeth's to the Scotch Crown' (V.454-5).

sor's touching for the 'king's evil' was also a compliment to James I, 'who was very fond of practising this *Superstition*' (V.453). Macbeth spoke of 'the English Epicures' because Shakespeare knew that Hardicanute, the Confessor's half-brother, 'would have his Table cover'd four times a day, and largely furnish'd. So that the *Englishmen* were said to have learn'd from him excessive Gluttony in Diet, and Intemperance in Drinking.'

Dealing with the Roman plays Theobald sometimes used 'the Old English Edition published in *Shakespeare's* Time' (North's), but more often another translation[11] to show 'how minutely *Shakespeare* used to follow his History in little particular Circumstance.' He loved to correct Pope: for example, Artemidorus was not a soothsayer but a rhetorician, as North made clear. Occasionally Theobald overreached himself, as when, rebuking Pope for asserting that the mild and philosophical Brutus would not stoop and bathe his hands in Caesar's blood (*Julius Caesar* III.i.106), he paraphrased Plutarch: '*Brutus* and his Party betook themselves to the *Capitol*, and in their way *shewing their Hands all bloody*, and their naked Swords ...' (VI.164). But Plutarch gave no account of the conspirators bathing their hands, though their hands were bloodied in slaying Caesar, and 'among them Brutus caught a blow on his hande, bicause he would make one in murdering of him' (*Sources* V.102). Like Pope, Theobald did not see the point of Shakespeare's invention.

Pope objected to what he called Theobald's pedantry in pointing out Shakespeare's many anachronisms, such as (in *Coriolanus*) the allusion to censors (not created until forty-six years later) and the title Censorinus (not given for over two hundred years). Menenius 'tells of Alexander the Great,' and elsewhere there is mention of Galen, as well as 'Roman aqueducts not built before 441, and the Marcian water, not brought in till 613.' Such an 'innocent Trespass' proved the limitations of Shakespeare's knowledge of Roman history.

Pope's irritation would be increased by Theobald's assertion that Caesar was unlikely, on the day of his murder, to have been wearing the mantle he had on 'That day he overcame the Nervii' – seventeen years before (*Julius Caesar* III.ii.173) – any more than *Hamlet* would be likely to know what armour his father was wearing 'When he th'ambitious Norway combated on the very day whereon young Hamlet was born.' But, wrote

11 *Plutarch's Lives, trans. from the Greek by Several hands. To which is prefixt the Life of Plutarch* (by J. Dryden) 5 vols, 1683-8

Theobald, 'These Circumstances and Strokes of Fancy dress up an amusing Picture for which the Poet, perhaps is neither accountable to Propriety, nor Probability' (VI.175).

Once more against Pope, who thought that in *Cymbeline* 'little besides the Names, is historical,' Theobald asserted 'that the Author has taken Pains to insert Points of History, both *British* and *Roman,* in the Detail of his Scenery. Indeed, he sometimes puts a change upon *Facts,* as well as subverts the *Chronology* of *Actions.*' Hence the jumble of names British and Roman, with others 'of a more modern Origin and Deflection.' Obviously Shakespeare knew what he was doing. Theobald gives accounts of the reigns of Cassibelan, Tenantius, and Cymbeline, and of Julius Caesar's invasions. He has actually seen a tribute coin bearing Cunobelin's name. He quotes several classical analogues to 'Britain, A Wall by itself' without claiming them as sources. He uses Holinshed to explain that it was not Cassibelan who was once 'at point to master Caesar's sword' (III.1.5-9) but his brother Nennius (*Sources* VIII.42). These scattered notes do not prove Pope wrong or help much in the interpretation of the play as a whole. He admits that 'our Author has jumbled Facts against the known Tenour of Chronology,' and although he finds that the war in *Cymbeline* cannot be before 'the forty-second year of *Augustus,* the year of Christ's birth,' he sees no significance in this date.

In editing *Hamlet* Theobald added little to what he had already put into his *Remarks.* He summarized *Saxo Grammaticus,* including nothing about Amleth's stay in England, his marriage, later journey to Scotland, bigamy, and death. He stated that 'the Time in which *Amlethus* liv'd was some Generations earlier than the Period of Christianity. And the Letters, which the Danish King's Messengers carried over to England, were wooden Tablets ... In fact, I'm afraid, our Author, according to his usual Licence, plays fast and loose with Time.' So Theobald now differentiated between the truly historical pieces and those which mingled legend with romance. No attempt was made to relate Shakespeare to Saxo,[12] and, although Theobald knew *The Spanish Tragedy,* he saw no connection between the two tragedies.

Othello is one of the few plays in which Theobald made some little attempt at critical use of the source. In particular he pointed out again that Cinthio's tale was 'a Document to young

12 '... and how happily the Poet has adapted his Incidents, I shall leave to the Observation of every Reader' (VII.226).

Ladies against disproportionate Marriages'; but Shakespeare had no such prejudice, and insisted on the beauty of the love between the Moor and Desdemona. All his remarks were not so percipient, for, commenting on 'A fellow almost damn'd in a fair wife' (I.i.21), which the text suggested was 'Michael Cassio, a Florentine,' he rightly pointed out that '*Iago*, not *Cassio*, was the married Man,' and this was borne out by Bianca's desire to marry Cassio. 'Besides, our Poet follows the Authority of his Novel, in giving the Villainous Ensign a fair Wife.' After citing Cinthio's Italian, Theobald concluded 'The Poet means, Iago had so beautiful a Wife, that she was his *Heaven on Earth;* that he *idoliz'd* her' – a view not supported by Iago's conduct in the play.

Theobald countered Rymer's sarcastic railing at Shakespeare's use of the handkerchief:

> So much ado, so much stress, so much passion and repetition about an Handkerchief! ... the Handkerchief is so much a trifle, no Booby, on this side *Mauritania*, cou'd make any consequence from it.[13]

He quoted Iago:

> Trifles, light as air,
> Are to the jealous, confirmations strong
> As proofs of Holy Writ.

He noted how the dramatist deviated from Cinthio, 'who only says that it was the Moor's Gift, upon his Wedding to *Desdemona*: that it was most curiously wrought after the *Moorish* Fashion, and very dear both to him and his Wife'; whereas Shakespeare 'makes his Handkerchief deriv'd from an *Inchantress*: *Magick* and *Mystery* are in its *Materials* and *Workmanship* ...' Here Theobald rises to his subject: 'Such Circumstances ... are the very Soul and Essence of *Poetry: Fancy* here exerts its great *creating* Power, and adds a Dignity, that surprizes to its Subject' (VII.447-8). Theobald also shows that Cassio's cries when wounded (V.i.27ff), 'I'm maim'd for ever' and 'My leg is cut in two,' were suggested by Cinthio, who wrote that the 'Antient' cut the Captain 'across the right Thigh in such a manner that with the Wound the miserable Gentleman fell to Earth' (VII.477).

13 *The Critical Works of Thomas Rymer* ed Curt A. Zimanski, New Haven 1956, p 160

Theobald omitted to add that henceforth the Captain 'went about with a wooden leg instead of the one that had been cut off' (*Sources* VII.251), whereas Cassio is present in the last scene, 'carried in a chair' (V.ii.282 sd).

Theobald had always had doubts about the fanciful nature of some of Warburton's emendations and notes, and on 15 September 1730 dared to say so, though he hastened to add, 'there is something extremely ingenuous in all you start.' The notes were both erudite and entertaining, but he proposed not to print them all; some should be kept over for another edition. Warburton, whose every word was gospel, did not like this, but as yet he did not suspect his friend of appropriating the fruits of his genius. However, the great success of the 1733 edition, which brought fame to Theobald, soon made the aspiring cleric consider that he had been robbed of public notice, as well as financial profit, that his part in the preface had been insufficiently acknowledged, and that the value of his notes had been underestimated.

On 2 June 1734 he sent Theobald fifty of his emendations which were, he declared, better than those Theobald had selected, and suggested that they should be printed in the edition of Shakespeare's *Poems* which Theobald was now proposing to make.[14] They included some of his wilder conjectures. He kept asking about the progress of this new venture, but the *Poems* never appeared. Theobald got involved in an edition of Beaumont and Fletcher, which was unfinished when he died in 1744. It was completed by T. Seward and Sympson (1750).

After 1734 the correspondence waned, as Warburton's self-induced suspicions of Theobald's good faith led him to invent reasons to support them. In addition, his ecclesiastical interests were now strong, and after tentatively starting an edition of Velleius Paterculus for which his classical learning was inadequate, he turned to his treatise on *The Alliance between Church and State,* which brought him into notice by its pungent defence of the Erastian position. With the publication of the first part of his *Divine Legation of Moses Demonstrated* in 1737, his fame as a heavyweight controversialist grew, although he had to wait twenty-two years for a bishopric.

The coldness between Warburton and Theobald arose origi-

14 Theobald made £650 by his edition of the plays, but poverty and hack-work for the theatre impeded him. In 1741 he proposed the edition of Beaumont and Fletcher, and had finished six plays before he died.

nally from the former's feeling that Theobald had not sufficiently acknowledged his contribution to the edition of Shakespeare, especially in the preface, although Theobald had paid tribute to

> the indefatigable Zeal and Industry of my ingenious and ever-respected Friend, the Rev. Mr. *William Warburton* of *Newark*-upon-*Trent* ... The number of passages amended, and admirably Explained, which I have taken care to distinguish with his Name, will shew a Fineness of Spirit and Extent of Reading, beyond all the commendations I can give them ... (preface I.lxvi)

But Theobald had not attributed to Warburton the many passages in his preface which derived from his part in their corresondence.[15] Moreover, Theobald had not printed enough of his friend's emendations to satisfy the avid annotator.

A letter from Theobald to Warburton (18 May 1736) shows their relations at breaking-point. Warburton had asserted, truly enough, that he had supplied many notes 'with a Generosity I could not complain of.' Theobald replied that he had confessed his obligations in the edition. Warburton had complained that 'I had all the Profit of my Edition.' To this Theobald answered that he understood 'that the Assistance of my Friends were designed gratuitous; and if I misunderstood this Point I should have been set right by some Hints before the Publication:

> I used, you say, what Notes I thought fit. I own as Editor,believ'dhad a discretionary Power of picking, and chusing my Materials: and I am certain, during the Affair, you conceded this Liberty to me.

Faced with such reproaches, Theobald foresaw, 'I am to be in the State of a Country conquer'd by its Auxiliaries.'

Warburton demanded the return of all his unused notes. This was reasonable, and in September Theobald returned his letters, renouncing any right to the notes in them. Further, he would revoke any of Warburton's notes which he had used. Accordingly, the second edition of Theobald's work omitted Warburton's notes and the parts of the preface contributed by him.

The breach was complete and final, but Warburton had by no means done with Shakespeare. He found a new partner in emendation and annotation with whom the course of his rela-

15 Cf Vickers II.475-90.

tionship followed the pattern of his friendship with Theobald: enthusiastic and generous assistance, gradual suspicion, then unbridled enmity and abuse. The new friend was Sir Thomas Hanmer, ex-Speaker of the House of Commons.

Late of Edinburgh

NEIL CARSON

Shakespeare and the Dramatic Image

Studies of Shakespeare's imagery have traditionally dealt with his poetic diction. Following the lead of Caroline Spurgeon, critics have cast considerable light on the imaginative world of the plays and on the associative characteristics of Shakespeare's mind. But these insights have been gained at some cost. By focusing almost exclusively on verbal images, some commentators have given the impression that the plays contain no other kind. The visual side of drama is often forgotten or totally ignored. Even when it is acknowledged that Shakespeare wrote for actors as well as readers, the admission is made grudgingly, as if a play's life on the stage were somehow of secondary and lesser importance. Frances Yates, for example, describes the performances of Shakespeare's day as if they were given to an audience of the blind. She writes, 'It was the voice of the players that mattered [and] it was upon the clearly heard words that they uttered that the *whole* appeal of the drama depended.'[1]

There is, of course, no justification whatsoever for the view that Shakespeare appealed exclusively to the ear (or even to that inner eye that responds to the visual component of poetic imagery). Roy Strong and others have made us keenly aware of the important role of pageantry and spectacle in many aspects of Renaissance life. It is impossible that Elizabethan audiences can have put aside their love of visual splendour when they entered

1 *The Theatre of the World* London 1969, p 124 (my italics)

the public theatres, and there is ample evidence that the playwrights catered to that taste to the limit of their abilities. The theatrical inventories which were part of the Alleyn-Henslowe papers at Dulwich College list elaborate costumes and properties used in productions on the Rose stage. These articles, along with the theatre in which they were displayed, have long since disappeared, and it is difficult (if not impossible) to form an accurate idea of the nature of spectacle in the Elizabethan public playhouses. But to say this is not at all the same as to imply that it did not exist or that Shakespeare (perhaps the most theatrical playwright of his time) was indifferent to the visual effects of his plays.

The tendency to treat Shakespeare primarily as a poet is understandable. The works undoubtedly do stand on their own, and the intelligent reader can often get more from a careful study of the text than he can from a mediocre performance. Furthermore, we can be reasonably certain that the surviving texts reflect fairly closely Shakespeare's intentions as a writer, whereas we can say virtually nothing at all about his intentions concerning the staging, costumes, and properties for his plays. Because of this we imagine that perhaps Shakespeare shared our own (and many of his contemporaries') contempt for the physical representation of his plays. To do so, however, is to distort Shakespeare's conception of the function of dramatic imagery.

A very ambivalent attitude towards visual images was widely prevalent following the Reformation. In religion, the iconoclastic sentiments of many Protestants stemmed from their conviction that the visual representation of sacred figures distorted truth and interfered with worship, which should be a spiritual exercise. In the drama, too, there was a growing prejudice against spectacle. Elaborate and visual effects had been prominent features of much medieval Catholic drama, which the English church and state were beginning to look on with suspicion. As the great cycle plays were gradually suppressed, a new kind of drama – rational and disputatious – began to take their place. Tudor moralities and interludes tended to put less stress on stage spectacle and more on argumentation.

An emphasis on the verbal (as opposed to the visual) dimension of drama was encouraged by ancient and modern authority alike. In their treatises on rhetoric and drama, classical commentators frequently distinguished between knowledge gained by sight and that acquired by ear. Aristotle, for example, considered spectacle to be the least important element of tragedy and thought that the full power of a drama could be experienced by one who only heard the incidents of the plot.[2] Plutarch, too, put a higher premium on knowledge gained by hearing. 'The only handle wherewith vertue may take hold of yong men,' he says, 'are the eares.'[3] During the Reformation, this bias was shared by writers who believed that hearing was a more reliable guide to truth because it alone could comprehend what George Hakewill calls 'vniversalls, immaterials, and the innward parts of things.'[4] Such writers believed not only that sight was limited to particulars, but that the very intensity of visual images was such that it constituted a danger to the unwary. As Thomas Wright explains,

> no sence hath such varietie of obiects to feed and delight it, as this; no sence imprinteth so firmely his formes in the imagination, as this; ... no sence sooner mooueth, than this; and consequently, no sence peruerteth more perilous than this.[5]

This age-old distinction between what Hamlet calls 'the faculties of eyes and ears' was well understood by the Elizabethans, and it is scarcely surprising that their attitude to the drama was affected by it. Puritan opponents of the stage directed their most virulent attacks against the spectacular elements of the theatre – the gorgeous buildings, the luxurious costumes, the visual examples of vice. Even defenders of the drama occasionally shared something of the Puritans' iconoclastic prejudice against the material image. For example, Jonson's scorn for creaking thrones and sieges to the music room is the negative side of his strong belief in the importance of the spoken word in the drama.

Shakespeare not only avoids the extremes of some of his contemporaries, he sees much more deeply into the complexities of the problem of dramatic illusion. The nature of that problem is most clearly set out in the 'mechanicals' scene in *A Midsummer Night's Dream.* There Bottom and Peter Quince are the individuals most vocally concerned, and it is significant that their preoccupations are very different. Bottom speaks from the actor's point of view and feels that the principal danger is that the per-

2 *The Poetics* VI.19
3 *Morals* trans Holland, 1603, p 52
4 *The Vanitie of the Eye* 1615, p 101
5 *The Passions of the Mind* 1604, pp 151-2

formance will be too convincing. His solution is to employ certain distancing techniques which will prevent the audience from becoming too emotionally engaged in the action. Peter Quince, on the other hand, looks at the play from the perspective of the producer. The creation of moonlight and a wall for the production strike him as 'hard things,' and it does not occur to him that any scenic illusion he might be able to create could be too powerful. Indeed, all his efforts are directed towards engaging the audience in such a way that they will accept the theatrical symbolism as a believable dramatic image.

The scene is delightfully satirical, and it is usually dismissed as being amusing but of no relevance to the kind of acting or staging that Shakespeare would have been familiar with in his own company. In fact, the problems encountered by Peter Quince are exactly the same as those that faced every stage manager in the Elizabethan theatre. Nor were there solutions available to the professional companies that were in any fundamental way different from those proposed for the Pyramus and Thisby interlude. Illusion on the open stage depended entirely upon the audience's willingness to participate imaginatively in the dramatic game. The actor, through a skilful imitation of emotion, could win that participation fairly easily. But it was another thing altogether to persuade an audience of the 'reality' of the actor's environment. The platform stage with its permanent tiring-house façade and natural lighting was inherently non-illusionistic. The images used to suggest the dramatic 'world' enclosing the actors were necessarily symbolic. It was the tension between this symbolic spectacle derived from a primarily emblematic tradition and a new realism in acting which, as much as anything, destabilized the Jacobean drama and led to the gradual adoption of movable scenery and the ultimate separation of poetry and drama. Beneath Shakespeare's playfulness in this scene, therefore, is a recognition of a fundamental problem of the Elizabethan drama – the discrepancy between the actor's ability to create a realistic illusion of psychological truth and the stage manager's failure to provide a similarly convincing stage environment. The ramifications of this problem are explored in several other plays.

One conceivable 'solution' of the discord betwen acting and staging styles would be to bring them into harmony by attempting the same kind of 'naturalism' in the scenery that is aimed at in the acting. This solution was never seriously proposed by Shakespeare, but he plays with the idea in *The Taming of the Shrew*. The Lord (who is probably the only advocate of total illusionism in the canon apart from Bottom) engineers a practical joke on Christopher Sly that is a kind of super-naturalistic drama. The ultimate purpose of the Lord's carefully staged playlet is not clear, but its immediate aim is to alter the consciousness of one particular viewer. His success in this respect is complete and it is worthwhile examining his methods.

The joke played on Sly is an example of complete illusionism, the theatrical equivalent of the trompe-l'oeil paintings and the tapestries the Lord admires. In describing these works the servants praise the life-likeness of the execution, which shows

> Adonis painted by a running brook
> And Cytherea all in sedges hid,
> Which seem to move and wanton with her breath
> Even as the waving sedges play wi'th'wind.
> ...
> Or Daphne roaming through a thorny wood,
> Scratching her legs, that one shall swear she bleeds;
> And at that sight shall sad Apollo weep,
> So workmanly the blood and tears are drawn.[6]

In instructing his servants, the Lord urges them to achieve a comparable level of illusion. Accordingly, they wrap Sly in sweet clothes, convey him to bed, put rings on his fingers, and place a banquet before him so that he is confronted by a myriad of 'facts' all attesting to his noble birth. The effect is a substitution of one set of sensory data for another, so convincing in its completeness that Sly is persuaded to accept the testimony of his eyes above the witness of his memory or reason.

> I do not sleep; I see, I hear, I speak;
> I smell sweet savours, and I feel soft things.
> Upon my life, I am a lord indeed. (ii.68-70)

Some apologists for the theatre (beginning with Thomas Heywood and continuing into our own day) seem to have persuaded themselves that drama can achieve an illusion as powerful as that which hypnotized Christopher Sly. There are others,

6 *The Taming of the Shrew* in *William Shakespeare, The Complete Works* ed Peter Alexander, London 1951, induction ii.48-51, 55-8

however, who believe that even if such a feat could be accomplished (which they doubt), it would be wrong-headed to attempt it. Critics such as Ben Jonson, for example, objected to the inadequacies of stage spectacle in the popular theatres on theoretical as much as practical grounds. To Jonson, the drama was essentially a medium of moral instruction, and as such its appeal should be primarily to the mind through the ears rather than to the emotions through the eyes. In his own work he wrote for an audience of what he called 'scholars,' who would

> judge and fair report
> The sence they hear above the vulgar sort
> Of nutcrackers, that only come for sight.[7]

Although Shakespeare obviously never subscribes to this theory of drama in his own work, he does give powerful expression to it through the mouth of one of his most sympathetic characters. Hamlet's aesthetic prejudices are revealed in two separate incidents – his first meeting with the actors, during which he is given a taste of their 'quality,' and the subsequent performance of the altered *Murder of Gonzago,* preceded by his own instructions to the players. The first clue to Hamlet's taste is his choice of a speech to be delivered by the First Player. Significantly, he asks to hear lines from a piece that was never a success at the box office and may never have been publicly acted. Hamlet's knowledge of the work presumably comes from a previous recital or reading, not a performance, and his appreciation of it is purely literary. What he admires is the structure of the work (the 'well-digested' scenes) and the restraint of the writing (done with 'as much modesty as cunning'). In other words, Hamlet's taste is essentially classical in that he prefers decorum to idiosyncratic originality. When he quotes part of the speech himself, we may imagine that he reflects this taste in his delivery, and it is probably meaningful that Polonius compliments him on his 'accent' and 'discretion' rather than on the truth or depth of his feeling.

For this reason, perhaps, the First Player's ability to become emotionally involved in the role seems to Hamlet a rebuke to his own intellectuality. His astonishment at the player's ability to be moved by a fiction is prompted by his aware-

7 *The Staple of News* prologue

ness of how it contrasts with his own apparent bloodlessness. It is not an admiration of romantic acting as such, and when he later advises the actors prior to their performance of *Gonzago,* he reiterates his classical precepts.

Hamlet's decision to use the players to alter the consciousness of his uncle bears a superficial resemblance to the Lord's practical joke on Christopher Sly. As we might expect, however, the prince's methods as well as his ultimate purpose are very different and much more clearly thought out. The theory that drama could betray a guilty spectator into self-incrimination was widely held during the Renaissance. It was based on a belief that an individual's conscience was never wholly dormant and could, in the proper circumstances, be stirred into active life. A pressing problem for Protestant theologians during the later sixteenth century was to enunciate the principles whereby an individual could take over the functions formerly performed by a priest. To assist in this process a considerable body of Protestant casuistry was produced in which it was emphasized that the devout Christian had a duty to subject his conscience to continual scrutiny and to apply general moral laws to his own life. According to this doctrine it was the 'applicability' of knowledge which made it conscionable knowledge.[8] To 'catch' the conscience of the king, therefore, Hamlet had to make Claudius understand the relevance of universal moral principles to his own actions. It was not sufficient to play 'something like' the murder of his father before the king; it was necessary to compel Claudius to see the 'applicability' of that story to his own case. This, presumably, was the purpose of the 'dozen or sixteen lines' which Hamlet felt he needed to add to a play which in its general outlines must have borne a very close resemblance to his uncle's deeds.

Hamlet's attitude towards spectacle in the drama, therefore, is consistent with his conviction that moral instruction is best communicated through language. The actor, with nothing but his voice and gestures, could 'amaze' the eyes as well as the ears of the listeners by persuading the audience to 'see' what was so vividly described. The trappings of production, in Hamlet's view, far from being an asset, constituted a distraction that might inhibit the function of drama – the consideration of 'necessary' questions. It is probably his anxiety that Claudius will be

8 See Richard Bernard *Christian See to Thy Conscience* 1613, pp 7-8.

distracted by the business of the action that prompts the prince to give the actors such detailed instructions. These instructions all accord with classical precept. Art is to reflect the ideal not the particular. Characters are represented according to the rules of decorum so that virtue's feature and scorn's image are never hidden or mistaken, as they are, for example, in the real world of Denmark. The ideal style is a 'modest naturalism,' in which 'grace' and 'smoothness' are preferred to violence or eccentricity. Hamlet's emphasis on the rhetorical aspects of drama is therefore a reflection of his conviction that spectacle is a subordinate and unimportant component of a play. It may or may not be a confirmation of these views that Claudius is 'caught' by the spoken version of the murder although apparently immune to the dumb show.

Both Hamlet and the Lord are narrowly practical in their dramatic aims. Prospero in *The Tempest* has a much broader concept of the drama's potentialities. While he too sometimes employs his art in order to change certain members of an audience, he also sees its value as pure gesture or celebration. And if the verbal component of his 'tricks' is important, it is primarily as a creator of what Glynn Wickham calls 'devices' that Prospero functions. In this respect Prospero differs significantly from the other theatrical producers we have been considering. The Lord and Hamlet were both seeking to awaken a sense of recognition in the spectator or listener. The 'mockeries' of the performance were intended to remind the audience of true things about which they had some previous knowledge. (Although Sly was never a lord, he presumably knew soft clothes and sweet savours when he experienced them.) Prospero's spirits produce images unlike anything in the audience's experience. The visions of Prospero's isle are not even conventional (like the Athenian mechanical's crude symbolism). His insubstantial pageants are based on dreams not reality; and the feeling they produce is not recognition but wonder.

With Ariel's assistance Prospero creates a wide variety of illusions during the play, but there are two 'revels' that best illustrate his particular methods and purposes. The first is the banquet proferred by the 'strange Shapes,' devised to catch the consciences of the 'three men of sin' – Alonso, Antonio, and Sebastian. Like *The Murder of Gonzago,* this curious play consists of a pantomime followed by a speech making clear the applicability of the actions. Whereas the plot of *Gonzago* closely resembles the circumstances of Claudius's crime, however, the gentle actions and salutations of the monstrous shapes seem unconnected to the lives of the spectators. The ironic contrast they suggest between non-human and human behaviour is too general to be understood by any but Gonzalo. Confronted by the spirits' dumb discourse, Alonso is led to muse but not to repent. It is only when Ariel gives a verbal explanation of the vision that the guilty spectators are overcome by conscience and sink into fits of distraction and ecstasy. In this strange pageant, spectacle serves a different function. There is no attempt on Prospero's part to create a realistic illusion. Instead, the aim seems to be to depart as far as possible from realism in order to make an emblematic statement about outward appearances and inward spirit. Prospero abandons the concept of art as a mirror and substitutes for it the idea of art as revelation.

The role of artist as visionary is given still greater emphasis in the engagement masque created to entertain Ferdinand and Miranda. Here Prospero seems to have no purpose beyond a desire to give pleasure to the young couple. There is no suggestion that the vision is intended to punish, instruct, or reprove. The masque is simply a revel, a celebration of the lovers' union, and an expression of Prospero's hopes for them. It is given for no reason but that the young people expect it. The meaning of the vision is communicated primarily by non-verbal means – allegory, music, dance – and Prospero thinks of it as a gift to be bestowed upon the watchers' eyes. As the entertainment is about to begin, he warns the audience, 'No tongue! All eyes! Be silent!' The vision itself is in the form of a masque, with classical-allegorical figures representing married love and fruitfulness, and it culminates in a dance symbolic of harmony and fertility.

It would be folly to single out any one of Shakespeare's 'stage managers' as representative of the playwright's own theory of the drama. The comic treatment of the subject of staging in *Shrew* and *Dream* and its more serious exposition by Hamlet and Prospero have led many commentators to see in the later figures an expression of Shakespeare's mature convictions. But the ideals of Hamlet are very much at odds with those of Prospero, just as the dramaturgy of the late romances is radically different from that of the tragedies. Superficially there does seem to be a shift of emphasis from rhetorical imagery in early plays such as *Love's Labour's Lost, Richard II* or *Romeo and Juliet* to 'theatrical' imagery in the later romances (a shift from what Cocteau calls 'poetry in the theatre' to 'poetry of the theatre'). But such an evolutionary theory hardly bears close examination. What study of the dramatic ideas of several characters in Shakespeare's plays does illustrate is that the playwright's conception of the nature of dramatic illusion is extremely complex. To understand those ideas fully it is necessary to treat Peter Quince's remarks a little more seriously and Hamlet's somewhat less so. For Shakespeare himself never falls into the trap of believing that the drama is primarily either visual or rhetorical. His work as a whole, no less than his discussion of dramatic principles in his plays, illustrates his wholeness. For Shakespeare, the true 'dramatic image' cannot survive in a single element (sight or hearing) alone, but must live simultaneously in the eye, the ear, and the imagination.

University of Guelph

T.W. CRAIK

'You that way; we this way': Shakespeare's Endings

This essay is concerned rather with the manner in which Shakespeare concludes a play's performance than with the manner in which he handles its dénouement, though it is not easy (or desirable) to consider these two aspects of dramatic technique separately. In both of them Shakespeare shows himself to be both artist and craftsman, aware of the final impression that he wants his play to make and equally aware of the conditions of the theatre in which he passes his daily life, as actor no less than as playwright.

While the comedies are to some degree admitted by Shakespeare to be fantasy, the tragedies and histories make a considerable claim, by their treatment, to be a realistic imitation of life. They therefore end with the powerful working-out of the human relationships upon which they have turned. To study their endings, then, is to see how Shakespeare theatrically reinforces the tragic fact, the death of the protagonist. His technique, however, varies from play to play.

The removal of dead bodies in a theatre without a curtain to lower between stage and spectators had usually to be written into the final lines. (*Romeo and Juliet* and *Othello,* which are exceptional, will be mentioned later.) In *Julius Caesar,* where Brutus's body is at the centre of the final tableau, its removal is not actually directed, merely implied, by Octavius's concluding speech, which follows Antony's tribute:

According to his virtue let us use him,
With all respect and rites of burial.
Within my tent his bones to-night shall lie,
Most like a soldier, ordered honourably.
So call the field to rest, and let's away
To part the glories of this happy day. (V.v.76-81)[1]

The somewhat similar ending of *Coriolanus* shows some interesting variations. Brutus's suicide, foreseeable yet attended by suspense as three of his friends refuse to kill him and the enemy draws nearer, is performed with resolute dignity. This is not a scene of violence. But Coriolanus's assassination, which Aufidius provokes him into inviting, is accompanied by mob outcries recalling the tearing of Cinna the poet, and when he falls, *Aufidius stands on him* (the direction is from the Folio). The shocked Volscian lords restore order and command Aufidius to remove Coriolanus's body with due honour. Aufidius assents:

My rage is gone
And I am struck with sorrow. Take him up.
Help, three o'th'chiefest soldiers; I'll be one.
Beat thou the drum, that it speak mournfully;
Trail your steel pikes. Though in this city he
Hath widowed and unchilded many a one,
Which to this hour bewail the injury,
Yet he shall have a noble memory.
Assist. [*Exeunt bearing the dead body of Coriolanus.*
A dead march sounded.] (V.vi.147-55]

The stage action here (unlike that at the end of *Julius Caesar*) is carefully written into the speech: three captains and Aufidius are to carry the body; a soldier is to beat a dead march on the drum; the rest are to trail their pikes. After the final couplet, the single word of command, 'Assist,' sets all the action going. It also, by putting a rough edge on the couplet, adds a touch of unexpected realism to the expected formal ending.

Shakespeare had given the same rough-edged finish to *Hamlet:*

1 All citations are to *William Shakespeare. The Complete Works* ed Peter Alexander, London 1951.

> Take up the bodies. Such a sight as this
> Becomes the field, but here shows much amiss.
> Go, bid the soldiers shoot. (V.ii.393-5)

The *'Exeunt'* of the Second Quarto is appropriately expanded in the Folio into *'Exeunt Marching: after the which, a Peale of Ordenance are shot off.'* The earlier part of Fortinbras's final speech, like Aufidius's, exactly specifies what is to happen so that the audience can fully absorb the respect which is being accorded to the dead hero:

> Let four captains
> Bear Hamlet like a soldier to the stage;
> For he was likely, had he been put on,
> To have prov'd most royal; and for his passage
> The soldiers' music and the rites of war
> Speak loudly for him. (V.ii.387-92)

The 'stage' (that is, scaffold) is the one on which he was asked by Horatio to expose the bodies to view; its mention shows that he has accepted Horatio's claim to speak authoritatively of the bloody spectacle. Horatio's importance has been strongly emphasized in the last sixty lines, most obviously by his impulse towards suicide and by Hamlet's reasons for staying him. It is also notable that Fortinbras's approach is heard off-stage before Hamlet dies, Osric explaining that 'this warlike volley' is his salute to the English ambassadors. This motivates Hamlet's recommendation of Fortinbras as the next king of Denmark (why else should he be in his thoughts?), and the preliminary announcement of his arrival prevents the audience's suspicion that dramatic convenience has dictated it. Shakespeare's concern for a realistic effect and a slow tempo at the end of the play appears in the 'after the which' of the Folio's stage direction (which must reflect the stage practice) and also in 'Go, bid the soldiers shoot.' The guns are fired not in response to Fortinbras's wish but to his command, which a soldier has to go and deliver to the gunners while others are removing the bodies of Hamlet, Claudius, Gertrude, and Laertes.

In *Othello* Shakespeare reverted to the couplet as conclusion. Lodovico, embodying the authority of Venice, speaks to Iago and, after him, to Gratiano and Cassio:

O Spartan dog,
More fell than anguish, hunger, or the sea!
Look on the tragic loading of this bed.
This is thy work. – The object poisons sight;
Let it be hid. Gratiano, keep the house,
And seize upon the fortunes of the Moor,
For they succeed on you. To you, Lord Governor,
Remains the censure of this hellish villain;
The time, the place, the torture – O, enforce it!
Myself will straight aboard; and to the state
This heavy act with heavy heart relate. (V.ii.364-74)

The finality of the couplet is emphasized by the balancing of 'heavy act' with 'heavy heart.' There are by now no bodies requiring removal. Desdemona, Emilia, and Othello have all died appropriately on the bed, and at 'Let it be hid' the bed's curtains are closed ('the object' is not the bed itself but its 'tragic loading'). It remains on stage after the actors have made their exit and probably also until after the spectators have left the theatre – unless the tragedy is followed by a jig, as was *Julius Caesar* when the Swiss traveller Thomas Platter saw it in 1599. The end of *Romeo and Juliet* is presumably to be managed in a similar way, though this is not made so clear by the lines. The dying Paris begs Romeo, 'Open the tomb, lay me with Juliet' (as he duly does), which indicates that Shakespeare is concerned to place all the bodies (of Paris, Romeo, and Juliet, not to mention Tybalt) where they can be conveniently allowed to remain at the final general exit. But the prince gives no order to close up the tomb ('Seal up the mouth of outrage for a while' V.iii.215, which might be interpreted in this sense, relates rather, in the context of his whole speech, to the passionate outcries of Juliet's parents and Romeo's father); furthermore, the visible presence of the bodies till the very end will provide a much-needed focal point while all the lengthy explanations are going on, and the prince's lines

Where be these enemies? Capulet, Montague,
See what a scourge is laid upon your hate,
That heaven finds means to kill your joys with love!
(V.iii.290-2)

seem to require the enemies to see, not merely to understand, the form that divine vengeance has taken. So if the tomb was closed – as it almost certainly was – this must have been done silently while the general exit was taking place, Shakespeare having missed his opportunity of writing it into the dialogue.

The dialogue culminates in the quatrain-and-couplet spoken by the prince, a lyrical conclusion in stylistic harmony with the sonnet which formed the prologue:

> A glooming peace this morning with it brings;
> The sun for sorrow will not show his head.
> Go hence, to have more talk of these sad things;
> Some shall be pardon'd and some punished.
> For never was a story of more woe
> Than this of Juliet and her Romeo. (V.iii.304-9)

These lines combine the functions of concluding speech and epilogue. The word 'story' is appropriate both to the recital of recent facts that the prince has just heard (as when Hamlet bids Horatio 'tell my story' or Kent tells Edgar 'the most piteous tale of Lear and him') and to the dramatized action that the audience has been witnessing. The prince's final couplet is directed outwards, to those in the pit and galleries as well as to those standing with him on the stage, and amounts to the rhetorical question, 'Have you ever heard a more pathetic story than this?'

The final speech in *King Lear*, by contrast, is wholly addressed to the characters on stage ('we that are young' referring to Albany and Edgar, upon whose shoulders – Kent having resolved to follow his master – the government of Britain has now fallen):

> The weight of this sad time we must obey;
> Speak what we feel, not what we ought to say.
> The oldest hath borne most; we that are young
> Shall never see so much, nor live so long. (V.iii.323-6)

'Exeunt with a dead march' is the Folio's direction, Albany's earlier command 'Bear them from hence' being now obeyed. The final tableau has had Lear and Cordelia at its centre; Goneril and Regan, after their violent deaths off stage, have been brought on earlier so that (as has often been noticed) Lear and his three daughters are all together on stage for the first time

since the opening scene. It was perhaps to emphasize this visual effect that Shakespeare had Edmund borne off stage to die. He may also have considered that four bodies were quite enough to remove at the close. Furthermore, since it was Edmund's remorse that had prompted the attempt to save Lear and Cordelia, Lear's entry with Cordelia's body would demand an emotional response of some kind from him – and yet any such response would be an unwelcome distraction of the audience's attention. For the sake of completeness his death has to be reported to Albany, whose comment, 'That's but a trifle here,' reinforces the stage's emphasis on Lear and Cordelia. But the bodies of Goneril and Regan are not forgotten, for Kent tries to draw Lear's attention to them. Shakespeare thus ensures that there is no superfluous element in the close of the tragedy.

Macbeth ends with couplets which look confidently to the future, not dejectedly to the past. This is an unusual tragedy in that the hero-villain has been slain off-stage, his 'cursed head' being now presented to Malcolm as a symbol of the end of his tyranny: 'The time is free' (V.viii.55). If Macbeth's death had been given the prominence of inclusion in the final scene, Malcolm's subsequent accession might have seemed like anticlimax. Shakespeare further separates the two events by beginning the last scene with Old Siward's poignant response to the news of his son's death. He handles all this far better than he had handled the somewhat similar last scene of *Richard III*, where Richmond is given the crown at the very beginning of the scene and the safety of young George Stanley can hardly be of much concern to the audience, however much Richmond's concern for it is to his credit.

There is little resemblance between the presentation of Macbeth's head to Malcolm and that of Mortimer's head to Edward III in the last scene of Marlowe's *Edward II*. Mortimer has been executed at the young king's order in retribution for the murder of Edward II, which he has very recently caused: Macbeth had murdered Malcolm's father almost at the beginning of the play, and after his death he is denounced not as a murderer but as a tyrant ('this dead butcher' [V.viii.69] is not readily applied to the butchery of Duncan). There is more resemblance between the ends of *Edward II* and *Richard II*. In Marlowe's play not only Mortimer's head is brought in but also (at the young king's command) the hearse bearing his victim, on which the head is placed as a sacrifice to revenge:

> Here comes the hearse: help me to mourn, my lords.
> Sweet father, here unto thy murder'd ghost
> I offer up this wicked traitor's head. (V.vi.98-100)[2]

When the coffined body of Richard is presented to Bolingbroke, the resemblance adds to the ambiguity of Shakespeare's play, for the new king is not the late king's rightful successor and avenger but his supplanter and murderer. Exton, whose hand struck the fatal blow, emphatically gives him the responsibility: 'From your own mouth, my lord, did I this deed.' But Bolingbroke sees himself, and the situation, quite differently:

> They love not poison that do poison need,
> Nor do I thee. Though I did wish him dead,
> I hate the murderer, love him murdered.
> The guilt of conscience take thou for thy labour,
> But neither my good word nor princely favour;
> With Cain go wander thorough shades of night,
> And never show thy head by day nor light.
> Lords, I protest my soul is full of woe
> That blood should sprinkle me to make me grow.
> Come mourn with me for what I do lament,
> And put on sullen black incontinent.
> I'll make a voyage to the Holy Land,
> To wash this blood off from my guilty hand.
> March sadly after; grace my mournings here
> In weeping after this untimely bier. (V.vi.38-52)

Being the king, he has the final word, and what he says goes. His grief and penitence may be perfectly genuine (though his relationship with Richard's actual murderer Exton is uncomfortably reminiscent of John's relationship with Arthur's supposed murderer Hubert), and his generous treatment of the Bishop of Carlisle has just raised him in our opinion, but even so, the end of the play is acutely uncomfortable. The final 'Exeunt,' I have little doubt, should take place in complete silence.

Richard III, culminating in Richmond's triumph, had probably ended with drums and trumpets. Parts 2 and 3 of *Henry VI* end in this way, with couplets so similar as to suggest that Shakespeare was falling into a formula:

2 *Edward II* ed H.B. Charlton and R.D. Waller, London 1933, in *The Works and Life of Christopher Marlowe* gen ed R.H. Case

Sound drums and trumpets and to London all;
And more such days as these to us befall! (V.iii.32-3)

Sound drums and trumpets. Farewell, sour annoy!
For here, I hope, begins our lasting joy. (V.vii.45-6)

But the end of *1 Henry VI,* with a soliloquy for Suffolk, and a soliloquy wholly in blank verse at that, is strikingly unusual, so much so that it hardly seems like an end at all. Shakespeare's tragedies and histories characteristically end processionally, with or without sound effects. This convention (seen, for example, in *1 Henry IV*) is subtly flouted in *2 Henry IV* in order to dramatize the rejection of Falstaff. If Falstaff had not bulked so large in the play and its precursor, the 'crown scene' between the prince and his dying father and the prince's scene with his brothers and the Lord Chief Justice could have led straight on to a formal 'coronation scene' ending in the usual exhortatory processional manner. Instead, Falstaff's entry with his companions leads on to the prince's rejection speech, in which he demolishes Falstaff's hopes in over twenty lines; these culminate in a typical couplet-and-rough-edge cadence:

Be it your charge, my lord,
To see perform'd the tenour of our word.
Set on. (V.v.71-3)

The effect is that of a false ending since, instead of the stage's being wholly cleared, Falstaff and his companions remain to resume their prose: 'Master Shallow, I owe you a thousand pound' (V.v.74). They in their turn must be got off stage, so we now have the return of the Lord Chief Justice to extinguish Falstaff's reviving hopes by ordering him to the Fleet. But this is not enough in itself to end the play, so we are also given his dialogue with Prince John about Falstaff's rejection and the prospect of a French campaign. I imagine that most readers, and many spectators, find this dialogue rather wooden, with Prince John telling the Lord Chief Justice what he knows already. The most that can be said for it is that it is a workmanlike way out of the difficulty that Shakespeare has made for himself by his striking dramatization of the rejection. The added epilogue – or choice of epilogues – seems a further indication that Shakespeare was doing his best to end his play in a definite manner as well as to advertise the forthcoming *Henry V*.

To end a play, as Haydn ends his 'Farewell' Symphony, with two players instead of the company's full complement is extraordinary for Shakespeare. He did it in *The Comedy of Errors* to make a comic point about the still-persisting confusion between each pair of twins; when the masters have left, the servants remain and, unable to settle the question of which is the first-born, depart hand in hand. The device is evidently appropriate to the dramatic material. But at the end of *Troilus and Cressida* Troilus's couplet

> Strike a free march to Troy. With comfort go;
> Hope of revenge shall hide our inward woe (V.x.30-1)

is followed by Pandarus's entry (a thoroughly incongruous one on the battlefield) and his indignant repudiation by Troilus (in a couplet which, in the Folio, also concluded the scene where he brought Troilus Cressida's letter). It seems that the ending has been revised, at considerable artistic violence to the original version, in order to drag in Pandarus's epilogue and replace a tragic dignified ending with a satirical undignified one. Whether the violent reworking is a justified theatrical effect is debatable.

Shakespeare's epilogues are usually introduced with great propriety:

> The King's a beggar, now the play is done.
> All is well ended if this suit be won,
> That you express content; which we will pay
> With strife to please you, day exceeding day.
> Ours be your patience then, and yours our parts;
> Your gentle hands lend us, and take our hearts.

This epilogue to *All's Well that Ends Well* resembles Jonson's epilogue to *Volpone*, where a principal actor speaks well-turned heroic couplets and alludes to his role. Others of Shakespeare's epilogues similarly exploit the shift from the world of dramatic illusion to that of everyday reality. Thus Puck, at the end of a play where magic and sleep have been intimately connected, invites the spectators to imagine that they 'have but slumb'red here / While these visions did appear' (V.i.414-15); Rosalind, who has spent much of *As You Like It* in the disguise of a youth and has not resumed her woman's dress till the final scene, says she would kiss the attractive men in the audience if she were a woman – being in reality a male actor; Prospero, having broken and buried his staff and drowned his book, appeals for favours that he now lacks the magic power to enforce. All three epilogues are distinct from each other in tone, and a brief summary can hardly suggest the subtlety of any of them, particularly Prospero's. But in all of them – as also in Time's prologue to the latter part of *The Winter's Tale* – a playful wit is an essential ingredient. The epilogue to *Twelfth Night* is exceptional in depending not upon wit but upon humour. The clown's song reveals itself to be an epilogue only in its final stanza:

> A great while ago the world begun,
>   With hey, ho, the wind and the rain,
> But that's all one, our play is done,
>   And we'll strive to please you every day. (V.i.391-4)

(Compare the same promise in the epilogue of *All's Well that Ends Well*.) The point, I think, is that until that stanza the clown's song, as a sequel to the final lines of the final scene, had seemed completely pointless.

To have an epilogue spoken 'in character' is far more consistent with the nature of comedy than with that of tragedy, where, even though the deaths are known to be 'fabulously counterfeit' (as Hieronimo expresses it in *The Spanish Tragedy*, preparatory to showing that in the case of his court entertainment they are not), there is little to be gained by underlining the fact. No one would wish for an epilogue spoken by Lear or Othello. The comedies, though each of them fully absorbs the audience into its world, are accorded a different kind of belief, the make-believe element being sometimes pointed by remarks like Fabian's 'If this were play'd upon a stage now, I could condemn it as an improbable fiction' (III.iv.121-4). Consistent with this is Shakespeare's trick of introducing blandly and suddenly some improbable event into the last scene, as when Don John's capture, Duke Frederick's conversion, and the imprisonment of Viola's sea-captain at Malvolio's suit are reported, and Antonio's ships are restored to him by a letter which Portia as good as admits to producing out of thin air. A curious feature of two of the last plays, *The Winter's Tale* and *The Tempest*, is that they end not with the usual couplet (as *Cymbeline* does) but with blank verse, which Shakespeare had hitherto used as a conclusion only in *1 Henry VI* and *The Two Gentlemen of Verona*. Perhaps this avoidance of the formality of rhyme reflects an absence of sententiousness from Leontes and and Prospero, the speakers of the final lines; and their final words, 'Hastily lead away' (V. ii.155) and 'Please you, draw near' (V.i.318), both imply further harmonious conversation between the stage personages once they have left our view. Prospero's return to the stage to speak his epilogue does not counteract that implication, since, as we have seen, he returns not as Prospero but as a subtle amalgam of Prospero and Actor-of-Prospero.

University of Durham

F.D. HOENIGER

Musical Cures of Melancholy and Mania in Shakespeare[1]

In several scenes in Shakespeare, characters are, with the help of music, restored to sanity from a severe state of depression or distraction and, in one instance, even from mania. How did Shakespeare hear about therapy of this kind, and were doctors actually applying musical therapy in Shakespeare's time or earlier? The best-known instance in Shakespeare is probably that in *King Lear*. Soon after her arrival in England in the fourth act, Cordelia learns of her mad father's wandering about the heath, 'Crown'd with rank fumiter and furrow-weeds,' but her physician gives her hope that he can be restored to sanity. Once Lear has been found and brought to camp, the doctor puts him to sleep with the help of herbal drugs. When after several hours the doctor urges that Lear be woken up in Cordelia's presence, she prays:

> O you kind gods,
> Cure this great breach in his abused nature!
> Th' untuned and jarring sense, O, wind up
> Of this child-changed father. (IV.vii.14-17)

1 This essay is an adaptation of a paper I gave in June 1981 at Halifax during the annual meetings of the Canadian Society for the History of Medicine, Learned Societies. Professor Rika Maniates saved me from more than one error in musical terminology, and Sheldon Zitner from infelicities in style.

The sleeping Lear is carried into her tent, and the doctor calls for music to be played. When it seems to have no effect, he urges, 'Louder, the music there!' After another sixteen lines, Lear begins to stir, whereupon Cordelia addresses him gently. Slowly, Lear responds that she must be some angelic spirit, a 'soul in bliss.' This elicits Cordelia's despairing comment, 'still far wide.' But stage by stage Lear comes to accept that she must be real, that she is indeed his daughter. His soul or mind and his jarring senses have been retuned. The physician remains duly cautious. Having given his patient as full assurance as possible, he advises that Lear not be troubled 'until further settling' (IV.vii.52).

This is the clearest instance in Shakespeare of a cure of acute mental illness with the help of music. But there are others. In *Pericles* the protagonist, having earlier lost his wife in childbirth, is led to believe sixteen years later that his daughter, whom he has not seen since she was a baby, has also died. As a consequence he falls into a deep depression, or melancholia as it was then called, and remains in it for three months. He does not cut his hair or shave his beard, and no one manages to get a word out of him. He sits in his cabin on his ship, with his head in his hands. The governor of Mytilene, hearing about this when Pericles' ship rests in his harbour, remembers a beautiful and virtuous young woman who has enchanted everyone in his city with her music:

> She questionless with her sweet harmony
> And other chosen attractions, would allure
> And make a batt'ry through his deafened ports
> Which now are midway stopped. (V.i.44-7)

That is, literally, her music may penetrate his sense of hearing and thereby move his psyche or soul. We in the audience know that the governor is speaking of Marina, who happens to be Pericles' daughter. But when Marina is brought to the ship, she is likewise unaware that Pericles is her father. She sings a beautiful song to him, accompanying herself on an instrument. For some time Pericles does not seem to react, but when she then speaks to him, he begins to stir. A happy recognition eventually follows. The play also includes a doctor called Cerimon who applies music therapeutically. But he uses it to awaken a woman who had been mistakenly given up for dead. That is a different subject, and involves a different, a rougher kind of music.

In my final example from Shakespeare, music is spoken of as sometimes having a negative effect. Richard II, having been deposed by Bolingbroke, is cast into prison. There he suddenly hears music played in a neighbouring room. At first he is delighted by the sound, but then he rejects it:

> This music mads me. Let it sound no more;
> For though it have holp madmen to their wits,
> In me it seems it will make wise men mad.
> Yet blessing on his heart that gives it me,
> For 'tis a sign of love! (V.v.61-5)

While here also alluding to the therapeutic power of music in treating the mentally ill, evidently Shakespeare based Richard's rejection of music on a view contrary to that of the tradition he used in *King Lear* and *Pericles.* And that such a different tradition existed is confirmed by a passage in *Midas,* a play by Lyly, where a young woman, Sophronia, speaking of her father laments:

> But that which maketh me most to sorrow and wonder is that music, a mithridate for melancholy, should make him mad. (IV.iv.49-50)

How did these opposed views of the effect of music reach Shakespeare? And can one perhaps even discover instances of the use of music in the medical practice of the time? In attempting to find an answer to these questions, one should begin by assuming that the traditions were not new but of either classical or medieval origin or both. Further, our very subject suggests that we may find the answers rather among writers on music than primarily in works by physicians. As we will see, we need to include some history of music in our investigation, though we will be particularly on the look-out for data in the history of medicine.

In ancient Greece, Pythagoras and his followers worshipped Apollo as the god of light, of healing, and of music; and Apollo's son was Aesculapius or Asclepius, the god of medicine. Pythagorean doctors developed a cult around Aesculapius and attributed to him cures of madness by means of musical incantations and also cures of deafness: healing music, they held, can restore our sense of hearing and thus open our spirit again to the influence of its harmony. Further, from the Pythagoreans derives the long-lasting belief, often echoed in the Renaissance, that the harmonies of music can purge and purify the passions, or at least mitigate the causes of the perturbation of mind in madmen. Inner disharmony, the theory ran, is cured by the affect of harmony. Some remarkable cures of this kind were attributed, for instance, to Empedocles, a philosopher and physician of the fifth century BC.

Pythagoras and his followers interpreted the whole universe in terms of interacting musical harmonies that move through the air in circular waves, and they sought to comprehend these movements and harmonies mathematically. From this developed a whole cosmology and astronomical theory which in the Renaissance crucially influenced both Copernicus and Kepler. Further, the Pythagoreans systematized the various modes of Greek music, the Dorian, the Phrygian, and so on, defining for each mode the intervals between notes in mathematical ratios. They further developed a theory of how the various modes lend themselves either to the arousal or the calming of particular passions. More than one ancient writer asserts that Phrygian music stirs up courage in soldiers while Dorian music makes men calm and peaceful. Thus the story arose that Timotheus, a musician, first aroused Alexander of Macedon's passion with his music and then, altering the mode, calmed him again. It is from this Pythagorean world view, echoed by Plato and his followers, that a tradition developed over many hundreds of years which claimed all sorts of powers for music, including therapeutical ones. However, even in classical times there was in practice some confusion about the precise effect of the various modes of music on the passions. Writers contradict one another on the subject. And much later in the Renaissance, when the humanists revived the Greek terms for the basic modes, the confusion was aggravated by the fact that the modes of music then familiar, inherited as they were from ecclesiastical medieval music, were completely different from the ancient Greek ones. The humanists' attempts to reconcile the classical modes with their own were doomed to failure from the start. And this, alas, means that we have no clear clue as to what mode of music was used, for instance, by the physician in charge of the cure of King Lear. It is a good guess that it was performed on neither krumhorn nor trumpet and that it was more harmonious than rock. But on this point we cannot get much farther, lacking as we do more precise documentation of the musical practice in Shakespeare's theatre.

Returning to classical times, we find that the most famous example for posterity of a physician applying musical therapy to madmen with remarkable results was Asclepiades of Bithynia,[2] who practised medicine in Rome during the first century BC. Unfortunately only tiny fragments of his writings have survived, but he is frequently mentioned by both medical and literary writers during the following three centuries. Censorinus of the third century AD reports that:

> the chief value of music, according to the opinion of Asclepiades, is to be found in those diseases in which the mind is affected. Hence the minds of phrenetics, disturbed by the disease, are often restored to their own nature by a symphony.[3]

Celsus in his *De medicina,* a work rediscovered and widely read in the Renaissance, also mentions musical therapy for melancholia, though only briefly; and Byzantine writers report that Archigenes treated the insane humanely and soothed them with music.[4]

On the other hand, Hippocrates many centuries earlier had already dissociated himself from the medical use of incantations because he considered them magical. Hippocrates advocated that all diseases have natural causes and that therefore only natural remedies should be used. For a similar reason, Galen rejected Asclepiades' views and practice completely, as did Soranus, who wrote, after citing the claims for music:

> But actually the sound of music congests the head, as is perfectly clear even in the case of healthy persons. In fact, it is abundantly attested that in some cases music arouses men to madness.[5]

Here, and in an often-cited passage by Plutarch, *musica magis dementat quam vinum,* is to be found the origin for the view

2 See Robert M. Green *Asclepiades, His Life and Writings (A Translation of Cocchi's Life of Asclepiades and Gumpert's Fragments of Asclepiades)* New Haven 1955.

3 Censorinus *De die Natali volumen illustre* chap 12, summarized in Green *Asclepiades* p 126. By 'symphony' is meant harmonious music.

4 See T. Clifford Allbutt *Greek Medicine in Rome* 1921; reprinted New York 1970, p 283.

5 Soranus, as in Caelius Aurelianus *On Acute Diseases and on Chronic Diseases* trans and ed I.E. Drabkin, Chicago 1950. The passage is from Chronic Diseases, bk I, sec v.

expressed by Shakespeare's Richard II.

At the same time, excessive claims for the powers of music were passed on from Greek thought via the neo-Platonists to early Christian writers on music, among them Cassiodorus of the sixth century[6] and his contemporary Boethius, author of the influential treatise *De Musica*. These writers and their successors in the Middle Ages included among examples for their claims not only Asclepiades' cures of the insane but also the famous Old Testament story told in the first book of Samuel of how David dispelled King Saul's depression by playing on his harp. From medieval writers on music, the tradition passed on in turn to poets, practitioners of an art akin to that of music. It was this way that Shakespeare learned about Asclepiades. Two generations after him, Rembrandt made David's playing on the harp to Saul the subject of one of his most famous paintings, thus providing another instance of the attractiveness to artists of a theory that allowed their work an influence and import beyond aesthetic effects.

But the influence of this tradition was not confined to poets and artists. Isidore of Seville, the Church Father and contemporary of Boethius, wrote:

> It is sometimes asked why the art of medicine is not included among the other liberal arts. It is because they deal with single causes, but medicine with all. For a medical man should know the *ars grammatica*, ... the *ars geometrica*, ... (etc) Moreover, he must know something of music, for many things may be done for the sick by this art ... Asclepiades restored a madman to his former health by means of a concord of sounds.[7]

Music was one of the seven liberal arts in which physicians were educated.

Jumping several centuries to the high and later Middle Ages we find that besides the continuation of the views just described, there were two further major developments. One of them is the association of Christ the physician with the thera-

6 Cassiodorus *Institutiones* bk II, v.9, in *An Introduction to Divine and Human Readings* by Cassiodorus Senator, trans Leslie Webber Jones, New York 1946, pp 195-6

7 Cited by Walter Clyde Curry, *Chaucer and the Medieval Sciences* 2nd edn, 1960, pp 4-5; Curry took the translation from H.P. Cholmeley *John of Gaddesden and the Rosa Medicina* pp 93-4. For Isidore's Latin text, see *Patrologia Latina* ed Migne, CXCIX.

peutic power of music. Music was then believed to be especially capable of dispelling demoniac influence or possession, widely held to be a cause of madness. Music indeed came to symbolize Christ's commandments, and the lyre to signify the Cross and its curative power. How familiar the tradition of Christ curing the sick with the help of music remained in the sixteenth century was shown in a paper given in 1981 by Philip Sohm[8] on church paintings (surrounding an organ) by the Venetian artist Veronese.

The other major development derived from Arabic medicine, which for several centuries dominated medieval theory and practice in the West. From early on, Arab physicians appear to have treated their mental patients humanely and to have used music widely for therapeutical purposes in hospitals. In a Latin manuscript translation of the *Handbook for Health, Tacuinum sanitatis in Medicina,*[9] by Albucasis, made at Verona near the end of the fourteenth century, we find a picture of a wealthy woman standing in a splendid Italian courtyard with what seems to be her waiting woman. The lady's look and stance suggest that she is suffering from acute depression. Hesitantly she allows herself to be taken by the hand, while three musicians with shawms and bagpipe strike up the healing dance.

This picture clearly suggests that by then the Arabic method had been adopted in Italy. It had presumably also become Christianized. In a document from about 1500 we learn about the following event in the life of the Flemish painter Hugo van der Goes, who had become mad. Believing himself to be damned, he was taken under guard to a father superior in Brussels called Thomas.

> After enquiry and examination, Thomas decided that the patient was agitated by the same evil as Saul. And recalling how Saul was relieved when David sounded his harp, he ordered for abundant music to be played at once before brother Hugo, ... by which he hoped to chase away his mental fantasies.[10]

8 May 1981, meetings of the Canadian Society for Renaissance Studies, Learned Societies, Halifax, NS

9 See Luisa Cogliati Arano *The Medieval Health Handbook, Tacuinum Sanitatis* trans and adapted O. Ratti and A. Westbrook, New York 1976. But the picture is not included in this edition. It is found in the ms of the National Library of Austria in Vienna.

This curious incident took place well after the famous Marsilio Ficino studied and practised medicine at Florence and founded the Neo-Platonic Academy. Ficino and other scholars edited, translated into Latin, and made widely available with the help of the new printers the dialogues of Plato, the works of several ancient neo-Platonists, as well as various hermetical writings and the Cabbala. These were to exercise an enormous influence on thought for two centuries. Ficino's own medical theories were strongly inspired by Pythagorean and neo-Platonic cosmology with its vitalist notions of interacting correspondences between the forces of the universe at large, the living cosmos, and the central creature in it, the little world of man. Both that phrase and the doctrine of correspondences are echoed in act III of *King Lear*.

Ficino was particularly concerned about types of melancholia or depression, especially the kind which can develop into mania, as Aretaeus and other classical writers had described it. As Ficino knew from experience and from one of the pseudo-Aristotelian *Problemata*, men of unusual talent and scholars are especially subject to such mania. Besides much sensible advice on preventative measures, his discussion of the disease includes interesting comments on the peculiar power of music on man. He notes

> a similarity between the material medium in which it is transmitted, air, and the human spirit; that is to the fact that both are living kinds of air, moving in a highly organized way, and that both, through the text of the song, can carry an intellectual content.[11]

Since the Pythagoreans, the spirit of hearing as part of the animal spirit had been, like music, associated with air and movement. We recall that the Pythagoreans claimed to be able to cure both deafness and madness with music. Through the sense of hearing, it was believed, the spirits in man can be moved more strongly than through any of the other senses. 'Musically moved air is alive ... and ... naturally has the most powerful effect on the hearer's spirit.'[12] By it the higher spirits

10 Jean Strabonski *Histoire du traitement de la mélancholie des origines à 1900* Basel 1960, who indirectly follows Hjalmar G. Sander 'Beiträge zur Biographie Hugo van der Goes' und zur Chronologie seiner Werke' *Repert. Kunstwissenschaft* 35 (1912) 519 (my translation)

11 Summarized from Ficino *De Triplica Vita* by D.P. Walker *Spiritual and Demonic Magic from Ficino to Campanella* London 1958, p 6

in man, animal and vital, are strengthened, thus counteracting the bad effect of excess and overheated melancholy on the brain. (Mania was thought to be caused by malignant vapours or smoke of melancholy adust rising from the abdomen and the cardia to the brain.) Further, the effort of intense scholarly study was supposed to be harmful to and reduce the animal spirit, which, according to traditional medical theory, was produced from the vital spirit in the brain.

> Musical sound, by its movement of air, moves the body; by its purified air, it excites the animal or aery spirit which is the link between body and soul; by its emotion, it affects the senses, and at the same time the soul; by its content and meaning (as in song with words) it touches the intellect; ... by its spiritual and material nature, it seizes the whole of man in a single stroke and possesses him completely.[13]

Music therefore is useful both as a preventative, to keep off disease, and as a means of restoring health after temporary insanity.

We recall that in *King Lear* Cordelia speaks of her father's untuned mind and jarring senses. In Ficino's theories we have a clear explanation for the therapeutic employment of music by Lear's doctor, and also particularly for the scene in Shakespeare's *Pericles* where Marina rouses her father from his condition of long-lasting depression by first singing and then speaking to him.

While Ficino emphasized the effect of music on the ear, the animal spirit, and the reason or intellect, its harmonious order also parallels as well as affects the physical order and movement of the body. Music counteracts dyscrasia. It can restore inner harmony or health. This ancient vitalist notion, newly developed by Ficino, included the view that the human pulse beats with a musical rhythm. So when Queen Gertrude in *Hamlet* attributes her son's strange behaviour and words after the renewed visitation of the Ghost, whom she cannot see, to the ecstacy of madness, he replies:

12 Ficino *De Triplica Vita*, cited by Walker *Demonic Magic* p 10

13 Ficino *Comment in Timaeum* vol I, chap xxviii, trans from citation in Strabonski *Histoire du traitement de la mélancholie* p 74

My pulse, as yours, doth temperately keep time
And makes as healthful music. It is not madness
That I have uttered. (III.iv.140-2)

Turning to the sixteenth century and closer to Shakespeare's contemporaries, one will not be surprised, after what we have learned, to find several writers repeating the high claims of their predecessors for the powers of music. These writers include references to Asclepiades, David and King Saul, and much else. And whenever poets turn to this subject, from the time of Queen Elizabeth to Milton in the seventeenth century, they similarly repeat the old material, as did Thomas Watson in 1582 in a sonnet beginning:

Esclepiad did cure with trumpets sound
Such men as first had lost their hearing quite:
And many such as in their drink lay drowned
Damon revived with tunes of grave delight:
And Theophrast when ought his mind oppressed,
Used music's help to bring himself to rest:
With sound of harp Thales did make recure
Of such which lay with pestilence forlorn:
With organ pipes Xenocrates made pure
Their wits, whose minds long lunacy had worn.[14]

As for medical men, we will recall Isidore of Seville's exhortation that physicians should include music among their studies and skills. Several of the Persian and Arab physicians, including the great Rhazes, were notable for their talent in playing musical instruments, and a number of physicians of the sixteenth century were skilful musicians, though it would be nice to know more exactly how widespread such expertise was. Ficino was a musician, and Paracelsus a notable player of the organ. Fracastoro, the author of the well-known poem on syphilis, was known also for his musical skills, and Felix Platter of Basel played the lute while studying medicine at Montpellier. Two Oxford physicians in the age of Queen Elizabeth, George Etherege and John Case,[15] were musicians. The latter was the

14 Sonnet 13 in *Hekatompathia* 1582; text modernized from edn by Cesare G. Cecioni, Catania 1964. The following sonnet begins with a reference to how Alexander was stirred by his musician.

15 For both, see DNB.

author of *The Praise of Musicke* (1586), in which he defends the art against the attack on it by Puritans just as Sir Philip Sidney had more eloquently defended the art of poetry against a similar attack. Case, besides repeating several stories we have mentioned, cites Macrobius the author of the Commentary on Cicero's *Dream of Scipio,* who described the effect of the various Greek modes of music on the passions. According to Macrobius, it is the Aeolian mode that allays and pacifies anger, quiets the mind, 'giveth sleep to the pacified senses.' It sounds like a proper mode for the cure of King Lear. Yet one wishes one knew exactly what Case understood by Aeolian music. He writes:

> as every disease is cured by his contrary, so music is as an Antipharmacon to sorrow ... Music assuageth and easeth the inordinate perturbations and evil affections of the mind; ... So Empedocles with his skilful playing on the cittern hindred a mad man, ready to slay himself ...[16]

One may assume, but cannot prove, that in practice Case sometimes aimed at similar results.

In some of the medical writings of the period, one encounters similar large claims for the powers of music to cure not only mental illness but also the effects of the bite of the tarantula, and even the plague. Among these are Ambroise Paré's *De diverses manières de Guarisons*[17] and André du Laurens's discourse on melancholic diseases, translated into English in 1599.[18] But it is very difficult to assess whether these doctors are merely repeating in their writings an age-old tradition or at times have actually experimented with it in practice. In Shakespeare's own time, the astronomer Kepler writes:

> It is the custom of some physicians to cure their patients by pleasing music. How can music work in the body of a person? Namely in such a way that the soul in the person, just as some animals do also, understands the harmony, is happy about it, is refreshed and becomes accordingly stronger in its body.[19]

16 John Case *The Praise of Musicke* 1586, pp 61-2

17 In *Oeuvres* 4th edn, 1585, bk I, chap 27, p 48. He chiefly alludes to the popular tradition of musical cures from the effects of the bite of a tarantula.

18 André du Laurens *A Discourse of the Preservation of the Sight; of Melancholike Diseases; of Rheumes, and of Old Age* trans R. Surphlet, 1599, in *Shakespeare Association Facsimiles* 15, ed Sanford V. Larkey, 1938, sig Q2, p 107

But this sounds very much like Ficino and more ancient writers, and can we be sure that by 'the custom of some physicians' Kepler does indeed mean a custom of his own time? I think that he does, because all the evidence I have presented points to the likelihood that such therapy was practised around 1600. Yet so far I have been able to discover only a single instance of a physician of the early seventeenth century actually trying out the effect of music on a patientand this patient was not suffering from mental illness, though he was in a state of raging fury after returning drunk from a wedding feast. Nicholas Bergier reports in 1623 in *La musique spéculative:*

> I decided to take my lute, and to play him a tune in the phrygian mode, composed ... with double spondees. I had not played ten or twelve chords, when the furious young man began to stop wandering about, returned his sword into its sheath, and listened to the lute with such intensity that shortly he became calm, capable of reason once more, and allowed himself to be peacefully conducted to his chamber ...[20]

Such a method might work as well today as it did then. Only it would have been nice to know whether this physician sometimes played his lute to patients who remained longer in their state of depression or manic excitement.

We do know that since Shakespeare's time music has been used in therapy. Over a hundred years ago Dr John Charles Bucknill, a leading English psychiatrist as well as author of two books on Shakespeare, referred to his colleague Dr Mason Cox as a great advocate for music in the treatment of insanity. In our own time, national and international conferences have been held in Britain and the United States on the use of music in psychiatric treatment. At one of these, held at the Uffculme Clinic in Birmingham, Dr Henry Rollin stated:

> The qualities of the ideal music therapist should include, in addition to dedication, the strength of Juno, the wisdom of Solomon, the patience of Job, the musical skill of David, and last but by no means least, the seductive charm of Cleopatra.[21]

19 Cited in M. Caspar *Kepler* London and New York 1959, p 63

20 My own translation; cited in original French from Bibl Nat ms fr 1359 by D.P. Walker in *Der musikalische Humanismus im 16. und frühen 17. Jahrhundert* Kassel und Basel, nd (ca 1947) p 20

The latter of course not so much for the patients as for the more sceptical doctors in the hospital. Moving still closer to home, in February 1980 Yehudi Menuhin is reported to have visited a psychiatric centre at Abbotsford in British Columbia. When interviewed, Menuhin said:

> Music is in fact therapy. The vibrations put us in touch with the whole of creation, with all the vibrations in the world.[22]

For Yehudi Menuhin, as we see, neo-Platonism is still a living philosophy.

Victoria College
University of Toronto

21 *Music in Psychiatric Treatment* ed Dr Newnham, Birmingham 1966. Dr Rollin worked at Epsom.

22 Quoted by Anne Roberts in *The Globe and Mail* (Toronto) early Feb 1980

J.A.B. SOMERSET

Shakespeare's Great Stage of Fools 1599-1607

Whatever may be our reaction to Shakespeare's earlier clown roles, Shakespeare clearly began to move in new directions with *As You Like It* (1599-1600) through to *King Lear* (1605-6). Usually, accounts of this change give much of the credit to Robert Armin, who joined the Lord Chamberlain's men sometime in 1599-1600 and, we are told, presented Shakespeare with a radically new 'line' of comic talents. As a result, the account goes, Shakespeare created his series of 'wise fools' – Touchstone, Feste, and so on – in response to Armin's proclivities. Such a brief outline as this cannot do complete justice to the idea, but I trust that it fairly presents the essentials of what has become a widely held orthodoxy of our time. A recent study presents a representative account suggesting that Kemp's departure from the Lord Chamberlain's men and Armin's advent account for the difference between Dogberry and Touchstone because 'Robert Armin not only surpassed the clownish witticisms and turns of the Tarleton-Kempe tradition, but originated a new style of witty, songful, intellectual, and socially mobile clowning.'[1] Also it is not unusual to find a Shakespearian wise fool discussed, as in a recent authoritative edition, as 'the Armin part.'[2] One could easily multiply instances of what has become a common view of the origin of Shakespeare's professional jesters. I wish to

1 Charles S. Felver *Robert Armin: Shakespeare's Fool* Kent Ohio, p 31
2 Touchstone, in *As You Like It* ed Agnes Latham, New Arden Shakespeare, London 1975, p liii

examine the origins and development of this belief. While readily granting the talents of the actors in the Lord Chamberlain's men, I wish to suggest that many recent treatments of Armin are overstated and tend to focus our attention upon the actor rather than upon the mature experimenting dramatist. Redressing the balance, placing the actor in the play rather than the play around the actor, will allow for a juster examination of Shakespeare's treatment of his five fools, their companions, and their worlds.

I

It has been many times suggested that Elizabethan clowns were in various ways separable from the actions of the plays. *Tarlton's Jests* provides evidence of contemporary popular delight at this, while Sidney's *Apology* and *The Pilgrimage to Parnassus* show that the delight was not universal. The seventeenth century settled fairly quickly on its response to Shakespeare's clowns; in 1647 William Cartwright praised Beaumont and Fletcher in these terms:

> *Shakespeare* to thee was dull, whose best jest lies
> I' the Ladies' questions and the Fooles replyes;
> Old fashion'd wit, which walkt from town to town
> In turn'd Hose, which our fathers call'd the Clown.
>
> (Commendatory verses to the 1647 Folio *Works* of Beaumont and Fletcher)

Our minds may boggle at Cartwright's calling Shakespeare 'dull.' This 'refinement' of taste was, however, reinforced by the increasing obscurity brought by time to many of Shakespeare's jokes. As well, neo-Aristotelian regard for decorum and the 'rules' could find no place for clowns and low comedy.

A remark by Coleridge typifies this critical tradition, and its attitudes in turn lie behind a great deal of later thinking about Shakespeare's comic parts. Dismissing the Porter scene in *Macbeth*, Coleridge suggests that it was 'written for the mob by some other hand, perhaps with Shakespeare's consent.' As the Variorum editor points out, Coleridge has recognized a verbal echo of *Hamlet* in the Porter's words; this is why he is prepared to admit, grudgingly, Shakespeare's possible agreement to the scene. The three ideas expressed by Coleridge, in any case, surface again and again in later writers as one or another of three reasons for 'comic relief.' First, the idea that the comedy is there 'for the mob' draws on the notion that Shakespeare's was an age of barbarism to which low comedy was a regrettable concession: the clear implication in a book such as Robert Bridges's *Influence of the Audience on Shakespeare's Drama* (1927) is that Shakespeare would have been a better artist had he been blessed with a better audience. However, we now agree that it is dangerous to use our incomplete knowledge of Shakespeare's milieu only to excuse alleged 'faults.' Second, the idea of 'some other hand' is found in the continuing attempts, lately waning, at disintegration of the text by finding other hands responsible for (or guilty of) 'suspect' passages. It seems to me that the disintegrators have worked with more energy and over a longer period on the comic passages than on other parts of Shakespeare's text. The clowns themselves have been more than once suggested as authors of their own material. Finally, the third idea we find again is that Shakespeare may have consented to the presence of others' irruptive comedy: modern critics have speculated about the relationship between author and comedian and have put forward theories about the partnerships between Shakespeare and Kemp and Shakespeare and Armin. Before assenting to this third idea it is necessary to have accepted the second, the presence of another hand, which in itself seems suspect: the sheer energy of Shakespeare's comic prose and the echoes one finds of it elsewhere in his verse lead most readers readily to grant Shakespeare's authorship. Modern sympathies are wider, and many are less ready now to reprehend or seek to excuse comic passages, or to entertain the idea that they are 'comic relief' – a term which raises more questions than it resolves.

Questions about the relationship between dramatists and clowns were stimulated by antiquarian investigation: Halliwell-Phillipps, Chambers, and Nunzeger (to name only three) amassed many details about actors' lives and the organization of theatrical companies. If parts might have been written *by* fellow actors, it is only a small step to suggest that parts might have been written *for* particular fellow actors. The 'lines' of particular actors were thoroughly investigated by T.W. Baldwin in his *Organization and Personnel of the Shakespearian Company* (1927), which put forward the view that 'Shakespeare cut his play to fit the actors of his company even in the details of age and physical appearance, fashioning for each actor a suitable principal part' (page 282). This did not win general scholarly agreement; as well, many of Baldwin's specific suggestions have been discarded. One which has not concerns Armin's 'line' as a comic actor. Undeniably, the dates of Will Kemp's departure (early 1599?) and Robert Armin's employment by the Lord Chamberlain's men (dates between August 1599 and mid-1600 have been suggested) occur at about the date usually suggested for *As You Like It*, wherein we meet Touchstone as the first of the witty professional jesters. While this might just have been coincidence, maybe not: it has been taken as clear evidence of the advent of Armin's 'line.' This part of Baldwin's theory has produced two corollary ideas. First, Armin has been considered in some way *necessary* for the parts he played – in spite of our sketchy knowledge of Kemp, it has usually been considered inconceivable that he could have played the parts. Second and more important, Armin is now considered to have been in some way the source or inspiration for Shakespeare's wise fools, as further tabulation of some recent representative views will make clear. Armin has been described as 'Shakespeare's source for Touchstone' and for Lear's Fool, for whose conception Shakespeare is said to have resorted 'to tradition, or ... to Armin, which was the same thing.'[3] Another writer includes Feste: 'everything, then, that one finds in a Touchstone, a Feste, or Lear's fool is foreshadowed [in Armin's writings] ... the mimicry, the sense of style, the delight in paradox, the singing, the nonsense rhymes, the pleasure in good living ...'[4] For some, the link between actor and dramatist intertwined comedy and philosophy: one writes, 'both men had come to inhabit a country of the imagination in which the notion of comedy as a mere laughter-maker had been put aside,'[5] while a second suggests that 'what Armin seems to have provoked in Shakespeare ... was the integrated comic vision of an Erasmus or a More of the world of fools.'[6] The tendency revealed in these quotations is clearly towards intimating that in some way (perhaps stopping short of actually holding the pen) Armin was the 'originator'

3 Robert H. Goldsmith *Wise Fools in Shakespeare* East Lansing 1963, p 60
4 Felver *Robert Armin* p 37
5 Gareth Lloyd-Evans 'Shakespeare's Fools: The Shadow and the Substance of Drama' in *Shakespearean Comedy* ed Malcolm Bradbury and David Palmer, Stratford-upon-Avon Studies 14, London 1972, p 152. His evidence, however, is the third (revised) quarto of one of Armin's works, *A Nest of Ninnies* (1608), on which see below.
6 M.C. Bradbrook *Shakespeare the Craftsman* London 1969, p 57

and inspired Shakespeare to write fool parts for him. In turn, this is a short step from suggesting that the comic actor created his own material; it brings us, in a strange way, back to Coleridge and inevitably leads towards seeing the comic parts as detachable from their plays. They have come to be often discussed more as actor's opportunities than integrated parts of a complex dramatic vision. The whole history of criticism, briefly outlined earlier, makes such a view seem the more reasonable. However, the evidence for Armin as source or inspiration, or even as co-author,[7] deserves fresh examination.

Aside from the date when he joined Shakespeare's company, Armin's proprietorship of the fool 'line' has rested upon two points. First let us examine his acting talents. No evidence survives from Armin's early acting career about what kinds of talents he may have had. He was apprenticed to a London goldsmith from 1580 to 1591 (from twelve to twenty-three years of age). He appears to have acted in the provinces with Lord Chandos's players, a minor troupe which never (as far as we know) graced the London stage and which indeed was so insignificant as to escape mention in E.K. Chambers's *The Elizabethan Stage.* After he gained employment with the Lord Chamberlain's men, the surviving documentary evidence, again scanty, suggests that Armin never became a major member of the company. He did not become a sharer in the Globe or Blackfriars; he received only a small remembrance in the will of Augustine Phillipps in 1605, and in turn he left nothing to his fellow actors in his own will (although he was styled 'player'). The objective evidence is sketchy and suggests little. When we examine allusions to Armin, we are struck by their scarcity in comparison with those to Kemp and the vastly better-known Richard Tarlton. In 1592 Armin had become, according to Gabriel Harvey, 'one of the common pamphleteers of London'; however, none of these early writings survives. A jest in *Tarlton's Jests* (1611; however, the 'second part' in which the jest is found was entered on the Stationers' Register on 4 August 1600) claims that Tarlton trained Armin and made him his adopted son 'to enjoy my clownes sute after me.'[8] This jestbook testifies to Tarlton's great reputation: the jests mingle fact, fancy, and fantasy to cre-

7 C.S. Felver, 'Robert Armin's Fragment of a Bawdy Ballad of "Mary Ambree"' *N & Q* 205 (1960) 14-16, suggests that Armin wrote the lyrics for some of his songs.

8 *Tarlton's Jests* ed J.O. Halliwell, London 1844, p 29

ate a wondrous portrait of the old clown twelve years after his death, but their verity has been more than once questioned. As for Armin, the jest shows at least that he enjoyed some reputation – it ends like an 'actor's puff,' advertising that Armin currently plays 'at the Globe on the Banks side' – and it also supplies a contemporary opinion that Armin's style was like Tarlton's. Another allusion seems to apply to Armin: Dekker in *The Guls Horn Book* (1609) refers to '*Tarleton, Kemp,* nor *Singer,* nor all the litter of Fooles that now come drawling behind them, neuer plaid the Clownes more naturally then the arrantest Sot of you all' (sig A2). Again Armin is compared with, not contrasted to, other clowns of the time.

When we look beyond allusions for evidence of Armin's talents, the works usually advanced first are Shakespeare's plays themselves: do not the roles betray the talents of the actor? But is it not a circular argument to proceed from the play to the player? When we say that Armin's style may be deduced from the parts Shakespeare created for him, have we not assumed what we are trying to prove – that Shakespeare created the parts *for him?* Is it not also risky to assume that an actor easily plays all parts of the roles he is given or that he can play nothing else? Such dangers, in my view, are in the way of those who advance the plays as evidence for the actor. If Touchstone, Feste, and company display Armin's special and successful 'line' which won audiences' favour, why, we may ask, is this company of wise fools so small in Shakespeare's plays? Only Lavache, Thersites, and Lear's Fool are to be added. (I omit Trinculo, even though he is called a jester. He is a reversion to the older type of clown within a sub-plot.) Indeed, we may examine the repertory of the Chamberlain's-King's men between 1599 and 1610 or so and again ask, why so few wise fools? (Passarello seems to be the only additional candidate). The scarcity of such roles suggests that fools were created by dramatists for artistic reasons, not theatrical ones arising from the presence of an actor.

To extract from the parts various ingredients of the fool role can also be risky. Armin's musical abilities have often been praised and included in his 'line' on the evidence of Feste – but why are there only two other singing fools, Lavache with a single song and Lear's Fool with a few scraps of song? Apparently Armin was asked to sing only a few times. Equally, those who assure us of Armin's talents in mimicry (on the evidence of Sir Topas in *Twelfth Night)* should explain why only one other fool,

Thersites, resorts briefly to the device. Another point is that in deducing from roles the talents of their player, one should limit discussion to physical characteristics which might refer to the actor – indications of stature, style, voice, and so on. To do otherwise, to point out that Shakespeare's fools often attend upon ladies or have considerable concern for the ranks of persons in society (two such examples), makes an interesting point about the dramatist's conception of the wise fool but nothing about the actor's theatrical talents. (Both traits mentioned, by the way, are also attributes of Erasmus's Folly). To sum up, from the company's whole repertory one gains an impression of the range and adaptability of Armin's talents rather than a limited 'line.' The two parts Armin specifically claims in his own writings are Shakespeare's Dogberry and his own Blue John, a natural fool. Dogberry reminds us that Armin would have been called upon to play older roles in revivals anyway, along with undistinguished comic parts like the clowns in *Othello* and *Antony and Cleopatra.* The opportunities to play a wise fool were few and far between.

The second area for investigation is Armin's writings, which, some suggest, contain the basis for the new wise fool. *Quips upon Questions* and *Foole upon Foole, or Six Sortes of Sottes* (little pamphlets published in 1600) and his *The Two Maids of Moreclacke* (published in 1609 but played in 1607-8 by the Children of the Revels) have no claims as great literature but shed some light on Armin's interests and possible influence. First, *The Two Maids* has the greatest claim to being extant early enough to have influenced Shakespeare, since two topical references in it stem from 1597-8; however, this does not allow us to date the whole play so early or to suggest as its latest editor does that 'Armin wrote and played in *Two Maids* as a means of bringing himself to the attention of the London companies after his years in the provinces.'[9] The play contains references which could not predate 1603-4, such as one to King James's forty-pound knights, along with clear echoes of *Hamlet* and *King Lear.* Once evidence of revision surfaces, a whole range of possibilities opens – one could argue, for example, that Armin in 1607-8 took an old play and refashioned it. In any case, echoes now detectable could result from Armin's borrowings, not Shakespeare's. As for Armin's motive for composition, I confess

9 Robert Armin *The Collected Works of Robert Armin* ed John Feather, New York 1972, I

myself dubious that the play as we have it would have brought anything but unfavourable attention for Armin in 1597: even allowing for its incredibly garbled and chaotic text, *The Two Maids* is an appallingly bad play. Perhaps it was a vehicle for him, however; it is thought that Armin doubled the parts of Blue John and Tutch, on the evidence of the epistle to the reader: 'I would haue againe inacted *Iohn* my selfe, but *Tempora mutantur in illis,* & I cannot do as I would, I haue therefore thought good to diuulge him thus ... Wherein I whilome pleased: and being requested both of Court and Citty, to shew him in priuate, I haue therefore printed him in public.' The part of Blue John as it is printed has no affinities to Shakespeare's wise fools – Blue John is a natural fool who appears a few times in the company of his nurse, and the pathetic entertainment he provides affords evidence only of Armin's continuing interest in such poor creatures. (Blue John also appears in *Foole upon Foole.)* The other part, Tutch, is a witty Italianate servant who again seems far from Shakespeare's conception of the wise fool.

Armin signed both of his 1600 pamphlets as 'Clonnico de Curtanio Snuffe' (Snuffe, Clown of the Curtain) – was he still at the Curtain in 1600? Their authorship is established by the 1605 edition of *Foole upon Foole,* which locates Armin as 'del Mondo': otherwise *Quips upon Questions* might never have been ascribed to Armin since it was long thought to be by John Singer. Does *Quips upon Questions* contain work 'characteristic' of Armin? It was, the title-page says, 'Clapt up by a Clowne of the towne in the last restraint, hauing litle else to doe' (probably Lent 1600), and in the dedication Armin refers to himself as being out of London. The work contains forty-five questions, each followed by a poem (often in dialogue) ranging from six to about sixty lines and a short 'quip' in verse set in italic type. Questions include: 'Why barkes that Dogge?' 'Two Fooles wel met,' 'Where is Ginking gone?' 'Who is happy?' and 'What ayles that Damsell?' Quotation best gives the flavour of these 'morrallised metamorphoses of changes upon interrogatories,' as the title-page terms them:

What is Shee?

What is that Woman: Sir she was a Mayde.
O, but she is not now. How happens this?
Yes sir she is, but therewith ill apayde:
Mayde is she, no Mayde by one deede amisse.

In deede, one deede which lately for she did,
From Maydes estate I must her needes forbid.
Is she a Wife? neither, not so blessed,
That honour last leape yeere escapt her too.
What, is sh'a Widdow, late by death distressed?
O no, nor that way wrongde: I know not how,
Onely thus much I say, and talke no more,
Not mayde, wife, widdow, but a common whore.

(*O beautie thou are wrongd thus euery hower*
(
(*Fro which this loues, thou'lt vanish like a flower;*
(
Quip (*And since tis so, this then became her thrall,*
(
(*Correction serues to quittance her for all.* (sig D2v)

The subject is not atypical: fornication, gambling, money-lending, and other social targets of the pamphleteers recur in these pages. Fools are mentioned, but interestingly Armin usually uses the term in its sense of reprehensible witlessness, and the concept of paradoxically wise folly does not appear. The verse is often laboured, and the rhymes forced – Armin admits to 'studying for a Rime' (sig C) and in the same verses to 'Writing these Embles on an idle time.' They do not claim to come from the theatre, and it would appear that Armin in these emblems was aiming at pithy sententiousness in the manner of other emblem writers. The second pamphlet, *Foole upon Foole* (1600), is also dated after *As You Like It.* The pamphlet concerns six different sorts of fools and mingles description and anecdote. Will Sommer, Henry VIII's legendary court jester, is the only one of the lot who is in possession of his right wits; the other fools are all naturals and the humour is almost always situational with the fool as victim, not perpetrator or critic. The book's latest editor sums up: 'It is well to admit at the outset that, despite some similarities, Armin's fools are not the source for the Shakespearian fool characters, except as Armin records a common tradition which the two authors share.'[10] In 1608 a new edition entitled *A Nest of Ninnies* appeared with additional material and a dedica-

10 H.F. Lippincott, ed *A Shakespeare Jestbook: Robert Armin's 'Foole upon Foole' (1600)* Salzburg Studies in English Literature, Elizabethan Studies no 2, Salzburg 1973, p 24

tion to the gentlemen of the Inns of Court and Universities. The additional material, moralizing verses by the fool to cure the world's sickness, strikes one as adventitious and out of keeping with the original, more modest conception. It is in this edition, however, that verbal parallels to *King Lear* and *Hamlet* are found: the borrower was almost certainly Armin, not Shakespeare.

The real interest of Armin's literary works lies elsewhere than in their supposed influence on Shakespeare. They were part of a vogue for fool literature after 1595, as F.P. Wilson's check-lists indicate.[11] One might, I suppose, survey the whole field in order to determine the degree of Armin's originality – if such things mattered in a genre where borrowings abounded. Armin's special interest in all this seems to have been in natural fools, and his works provide us with six lively portraits of these poor unfortunates whose antics were then apparently more amusing than we can find them today. When we survey the whole corpus of fool literature, looking at both natural and artificial fools recorded from life in the sixteenth century, we must conclude, with Nevill Coghill, that 'they are a disappointing lot.'[12] Shakespeare was to transcend, not imitate, the recorded tradition.

II

Will Kemp's departure in 1599 from the Lord Chamberlain's men probably was due to his retirement. Although still fit enough to dance a nine days' wonder from London to Norwich, he had probably been on the stage for over twenty years (he was referred to as a 'jesting player' early in the 1580s, we remember), and he is last recorded in 1603. To notice that tastes were changing by 1599 is not to attack Kemp; he awaits his due as the actor of Shakespeare's early clowns. The Elizabethan theatre was notoriously quick in its changes of fashion, and by 1599 chronicle history, heroic tragedy, and romantic comedy were becoming passé, while the 'little eyasses,' citizen comedy, and satire were soon to strut and fret their hour. This situation no doubt affected Shakespeare at least as much as Armin; we

11 F.P. Wilson 'English Jestbooks of the Sixteenth and Seventeenth Centuries' in his *Shakespearian and Other Studies* ed Helen Gardner, London 1969, pp 285-324

12 Nevill Coghill 'Wags, Clowns, and Jesters' in *More Talking of Shakespeare* ed John Garrett, London 1959, p 5

remember that by 1599 Shakespeare had reached maturity with (Meres tells us) a string of successes to his credit. He was 'a man who knows that he has altered the shape and scope of English drama and who expects his audience to be aware of the fact.'[13] While we have no reason to doubt the histrionic talents of the new comic recruit, the evidence on balance suggests that it was Shakespeare who forged the new conception of the wise fool.

Hamlet is unique in having both a clown and a fool, though neither speaks; the hero's ideas about them, however, give us some access into the range of possibilities open for both. The clown, of course, is a member of the travelling players, and Hamlet begins by praising his special talent to 'make those laugh whose lungs are tickle a th'sear' (II.ii.322-3).[14] Hamlet has a refined taste; he attacks Polonius as a dullard for preferring 'a jig or a tale of bawdry' to the heightened rhetoric of the player's speech of Hecuba. Later, during Hamlet's excited 'green-room' advice to the players, comes his famous attack on clowns' extemporizations. While this may be a gratuitous attack on the departed Kemp (as many have thought), it seems a strange place to mount it: the primary effect seems to me to emphasize Hamlet's over-excited determination that *his* interpolation will succeed. To forbid 'gagging' (a not unusual practice) makes the point well about Hamlet's 'necessary question' and perhaps makes the point again about his aristocratic tastes. Later we encounter Yorick, a dead presence from the past recalled by Hamlet first of all in terms which emphasize his entertaining:

> a fellow of infinite jest, of most excellent fancy. He hath bore me on his back a thousand times ... Where be your gibes now, your gambols, your songs, your flashes of merriment, that were wont to set the table on a roar?
>
> (V.i.178-85)

But for Hamlet the fool has a message as well – an unwelcome one, but none the less necessary: 'Now, get you to my lady's chamber and tell her, let her paint an inch thick, to this favour she must come. Make her laugh at that.' The message of mortal-

13 G.R. Hibbard '*Henry IV* and *Hamlet*' *Shakespeare Survey* 30, Cambridge 1977, p 11

14 All references to Shakespeare are to the New Arden Shakespeare: *Hamlet* ed Harold Jenkins, London 1982; *2 Henry IV* ed A.R. Humphreys, 1966; *As You Like It* ed Agnes Latham, 1975; *Twelfth Night* ed J.M. Lothian and T.W. Craik, 1978; *All's Well that Ends Well* ed G.K. Hunter, 1967.

ity, of the skull beneath the skin reminding us of our irreducible physical natures, is one we hear again from Shakespeare's fools.

The presence of the clown and fool in Hamlet's consciousness follows hard upon Shakespeare's memorable comic creation, Falstaff. In *1* and *2 Henry IV* the fat knight embodies shrewd commentary and buffoonery, at times setting the table on a roar and at others speaking out of turn; significantly, Hal finally comes to rebuke him as a 'fool and jester' (*2 Henry IV* V.v.48). Here again we have evidence that between 1597 and 1600 Shakespeare was turning over in his mind the possibilities and range of folly, which were to issue in the five wise fools he created between 1599 and 1607. To consider these characters fully would require (at least) a separate essay, because each is a unique conception and inhabits a unique world. One common characteristic is that, like Yorick, the fools appear to have disordered or troubled relationships with their societies. Two of them, Feste and Lavache, like Yorick were fools to characters who have died, but unlike Yorick it remains for them to settle their relationships with the living. Feste, Lavache, and Lear's Fool enter after unexplained absences of some length which occasion reproof. We also note that Lear's Fool leaves unexplainedly, with his gnomic aside about going to bed at noon. Reproof awaits Touchstone, because as Celia remarks the world has changed: 'since the little wit that fools have was silenced, the little foolery that wise men have makes a great show' (*As You Like It* I.ii.80). Touchstone is easily won to abandon this court world to accompany its latest refugees to Arden. Similarly Thersites, physically reproved by the fists of the cobloaf, Ajax, is inveigled from him to follow Achilles. These ways of presenting the characters detach the fools from their surroundings and puzzle us about them while underlining the fools' freedom (claimed often) to walk freely about the orb like the sun: they remain somewhat apart from the action, and their only link to the other characters is their good fooling.

Hamlet's eulogy on Yorick recalls other overt comments on the fools' abilities; these have sometimes been proposed as Shakespeare's advertisements for Armin, the new actor with a new line, but I think that they are mainly effective in two other ways. Characters reveal themselves in speaking of the fool, as *Twelfth Night* illustrates. Malvolio's dismissal of Feste shows us, and Olivia, that he is 'sick of self-love,' while her own comment is similarly self-revelatory: 'there is no slander in an allow'd fool, though he do nothing but rail; nor no railing in a known discreet man, though he do nothing but reprove' (I.v.87-90). Aside from her self-congratulatory view of herself as 'generous, guiltless, and of free disposition,' her speech reveals her love for settled order, where everyone is known, where place governs function and everything stays the same. Erasmus's Folly agrees with Olivia about the fool's office: 'What woorde comyng out of a wisemans mouth were an hangyng mattier, the same yet spoken by a fool shall much delight evin hym that is touched therewith.'[15] Viola also comments on the fool:

> This fellow is wise enough to play the fool;
> And to do that well craves a kind of wit.
> He must observe their mood on whom he jests,
> The quality of persons, and the time;
> And, like the haggard, check at every feather
> That comes before his eye. This is a practice
> As full of labour as a wise man's art:
> For folly that he wisely shows is fit;
> But wise men, folly-fall'n, quite taint their wit. (III.i.57-65)

Viola discerns a trait in Feste which we see in her – an ability to see, beneath surface appearances, the real qualities of those she attends. Such comments as these also hint at why one would play the fool, by recalling the tradition of wise folly. We detect Erasmus behind a comment like Duke Senior's in *As You Like It*: 'He uses his folly like a stalking-horse, and under the presentation of that he shoots his wit' (V.iv.105-6). Folly here means 'the office of fool' – Duke Senior's comment follows an acquaintance of only sixty-five lines, during which he discerns that Touchstone's allowed office provides an ironic vantage point to observe the world, free from charges of self-interest or bias. Shakespeare took up the fool, I think, in order to exploit this freedom to observe, and in comments like these he draws attention to his new departure.

The reasons Shakespeare created a great stage of fools between 1599 and 1607, culminating in his unique inclusion of the fool in tragedy, are to be found in the parts themselves. The variety, the values, and the limits of Erasmian folly are explored

15 Erasmus *The Praise of Folly* trans Thomas Chaloner, ed Clarence H. Miller, Early English Text Society no 257, 1965, p 50

in the five characters. Shakespeare's fools differ widely in their attitudes to comic or tragic inadequacy, comic or tragic suffering. The more violent or disordered are their worlds, the more folly is tinged with morbidity, bitterness, or disgust. The actor called upon to play these five parts must have possessed considerable talents; finally, he should be celebrated for his astonishing range and variety, not for his 'comic line.'

University of Western Ontario

JAMES BLACK

Shakespeare's Mystery of Fooling

Be sure to give all thy sons a vocation.
- Sir John Oglander's notebook 1632[1]

Out of the vast and cloudy charivari of folk, religious, and aristocratic rituals exhaustively and yet at the same time sketchily described by Enid Welsford[2] and, somewhat more recently in the context of Rabelais's art, by Mikhail Bakhtin,[3] there 'emerges' Shakespeare's stage and court fool. In a general way we know a good deal about this fool. Thanks mainly to Welsford we can track him through Tudor moral plays, French *soties*, Erasmus, and medieval literature. Leslie Hotson has tried to work out details of fools' dress (so did Francis Douce),[4] the distinction between real and artificial fools, and the legal status of a certain class of idiot wards or kept fools. We also have a sort of contemporary Tudor history of six prominent court fools in Robert Armin's *Foole upon Foole* (1605).[5] We know that many court fools were paid expenses and board wages, for Welsford has found

1 Francis Bamford, ed *A Royalist's Notebook: The Commonplace Book of Sir John Oglander* New York 1971, p 235
2 Enid Welsford *The Fool: His Social and Literary History* Garden City NY 1961
3 Mikhail Bakhtin *Rabelais and His World* trans H. Iswolsky, Cambridge Mass 1968
4 Leslie Hotson *Shakespeare's Motley* London 1952. See esp chap 1 'The Mystery of Motley.' Francis Douce *Illustrations of Shakespeare* London 1839; reprinted New York 1968. See esp pp 497-517.

royal account-book entries (two shillings a month to William Worthy, otherwise called Phip[6]), and we know also that the keeping of fools was not confined to royalty, for when Sir John Oglander (1585-1655) was deputy governor of Portsmouth, his wife engaged one:

> He was a poor, lame, decrepit fellow, one Stockwell, a Gunner's son, but of a bold spirit and excellent wit. My wife, having compassion on him, took him into the house and made of him a kind of jester.[7]

Stockwell called himself the Earl of Newport, thereby inspiring derision for the real Earl of Newport and actually impeding the earl's advancement. He also talked familiarly with the Duke of Buckingham and with King James. Yet with what we know of them, court fools, and especially Shakespeare's court fools, are – as Gareth Lloyd Evans points out – conspicuously classless or at least difficult to place with confidence in the social hierarchies.[8] Somehow from the mists of social history Shakespeare's fools appear ('Emergence of the Stage Fool' is a chapter in R.H. Goldsmith's study[9]); like the poor relatives of a great, decayed family they seem to have an immense pedigree but little recognition in their own time. Feste and Touchstone, with their teasing, almost anthropological names, have been scrutinized in appreciative but not especially descriptive ways. Perhaps what we need is a sort of job description for Shakespeare's fools in their working-day world, and to some extent this is what I am going to attempt.

All four of Shakespeare's major clowns – Lavache, Touchstone, Feste, and Lear's Fool – are displaced professionals – that is to say, whatever atmosphere of everyday or holiday festival might have existed in Illyria, Rossillion, or the other courts already is dissipating or dissipated by the opening of each of the four plays. The sports in Duke Frederick's court consist of breaking

5 H.F. Lippincott, ed *A Shakespeare Jestbook, Robert Armin's 'Foole upon Foole' (1600): A Critical, Old-spelling Edition* Salzburg Studies in English Literature, Elizabethan Studies no 20, Salzburg 1973

6 Welsford *The Fool* p 159

7 Bamford *A Royalist's Notebook* p 326

8 Gareth Lloyd Evans 'Shakespeare's Fools: the Shadow and the Substance of Drama' in *Shakespearian Comedy* ed Malcolm Bradbury and David Palmer, Stratford-upon-Avon Studies 14, London 1972, p 147

9 R.H. Goldsmith *Wise Fools in Shakespeare* East Lansing Mich 1963

of ribs; Illyria and Rossillion are in mourning; Lear's kingdom is being divided and a new order is emerging. All four fools have to come to terms with these transitions, which mean that in various degrees their occupation's gone. At best, they face the same imposition as that placed by the Princess of France on Biron, who for a twelvemonth is to use 'all the fierce endeavour of [his] art / To enforce the pained impotent to smile' (*Love's Labour's Lost* V.ii.863-4).[10] All four accept the assignment.

The four fools were played by Armin, and by a paradox their situations are exactly the reverse of the professional opportunity which was offered to Armin himself. It is assumed that Armin's replacement of Will Kemp in the Lord Chamberlain's company was a result of the development of the company and of theatrical taste. He brought talents – for verbal wit, for singing – that Kemp may not have had, talents which in fact are thought to have influenced Shakespeare's own writing and hence the further development of the company's scope. Whether or not these assumptions – Kemp's lack of adaptability, Armin's influencing talents – are reasonable, it is a fact that Kemp departed and Armin arrived at about the time of *As You Like It*. *As You Like It* has a clown who finds that the world around him has changed. In a way – and Shakespeare must have perceived this – Kemp's plight is implicit in the roles written for his successor. The physical Kemp of course could have accommodated to the rib-cracking sports of Duke Frederick's court or to an Arden as rude and uncivil as some of *As You Like It*'s expatriates think it is. But the mysterious and metamorphosing aspects of Arden, Illyria, and even Lear's heath were beyond his wit to conceive. It is intellectual and not merely physical comic energies with which the Armin fools are to hold out against their fates. They all would ruefully recognize the Princess's challenge to Biron:

> A jest's prosperity lies in the ear
> Of him that hears it, never in the tongue
> Of him that makes it; then, if sickly ears,

10 The general text used for references to Shakespeare's plays in this essay is *The Complete Plays and Poems of William Shakespeare* ed W.A. Neilson and C.J. Hill, Boston 1942. The New Arden texts are cited for the four plays discussed in detail: *All's Well that Ends Well* ed G.K. Hunter, London 1967; *As You Like It* ed Agnes Latham, 1975; *Twelfth Night* ed J.M. Lothian and T.W. Craik, 1978; *King Lear* ed Kenneth Muir, 1963.

> Deaf'd with the clamours of their own dear groans,
> Will hear your idle scorns, continue then.
>
> (*Love's Labour's Lost* V.ii.871-5)

I am going to examine how each of these fools sees his profession and plies it in unpropitious circumstances and surroundings simply by being 'the thing he is.' I also hope to show a quality in Lear's Fool that is special not only in contrast to the other three characters but in contrast to the general situation of Tudor professional fools.

In *All's Well* Lavache, 'a shrewd knave and an unhappy' (IV.v.60), is a relic of former and grieved-for days in Rossillion. The Countess's household and the court languish in mourning or in impotence, waiting for the dead Count's heir to find himself and galvanize them or – the same thing – for Helena's qualities of healing and optimism to rejuvenate them. Lavache is sadly tolerated: the Countess says, 'My lord that's gone made himself much sport out of him. By his authority he remains here, which he thinks is a patent for his sauciness; and, indeed, he has no pace, but runs where he will' (IV.v.61-4). 'Where he will,' 'What You Will' – neither Lavache nor Feste is quite an all-licensed fool; but neither Rossillion nor Illyria quite knows what to do with their entertainers during periods of extended mourning, so both fools have a large measure of freedom.

In Lavache's first scene (I.iii) he actually is an intruder on his mistress's quiet, stolidly at first resisting her efforts to drive him from her serious presence and engaging her much against her will in one of those catechizing exchanges where no one ever bests a fool. (It was one of Armin's routines, as in his published *Quips upon Questions* [1600], to give spontaneous witty answers to questions thrown from the audience.) Before the Countess knows it, she is an audience asking Lavache questions, and he is in temporary charge of the situation, turning the conversation and the household's thoughts to the topics of marriage and life. We already have been introduced to a mourning Countess and a sick, weary King. Lavache's is the first really warm blood in the play, and in the indecorous but practical way of turning the Countess's thoughts to his physical urges ('COUNTESS Wilt thou ever be a foul-mouth'd and calumnious knave?' I.iii.54-5) he is enforcing a lesson that Lafeu earlier could only politely word: 'Moderate lamentation is the right of the dead; excessive grief the enemy to the living' (I.i.51-2). Lavache with his cheerful bawdry helps keep both good humour and life itself flickering in the Rossillion household. In this function he is like the gravedigger in *Hamlet,* who even while standing in a grave reminds us that the geography of Elsinore includes not only yawning churchyards and haunted battlements but also Yaughan's hostelry with its take-out or off-licence service (V. i.67-8). Lavache's adroit playing of both knave and fool keeps everyone guessing as to which he is:

> LAFEU Whether does thou profess thyelf – a knave or fool?
> CLOWN A fool, sir, at a woman's service, and a knave at a man's ...
> LAFEU I will subscribe for thee; thou art both knave and fool.
> CLOWN At your service. (IV.v.20-31)

Lavache has other themes to impart, for he is a prophet who '[speaks] truth the next way' (I.iii.56-7). 'I do marry that I may repent' (I.iii.34-5), he says. This will be Bertram's case when he weds Helena, his 'clog,' against what he thinks are his inclinations and again when he comes to the realization that repentance will make a far better marriage. As Lavache, with a bawdy meaning, announces that he hopes to have friends for his wife's sake (I.iii.37-8), Bertram also will restore his credit with King and Countess through their love for Helena. Lavache's function here is choric. His qualification for the office of fool is a witty perspective that clearly comes out of a very sure sense of who he is. He knows his erotic urges, admits them, and his central teaching to others is:

> If men could be contented to be what they are, there were no fear in marriage. (I.iii.48-9)

This art of being contented with what one is is a lesson hard-learned by Parolles and Bertram. Parolles professes a 'mystery in strategem' (III.vi.61) but is a coward. As Lavache is a prophet who speaks the truth the next way, Parolles is his obverse, a 'double-meaning prophesier' who deceives (IV.iii.96-7). Fool and *miles gloriosus,* each living by his wits, are mirrors of one another in the play, as Lavache clearly sees:

> PAROLLES Go to, thou art a witty fool; I have found thee.
> CLOWN Did you find me in your self, sir, or were you taught to find me? ... The search, sir, was profitable; and much fool may you find in you, even to the world's pleasure and the increase of laughter. (II.iv.31-6)

In the 'dialogue between the Fool and the Soldier' (IV.iii.95), a set piece of the play, there are wrung from Parolles under cross-examination those very truths which Lavache imparts so freely. As suggested, Lavache habitually speaks out of an honest corporal urge, and here at least so does Parolles – in his case out of the honest corporal urge to save his skin. Central to this dialogue of the fool and the soldier is the truth which is told about Bertram. Bertram is characterized in the punning verses (IV.iii.203-24) which Parolles has written to Diana, Bertram's sexual prey, 'Dian, the Count's a fool, and full of gold ...,' and also in Parolles' defence of these verses, 'Count Rossillion [is] a foolish idle boy, but for all that very ruttish.' The only time therefore when Parolles publicly speaks the truth is when he is made a fool. Having been made a fool he determines to live by exactly the same truth which Lavache has uttered, the truth of being what one is: 'Simply the thing I am / Shall make me live' (lines 322-3). The play now has two enlightened fools.

In his new role of enlightened fool Parolles actually tries to defend Bertram before the King – and his dexterity in evading is nearly equal to Lavache's own:

> PAROLLES He did love [Diana], sir, as a gentleman loves a woman.
> KING How is that?
> PAROLLES He lov'd her, sir, and lov'd her not. (V.iii.243-5)

Bertram, fool and soldier, is one with the other self-deceived of the play. Lavache saw this when he considered Bertram's moody behaviour at court, and he compares his own dissatisfaction with Isbel and Bertram's with Helena. His complaint that 'I have no mind to Isbel since I was at court ...' is spoken as the Countess reads the letter he has just delivered from Bertram, and the letter says that Bertram has no mind to Helena. The Countess's question 'What have we here?' applies equally to Lavache's love-complaint and Bertram's: the fool takes it as asking about his own situation and, indicating the letter, says 'E'en that you have there' (II.ii.12-25). Question and answer can be taken as 'What's the matter with you?' and 'Just the same thing that's the matter with him.' The amorous soldier-hero and the amorous fool are merely putting on airs, but Lavache knows he is doing so and also knows why.

To say all this is to say how Lavache 'holds his place' in the play. And he holds his place in the Rossillion household by exactly the same qualities: by being, as the wise Countess and Lafeu recognize, a life-force in the midst of gloom, mourning, and dismay. It is striking to see how attempted consideration of the bawdiness of Shakespeare's clowns often leads critics away from the plays into something like social anthropology – an instance is Goldsmith's exegesis of Lavache's description of himself as 'A fool, sir, at a woman's service, and a knave at a man's ... And I would give his wife my bauble, sir, to do her service' (IV.v.22-8). Goldsmith says:

> Is it not conceivable that the medieval fool's bauble was but a vestige of the exaggerated phallus worn by the Dorian mime and the Mimic fool of the later *phylakes*? In the procession of the *phallophoroi*, it should be noted, the participants carried the symbol of male fertility, mounted upon a pole. If an association can be established between the fool's bauble and the phallus of the bald-headed mime, we should have one more proof of the ancient origin of the fool's costume.[11]

I think the association which Shakespeare is establishing is between the fool's bauble and the situation in the household where he lives, and the point is that Lavache insistently speaks of – for a time is in fact the sole voice of – generation. To paraphrase Sonnet 2, he feels his blood warm when others around him see theirs cold. Cheerfully agricultural, he knows what it is that makes land and people yield:

> He that ears my land spares my team, and gives me
> leave to in the crop; if I be his cuckold, he's my
> drudge ... He that kisses my wife is my friend. (I.iii.43-8)

One of Hamlet's tragic questions is 'Why would'st thou be a breeder of sinners?' (*Hamlet* III.i.122-3); one of Lavache's comic responses is 'Why not?' Set against his cheerful commitment to fertility is Parolles' and Bertram's empty-as-a-drum bellicosity towards Helena: Parolles, 'Man setting down before you will undermine you and blow you up' (I.i.116-17); Bertram, 'Go thou toward home, where I will never come / Whilst I can shake my sword or hear the drum' (II.v.90-1).

In *As You Like It* Touchstone, like Lavache, feels the insistent spurring of 'love's prick' and expresses his discomfort comi-

11 Goldsmith *Wise Fools* p 4

cally and wisely. As I have tried to show elsewhere,[12] Touchstone amplifies *As You Like It*'s comedy-of-manners theme of 'forked heads' (II.i.24) and other urban dangers which lurk even in the pastoral setting. Being himself actually visited in this comic sexual plague and fatalistically aware of what is happening to him ('I press in here sir, amongst the rest of the country copulatives' V.iv.54-66), Touchstone is not nearly so objective as Shakespeare's other three great fools. Shakespeare may have started out with the idea of making him play the solacer and instructor to his displaced and troubled mistress Celia and her friend Rosalind. He clearly is ill at ease in Celia's father's court, where 'the little wit that fools have [has been] silenced' (I.ii.82-3) because the usurping Duke will not tolerate 'taxation' or criticism, and verbal or witty entertainment has been replaced by wrestling – a court, indeed, for Will Kemp's talents. Touchstone is taken away by Celia and Rosalind to 'be a comfort to [their] travel' (I.iii.127), but after this familiar opening phase Shakespeare varies the pattern somewhat. On the journey Touchstone needs nearly as much encouraging from Rosalind as Celia does (II.iv.1-16). He is at first however a promising corrective to Rosalind's romantic expectations in Arden and also a cheerful satirist of Orlando's love-struck frenzy. But soon, like so many of his fellows in Arden, he too is smitten with love and takes his place with Audrey among the 'couples' whom Jaques mocks:

> There is sure another flood toward, and these couples are coming to the ark. Here comes a pair of very strange beasts [that is, Touchstone and Audrey], which in all tongues are called fools. (V.iv.35-8)

Though Touchstone does for his betters the somewhat rueful office of standing between them and Jaques's scorn, the very fact that his duties as intercessor are so light says a good deal about the essentially serene mood of *As You Like It*. He never could be called 'a shrewd knave and an unhappy,' or if the first then hardly the second, and he scarcely seems to notice whether the rain rains every day. But then, the boughs of Arden never are melancholy for long – even for Jaques, who will admit to laughing at Touchstone 'sans intermission, / An hour by his dial' (II.vii.32-3).

In Illyria, Feste is as much a reminder of life – a *memento*

12 James Black 'The Marriage-Music of Arden' *English Studies in Canada* 6, no 4 (Winter 1980) 385-97

vivere – as Lavache in Rossillion. *Twelfth Night* proceeds as an answer to the question 'What should I do in Illyria?' The question is asked explicitly by Viola (I.ii.3) and implicitly by Feste when he steels himself for the first encounter we see between him and Olivia: 'Well, God give them wisdom that have it; and those that are fools, let them use their talents' (I.v.14-15). Viola's assessment of her own talents is to serve this duke,

> For I can sing
> And speak to him in many sorts of music,
> That will allow me very worth his service.. (I.ii.57-9)

(Inventories of this kind are frequent in *Twelfth Night*: see for instance Olivia's schedule of her beauty, 'every particle and utensil labelled,' at I.v.247-52, or Malvolio's totting-up of his qualifications and chances as Olivia's husband, II.v.23-40.) Feste also can sing, of course, and speak in many kinds of nonsensical music. Like Lavache he has to go directly against the prevailing mournful moods of the households where he performs (though he knows how to humour Orsino, whose case he has accurately diagnosed, with a fine strain of melancholy). And his situation is far more difficult than Lavache's in another way, for anyone trying to market a fool's talents in Illyria has an astonishing amount of competition. Besides the 'proven' foolishness (I.v.55-70) of Olivia and Orsino's foolish determination to do something like die of a rose in aromatic pain, there also are fools everywhere. When Toby Belch is drunk, he puts on a show of active and verbal foolery that draws Feste's professional admiration and Aguecheek's envy:

> CLOWN Beshrew me, the knight's in admirable fooling.
> SIR ANDREW Ay, he does well enough, if he be disposed, and so do I too: he does it with a better grace, but I do it more natural. (II.iii.81-4)

In Feste's fairly long silence after Aguecheek's reply we might well consider him to be reflecting on Sir Andrew's qualifications as a 'natural.' And he also could be thinking of something like the complaint expressed by King Lear's Fool:

> Lords and great men will not let me [be altogether fool]; if I had a monopoly out, they would have part on't: and ladies too, they will not let me have all the fool to myself; they'll be snatching. (I.iv.166-9)

Along with competition, Feste also has fierce opposition from Malvolio. It is difficult enough to combat Olivia's unnatural grief for her brother and to overcome her weariness of Feste at the beginning of the play by turning what hardly can be called a promising feed line, 'Take the fool away,' into a witty catechism (I.v.36-70); the snarling presences of Malvolio, a very *memento mori,* is an even greater obstacle and challenge:

> OLIVIA What think you of this fool, Malvolio, doth he not mend?
>
> MALVOLIO Yes, and shall do, till the pangs of death shake him. (I.v.71-4)

Pointed in this encounter and in this scene is a struggle (on Malvolio's side a struggle for domination) between offices, fool and steward; and between opposed spirits of life, the comic and the repressive or even life and death themselves. Lavache in his way had to inspire a moribund household. Feste, who literally wanders between two worlds – Olivia's wilfully dead and Orsino's powerless to be born – also has to contend with Malvolio's belligerent spirit. A.L. Rowse has suggested that the Puritans amplified the English Bible's trumpet-note to such a pitch that eventually it became the deafening crash of civil war.[13] In this first scene of *Twelfth Night* in which Feste and Malvolio ('a kind of Puritan' who actually has nothing to do with the English Bible) confront one another we can hear a rattle of warfare: 'That saying was born ... in the wars' (lines 9-12); 'He's out of his guard' (84); 'Take those things for bird-bolts that you deem cannon-bullets' (91-3). In that movement of the play that may be called Feste's Revenge, Malvolio is brought through motley-clad 'madness' to be a fool. It is a shattering experience for him, who at his first appearance dismissed Feste as having been 'put down the other day with an ordinary fool, that has no more brain than a stone' (I.v.82-4), to be greeted, however sympathetically, by Olivia with 'Alas, poor fool, how have they baffled thee!' and to have Feste instantly rub it in by repeating Malvolio's own words, 'Some are born great ...' (V.i.368-76). But if Malvolio's ambitions had been fulfilled, Feste's way of life would have been at an end, in Olivia's household at any rate.

Feste's is a way of life which is carefully characterized in the play as a trade. In Viola's speech 'This fellow is wise

13 A.L. Rowse *William Shakespeare: A Biography* New York and Evanston 1963, p 47

enough to play the fool ...' (III.i.61-9), Feste's powers of observation and his humouring of people are designed as 'practice,' 'labour,' and 'art,' words applicable to a profession. By his profession he is 'kept' (III.i.34) and of course is on various occasions seen being rewarded – and cleverly improving the reward (III. i.44-54; V.i.26-38). As mentioned, Feste, like any thorough professional who has built up a practice, is very much aware of the competition. In Illyria the competition mainly is from amateurs such as Sir Toby and Andrew, and Feste recognizes this. But it is especially striking to see him very carefully size up the newcomer Viola-Cesario, whom Olivia has been pursuing. A husband, after all, could change the balance and the possibilities of Olivia's household. Even if most such changes would not be so drastic as that which Malvolio could cause by marrying Olivia, and even though a happily married Olivia would no longer be a mourning Olivia, husbands may represent difficulty or even competition. Husbands, after all, are their own (and their wives') fools, for 'fools are as like husbands as pilchards are to herrings' (III.i.34-5).

In the long exchange between Feste and Viola (III.i) Feste cleverly evades Viola's questions about himself and, as Shakespeare's fools so often do when they are being evasive, appraises her. As he gives his deflective responses to Viola's cross-examination, Feste uses the form of address 'sir' in the opening sentence of every answer. In his thirty-nine lines through their scene together he says 'sir' seventeen times, moving the word around in his sentences for emphasis. Perhaps the address is at first polite; in its recurring use it seems to be questioning, even sardonic, especially when we read the sly observation (in his only sentence where 'sir' isn't used, possibly because it isn't needed for mocking emphasis), 'Now Jove, in his next commodity of hair, send thee a beard!' (lines 45-6). Viola in her turn is not insensitive to the scrutiny and challenge she apparently is receiving, for she begins to give back a word – 'man': 'Why, man?' 'Thy reason, man?' Her tone seems to be artificially hearty, her intention to imitate 'man-talk.' When Feste at last agrees to announce Viola's arrival to Olivia's attendants, he says:

> I will conster to them whence you come; who you are and what you would are out of my welkin. I might say 'element,' but the word is overworn. (57-60)

It is quite possible that he has thoroughly satisfied himself that 'Cesario' is no serious prospect as a husband and no threat to the balance of things in the household. Viola in turn has felt the closeness of his appraisal, hence 'This fellow is wise enough to play the fool ...' When one thinks about it – and I believe III.i suggests that Feste has thought about it – the best husband for Olivia from Feste's point of view would be Orsino, who is well established as part of the fool's support system. Having so carefully appraised Cesario, Feste very securely and playfully glances at his role of go-between for Cesario and Olivia when, taking Cesario's offered coin and attempting to add to it, he says, 'I would play Lord Pandarus of Phrygia, sir, to bring a Cressida to this Troilus' (523). He seems perfectly comfortable about bringing or leaving Cesario and Olivia together. So it is a great comic twist of *Twelfth Night* when in IV.i Feste actually does bring together Olivia and Sebastian (who calls him 'foolish Greek,' 18). But then, in Illyria fools have to look after madmen.

So too, but sadly, in *King Lear*. Although in *Lear* the duties performed on Lear's behalf by Kent and the Fool are of the nature of that 'constant service of the antique world, / When service sweat for duty, not for meed' (*As You Like It* II.iii.57-8), there also is a strong vein of professionalism and practicality in Lear's Fool. Strongly associated with Cordelia, who unstintingly gives her love for 'nothing,' the Fool none the less actually first enters the play at the instant when Lear clinches his agreement to hire the disguised Kent. Kent has disguised himself with the intention of seeking some way of serving the king, who has banished him: 'So may it come, thy master, whom thou lov'st / Shall find thee full of labours' (I.iv.6-7). Presenting himself to Lear as a servant looking for a place, he is comprehensively interviewed:

> LEAR What dost thou profess? What would'st thou with us?
> KENT I do profess to be no less than I seem; to serve him truly that will put me in trust; to love him that is honest; to fear judgement; to fight when I cannot choose; and to eat no fish.
> LEAR What art thou?
> KENT A very honest-hearted fellow, and as poor as the King.
> LEAR ... What would'st thou?

KENT Service.
LEAR Who would'st thou serve?
KENT You. (I.iv.12-27)

Shortly after, when Kent has bowled Oswald over for being impertinent to the king, Lear offers him earnest-money to seal the hiring agreement, and it is here that the Fool comes in, with the words, 'Let me hire him too: here's my coxcomb' (I.iv.100). The coxcomb is an implement of the Fool's trade or emblem of his office. As he goes on to suggest, to give it away to Kent (anyone who serves the declining Lear is a fool and may as well wear the badge) is to part with his living, as Lear himself has done. Yet, the Fool also suggests, the property of a fool is inexhaustible; there always will be more than enough coxcombs to go around, and foolishness is mysteriously an endlessly renewable resource: 'If I gave them [my daughters] all my living, I'd keep my coxcombs myself' (I.iv.113-14).

Immediately after his gesture of 'hiring' Kent as fool, and Lear too, for both are qualified, the Fool turns to what logically would follow in any apprenticing association, the training program: 'Sirrah [that is, Lear], I'll teach thee a speech ... Mark it, Nuncle' (I.iv.121-3). Actually, the rhyme which the Fool then repeats is a kind of aptitude test and certainly is delivered in that spirit, for when Lear rejoins 'This is nothing, Fool,' the Fool's next question is 'Can you make no use of nothing, Nuncle?' and he explains the riddle for him. The next lesson, to which Lear submits ('teach me' line 145) is how to know the difference between a bitter fool and a sweet one; and gradually Lear is edged towards his first insight: 'Dost thou call me fool, boy?' (154).

As I have mentioned, Lear's Fool has a strong sense of his vocation and like Feste recognizes that it is difficult to keep the profession free of interlopers, including kings: 'If I had a monopoly out, they would have part on't' (I.v.159-60). But whatever qualification or pretence the king might have to be a fool, he has not yet succeeded to the office. As the Fool tells him, 'I am better than thou art now; I am a Fool, thou art nothing' (I.v.201-2).

From what we know of Tudor and Stuart clowns of the court and stage it would seem that professional fools guarded their places very jealously. In *Foole upon Foole* Armin affirms that 'indeed lightly one foole cannot indure the sight of another' and tells a story of how Will Summers watched his chance to disgrace a rival who had been employed in Henry VIII s court and was prospering.[14] He gives Jack Oates as another example:

> One time being very melancholie, the Knight to rouze him up said, hence foole hence, Ile have another foole, thou shalt dwell no longer with me: Jacke to this answered little, though indeede ye could not anger him worse: A Gentleman at the boord answeres, if it please you sir Ile bring ye another foole soone: I pray yee do quoth the knight, and he shall be welcome. Jacke fell a crying and departed mad and angry downe into the great Hall: and being strong armed as before I described him, caught the Bagpipes from the Piper, knockt them about his pate, that he laid the fellow for dead on the ground, and all broken, carries the pipes up into the great Chamber, and layes them on the fire.[15]

The single known example – and we have this only from a questionable story in *Tarlton's Jests and News out of Purgatory* – of one clown's being apprenticed to or assisted by another is the tradition of Armin having been 'adopted' by Richard Tarlton, who died in 1588. Tarlton is supposed to have been impressed by some extempore verses scribbled by Armin on the wainscot of a house occupied by Tarlton and a man from whom Armin unsuccessfully tried to collect a debt. The story tells how the old clown improvised some additional lines:

> A wagge thou art, none can prevent thee;
> And thy desert shall content thee.
> Let me divine. As I am
> So in time thou'lt be the same,
> My adopted sonne therefore be,
> To enjoy my clownes sute after me.[16]

Whether or not this story is true, it hardly seems likely that Kemp later could have regarded Armin with anything like Tarlton's generous enthusiasm.

The examples that we do have of professional jealousy

14 *Foole upon Foole* pp 131-2

15 Ibid, pp 63-4

16 *Tarlton's Jests, and News out of Purgatory* ed J.O. Halliwell, London 1844, p 29

between court fools make the reaction of Lear's Fool all the more striking when he sees that his 'monopoly' is being infringed by amateurs, and how

> Fools had ne'er less grace in a year;
> For wise men are grown foppish,
> And know not how their wits to wear
> Their manners are so apish. (I.iv.173-6)

King Lear, in a much more serious way than *Twelfth Night,* is a play in which 'What should I do?' is an all-important question. Besides the Fool's clear references to his living and Kent's hiring himself out there is the gruesome saying-and-getting or performance-reward nexus of Lear's competition – 'What shall Cordelia speak?' (I.i.62). Even Edgar as mad beggar, or 'nothing,' recognizes that he is not outside this process of plying a trade when he says,

> Bad is the trade that must play fool to sorrow,
> Ang'ring itself and others, (IV.i.39-40)

and suggests that in playing a part both to conceal himself from Gloucester and to give Gloucester some hope he is 'daubing' (IV. i.51) – that is, plastering over a collapsing structure like a foolish workman.

But as Lear does with Kent, Gloucester all as unwittingly finds Edgar 'full of labours.' And while they are together, even in the storm, the Fool 'labours to out-jest [Lear's] heart-strook injuries' (III.i.16-17). Splendid as the performances of Shakespeare's other fools are in their affirmations against adversity, it is Lear's Fool who most heroically of all marshals the 'fierce endeavour of ... art / To enforce the pained impotent to smile.' Hence the virtuoso performance in I.v, which is practically all a dialogue between the Fool and the king, in which the Fool tries to prepare Lear for the disappointment that awaits him when he tries to enlist Regan's sympathy. He gives the king a brilliant exhibition of what Hamlet calls speaking tropically; every one of his topics, no matter how outlandish – chilblains, crab-apples, oysters and snails – comes round to Lear's foolishness and vulnerability. And having 'proven' that the king has not the common sense of the lowest creatures, the Fool turns their exchange into another of his interviews or aptitude tests:

FOOL The reason why the seven stars are no mo than seven is a pretty reason.
LEAR Because they are not eight?
FOOL Yes. indeed: thou would'st make a good Fool.
...
If thou wert my Fool, Nuncle ... (I.v.74-7)

It is as if, in the Fool's eyes, Lear's answer has indicated a satisfactory level of aptitude or attainment in fooling, and now it is time for a word or two about conditions of employment. The king is a shadow of himself and, having a little tiny wit, must make content with his fortunes fit (so the Fool's song, echoing one of Feste's, goes at III.ii.74-7). He therefore is ready to be admitted to the only brotherhood into which the Fool is qualified to admit him, the trade or mystery of fooling: 'This [coxcomb] part between you' (compare I.i.139).

In their sufferings during the storm the Fool protects Lear as best he can (compare III.iv.113-14) and sees Poor Tom engaged as court philosopher (III.iv.180; III.vi.80). With his retinue of fool and pretended madman, Lear, the now-insane lord of misrule, directs the mock trial of Goneril and Regan in which the Fool, who must logically be in a very advanced state of exhaustion, humours the king more than Edgar or Kent can do. The famous exchange of nonsense lines after which he falls silent and shortly leaves the play could in this process of engaging, initiating, and 'training' the king to be fool be a final rite of passage, a challenge, and password into the mystery of fooling:

LEAR Make no noise, make no noise; draw the curtains: so, so. We'll go to supper i'th'morning.
FOOL And I'll go to bed at noon. (III.vi.85-8)

At his re-entrance in the play (IV.vi), fantastically dressed (the stage direction is Capell's but perfectly apt), Lear immediately will set about the mad yet logical business of hiring and training soldiers and will challenge Edgar: 'Give the word. EDGAR Sweet marjoram. LEAR Pass' (IV.vi.93-5). In his towering and obsessive madness during this scene the king also has an early paragraph full of echoes of the Fool's astute teachings: about not being old before one is wise ('They flattered me like a dog, and told me I had white hairs in my beard ere the black ones were there' lines 97-100); about how the wind and the rain of everyday adversity bring their lessons ('When the rain came to wet me once and the wind to make me chatter ... there I found 'em' 102-5); and about how when one is unable to see things one can smell them out (105; compare I.v.19-23). Lear also mirrors the Fool's generosity when he counsels Gloucester on how to make something out of nothing:

> Get thee glass eyes;
> And, like a scurvy politician, seem
> To see the things thou dost not. (172-4)

And he of course recognizes what the Fool knew and accepted from the very first, that the world is no more than 'this great stage of fools' (185).

From the third act onwards Lear has become more and more the inheritor of the Fool's living and speaker of reason in madness. Having been a fool, he has been initiated and become a Fool, a profession for the very wise. And Lear retains something of the Fool's wisdom after his storm of madness has passed, for he too can make an affirmation of life in the teeth of calamity. His reassurance of Cordelia, 'Come let's away to prison ...' (V.iii.8-19), is a Song of Innocence with its internal rhymes ('sing ... blessing ... sing') and its catalogue of children's benedictory gestures: singing like birds, asking blessing and forgiveness, praying, singing, telling old tales, laughing at butterflies. Goneril would sneer at this, as before ('Old fools are babes again' I.iii.20), but the Fool would say otherwise.

It now is time to write the job description which is deducible from this survey of the work of these four Shakespearian fools, and especially from that of the Fool in *King Lear*. The candidate: must be able to speak for life in the face of morbidity or even of death itself; should be aware of and able to direct his own urges to the benefit of others; should be able to sing (this qualification, like madness, is not an absolute requirement); must be able to enforce the pained impotent to smile, be alert to competition but utterly generous in sharing trade secrets with promising newcomers, and when convinced that a worthy successor is ready must uncomplainingly quit the scene. Compensation: successful practitioners of the fool's mystery ultimately may have a glimpse of the 'mystery of things.'

University of Calgary

CYRUS HOY

The Language of Fletcherian Tragicomedy

The chief element in the rhetorical style of John Fletcher's plays is repetition, and the patterns of repetition on exhibit in his work are classic in their origin.[1] According to Quintilian, 'figures of speech fall into two main classes. One is defined as the form of language while the other is mainly to be sought in the arrangement of words.' The former tends more to the grammatical, the latter more to the rhetorical[2]; and it is the latter which is the 'more striking class.' The first figure in it 'which calls for notice is that which is produced by *addition*. Of this there are various kinds.'[3] And Quintilian proceeds to set forth the several patterns of verbal repetition which had come, by his time, to be formulated in a rhetorical tradition extending from Aristotle to Cicero. All Renaissance students of the arts of poetry and rhetoric were familiar with it. Patterns of repetition are described in the pseudo-Ciceronian *Rhetorica ad C. Herennium,* one of the standard school-texts throughout the Middle Ages and the Renaissance,[4] and English readers could find them demonstrated in

1 Eugene Waith has noted of Fletcher's style: 'He concentrates narrowly upon certain devices of which repetition is the most conspicuous' (*The Pattern of Tragicomedy in Beaumont and Fletcher* New Haven 1952, p 192). But Waith makes no attempt to trace out Fletcher's use of the traditional repetitional schemes.

2 *Institutio Oratoria* IX.iii.2, trans H.E. Butler, London and New York 1922, III.443

3 *Institutio Oratoria* IX.iii.28 (Butler, III.461)

4 *Ad Herennium* IV.xiii.19ff, trans Harry Caplan, Cambridge Mass and

treatise after treatise during the latter half of the sixteenth century: in, for example, Thomas Wilson's *Arte of Rhetorique* (first published in 1553 and reprinted seven times by 1585), in *The Garden of Eloquence* by Henry Peacham the elder (1577; reprinted 'corrected and augmented' in 1593), in Abraham Fraunce's *Arcadian Rhetorike* (1588), in George Puttenham's *Arte of English Poesie* (1589), in John Hoskyns' *Directions for Speech and Style* (written circa 1599).

Book three of Puttenham's treatise deals with poetical ornament and chapter nineteen with rhetorical figures, and the focus here is frankly on the sound of poetry: how by means of the 'copious amplification, or enlargement of language'[5] to enable it to make the most effective possible impression on the ears and so on the mind of the hearer. Puttenham explains the rationale that is the motive to his discussion:

> For like as one or two drops of water perce not the flint stone, but many and often droppings doo: so cannot a few words (be they neuer so pithie or sententious) in all cases and to all manner of mindes, make so deepe an impression, as a more multitude of words to the purpose discreetely, and without superfluitie vttered: the minde being no lesse vanquished with large loade of speech, than the limmes are with heauie burden. Sweetenes of speech, sentence, and amplification, are therfore necessarie to an excellent Orator and Poet, ne may in no wise be spared from any of them.[6]

Of all rhetorical figures tending to the poet's purpose, that which 'worketh by iteration or repetition of one word or clause' heads Puttenham's list; it 'doth much alter and affect the eare and also the mynde of the hearer, and therefore is counted a very braue figure both with the Poets and rhetoriciens.'[7] Of repetition there are seven sorts, according to Puttenham, and in describing them in what follows I will replace his examples with illustrations from Fletcher's plays by way of suggesting just how fundamental these classic repetitional schemes are to the structure of Fletcher's dramatic language.

The first figure of repetition Puttenham cites is *anaphora*, wherein the same word stands at the beginning of successive

London 1968, pp 275ff

5 George Puttenham *The Arte of English Poesie* ed Gladys Doidge Willcock and Alice Walker, Cambridge 1936, p 196

6 Puttenham *Arte of English Poesie* pp 197-8

7 Ibid, p 198

lines of verse or, as Henry Peacham the elder had put it in *The Garden of Eloquence* some dozen years before the publication of Puttenham's treatise, 'when one word is repeated in the beginning of diuers clauses, or thus, when we begin manye members still with one and the same worde.'[8] Here is an example from Fletcher's tragedy *Valentinian* (written sometime between 1610 and 1614), where the Emperor shamelessly sets about rationalizing his rape of Lucina:

> If I have done a sin, curse her that drew me,
> Curse the first cause, the witchcraft that abusd me,
> Curse those faire eyes, and curse that heavenly beauty,
> And curse your being good too. (III.i.54-7)[9]

There is another example in Fletcher's tragicomedy *The Loyal Subject* (1618), where Archas, the titular character, is addressing his rebellious son:

> Downe with that heart, downe suddenly, down with it,
> Downe with that disobedience; tye that tongue up ...
> (I.iii; Folio 1647, 25b)

And still another from a bit farther on in the same scene (Archas is saying farewell to his troops):

> when ye fight next,
> When flame and furie make but one face of horror,
> When the great rest of all your honour's up,
> When you would thinke a spell to shake the enemy,
> Remember me ... (26b)

8 Henry Peacham *The Garden of Eloquence* edn 1577, sig H4V

9 Act, scene, and line numbers refer to R.K. Turner's edition of *Valentinian* in vol IV of *The Dramatic Works in the Beaumont and Fletcher Canon* gen ed Fredson Bowers, Cambridge 1979. In the following discussion, quotations accompanied by act, scene, and line references are drawn from texts in the New Cambridge edition. Quotations from plays that have not yet appeared in the New Cambridge edition are drawn from the text of the 1647 Beaumont and Fletcher Folio and are accompanied by parenthetical references to folio page and column (the letters 'a' and 'b' following each number referring respectively to the left and right column of the folio page).

One effect of anaphora is suggested by John Hoskyns when he declares: 'This figure beats upon one thing to cause the quicker feeling in the audience, and to awake a sleepy or dull person.'[10]

The reverse of anaphora is *epistrophe,* Puttenham's second figure of repetition, wherein, as he describes it, 'ye make one word finish many verses in sute, and that which is harder, to finish many clauses in the middest of your verses.'[11] There is an example in Fletcher's *Monsieur Thomas* (circa 1615):

> alas consider,
> Play but the woman with me, and consider
> As he himselfe do's, and I now dare see it,
> Truly consider sir, what misery (III.i.94-7).

There is an even more striking instance in *Valentinian,* in the course of Lucina's denunciation of the Emperor who has ravished her:

> Women, and fearefull Maids, make vows against thee:
> Thy own Slaves, if they heare of this, shall hate thee;
> And those thou hast corrupted, first fall from thee;
> And if thou let'st me live, the Souldier,
> Tyrde with thy Tyrannies, break through obedience,
> And shake his strong Steele at thee. (III.i.47-52)

Sister Miriam Joseph has observed that 'anaphora and epistrophe, the most obvious of rhetorical devices, appear ... in stiff profusion' in Shakespeare's early plays but are rarely used in his later ones.[12] This is not the case with Fletcher's plays, where both figures commonly appear in mature work.

10 John Hoskyns *Directions for Speech and Style* ed Hoyt B. Hudson, who spells the author's name 'Hoskins' (Princeton 1935), p 13. Hoskyns's essay was not printed in its entirety until Hudson's edition, but it had circulated in manuscript during the early decades of the seventeenth century. For an account of the portions of it printed in Ben Jonson's *Timber* (1641), Thomas Blount's *Academy of Eloquence* (1654), and John Smith's *The Mysterie of Rhetorique Unvail'd* (1657), see the introduction to Hudson's edition, pp xxvii-xxxviii.

11 Puttenham *Arte of English Poesie* p 198 (where the figure is called *antistrophe*). It is called epistrophe in Fraunce *Arcadian Rhetorike* edn 1588, sig D1v, and Hoskyns *Directions* p 13. Peacham in *The Garden of Eloquence* (sig I1v) labels it *epiphora.*

12 Sister Miriam Joseph *Shakespeare's Use of the Arts of Language* New York 1947, p 80

Puttenham's third figure of repetition, *symploce,* combines the features of the two previous ones: a series of lines which both begin and end with the same word or words[13]; or as Hoskyns puts it, 'when several sentences have the same beginning and the same ending.' According to Hoskyns, 'This is the wantonest of repetitions, and is not to be used in matters too serious.'[14] Fletcher employs it appropriately enough in *The Humorous Lieutenant* (circa 1619), where Demetrius laments the defeat of his army and (as he supposes) the loss of all his companions who comprised it:

> I have lost my friends, those worthy soules bred with me,
> I have lost my selfe, they were the pieces of me;
> I have lost all Arts, my Schooles are taken from me ...
>
> (II.iv.51-3)[15]

And a bit later in the same scene, after Demetrius learns that his enemy has generously freed all the prisoners taken in the defeated army:

> At mine owne weapon, Courtesie, h'as beaten me,
> At that I was held a Master in, he has cow'd me ...
>
> (lines 126-7)

Peacham had said of symploce: 'This figure is more pleasaunt, if euery repetition following haue one worde more then the repetition going before, thus. Remember *Sodom* and *Gomer,* remember the sinne of *Sodom* and *Gomer,* remember the sinne and destruction of *Sodom* and *Gomer.*'[16] Symploce thus considered closely partakes of Puttenham's fourth figure, *anadiplosis,* one of the most common in Fletcher. In it, the word that ends a line (or a clause or sentence) is repeated at the beginning of the following line (or clause or sentence).[17] There are some relatively simple examples in *The Humorous Lieutenant:*

13 Puttenham *Arte of English Poesie* pp 199-200
14 Hoskyns *Directions* p 13
15 Quotations from *The Humorous Lieutenant* in this paper are based on my forthcoming edition of the play in vol v of the New Cambridge Beaumont and Fletcher.
16 Peacham *Garden of Eloquence* sig I2
17 Puttenham *Arte of English Poesie* p 200

I grieve truly,
Truly and heartily to see you thus sir: (IV.iv.88-9)

and in the triumphant cry of the heroine of *Bonduca* (circa 1613):

a woman,
A woman beat em, *Nennius;* a weak woman,
A woman beat these *Romanes.* (I.i.15-17)

More elaborate is such a passage as the following from *A Wife for a Month* (1624), with its augmentation of the repeated words ('old,' 'fellowship,' 'a maid') and its *polyptoton* on 'piously / pious'[18]:

Now I see I am old Sir,
Old and ill-favour'd too, poore and despis'd,
And am not worth your noble Fellowship,
Your fellowship in Love, you would not else
Thus cunningly seeke to betray a maid,
A maid that honours you thus piously;
Strive to abuse the pious love she brings ye.
(III.i; Folio 1647, 57b)

Later in the same play there occurs a comparable elaboration on the three words 'speak unto her':

speake unto her,
You are familiar; speake I say unto her,
Speake to the purpose ... (IV.i; Folio 1647, 59b)

A continued anadiplosis, as Sister Miriam Joseph has noted, amounts to another repetitional figure, *climax,* or *gradatio,*[19]

18 'Polyptoton is the repetition of words derived from the same root' (Sister Miriam Joseph *Shakespeare's Use* p 83). Puttenham does not consider it among his 'seuen sortes' of figures of repetition but discusses it later (pp 203-4), where he refers to it as '*Traductio,* or the Tranlacer' and describes the figure thus: 'when ye turne and tranlace a word into many sundry shapes as the Tailor doth his garment.'

19 Sister Miriam Joseph *Shakespeare's Use* pp 83, 306. Thomas Wilson describes 'Gradatio' thus: 'Gradacion is when we reherse the worde that goeth next before, and bryng another woorde thereupon that encreaseth the matter, as though one should go vp a paire of staiers, and not leaue til he come at the toppe. Gradacion is when a sentence is disseuered by

described by Puttenham as 'the *marching*' or 'the *clyming*' figure, 'for after the first steppe all the rest proceede by double the space, and so in our speach one word proceedes double to the first that was spoken, and goeth as it were by strides or paces.'[20] In *The Loyal Subject* the valiant Archas describes his past military exploits by means of a continued anadiplosis which, with the elaboration worked on the words 'Volga' and 'ruines,' reminds one of the effect that Peacham found especially pleasant in symploce:

> I yet remember when the *Volga* curl'd,
> The aged *Volga*, when he heav'd his head up,
> And rais'd his waters high, to see the ruines,
> The ruines our Swords made, the bloudy ruines ...
> (I.iii; Folio 1647, 25a)

A passage such as this suggests something of the rhetorical complexity that Fletcher's repetitional schemes can take on. In addition to the anadiplosis built on the repetition of Volga and ruines, the use of ruines at the end of the penultimate line forms an epistrophe with the repetition of the word at the end of the last line. Moreover, the repetition of ruines at the beginning and end of the last line represents (as does the repetition of the word 'woman' at the beginning and end of the middle line of the passage quoted above from *Bonduca*) an *epanalepsis*, Puttenham's fifth figure of repetition,[21] where a single verse line begins and ends with the same word. There is an example in *A Wife for a Month* in the cry of one suffering the feverish heats of poison: 'Drinke, drinke, a world of drinke' (IV.i; Folio 1647, 63a). And a characteristic passage in *The Loyal Subject*:

> Take heed, take heed young Ladies: still take heed,
> Take heed of promises, take heed of gifts,

degrees, so that the worde, whiche endeth the sentence goyng before, doeth begin the nexte' (*The Arte of Rhetorique* facsimile edn 1553, prepared by Robert Hood Bowers, Gainesville Fla 1962, p 229). Cf *Ad Herennium* IV.xxv.34: 'Climax is the figure in which the speaker passes to the following word only after advancing by steps to the preceding one' (p 315).

20 Puttenham *Arte of English Poesie* p 208

21 Puttenham *Arte of English Poesie* p 200. Hoskyns (*Directions* p 14) notes the similarity of epanalepsis and symploce: 'Epanalepsis is the same in one sentence which symploce or *complexio* is in several sentences.'

Of forced feigned sorrowes, sighes, take heed.
(IV.iii; Folio 1647, 43a)

Here the alliteration in the last line is a reminder that alliteration itself (*paroemion*) is a figure of repetition. Rhetorical injunctions of the kind issued in this passage are recurrent in Fletcher; for example, in *The Mad Lover* (1617): 'Take heed for honours sake take heed' (IV.i; Folio 1647, 16b) or *Valentinian*: 'Take heed, by all our love take heed' (III.iii.137).

Puttenham defines the sixth rhetorical figure of repetition, *epizeuxis*, as occurring 'when in one verse or clause of a verse, ye iterate one word without any intermission.'[22] There are a number of examples in the sick-bed speech of the poisoned Alphonso in *A Wife for a Month:*

Give me more ayre, ayre, more ayre, blow, blow,
...
I am all fire, fire, fire,
...
Dig, dig, dig, till the springs fly up,
The cold, cold springs ... (IV.iv; Folio 1647, 62b)

Finally, there is the figure which Puttenham calls *ploce*, or 'the Doubler.' Like epizeuxis, it is 'a speedie iteration of one word' but with the difference that here there is 'some little intermission by inserting one or two words betweene.'[23] But ploce, as Sister Miriam Joseph has pointed out, is usually taken to mean a figure whereby a proper name is repeated in order both 'to designate a person and to signify his qualities.'[24] Puttenham's ploce is termed *traductio* by Peacham ('when one word is sundry tymes repeated in one sentence, to make the Oration more trimme'[25]) and *epanados* by Fraunce ('regression, turning to the same sound, when one and the same sound is repeated in the beginning and middle, or middle and end'[26]) and Hoskyns ('when the midst and the end or the midst and the beginning

22 Puttenham *Arte of English Poesie* p 201. 'This figure,' says Hoskyns (*Directions* p 12), 'is not to be used but in passion.' Fraunce (*Arcadian Rhetorike* sigs C5v-C6) says that epizeuxis is also called *palilogia*.

23 Puttenham *Arte of English Poesie* p 201

24 Sister Miriam Joseph *Shakespeare's Use* p 84

25 Peacham *Garden of Eloquence* sig 13v

26 Fraunce *Arcadian Rhetorike* sig D4

are the same'[27]). Fletcher's plays abound in this sort of thing; for example, in *The Loyal Subject*:

> O we are too honest,
> Believe it sir, too honest far too honest,
> (IV.iii; Folio 1647, 42a)

or the repetition of the word 'speak' in the passage already quoted from IV.i of *A Wife for a Month*, or the repetition of the word 'woman' in the passage already quoted from I.i. of *Bonduca*.

These seven figures of repetition comprise what may be thought of as the classic ground-plan for Fletcher's rhetorical style,[28] but in the perfection of this he proceeds to combine and elaborate the classic elements of his art and in doing so achieves ornate and often fantastic effects of verbal display that go far beyond any purely classic aim; Fletcher is clearly as much concerned with creating patterns of sound, rhythmic designs, as he is with embellishing or diversifying his blank verse. One way in which he manipulates his metrical rhythms is to endow virtually all the principal parts of English speech with repetitional patterns of their own. Nouns, for example, are regularly repeated with an intervening adjective:

27 Hoskyns *Directions* p 14

28 The seven figures that Puttenham singles out for discussion are by no means all the figures of repetition known to rhetoric. Some he omits: eg *diacope* (see below, p 163). Some he discusses elsewhere in his treatise: eg polyptoton (see above, n 18) and alliteration (paroemion), which he treats in bk III, chap 16, with 'auricular' figures. At the end of his account of the seven, he says:

> Now also be there many other sortes of repetition if a man would vse them, but are nothing commendable, and therefore are not obserued in good poesie, as a vulgar rimer who doubled one word in the end of euery verse, thus:
>
> *adieu, adieu,*
> *my face, my face.*
>
> And an other that did the like in the beginning of his verse, thus:
>
> *To loue him and loue him, as sinners should doo.*
>
> These repetitions be not figuratiue but phantastical, for a figure is euer vsed to a purpose, either of beautie or of efficacie: and these last recited be to no purpose, for neither can ye say that it vrges affection nor that it beautifieth or enforceth the sence, nor hath any other subtilitie in it, and therfore is a very foolish impertinency of speech, and not a figure. (p 202)

The seven figures that Puttenham does discuss are the crucial ones.

this Ladie,
This goodly Ladie (*The Mad Lover* Act III; Folio 1647, 13a)

Upon thy Fathers charge, thy happy Fathers
(*A Wife for a Month* Act IV; Folio 1647, 60b)

the wounds I suffer,
The smarting wounds of losse
(*The Humorous Lieutenant* II.ii.53-4)

The pattern can be extended, thus:

That was the bloud rebel'd, the naughty bloud,
The proud provoking bloud
(*The Loyal Subject* IV.vi; Folio 1647, 46a)

Come kisse the Prince, the vertuous Prince, the good
Prince (*The Loyal Subject* IV.iii; Folio 1647, 42b)

through the world, the wide world thus to wander,
The wretched world alone
(*Women Pleased* V.i; Folio 1647, 43b)[29]

the wrong you have offred me,
The most unmanly wrong, unfriendly wrong
(*The Little French Lawyer* II.i; Folio 1647, 59a)[30]

such a love she beares to me, a chaste love,
A vertuous, faire, and fruitfull love
(*Beggars' Bush* IV.vi.83-4)[31]

What these amount to are examples of another of the classic figures of repetition (but one not mentioned in Puttenham), the figure of *diacope*, 'the repetition of a word with one or more

29 The date of *Women Pleased* is ca 1620.

30 The date of *The Little French Lawyer* (a Fletcher and Massinger collaboration) is ca 1619. For Fletcher's authorship of act II of this play, see my 'Shares of Fletcher and his Collaborators in the Beaumont and Fletcher Canon, Part II' *Studies in Bibliography* IX (1957) 150-1.

31 The date of *Beggars' Bush* (which contains the work of Beaumont, Fletcher, and Massinger) is ca 1615. For Fletcher's authorship of act IV of this play, see my 'Shares of Fletcher and his Collaborators ... Part III' *Studies in Bibliography* XI (1958) 87-9.

between.'[32] Sometimes the noun is immediately repeated and the adjectival phrase follows the repetition; this is often managed in such a way that the noun is first stated at the end of one line and repeated at the beginning of the following line, and so amounts to a version of anadiplosis:

> that day,
> That day so long expected
> (*The Loyal Subject* I.i; Folio 1647, 23b)

> a teacher,
> Teacher of these lewd Arts
> (*The Loyal Subject* III.vi; Folio 1647, 40a)

> when I put these things to her,
> These things of honest thrift
> (*The Humorous Lieutenant* II.i.52-3)

> since you have conceiv'd an evill against me,
> An evill that so much concernes your honour, That honour
> aim'd by all at for a patterne
> (*The Humorous Lieutenant* V.v.4-6)

Adjectives themselves will often be repeated, and it is typical of Fletcher's refinement on his classic models that with him repetitions do not merely repeat but serve to augment and intensify the patterns both of sound and sense; as the repeated noun came equipped with an adjective, so repeated adjectives are often provided with an intervening adverb:

> She was too good for me, so heavenly good sir
> (*The Loyal Subject* V.v; Folio 1647, 49a)

> a loving heart
> A truly loving heart (*The Mad Lover* Act I; Folio 1647, 5a)

> I should grow envious,
> Extreamely envious of your youth, and honour
> (*The Humorous Lieutenant* I.ii.20-1)

32 Sister Miriam Joseph *Shakespeare's Use* p 87. Cf Peacham *Garden of Eloquence* 13v: 'Diacope, when a word is repeated, and but one word put betweene.'

Repetition of verbs follows the now familiar pattern which includes augmentation: sometimes the verb will be repeated with one or more intervening adverbs:

> your grace would love us,
> Most dearely love us
> (*The Loyal Subject* IV.iii; Folio 1647, 42a)

> I know you have suffer'd, infinitely suffer'd
> (*A Wife for a Month* Act IV; Folio 1647, 60a)

> Thus led away, thus vainly led away (*Valentinian* I.iii.45)

And sometimes the adverb will follow the repetition:

> I shall then remember,
> I shall remember truely
> (*The Loyal Subject* I.i; Folio 1647, 23b)

> I tell ye, ye shall have her: have her safelie
> (*The Mad Lover* Act IV; Folio 1647, 16a)

> The Gentleman will cast himselfe away,
> Cast himselfe wilfully (*Women Pleased* II.v; Folio 1647, 30a)

What, one may ask, is the effect of these patterns of repetition on passages of sustained dramatic speech in Fletcher's plays? The answer, of course, is that the effects are various, but a property common to them all is the air of often hysterical urgency imparted by these reiterated and steadily augmented rhythms. And it is notable – especially in the passages quoted below – that for all the impression of headlong, unpremeditated passion which it is the first intention of these speeches to convey, they all fairly flaunt the highly mannered artifice of their verbal arrangement. Feeling thus elaborately expressed, no matter how deeply felt its dramatic occasion may proclaim it to be, has about it a quality of edgy shrillness which contributes an essential feature of the dramatic climaxes of Fletcherian tragedy and tragicomedy. In them, passion regularly lifts its voice in the accents of the most ingenious artifice, and the tension created between the clashing impressions of spontaneity and contrivance may represent one of Fletcher's most significant claims to the baroque style, qualities which his work has often been said to display. Here are some examples.

The second act of *The Queen of Corinth* (which Fletcher wrote in collaboration with Massinger and Field circa 1617)[33] opens with the stage direction '*Enter Merione (as newly ravished)*,' and that sufficiently explains the cue to her impassioned outburst that follows:

To whom now shall I cry? What pow'r thus kneele to? 1
And beg my ravisht honour back upon me? 2
Deafe, deafe, you gods of goodnesse, deafe to me, 3
Deafe Heaven to all my cryes; deafe hope, deafe justice, 4
I am abus'd, and you that see all saw it; 5
Saw it, and smil'd upon the villaine did it: 6
Saw it, and gave him strength: why have I pray'd to ye, 7
When all the worlds eyes have been sunk in slumbers? 8
Why have I then powr'd out my teares? kneel'd to ye? 9
And from the Altar of a pure heart sent ye 10
Thoughts like your selves, white, innocent, vowes purer 11
And of a sweeter flame then all earths odours? 12
(Folio 1647, 5b)

The passage is built on the classic figures of repetition, five of which are demonstrated at least once in its twelve lines. The first line, beginning and ending with the same word ('to'), is an epanalepsis. Lines 2 and 3, both ending with the same word ('me'), compose an epistrophe which is set in balance against the anaphora of lines 3 and 4, both beginning with the word 'deafe.' But lines 3 and 4 also provide a good example of epanodos; in addition to standing at the beginning of each line, the word 'deafe' is repeated twice again in each, the repetition separated by other words in each case. The use of 'it' at the end of lines 5 and 6 comprises another epistrophe; and the lines also exhibit an anadiplosis, with the 'saw it' which ends line 5 repeated at the beginning of line 6; when it is repeated again at the beginning of line 7, we have another anaphora. The remaining lines are not so stiffly patterned, though further repeated words are loosely sprinkled throughout them. The 'why have I' query of line 7 is repeated in line 9, and the terminal 'ye's are worth noting at the end of line 7 and of lines 9 and 10, which

33 For Fletcher's authorship of act II of this play, see my 'Shares of Fletcher and his Collaborators ... Part IV' *Studies in Bibliography* XII (1959) 98-100.

comprise another epistrophe. Also worth noting are the 'and's which open lines 10 and 12.

Here is another example, from the third act of *The Mad Lover,* where a young man reproaches a lady for her rejection of his brother's love, a rejection that has apparently (but not really) resulted in the brother's death.

> Live then I say famous for civill slaughters, 1
> Live and lay out your triumphs, guild your glories[,] 2
> Live and be spoken this is she, this Ladie, 3
> This goodly Ladie, yet most killing beautie; 4
> This with the two edg'd eyes, the heart for hardnes 5
> Out doing rockes; and coldnes, rockes of Christall[,] 6
> This with the swelling soule, more coye of Courtship 7
> Then the proud sea is when the shores embrace him [;] 8
> Live till the mothers find ye; read your story 9
> And sowe their barren curses on your beauty, 10
> Till those that have enjoy'd their loves despise ye, 11
> Till Virgins pray against ye, old age find ye 12
> And even as wasted coales glow in their dying 13
> So may the Gods reward ye in your ashes 14
> (Folio 1647, 13a-b).

Immediately evident is the anaphora involving the word 'Live' at the beginning of the first three lines. There is an anadiplosis, Fletcherian variety, in lines 3 and 4, where the phrase 'this Ladie' at the end of line 3 becomes 'This goodly Ladie' in its repetition at the beginning of line 4. The repetition of 'This' at the beginning of both lines 4 and 5 forms another anaphora. There is an epanodos involving the word 'rockes' in line 6. The anaphora on 'This' in lines 4 and 5 is echoed in line 7, just as the anaphora on 'Live' of lines 1 through 3 is echoed in line 9. Lines 11 and 12, beginning and ending with the same words ('Till' and 'ye') comprise a good example of the figure symploce: and the medial repetition of 'ye' in lines 9, 12, and 14, together with its terminal position in lines 11 and 12, contribute to the figure epistrophe, which as Puttenham has described it involves not only one word finishing 'many verses in sute' but also 'that which is harder,' one word finishing 'many clauses in the middest of your verses.'

The tendency in both these passages is towards what is at once a larger and more specified verse utterance, with the attitude or emotion that is expressed subject to what is often an extreme degree of amplification. Fletcher's patterns of repetition enable him to retain poetic control over his wide-ranging and generally turbulent dramatic materials; and the rhetorical strategies of his language, with its intricate reiterations and augmentations, are crucial factors in making it so extraordinarily right for the purposes of tragicomedy. Fletcher's tragicomic plots are expressly designed to explore labyrinths of feeling, real and feigned, and his characters' twisting, convoluted speech, backtracking on itself and then surging forward in repetitious waves, is but the verbal equivalent of the emotional states that impel them from one remarkable extreme to another. It is Fletcher's way of suiting words to action.

University of Rochester

RALPH BERRY

Richard III: Bonding the Audience

The first thing that we know of *Richard III* is that it was a success, and remained so. From the days of its mentions in Henslowe's diary and the five quartos by 1612, through two centuries of Cibber's version to the triumphs of Olivier's film and the opening night of the Festival Theatre at Stratford, Ontario, *Richard III* has commanded popular success. It is not only a hit but a play intended and designed as a hit (as some of Shakespeare, in the second half of his career especially, is not). In *Richard III* Shakespeare seems to have expressed all that he knew of the means of controlling an audience: of creating, for the first time in his career, a star part and of welding the audience into a fascinated and delighted unity. The relations between Richard and his audience are my subject.

I

The ground-plan of *Richard III* is that the audience supports the villain-hero, then abandons him. The formal action can be called the working of 'retributive justice'[1]; the audience experiences it as the waning of an affair and a demonstration that actions will have consequences that include our emotional reactions to those consequences. Gloucester is in the first place a channel for the

Citations are to *The Complete Works of Shakespeare* ed David Bevington, Glenview Ill 1980.

1 A.P. Rossiter *Angel with Horns* London 1961, p 2

energies of the drama, impulses transmitted from stage to audience and back. Those energies are dark and primitive, emerging from a stratum of folklore and desire in the collective mind. Richard, clearly, permits the acting-out of desires in the audience. He makes himself king; he takes his sexual rewards; he plans (but is unable to commit) incest. Against all the structures of morality, kinship, the needs of the tribe itself, the individual asserts himself. The process is made profoundly attractive and, in the end, as profoundly repellent. The atavistic forces tapped by Richard are never far below the surface of the action. The folklore element suggests, for instance, that Richard's status is that of imposter. He is the Man Who Would Be King, behind whom stretches a long line of tricksters. Then, in the wooing of Lady Anne, we become conscious of another myth: Beauty and the Beast. (It is a myth Middleton also exploits, in *The Changeling.)* Nicholas Brooke finds echoes of de Sade in Richard's treatment of Lady Anne. As Brooke remarks, the play's 'sexual current, prominent in this scene and equally so later in the wooing of Queen Elizabeth for her daughter, is elsewhere frequently felt, but very much as an undercurrent.'[2] This is true, but it is interesting that the sexual current is strong and explicit in Richard's apotheosis, his address to the troops:

> You having lands, and blest with beauteous wives,
> They would restrain the one, distain the other ...
> Shall these enjoy our lands? Lie with our wives?
> Ravish our daughters? (V.iii.321-2, 336-7)

The appeal to the sexual and racial instincts of the soldiery and the proposition that the end of war is to get at the enemy's womenfolk can be looked at as a tactic of rhetoric: they can also be taken as a straightforward exposition of Richard's psychology and values. The soldiery / audience is appealed to at a certain level of its psyche. The appeal is rejected, as it happens; but the intensity of the current is fully registered.

From these hints of a dark prehistory to Richard, a shadowy impression of his identity begins to emerge. That identity is, however, based on an immediately available tradition. The great container for Richard is the Vice figure. The explicit reference does not occur until III.i, but the Vice governs the frame of

2 Nicholas Brooke *Shakespeare's Early Tragedies* London 1968, p 67

reference within which Richard engages the audience. Richard alludes to a network of devices, stratagems, traditions with which his audience is well familiar. He can, for instance, be looked at as a mutation of Herod in the mystery plays, a role 'rooted in the tension and interaction of the horrible and the comic.'[3] The comic is the means by which the audience both approaches the tyrant and revenges itself upon him. Richard, for his part, seeks to seduce the audience. Audience rapport is the key to the early structuring of this play, and we need to touch lightly on the obvious features of Richard's wooing of his public.

Soliloquies and asides

It is generally accepted that the soliloquies in *Richard III*, prior to the last one (V.iii), should be played as direct address to the audience.[4] The tone is ingratiating, and the audience flattered by being taken into Richard's confidence. We become accomplices. But these soliloquies cluster most densely around the early scenes, and they later fade. Thus the audience's regard for Richard is insidiously weakened. In the opening phase Richard confides in us; in the second, in Buckingham; in the third, in no one.

The aside in *Richard III* is not really a miniature soliloquy, merely a joke that maintains good relations with the audience.

> Amen! And make me die a good old man!
> That is the butt-end of a mother's blessing;
> I marvel that her Grace did leave it out. (II.ii.109-11)

3 Robert Weimann *Shakespeare and the Popular Tradition in the Theatre: Studies in the Social Dimension of Dramatic Form and Function* ed Robert Schwartz, Baltimore 1978, p 68

4 The practice is codified in Laurence Olivier's film. It is accepted as correct by Brooke *Shakespeare's Early Tragedies* p 56. Bernard Spivack cites an interesting anecdote on this point: it was the experience of Margaret Carrington, who prepared John Barrymore for his Richard III. Barrymore delivered the soliloquy at the end of the Lady Anne wooing scene to himself, with a mediocre response from the audience. Margaret Carrington suggested that he speak directly to the audience; he did, and the reaction was tremendous. *Shakespeare and the Allegory of Evil* New York 1958, p 456

This aside presents Richard as Peck's bad boy, an endearing-enough figure.

> So wise so young, they say, do never live long. (III.i.79)

The aside is transmitted to Catesby and Buckingham, who illustrate a tactic of their master's:

> CATESBY The princes both make high account of you –
> For they account his head upon the bridge. (III.ii.69-70)

> HASTINGS Nay, like enough, for I stay dinner there.
> BUCKINGHAM And supper too, although thou know'st it not. (III.ii.121-2)

All instances of the aside occur in the first half of the play. Its lapse marks a weakening of the bond between Richard and audience.

Double meanings

The double meaning is a joke shared between Richard and the audience. While the remark is addressed to another character on stage, its import is clear and will be pointed up by the actor. Thus:

> We are not safe, Clarence, we are not safe. (I.i.70)

> Meantime, this deep disgrace in brotherhood
> Touches me deeper than you can imagine. (I.i.111-12)

> I will deliver you, or else lie for you. (I.i.115)

> For they that were your enemies are his. (I.i.130)

> Some tardy cripple bare the countermand. (II.i.90)

Buckingham is presumably the audience for whose benefit the last remark is passed; the others are all for the playhouse audience. Again, the pattern holds of an opening blaze of instances, soon extinguished. But while the immediate tactic lapses, the idea of double meaning broadens out into the superlative continuous jest of III.vii.

Word-play

Richard enjoys word-play, usually of a rather obvious and mechanical type. The most advanced instance I can find is the reference to the 'new-delivered Hastings' (I.i.121), a neat hit at the innocent-babe aspect of Hastings. Otherwise Richard's word-plays do not test the powers of the audience:

> Since every Jack became a gentleman,
> There's many a gentle person made a Jack. (I.iii.71-2)

> while great promotions
> Are daily given to ennoble those
> That scarce some two days since were worth a noble.
> (I.iii.79-81)

> What, marry, may she? Marry with a king ... (I.iii.99)

These (with which one can include the oath-substitute of 'Margaret') are broad and easy games with words, much in the Vice tradition and sure to win the approval of the audience. Shakespeare extends their use into the second half of the play, presumably because he finds them psychologically interesting. Richard, in the bad-news scene, has three in rapid succession:

> STANLEY Richmond is on the seas.
> RICHARD There let him sink, and be the seas on him!
> (IV.iv.462-3)

> STANLEY Unless for that, my liege, I cannot guess.
> RICHARD Unless for that he comes to be your liege,
> You cannot guess wherefore the Welshman comes.
> (IV.iv.474-6)

(The word 'liege' evidently touches a nerve: Richard had played on 'true noble Prince' with Buckingham, IV.ii.20.)

> STANLEY No, my good lord, my friends are in the north.
> RICHARD Cold friends to me! What do they in the north,
> When they should serve their sovereign in the west?
> (IV.iv.483-5)

These attempts to wrest words from their meaning show a mind trying to impose order on a dissolving reality.

Word-play is the critical term for locating the traditions energized by Richard. It is focused to the clear exposition of

> GLOUCESTER So wise so young, they say, do never live long.
> PRINCE What say you, uncle?
> GLOUCESTER I say, without characters fame lives long.
> Thus, like the formal Vice, Iniquity,
> I moralize two meanings in one word. (III.i.79-83)

'Gloucester's reference to the "formal vice, Iniquity" is – like Speed's – itself in the form of a pun, and it is a vicious and highly sophisticated kind of "contrarie sence" in which Gloucester uses the verb "moralize."'[5] Weimann marks the first and fourth lines in the passage cited as 'aside.' That is precisely the point, left open for performance, which characterizes the openness of the text to the traditional allusion. Richard may deliver the lines broadly, to the audience; or he may speak them covertly, to Buckingham. The one mode is the non-representational use of the *platea* (platform), a direct address to the audience. The other way assents to the realistic *locus*-centred style. It is impossible and unnecessary to determine the matter; no doubt the actors' way of playing this passage (and others raising parallel problems) varied over the years in Shakespeare's lifetime. These options raise the question of the degree of obsolescence associated with the tradition. Weimann emphasizes the word 'old' used of the Vice in *Twelfth Night* and *The Two Gentlemen of Verona.*

> These qualifications are, in Shakespeare, perhaps the most illuminating: The Vice was the *old* Vice, but *still* he could be used or referred to; and the words 'old' and 'still' indicate the dialectic of innovation and tradition by which Shakespeare's wordplay actually thrived upon the diminishing tensions of *mimesis* and ritual, matter and impertinency.[6]

The psychology of the role adapts easily to the dualism of the tradition. There is nothing improbable in the notion of a person modelling himself upon a stereotype of conduct or using this

5 Weimann *Shakespeare and the Popular Tradition* p 150. '"Moralize," in this sense, is a metaphorical statement about the literary history of the verbal figure ...'

6 Ibid, p 151

stereotype as a point of departure. 'And what's he then that says I play the villain?' demands Iago. It seems likely that the development of dramatic style was able to assimilate the traditional Vice. The villain-hero who takes the audience into his confidence – for whom an antecedent can be found as far back as the Chester cycle[7] – is absorbed into the self-consciousness of Richard. Even at the very end there is no contradiction between tradition and psychology. The demoniac energy of Richard –

> March on, join bravely, let us to it pell-mell;
> If not to heaven, then hand in hand to hell (V.ii.312-3)

– calling for a horse with his last breath, is simply the 'terrible exuberance' of the Vice, riding off like Nichol Newfangle to hell.[8] On all counts, traditional, tactical, and psychological, the Vice material strengthens Richard's bond with the audience.

The Vice is a technical means of establishing rapport. It will not in itself guarantee success. Richard remains, a man. His links with the audience must consist of something other than jokes and direct appeals. Behind the tricks is a sensibility; and Shakespeare develops in that sensibility a sympathetic exploitation of class attitudes. One cannot adequately discuss the core of this play without reference to class.

II

Richard is an aristocrat. And some of his utterances assert an aristocratic sensibility, one founded on pride of family and class:

> Unmanner'd dog, stand thou, when I command! (I.ii.39)

> Ay, and much more; but I was born so high.
> Our aery buildeth in the cedar's top,
> And dallies with the wind and scorns the sun. (I.iii.262-4)

7 Weimann quotes a 'Tyrant' who introduces himself thus:
I am full of sotelty,
ffalshed, gyll, and trechery;
Therfor am I namyd by clergy
As mali actoris. (Ibid, p 69)

8 Ibid, p 155

> Madam, I have a touch of your condition,
> That cannot brook the accent of reproof. (IV.iv.158-9)

But this is not his norm. The substantive mass of Richard's expression is not aristocratic or is so only in a highly qualified sense. Richard habitually expresses himself in a mode that is highly accommodating to his audience, one that is in essence bourgeois. Let us explore this class sensibility. Richard's imagery and turns of speech are often colloquial and often suggest the attitudes of businessmen. Thus the 'pack-horse,' 'post-horse' references; and 'But yet I run before my horse to market' (I.i.160). Financial and monetary terms crop up: 'then must I count my gains' (I.i.162); 'And yet go current from suspicion' (II.i.95); 'Repair'd with double riches of content' (IV.iv.319). Buckingham adjures him to act 'Not as protector, steward, substitute, / Or lowly factor for another's gain' (III.vii.133-4): Queen Margaret repeats the perception in

> Richard yet lives, hell's black intelligencer,
> Only reserv'd their factor to buy souls
> And send them thither (IV.iv.71-3).

A consistent strain of language suggests the concerns of a businessman. I do not conclude, as does Paul N. Siegel in his Marxist reading, that Shakespeare is drawing a blackly negative picture of bourgeois values and using it to establish Richard's evil.[9] The *dramatic* function of this bourgeois language is to maintain contact; it is in the main jocular, ingratiating, reaching to the concerns and awareness of the general audience. It is oddly reassuring, as though Richard were saying, 'I am really one of you, you know.' Richard's is the language of the common man rather than the grand seigneur.

Moreover, this linguistic quality reinforces certain class attitudes that the play on occasion calls upon. In I.iii Richard seeks to unite his stage audience behind him and against the queen's kindred, the Woodvilles; and in this the stage audience is the model of the larger audience. 'The world is grown so bad / That wrens make prey where eagles dare not perch' (I.iii.69-70); for a moment there's a hallucinatory resemblance between Richard and Third Citizen, each crying woe! on social

9 Paul N. Siegel 'Richard III as Businessman' *Shakespeare Jahrbuch* (Weimar) 114 (1978) 106

dissolution. The hits at 'Jacks' and 'nobles,' already quoted, extend the point. At bottom Shakespeare traces a commonplace of history, the alliance between nobles and people. No positive values are imparted to the Woodvilles. There is nothing in stage terms to counter Richard's stated view of them. Thus the Woodvilles focus whatever class resentment is in the audience: they are jumped-up gentry, a category which by definition no one (noble, popular, or simple bourgeois) cares for. So Richard succeeds in rallying the audience behind him.

Again, take Richard's relations with his subordinates. For most of the play he is affable enough, if with an edge. 'How now, my hardy, stout, resolved mates! ... I like you, lads, about your business straight' (I.iii.339, 353). Richard's excellent relations with the workers reaffirms the audience rapport: 'no side' about Richard, one might say, a jovial and understanding employer. (Note how his word 'business' conflates the suggestions of trade and stage.) Not till IV..iii do these master-servant relations appear repellent ('Kind Tyrrel,' 'gentle Tyrrel,' which is altogether disgusting), and not till the last speech of all does Richard address Catesby as 'slave,' a word that reveals all by reducing Catesby from a name to an object. In sum, Richard for most of the play seems the sort of aristocrat of whom the general audience could reasonably approve, a noble with the common touch.

And this common touch emerges most subtly, I think, in the attitudes which Richard constantly invokes, sometimes by way of proverb. These attitudes I characterize as citizen morality. They are promoted (and of course subverted) by the very personae that Richard assumes: pious contemplative, unworldy innocent, country boy. All of them seem to me broadly bourgeois in origin, though I do not take the term literally as applying to a town resident. Take the country boy: the persona Richard affects in I.iii – one unused to the traffickings of court politics – sorts well with the rustic quality of some of his lines. 'But yet I run before my horse to market' (I.i.160); 'He is franked up to fatting for his pains' (I.iii.313); 'Small herbs have grace, great weeds do grow apace' (II.iv.13); 'Short summers lightly have a forward spring' (III.i.94); 'A milksop, one that never in his life / Felt so much cold as over shoes in snow' (V.iii.325-6). The 'strawberries' episode suggests a man more at home in a garden than the court, and 'Chop off his head' is a woodman's phrase. Beyond the suggestions of milieu lie those of values. The wooing of Lady Anne is conducted by the ardent lover; nothing in Shakespeare is closer to the world of Colley Cibber, and the language of Richard here is eighteenth century, pure drama of sensibility. It illustrates a vein of popular morality and moralizing easily detectable elsewhere: 'Now by St. John, that news is bad indeed! / O, he hath kept an evil diet long, / And overmuch consum'd his royal person' (I.i.138-40); 'God will revenge it' (II.i.139); 'O, do not *swear,* my lord of Buckingham' (III.vii.220; Buckingham has just said 'Zounds'). The marketing of the candidate to the citizenry is founded on the proposition that Richard 'is not an Edward! / He is not lulling on a lewd love-bed ... Not dallying with a brace of courtezans ...' (III.vii.71-4) No phrase sums up this aspect of Richard's appeal better than Buckingham's 'I never look'd for better at his hands / After he once fell in with Mistress Shore' (III.v.50-1). This is proto-Pecksniffianism, a homage to moralizing, bourgeois righteousness. A picture emerges from all this of a reformist Richard, clean of speech and living, dedicated to restoring the standards of civic morality that have so sadly lapsed during the reign of Edward the Lustful.

It is high comedy, reaching its zenith in III.vii. Just how much of an edge there was in the presentation, then guying of these bourgeois attitudes is hard to say. I suspect that the satirical bite may have been fiercer than is commonly imagined.[10] After all, the Vice tradition was rooted in challenge to the status quo, in a 'moral scepticism' directed at the conventional pieties: 'I pray thee, tel me what meneth this word charity? / Because thou doest make it so holy.'[11] Weimann suggests that the jingling language of the Vice may have recalled Lollard heresies[12]; and the 'deep divines' who flank the Protector in the draft-Richard convention may hark back to older traditions. It is not hard to see a vein of popular anticlericalism touched on here.[13] One cannot dogmatize on such matters, but I propose a formulation of audience response along these lines: Richard and his accom-

10 Wilbur Sanders, in *The Dramatist and the Received Idea* (Cambridge 1968), gives full weight to the ironic and satiric content of *Richard III.*

11 *King Darius* printed in 1565; cited by Weimann *Shakespeare and the Popular Tradition* p 111

12 Weimann *Shakespeare and the Popular Tradition* p 147

13 There is also a tradition in the visual arts of such a grouping. The iconography of the king flanked by bishops is discussed by Bridget Gellert Lyons, in 'Stage Imagery and Political Symbolism in *Richard III,*' *Criticism* XX (1973) 21-3.

plices promote a broad vein of citizen morality, bourgeois attitudes which are presented in an engagingly comic light in the early scenes; they culminate in the high-pressure, satiric comedy of III.vii which simultaneously delights and appals. Thereafter the mode changes. The comedy turns sour. (The formula is not so very different from *Romeo and Juliet.*) Buckingham's threnody on All Souls' marks a late conversion to conventional morality. Proverbs are extensions of 'they say,' and in the end it turns out that 'they' are right. Citizen morality, like God, is not mocked for five acts.

In all this, the movement of audience response is governed by an ancient formula: 'The Vice criticizes from the audience's point of view.'[14] Richard reaches out towards the platea: he is the presenter, the commentator on the locus scene. His genial mockery of civic values, his command of proverbial lore, his mode of delivery, all create a special relationship with his audience. But that is for three acts. The Vice stands outside the action to begin with and is then gradually sucked into it. The proverbs, jokes, word-plays die away. The audience becomes progressively more detached, then alienated. The Vice's ultimate dialogue (the V.iii soliloquy) is with himself, not the audience. The story of the last two acts is the turning of the audience against Richard. Much of this needs no comment; it is a simple revulsion against a monster. But I want to trace the lines of Shakespeare's technique in this matter. If class attitudes influence the bonding process in the early stages, the later stages rely on the imperatives of place. It is location, region, and ultimately nation that define the audience of *Richard III*

III

No play of Shakespeare's is so strongly imbued with a sense of place, of national identity as the sum of many locations. Counting indifferently together names of places and titles (I shall come to the distinction later), I find some fifty English locations mentioned, whether of house (Crosby House), county (Devonshire), or city (Exeter). Of these fifty, many are referred to on several occasions. The Tower of London is mentioned no fewer than twenty-five times. All the major regions of the country are covered. The cumulative effect is of a massive impregnation of

14 Weimann *Shakespeare and the Popular Tradition* p 153

the text with a sense of England, the full extent of the land.

The broad effect is one thing. The individual references are something else. For each single allusion to a place there is a justification peculiar to drama: some member or members of the audience will know it or have some connection there. Shakespeare must have learned early that the chances of striking a chord in a spectator's mind through the allusion to some out-of-the-way place are fairly high. Someone always turns out to have come from Haverfordwest. It is not unlike the well-known odds against finding two people with identical birthdays in a quite small group. And all London references must connect with virtually the entire audience. The effect of each reference is a minor shock of recognition. The place-names are tiny foci of dramatic energy, pellets of meaning released into the audience's bloodstream. 'I used to live near Baynard's Castle.' 'You *can* stay at Stony Stratford, but I wouldn't, not with the inns there.' 'Curious how you always get good strawberries in Holborn.' 'My mother came from Hereford!' And so on. There is much dramatic energy stored in these innocent namings.

If that were all, it would at least justify raising the matter. But Shakespeare does not deploy place-names on a scatter principle. He organizes these far-flung places into patterns which are, as I take it, the final index to his sense of the audience's identity.

In act I, *Richard III* is above all a London play. Set in London, the milieu has great solidity of impression. The many references to the Tower, with all its associations, symbolize the dramatic centre of London; and we hear of Chertsey, St Paul's, Crosby House, Whitefriars. The provinces exist only through the references to St Albans and Tewkesbury (and thus, the past of the civil wars). Titles aside, that is all. Through this phase the audience enjoys the greatest rapport with Richard. Broadly, then: in the first act we are Londoners in London, and we approve of Richard.

Act II begins the move away. Although the play is still set in London, the impress of topography is much weaker. The talk is of travel, of Ludlow, Stony Stratford, Northampton. It is an undular strategy, in which Shakespeare creates a psychic wave away from London.

Act III anchors itself very firmly in London. All the manoeuvrings take place there, and the citizenry must establish itself as belonging to the capital. Similarly with the Recorder and the Lord Mayor of London. The Tower, of course, dominates all. The local allusions continue, and we are reminded of Holborn, the Crown, Baynard's Castle, Tower Bridge, Paul's, Crosby House. The provinces (Pomfret, Hereford) are still at the margin of this play's consciousness. The general audience, at the height of its pleasure in Richard, is continually reminded: this is London, our city.

The peremptory 'Stand all apart' (IV.ii.i) announces the second part of the play. That order to the courtiers figures Richard's relations with the audience. From now on he is distrustful, paranoid; the old rapport is gone. The allusions to place impart the new reality. We have no sense of London, though the play is still set there. All the talk is of the provinces, which now come to the fore of the play's consciousness. The roll-call is impressive: Exeter, Brecknock, Salisbury, Devonshire, Kent, Yorkshire, Dorsetshire, Milford, Pembroke, Haverfordwest. The west, Wales, even Kent are in arms. The north (of the 'cold friends') is the distrusted, hostage-enforced alliance with Derby. The drama, then, composes a map which we can discern without much difficulty: the great rough triangle of the British isle has arrows pointed, threateningly, towards London. And with them the psychology of the play changes. The provinces are right, and London is wrong.

With these harsh explicit indications come subliminal suggestions all tending to the same end. For we cannot confine our assessment of place-names to a simple symbolism of region and rebellion. We have to recognize the soft mutation of *place* to *title*. This play often broods on 'title' as Brackenbury does – Richard, the Duchess of York, Queen Elizabeth all talk about it – and the union of place and name has its significance. We have largely lost our sense of it today with our later traditions of title based on surname or battle-honour or simple euphony allied to tenuous local connection (Attlee, Alamein, Avon). It is salutary to be reminded, as one can still be in England today, that a local magnate counts for something in the area bearing his name. Titles were based on the possession of land; they were not empty honorifics. A name signified a reality. Thus insidiously the play makes its point along these lines: Dorset may be a cipher, but Dorsetshire (IV.iv.522) matters. The titles, hence the land, are in arms against the king.

And who supports the king? The symbolism of act V is clear. Only from the south-east is there any support: the Duke of Norfolk and the Earl of Surrey, his son. (The name of Richard's horse, 'White Surrey,' underlines the symbolism.) Outside the south-east only Northumberland sides with Richard, and he is dubious, stigmatized as 'melancholy' and having his comments repeated for Richard's benefit. ('What said Northumberland as touching Richmond?') Derby has already made his arrangements. The titles offer a diagram of forces here.

The conclusion is a boar-hunt, conducted in the middle of England.

> Thus far into the bowels of the land
> Have we march'd on without impediment; ...
> The wretched, bloody, and usurping boar,
> That spoil'd your summer fields and fruitful vines,
> Swills your warm blood like wash, and makes his trough
> In your embowel'd bosoms, this foul swine
> Is now even in the centre of this isle,
> Near to the town of Leicester, as we learn. (V.ii.3-4, 7-12)

Bosworth is almost the dead centre of the land. There the forces of the south and west, united with the symbolic representatives of London and the midlands (Richmond and Oxford), defeat the tyrant, who is let down by the north and inadequately defended by his own south-east. The land renews itself, gathering together to kill the usurper to its title. (Again, as in *King John*, Shakespeare plays on the synecdoche of 'England' and 'king of England.') The triumph of right is also the triumph of the provinces. The alienation of the London audience is now complete: it detaches itself from 'the bloody dog'[15] and declares itself for the morality of the provinces, and thus the nation. Title (the Crown), land, people, and audience unite. In the end, the bonding principle of the audience is that it is English.

University of Ottawa

15 '"The bloody dog is dead" replaces the customary obituary on the tragic hero; "from the dead temples of this bloody wretch" Derby has plucked the now superfluous crown.' Wolfgang Clemen *A Commentary on Shakespeare's 'Richard III'* London 1968, pp 235-6

BERNARD BECKERMAN

Playing the Crowd: Structure and Soliloquy in *Tide Tarrieth No Man*

That the study of Renaissance drama is also the study of the performance of Renaissance drama is no longer disputed. But exactly how the study of performance illuminates the drama is not always so apparent. Fairly widespread is the notion – and the scholarly demonstration – that sensitivity to performance features of a play makes us aware of aspects of drama otherwise ignored. This notion has led to fruitful examination of the non-verbal, visual elements in Shakespeare's plays. Also widespread is the tacit assumption that reading a play with its performing qualities in mind alerts us to alternate ways in which we may interpret a play's lines and action. In addition to these two premises there is a third that has yet to be sufficiently elaborated. It is the premise that the aesthetic character of a play is embedded in its performing structure, a structure not merely of words but of theatrical actions. Performance, from this point of view, does not merely enhance a drama; it is the manifestation of the very nature of a drama.

Demonstrating this proposition, especially at a time considerably removed from the date of original performance, is chancy at best. Yet in certain respects Renaissance drama is conducive to this attempt. By relying so thoroughly on the actor to sustain the narrative and by minimizing the scenic context, Renaissance play texts capture many of the performing elements in the language of the characters. This is particularly true of Tudor drama, above all of the moralities. So large a proportion of these plays involve exchanges between players-as-characters and audience that explicit performing clues are richly distributed through many of the texts. Of all the clues, those pertaining to the Vice offer us the best material for examining the connection between dramatic structure and performance.

The Vice's by-play with the audience is familiar to any reader of the moralities. Often the Vice appears alone on stage, and when he does, he usually makes direct contact with the spectators. This contact, of course, has a double nature. It is made by the player on behalf of the Vice persona while the audience remains itself. This is in contrast to some productions in the modern theatre, such as that of *Marat/Sade,* where the frame character, the Governor of Charenton, promotes the fiction that we the audience are spectators at his asylum early in the nineteenth century. Such transposition is never sought by the sixteenth-century Vice. Instead, he is content to take the audience as it is. He calls out to the masters and the sirrahs and with such sorts of tags establishes and maintains contact with the playgoers.

But though these tags are handy devices for promoting contact between player and audience, the real substance of the contact resides in the distinctive quality of exchange that the Vice stimulates. As a popular stage figure the Vice plays a repertory of familiar games with audiences. He entertains them with tricks and songs, but more significantly, he will surprise them by intimidating, teasing, or in some other way unsettling them.[1] Often he will make assumptions about what they are thinking or feeling. That is, he will project upon them a persona, an attitude, or a response that they may not or indeed cannot express openly. And once he assumes something about the audience, he is free to mock, challenge, or shame it. Ill Report in *The Most Virtuous and Godly Susanna* teases the playgoers by feigning to read obscene thoughts in their eyes; 'Why, why, do you winke, / Shame to you that shame thinkes.'[2] In effect, Ill Report thrusts upon the audience a notion it may or

1 Bernard Spivack, *Shakespeare and the Allegory of Evil* (New York 1958), notes the intermixture of jocularity and 'homiletic mordancy' in the Vice (p 119). A fuller discussion of the 'varying structural functions of the Vice' appear in Robert Weimann's book *Shakespeare and the Popular Tradition in the Theater* ed Robert Schwartz, Baltimore and London 1978, pp 156ff.

2 Thomas Garter *The Most Virtuous and Godly Susanna* Malone Society Reprint 1937, ll 915-16

may not hold. This practice is both common and necessary. Because the stage player must continually project a flow of energy in order to make his presence felt, he does it by concentrating upon a fellow actor or upon the audience. A fellow actor maintains the vibrancy of the mimetic game by sending back signals. The audience, however, is in no position to send back the precise and appropriate signals that the player demands, and therefore, to keep the show going, he has continually to modulate his image of the audience upon which he exerts the force of his personality.

Through the relatively abundant examples we have of the Vice, we are able to see how the forms of address were varied. Presumably the extant ones we have are but a small sample of what once existed. Welcome as the Vice persona must have been to the audience, however, he must also have presented a challenge to the players. How to vary the routine? How to surprise the audience once again? One way we find was for the Vice to work against the very convention of direct address, as where Iniquity (*King Darius*)[3] bursts on stage only to act surprised that no one – that is, no audience – is present (which, of course, it is). More frequent was the way the Vice teased the audience about his identity – 'You know me, sure you do' – or insisted on respect. In *All for Money*, Sin turns on the audience: 'What, of[f] with your cappes sirs, it become you to stande bare.'[4]

At root of the Vice-audience exchange was the very nature of the Vice. Although he is clearly associated with the Devil (Ill Report in *Susanna*, Nichol in *Like Will to Like*, Hypocrisy in *The Conflict of Conscience*), his primary qualities are not necessarily reflective of malevolence itself. In the second half of the sixteenth century the Vices are characterized by such names as Haphazard, Courage (Contagious and Contrarious), Common Conditions, and Subtle Shift as well as by Iniquity and Sin. Most characteristic of these figures is instability. Increasingly, as with Subtle Shift and Common Conditions, they readily change sides and even have a conscience. Essentially they are agents of anarchy, and consequently in their contact with the audience they promote disruption. Most important, they do not promote it by depicting disruption mimetically but by acting upon the audience directly.

To appreciate how the Vice works on an audience, we need

3 *King Darius* Students' Facsimile edition, A2v12-33
4 *All for Money* Students' Facsimile edition, B2v35

to consider not only the moments when he addresses the audience directly but also the way those moments are arranged sequentially. The moments that I am speaking of are, in effect, soliloquies.[5] They are abundant in the moralities, far more abundant than they are in the later drama. More important, they occupy a greater number of the total lines of a play. For example, in many plays of the 1560s and 1570s, the proportion of lines of soliloquy to total number of lines runs about 20 per cent.[6] In the 1580s, the percentage is likelier to be about 7 per cent. These differences are not insignificant. While the precise number of lines is of little consequence, the proportion between soliloquy and scene is not. As the proportion of solo scenes grows, especially scenes of intimate contact between player and audience, the more decisive is the effect of that contact upon the structure of a play. In those plays where one-fifth of the length is given to soliloquy, direct address appears frequently enough and at sufficient length to influence the shape of the play decisively.

Not all soliloquies are spoken by the Vice. Nor do they all involve explicit exchange with the audience. But it is in those plays where the Vice is the principal solo performer that we can see how direct contact is used as a structural factor. For example, in the period 1565-80 there are a number of plays (*King Darius, Like Will to Like, The Trial of Treasure, All for Money, Wit and Wisdom,* and *Tide Tarrieth No Man*) in which the bulk of the soliloquies are spoken by the Vice or the Vice and his cronies. In *Darius* four out of five soliloquies are delivered by Iniquity the Vice; in *Like Will to Like* Nichol Newfangle speaks five out of eight; in *The Marriage of Wit and Wisdom,* Idleness six out of ten. In *The Trial of Treasure* all six soliloquies are spoken by Vices, four by the principal Vice Inclination. Since the Vice figures engage in direct contact with the audience more frequently than any other characters, these plays use the Vice's intimacy with the audience as the spine of the play. In them, it is not uncommon for the Vice to deliver the early soliloquies, thus establish-

5 Authorities use the terms soliloquy and monologue for the speech delivered by a solo actor whether or not directed to the audience. Spivack insists on monologue (p 119 and passim). In a title to an essay, Neil Carson employs the term soliloquy to embrace direct and indirect address (see his 'The Elizabethan Soliloquy – Direct Address or Monologue?' *Theatre Notebook* xxx [1976] 12-18).

6 *Apius and Virginia, Damon and Pithias, Like Will to Like, Tancred and Gismond, Sir Clyomon and Sir Clamydes, Common Conditions,* among others

ing a ground of understanding with the audience. Only later in the play do the Virtues deliver their soliloquies and so break or attempt to break the hold of the Vice on the onlookers. In this way the play induces a struggle in the audience that leads to moral triumph at the end.

The fullest elaboration of this alternating pattern of soliloquy and scene occurs in George Wapull's *Tide Tarrieth No Man.*[7] In this play Wapull utilizes an unusually large number of soliloquies, many of which contain explicit signs of direct address. Altogether there are twenty-one soliloquies, eleven of which are delivered by the Vice Courage.[8] Of the remaining ten, four are delivered by the Virtues Christianity and Faithful Few, and six are distributed among profligates and victims.[9] These last soliloquies are the ones that exhibit the least overt signs of contact with the audience, and, as may be expected, those by the Vice the most overt indications. Moreover, the importance of the soliloquies to the structure of *Tide Tarrieth* is most clearly demonstrated by the fact that roughly 30 per cent of the total lines in the play are spoken by a solo performer on the stage.

Like his forebears, the Vice Courage preens for the audience, plays with it, and ultimately attempts to change it. As his name suggests, he is chameleon-like. He explains in his fifth address 'how he can encourage, both to good and bad' (C3v2), illustrating this by his urging men to be greedy but also to win fame.

> Thus may you see Courage contagious,
> And eake contrarious, both in me do rest:
> For I of kind, am alwayes various,
> And chaunge, as to my mind seemeth best (C3v9-12).

Variable and unstable as he is, Courage still retains a propensity for disruption and the flesh. He is thus allied to all the devilry of the past and, and as he acts through the play, promotes cor-

7 George Wapull *Tide Tarrieth No Man* Students' Facsimile edition. Citations in the text refer to this facsimile.

8 In addition to the twenty-one soliloquies, there is a lengthy prologue. Three of Courage's soliloquies are very brief, one being six lines in length, the other two four lines (B3v1-6; C4v26-29; E1v2r1). His remaining soliloquies vary in length from 12 to 28 lines with the very first being much longer (either 102 half lines or 51 full lines). See text below for specific discussions of the individual speeches.

9 See text below for specific discussions of these speeches.

ruption. At the same time, in using the idea of misplaced Courage, Wapull the author stresses the twisting of virtue rather than the prevalence of inherent evil.

Because he is 'alwayes various,' the Vice repeatedly exploits the unexpected in playing with the crowd. Because he appears so frequently in these solo displays, his sequence of exchanges crucially shapes the entire play. Previous discussion of *Tide Tarrieth No Man,* such as that of David Bevington in *From Mankind to Marlowe,* pays little attention to the solo structure with its modulations in audience contact.[10] While Bevington gives an excellent account of the scene action, an account that one must keep in mind to gain a full perspective on this play, it is equally necessary to see how Wapull handles the solo speeches in order to gain an adequate appreciation of his dramatic skill.

Wapull gives his Vice Courage eleven soliloquies, bunched into a sequence of ten in the first half of the play and the eleventh, a significant eleventh, near the end. While various soliloquies by others are interspersed among the first ten, only after these first ten do we find the initial soliloquy by one of the Virtues. The distribution traces the increasing dominance of the Vice in the play, the revelation of his influence through the speeches of victims, and finally the restitution of morality in the figures of Christianity and Faithful Few.

Wapull is also skilled in varying the style and content of Courage's soliloquies. He moves from an opening chant-like speech where, like a huckster, Courage invites all to the barge of sin. Ironically, he bids all sail with him 'to the Divell of Hell' (A3r36b). As he goes from soliloquy to soliloquy, he becomes more direct and specific in his address to the audience. He tells an illustrative story about himself in his second speech (B2r4-27); in his third he briefly asks audience approval for his shrewdness (B3v1-6); and he expatiates on his friends in the fourth, confidently affirming that 'I thinke there is no man within this place' who would not embrace them (C1v10). This inclusion of the audience as welcome sharers in his kind of courage continues as he describes good wives as 'hardy and stoute,' challenging them to agree: 'How say you good wives, is it not so?' (C3v21) At this point he attempts to incite dissension between the men and women by appealing to the men to confirm the fact that 'the best [of women] are but shrewes'

10 David Bevington *From Mankind to Marlowe* Cambridge Mass 1962, pp 149-50

(C3v27). Later, in rejoicing over his influence upon the maid Wanton, he turns to some in the audience and teases, 'How say you my virgines everyone' (D3r25). By the time he comes to his ninth speech, he is ready to promote disruption in the audience midst. Addressing his supposed good cousin Cutpurse, 'if you be in place' within the crowd, he bids him get to work. 'I beseech you now, your business to plye, / I warrant thee I, no man shall thee espye.' The 'coz' might risk hanging, but what does that matter since he might well filch a purse 'worth a yeres spending.' Courage is eager to encourage him: 'Come hyther, let me clap thee on the back' (D4v27-33). Presumably the Vice will seem to speak to someone in the crowd, perhaps shifting his gaze from one part of the place to another or even addressing specific members of the audience, and thus play one person against another, fostering the notion that a thief is mingling with the entire assembly and threatening it. After promoting the disturbance, Courage concludes to the audience,

> Well syrs it is time, that hence I doe pack me,
> For I am afrayde, that some men doe lack me (E1r9-10).[11]

Several things are to be noted about this sequence of soliloquies. First there is, as I have said, a progressive intimacy with the audience and an intensifying effort to divide and fracture the group. Directness of address increases, not only as a result of specific tags but also in the shift from display to teasing. Second, while continuity is sustained through the Vice's promotion of disruption in the audience, the individual sequences are set speeches that work as separate entertainments. There is little plot continuity, and whatever there is relates more to the Vice's rejoicing in his mischief than in his advancement of the action. The development of the play therefore moves from the Vice corrupting on-stage characters to the Vice provoking or trying to provoke disorder in the watching crowd.

The counteraction overlaps Courage's soliloquies. First comes a solo speech where Courage overhears a would-be courtier's internal debate over whether to stay at court or return home (C1v28-2v34), only to be persuaded subsequently by Courage to remain at court. Next comes a generic Tenant, newly

11 This ninth speech in effect ends the first half of the action. The tenth soliloquy is merely a transitional quatrain (E1v33-2r1).

evicted, bewailing his state and seeking the lost Christianity. After Courage's ninth soliloquy the courtier returns to point to himself as deceived and to moralize on the proverbial title of the play (E1r14-1v14). Then follows Wastefulness at the height of joy and riot. Only then, when we have seen evidence of Courage's success on stage and have felt his effects among us, does the lost Christianity appear. He speaks directly to the audience, explaining the meaning of his two emblems, the sword of policy and the shield of riches, which he must bear as parodies of the sword of faith and the shield of God's word. The direct presentation to an audience is an ironic exposition of contemporary Christian values. He hammers home the audience's responsibility by his use of the first-person plural: 'We say by policy, ourselves we can save ... for riches, we sell all that we have' (F2v27-30). Reduced to this state, Christianity must rely on Faithful Few, who now speaks a sequence of three soliloquies separated only by one of Wastefulness's speeches. Faithful Few laments the prevalence of greedy citizens (F2v33-3r16), emphasizing the audience's involvement: 'some among us there be, / For whose sake the whole number beareth great blame' (F3r5-6). Are those 'some,' like cousin Cutpurse, lurking in the crowd? Here Faithful Few provides a yardstick for discerning the dangerous ones. They live without the love that Plato and Seneca teach. 'God graunt we therefore of them may beware' (G1v11). He then overhears Wastefulness's sad soliloquy, plucks him from the claws of Despair, and teaches him repentance. The address to the audience takes Wastefulness's recovery as a topic for illustration. It is Faithful Few's last soliloquy: 'See,' he says to the audience, 'how the time makers their fact doth repent' (G2v24), for without repentance prodigality leads to beggary. But though he has redeemed Wastefulness, his work is not over and he goes off to seek Authority.

So far we see how the soliloquies provide the fundamental structure of the action and induce the distinctive experience of a moral by playing with the audience. Through cajoling, taunting, admonition, and demonstration, Wapull moves us through the action. He caps the use of presentation by his final soliloquy, the eleventh by Courage. As we might expect, it reflects Courage's defeat in the face of Christianity and Faithful Few. But even more interesting is the form itself. Courage enters, lamenting the tidings that his friend Greediness is dead. Yet he cannot believe the news, and as an unusual stage direction specifies, he begins 'reasoning with / himselfe' (G3r10-11). He goes from belief to disbelief:

> Why but is Greediness dead in good sadnesse,
> Why thinkes these newes are not true which you [that is, he] tell (G3r11-12).

While one part of him argues that Greediness can never die, another side confesses that he saw him buried, and at last he seems to confess to the audience that it must be so.

This soliloquy is doubly significant. If intensified direct presentation by Courage promotes disruption, then the revelation of inner debate which diverts the player's energy from the audience to himself is an acting-out of his defeat. Of larger import is the fact that, almost symbolically, the shift to inner struggle in the soliloquy follows a demonstration of the Vice's full panoply of entertainment. Wapull has the Vice try many tricks that we find in earlier figures of this type. But there are limits to the power of direct presentation, and when these limits are reached, the action turns inwards.

To what extent the pattern of *Tide Tarrieth No Man* influenced later drama is impossible to say. But one striking similarity may be worth mentioning. Seen in its broadest strokes, the sequence of soliloquies in Shakespeare's *Richard III* parallels that in Wapull's play. True, the number of lines of soliloquies and the total number of soliloquies in Shakespeare are much fewer. Although *Richard III* does contain twelve soliloquies, their total lines only come to 220, or about 6 per cent of the lines of the play. Once this difference is granted, the structural parallels leap out at us. Of the twelve soliloquies, Richard speaks seven. Most of these come early in the play. Indeed, he speaks the four main soliloquies of the play – the most memorable ones and the ones most explicitly directed at the audience – in the first three scenes of the play. Five speeches by others than Richard first convey the anguish of the victims and then prophesy retribution. Queen Margaret sees how prosperity is falling 'into the rotten mouth of death' (IV.iv.2), and Richmond prays for victory (V.iii.109-18).[12] Most suggestive, however, is the similarity between the final soliloquy by Courage and the one by Richard.

In both instances, after each of the 'Vices' commands and

12 Line references for *Richard III* are to the Pelican edition of *The Complete Works of William Shakespeare* ed A. Harbage, Baltimore 1969.

taunts the audience in the early soliloquies, each reveals a schizoid anguish in the final speech. As the stage direction specifies, Courage 'reasons' with himself: 'Yes truely [Greediness] dyed in a great madnesse ... / Why foole, Greedinesse will never dye' (G3r13, 15). Is not this echoed in Richard's 'I am a villain. Yet I lie, I am not. / Fool, of thyself speak well. Fool, do not flatter' (V.iii.192-3). Whether Shakespeare has followed Wapull's lead or devised by chance an analogous pattern, who can say?

Two conclusions emerge from this brief examination of the interplay between the Vice and the audience. First, the dramatic coherence of the moral interlude is inseparable from its theatrical structure, and where that structure utilizes direct contact, an understanding of patterns of contact is indispensable to an understanding of the drama. Second, once we appreciate the theatrical structure, we can better assess the achievement of a man like George Wapull, who, it appears, was a conscious theatrical artist. It is evident that his play *Tide Tarrieth No Man* not only has a thematic unity pertaining to economic questions of the 1570s but also an aesthetic unity governing the interplay between performer and crowd.

Columbia University

S.P. ZITNER

Staging the Occult in *1 Henry IV*

From early in 1700, when Betterton's cut version opened at the Little Theatre in Lincoln's Inn Fields, until the Falconer-Chatterton revival during the Shakespeare tercentenary in late March of 1864, *1 Henry IV* was played without much of act III, scene i.[1] The section generally excised begins at line 135, after Hotspur's 'Are the indentures drawn, shall we be gone?'[2] For the eighteenth and much of the nineteenth century, the conspirators were deprived of some of their best speeches; one of Shakespeare's happiest pictures of love in marriage went unobserved, and the suggestion – so important to the second tetralogy – that the capacity for rule and the capacity for human intimacy are perhaps mutually exclusive was lost to the theatre. As late as 1896, William Archer, while urging Beerbohm Tree to produce the play in 'its integrity,' tried to persuade him to eliminate the latter part of the scene on the ground that the theatre was no place for either the 'archaeology of humour' or the Elizabethan enthusiasm for Welsh gibberish.[3] Tree, probably with song-loving matinee-goers in mind, stood by the text. Yet for all our wonder at these excisions in vogue for over a century and a half, we must admit that cutting the scene may have had its

1 Harold Child 'The Stage-History of *King Henry IV*' in *Henry IV, Part I* ed J. Dover Wilson, Cambridge 1946, xxxiii, xl; A.C. Sprague *Shakespeare's Histories* London 1966, p 64

2 Throughout I use the New Arden text, ed A.R. Humphreys, London 1970.

3 Quoted in Sprague *Shakespeare's Histories* pp 64-5

uses. Perhaps one could not recruit Welsh sopranos as easily as one can nowadays at a football match in Cardiff. For directors the cut certainly had the important advantage of eliminating some nagging problems of staging and interpretation presented by the passage beginning at line 223.

In these lines Glendower asks Mortimer, who knows no Welsh, to rest his head in the lap of Mortimer's wife, who knows no English, while the lady is to sing a song that will charm his blood 'with pleasing heaviness.' Mortimer agrees, observing, no doubt for the benefit of devotees of flat-out historical drama, that by the end of the musical interval the contract for the division of the kingdom will have been drawn up. As if for further diversion, Glendower offers to exercise his magic art:

> those magicians that shall play to you
> Hang in the air a thousand leagues from hence,
> And straight they shall be here. (lines 218-20)

There follows a bawdy exchange about laps and lying down between Hotspur and Kate. Then the music plays and the Welsh lady sings.

The passage has prompted some interpretative comment. Samuel B. Hemingway, the editor of the New Variorum edition of *1 Henry IV*, censured Malone for not being quite fair in stating that Glendower '*pretends* [italics mine] to ... power over the spirits of the air.' He quotes Cowden Clarke's suggestion that Hotspur's 'sly comment ... lets us into the secret that probably the Welsh chieftain has some such instrument as an Aeolian harp placed under the control of one of his people commissioned, at a signal, to set it playing ...' Hemingway decries this too and goes on to beg the question. In no other passage of 'supernatural music,' he states, citing *The Tempest, Midsummer Night's Dream, As You Like It, Antony and Cleopatra,* and *Pericles,* 'is the authenticity of the supernatural quality of the music questioned by author or reader, nor should it be in this passage.' In short, 'Shakespeare believed in Glendower's magic powers, whatever Hotspur's opinion may have been.' Hotspur's comment was – so the editor continues – a 'somewhat embarrassed confession that, after all, there seems to be something in Glendower's claim to supernatural power.'[4] Some recent editors of the play agree,

4 New Variorum *1 Henry IV* ed S.B. Hemingway, Philadelphia 1936, pp 200-1

among them J. Dover Wilson, whose note to lines 223-5 tells us that 'Glendower is clearly a genuine magician, like Prospero.' His note to line 24 observes that the music comes 'from the music-gallery in the third story of the tiring-house.' Most modern editions, such as the New Arden, are silent, and here silence seems to give assent. Professor John H. Long, concerned primarily with the musical aspects of the scene, is content to state that 'Whether Shakespeare believed that Owen Glendower was a genuine sorcerer or a charlatan is a moot question.'[5] We can conclude this survey with Francis Gentleman, who provided the commentary for Bell's 1773 edition of the play. He thought act III, scene i, 'a strange, unmeaning wild scene ... which is properly rejected'[6] – a rather harsh refusal to deal with matters, among them the question of Glendower's magic, that possibly appeared nonsensical to an eighteenth-century rationalist.

Questions of interpretation – was Glendower represented as an authentic magician? just what was Hotspur's reaction to the Welsh chieftain's 'powers'? – and a question of staging – where did the music come from? – are neatly connected. Small questions – perhaps even taken together they hardly make up a mote to trouble the mind's eye. Yet attention to details here illuminates not only Shakespeare's own attention to them but helps clarify a mastery of theatrical resources that led to the unmatched ebullience of *1 Henry IV*.

Staging depends, or ought to, on interpretation; first, then, is the question of Glendower's magic. Its authenticity – that is, whether we are to see Glendower as a magician – is to be judged in the context of Shakespeare's conception of Glendower as a 'part' in the action of the play rather than in such other contexts as the available Elizabethan notion of the historical Glendower, the way he is presented in early English or Welsh accounts of him, or the likelihood of Shakespeare's or any Elizabethan's belief in magic.

Shakespeare's portrait of Glendower is the subject of some differences of opinion. Gareth Lloyd Evans seems to think that Hotspur's behaviour towards Glendower is to be condemned as disrespectful of the Welsh hero.[7] For the most part, however,

5 John Long *Shakespeare's Use of Music: The Histories and Tragedies* Gainesville Fla 1971, p 76

6 *1 Henry IV* Bell edition, London 1773, p 31

7 Gareth Lloyd Evans 'The Comical-Tragical-Historical Method: *Henry IV*' in *Stratford-Upon-Avon Studies* 3 (1961) 154

Welsh commentators are pleased with Shakespeare's presentation of Glendower as a 'courtly, gracious figure.'[8] Arthur E. Hughes goes so far as to suggest that the English chronicle accounts available to Shakespeare were so unfavourable that he must have heard more sympathetic views of Glendower from Welsh acquaintances in London at some time between the composition of the first and third acts of the play.[9] At best this is undemonstrable; at worst it obscures Shakespeare's procedures in characterization. Only rarely does Shakespeare simplify an important character from his 'source' by elevation or reduction. With 'historical persons' he often – as is the case with Brutus – puts on stage a character at once better than, worse than, and recognizably similar to the figure presented by a Holinshed or a Plutarch. This procedure is, I think, less interesting as a personal manner or as the outcome of a profound observation of men than as a response to the needs of particular plays. Perhaps one ought not ground one's impression of the character, then, on Hotspur's baiting of Glendower, or on Mortimer's praise of him as

> a worthy gentleman,
> Exceedingly well read, and profited
> In strange concealments, valiant as a lion,
> And wondrous affable, and as bountiful
> As mines of India (lines 160-4)

any more than on King Henry's imprecations. It is the sum of such evidences in their variety that contributes to Glendower as a 'part' and leads to the vividness of our perceptions of him. That variety results no doubt in part from settled convictions on how men are variously perceived by others, in part from a sympathy for the 'mingled yarn' that constitutes the character of any man, but in the first instance it results from the demands of the play. The comic tone and outcome of *1 Henry IV* dictate that the rebels seem dangerous but not critically so, unworthy of rule but formidable presences – not to be destroyed casually and (hence) without the consequent impression of satisfaction and loss. If the action of the play is to be comic rather than tragicomic, Hal's triumph must be neither in doubt nor perfunctory,

8 J.E. Lloyd *Owen Glendower* Oxford 1931, p 5

9 Arthur E. Hughes 'Shakespeare and His Welsh Characters' *Shakespeare Association Papers* III, Oxford 1919, pp 16-17

and the rebels' defeat neither unexpected nor trivial. These are the outer limits for the characterization of Glendower and also of Hotspur, Blunt, Mortimer, and Worcester. How variously they occupy the dramatic space appropriate for their parts is one of the achievements of the poet's invention.

The first view we are given of the character is Westmoreland's account of 'the irregular and wild Glendower' (I.i.140) who at the least allow 'the beastly shameless transformation,' that is, the mutilation of the English troops his men had killed in battle. King Henry's epithet, 'the great magician, damned Glendower' (I.iii.83), is the first reference to the Welshman's occult powers, which, with his more conventional military abilities, the king insists on in part as a means of belittling Mortimer to Hotspur later in the scene.

When next we hear of Glendower, it is through Falstaff's mocking sketch of the conspirators. There Glendower is 'he of Wales, that gave Amamon the bastinado, and made Lucifer cuckold, and swore the devil his true liegeman upon the cross of a Welsh hook' (II.iv.331ff). Both Falstaff and Hal are of course amusing themselves at the expense of the conspirators. But in each case – Douglas's running 'a-horseback up a hill perpendicular' or killing 'with his pistol ... a sparrow flying' – we are invited to doubt the conspirator's reputation. Douglas is valiant enough to be called later by Hal 'the noble Scot' (V.v.17), but though he defeats Walter Blunt at Shrewsbury, the last we hear of him is his capture as he flees the field during the rout of the rebels. 'Falling from a hill, he was so bruised / That the pursuers took him' (V.v.21-2). This recalls ironically not only the gravity-defying perpendicularity of Falstaff's send-up but the rest of the exchange with the prince, in which Falstaff declares that the Douglas 'will not run' on foot. Douglas's fate at Shrewsbury both sustains and undercuts his reputation and hence as much justifies Falstaff's satire as it does the complimentary terms applied to the Scots leader. Shakespeare's treatment of Douglas argues a remarkable attention to detail as the instrument of the studied placement of characterization required by the play.

A quite different but relevant point of interest in Falstaff's remarks on 'he of Wales' is the name of the devil Amamon and the ludicrous achievements Falstaff attributes to Glendower, such as the cuckolding of Lucifer. We come on Amamon again, and together with Lucifer and cuckolding, in *The Merry Wives of*

Windsor (II.ii.267ff) just after Falstaff has promised the disguised Ford an illicit meeting with Ford's wife. In the outraged soliloquy that follows Falstaff's departure, Ford deplores the possibility of being not only cuckolded but of standing 'under the adoption of abominable terms.' 'Terms! names! Amamon sounds well.' Again a comic context, and an appreciation of the magniloquence of nether-worldy lingo. One doubts it only an accident that Shakespeare seems to have gone to Reginald Scot's sceptical and rationalistic *Discovery of Witchcraft* (XV.iii) for Amamon and some other details of Falstaff's sketch.

Something of the balance and the complexity that characterize Shakespeare's creation of Douglas appears in the representation of Glendower during the rest of the play. From the tenor of the English chronicles (we get a very different picture from Welsh sources)[10] and from Westmoreland's description we might have expected a much less attractive Glendower than the one who at last appears on the stage. This Glendower is no hulking ruffian out of *Tamburlaine* or *Cambyses*. Nor is he 'that devil Glendower' Falstaff matches with 'that fiend Douglas' and 'that spirit Percy' (II.iv.363-4), nor the even more ludicrous butt of Falstaff's satire. Yet he is not quite Dover Wilson's 'gentleman and scholar' either. Further, the complimentary judgment of Glendower that Mortimer gives Hotspur is only in part like the Glendower we see on stage.

Act III, scene i, begins in Wales. Neither the Folio nor the quartos specify a location. Most modern editions, including the New Arden, follow Theobald's suggestion, based on Holinshed, that the conspirators met at Bangor in the home of the archbishop or archdeacon. However, Dover Wilson's argument for localizing the scene, if one must, in Glendower's own house, on the ground that 'It is a family party; [and] Glendower behaves like a host,' is congenial and catches one of the tones of the scene. The charming domesticity of the usually excised part of the scene after line 135 pleasantly colours our view of Glendower. He remarks that his daughter's concern for the safety of Mortimer has made her an example of 'a peevish, self-willed harlotry, one that no persuasion can do good upon' (lines 192-3). This itself is a bit peevish. But for the most part Glendower is here the moderate host and paterfamilias, attracting a share of

10 For English chronical sources see New Arden, xxiff; for Welsh sources Lloyd *Owen Glendower* pp 147ff, and Hughes 'Shakespeare and His Welsh Characters' pp 14ff.

the warmth of Shakespeare's portrayal of two well-suited married couples. The Welsh lady's song, whose lyrics were unintelligible to most of the audience, conveys a generalized but deep intimacy of feeling, which Hotspur's tart exchanges with his wife keep from seeming cloying. Not only is the tone finely adjusted, but the 'wordlessness' of the song and the absence of dialogue forestall either the poet's or the audience's investment of interest in the precise character of a relation whose function is momentary effect, and one which will not be taken up further in the play.

The first part of the scene, however, is vastly different from the second, not only in tone but in import. After Hotspur's significant but ludicrous misplacing of the map (this is a conference on the division of the kingdom!) the scene becomes a shouting match between two eccentrics: a stuffy and rhetorical Glendower insisting on the portents attending his birth and on the fearsome extent of his occult powers; and a pugnacious and colloquial Hotspur playing the rationalist, the sceptic, and the Philistine by turns, declaring the portents to be meaningless and urging his host to shame the Devil by telling the truth. Their argument – 'this unprofitable chat,' as Mortimer calls it – is diverted to a discussion of the proposed division of the kingdom at just the most interesting point, when Mortimer interrupts Hotspur's challenge to Glendower to raise the Devil on the spot. In this match between Hotspur and Glendower, the former seems the victor since he wields the sharper weapon, wit. Gareth Lloyd Evans's negative reaction here is significant; Glendower is indeed presented as the windbag that Hotspur hints the earth vented at the Welshman's birth. Through their exchange, however, we see the division of the kingdom as a futile exercise, hence both amusing and reassuring, since the chief conspirators display a comic incapacity not only for rule but even for victory. The later part of the scene humanizes them through their domesticity, 'elevating' them through the strength and rightness of private relations which have no bearing on their political stature. We cannot, therefore, simply dismiss them as trivial.

It is in the context of this conception of the conspirators – dictated by the needs of the action – that one has to view Glendower's 'magic.' Shakespeare lets pass without emphasis and without clarification at least one occasion to suggest the awesome military or political implications of Glendower's supposed occult powers. In lines 60 to 63 Glendower tells of having three times repelled Harry's forces from the banks of the Wye and the Severn and sent them 'Bootless home, and weatherbeaten back.' The lines are based on passages in Holinshed and possibly Hardynge. In Holinshed Glendower is credited with having used 'art magike' to cause weather so bad as to force the English into retreat. In the play the military implications of Glendower's magic are suppressed. Mortimer's peacemaking intervention seems to close the issue of Glendower's magic by ending for the moment the contention between the Welsh leader and Hotspur. It is just after this intervention that the king's retreats from Wales are described by Glendower and therefore made to seem a boast of general skill in battle rather than in occult art.

The occult is used later in the play to weaken our impression of Glendower as man and as military leader rather than to strengthen it. He does not join in the battle at Shrewsbury because he is 'o'er-ruled by prophecies.' According to Holinshed the Welsh forces actually joined in the battle; according to Daniel they were absent.[11] Daniel is correct. Apparently Henry's march to Shrewsbury was a logistical lightning stroke; Glendower was simply unable to move his troops rapidly enough to reach the field of battle in time.[12] But the reason Shakespeare gives for Glendower's absence departs from both Holinshed and Daniel. It is the poet's own invention and focuses on the negative side of Glendower's occultism, here seen as an enervating superstition. Like the suppression of the 'magical' cause of Henry's Welsh retreats and the puncturing of Glendower's boasts by Hotspur's witticisms and Falstaff's, this invention seems part of an intent to keep us from taking Glendower's magic seriously in the play and, rather, an intent to use the Welshman's reputation as a means of localizing his inadequacy, an especially significant inadequacy when one reflects on the weight given to the pragmatic use of power in the reign of Henry IV, the first of the 'unanointed,' wholly temporal kings. In this context one turns to the supposed magical concert of of act III, scene i.

Late 1597 is usually accepted as the time of the first performances of *1 Henry IV* by the Chamberlain's men. Thus the play might have been introduced at either the Theatre or the Curtain, to which Shakespeare's company moved sometime during 1597. Both had traps and both – so the account of Samuel

11 See New Arden, p 138, n 18.

12 Lloyd (*Owen Glendower* pp 70-1) provides an account from Welsh sources.

Kiechel, a German visitor to London, seems to indicate[13] – had three tiers of galleries, the highest of which over the tiring-house was used by the musicians, who were generally, but not necessarily, concealed from public view. The most casual Elizabethan theatre-goer is likely to have known at least as much about the music gallery in Elizabethan theatres as we do. To have Glendower promise that musicians hanging in the air a thousand leagues away will play nearby at once, to have him, as he makes the promise, make also the appropriate upward gesture the lines call for, is to have him promise and produce – what? How an Elizabethan or indeed any spectator would take this promise would depend on his wit, on his expectations of the character as presented so far, and on his sense of the resources of the playhouse. I am suggesting that there are valid reasons for thinking that the appropriate response to Glendower's promise of magical music is the First Carrier's reply to Gadshill in II.i.35-6: 'Nay, by God, soft, I know a trick worth two of that' – a trick like making the moon disappear behind a handkerchief. One needed nothing more than a glimpse of the musicians in the music gallery to make the point explicit.

Hotspur's response to the music suggests the possibility of an even more explicit comic staging:

> Now I perceive the devil understands Welsh,
> And 'tis no marvel he is so humorous,
> By'r lady, he is a good musician. (lines 224-6)

Earlier Hotspur had threatened to drive off any devil Glendower could raise; one would have been delighted to see him do so here. Evidently it is not necessary. His reaction seems on the evidence of the lines neither embarrassed, pugnacious, repentant, nor amazed. He does not ask Glendower: if you can get the Devil to play music, what else, preferably useful to our cause, can you get him to do? Hotspur's response is amused and amusing; the occult music is taken as a joke, or worse, a triviality. Perhaps it has even come not from the heavens of the music gallery but (with the playwright's direct intervention) from below stage, whence the Devil's infernal music issued in old plays, as did the music signifying the tutelary god's departure from Antony.

13 E.K. Chambers *The Elizabethan Stage* Oxford 1923, II, 358

The historical question of how the scene was actually staged can probably never be answered. But the comic spirit in which it probably was and should be staged seems to me demonstrable. To take the music as an exhibition of Glendower's magical power is to undercut Shakespeare's conception of the conspirators as essentially comic, to overlook the details of Shakespeare's specific treatment of Glendower's occultism earlier and later in the play, to impose on Hotspur's reaction a construction other than the obvious one, and to have Shakespeare puzzle the spectator with questions about Glendower's power that would remain unresolved elsewhere and only work against the impression of delicious intimacy created in the scene itself.

There is perhaps also a larger conceptual system illustrated in Glendower's superstitious pretensions to occult powers. In several ways Henry IV stands in the second tetralogy as a middle term between Richard II and the rebels against his own rule. Henry IV's successful use of mundane forces is bracketed by Richard's vain dependence on celestial powers and Glendower's on infernal ones. In all three cases, off-stage music figures at crucial moments in their characterization: for Richard (*Richard II* V.v.41ff) as the disturbing symbol of harmony unachieved in his 'state and time'; for Glendower as the evidence of his limitation. When in *2 Henry IV* (IV.v.1ff) music plays for the pragmatic king, it is both literally and figuratively instrumental, that is, a medicine for his illness.[14]

The interpretation proposed here has some other implications worth exploring. In *1 Henry IV* the resources of the theatre are used openly and consciously as resources of the theatre – rather than as means hidden or subdued in the course of creating a theatrical illusion. Here Shakespeare seems to be waving the dyer's hand to his audience rather than trying to conceal it; the players' instruments are used not only for delight but as a means of commenting on the action and – perhaps – as a means to the author's self-delight. They suggest a freedom, an at-homeness in the dramaturgy that defines the special ebullience of the play. Such freedom in the use of the 'arts of the theatre' is paralleled in Shakespeare's use of language and impersonation. Literary satire – the send-up of Euphuism – is pressed into service as part of the satire of the pomposity of statecraft; impersonation – the theatre's central artifice – is used in the play extem-

14 Cf Long (*Shakespeare's Use of Music* pp 85-6) for another view.

pore between Falstaff and Hal, not only as a justification of the role-playing that makes Hal the master of 'all humors' and the 'sworn brother' of those who will gain the victory at Agincourt, but – in effect – as evidence that impersonation, far from justifying Plato's condemnation of it as diversion from the task of 'playing one's own part,'[15] is a means of self-knowledge. In playing his father, Hal begins to play himself. Shakespeare's apparent earlier dissatisfaction with the theatre and the professions of actor and writer is expressed in Sonnets 110 and 111. These sonnets present the theatre as trapping the poet in depersonalization, opportunism of expression, and an abandonment of disinterestedness. In this play such dissatisfactions seem to have given way to a delight in the theatre's resources, to an acceptance of them as means for the expression of personal taste and the exploration of essential truths. No doubt the reservations presented in the sonnets had been thought through even earlier. But the poet's confidence in the spaciousness and integrity of the theatre and its resources had not been so clearly or so gaily expressed. And the charming poetry of Hotspur's Philistine rejection of 'mincing poetry' (III.i.122-9) suggests that he had made – as of so many other deep contentions – a peace of paradox between the confidence and the reservation.

Trinity College
University of Toronto

15 *Republic* 3.394-8

C.E. McGEE

2 Henry IV: The Last Tudor Royal Entry

What might have been the last splendid reception of Elizabeth by the city fathers of London was planned and performed but never enjoyed, for Rumour played a decisive part in the world of Elizabeth, just as it played a primary role in the imaginative environment of *2 Henry IV* John Chamberlain shared his knowledge of the ill-fated proceedings with Dudley Carleton in a letter 19 November 1602, noting that 'The Quene came to Whitehall on Monday by water, though the Lord Mayor and his troupes of 500 velvet coates and chaines of gold was already mounted and marching to receve her at Charing Crosse. The sodain alteration grew upon inckling or suspicion of some dangerous attempt.'[1] As a result of this 'sodain alteration' in the queen's plans, the dreadful passage of King Henry V in the closing scene of *2 Henry IV* stands as the last Tudor royal entry into London. Obviously, this entry was not one by a Tudor monarch, but the design of the affair – both in its little show of Zeal[2] sketched by Falstaff and in its climactic encounter of sovereign and subject, Henry V and Falstaff – is typically Tudor.

No Shakespearian character is better suited by sensibility than Falstaff to master the art of Tudor royal entertainments, frequently the art of getting out of trouble, political or economic,

1 *The Letters of John Chamberlain* ed N.E. McClure, Philadelphia 1939, I, 171-2

2 Alice S. Venezky, *Pageantry on the Shakespearean Stage* (New York 1951, pp 150-2), notes the features of Falstaff's proposed show which are standard in such entertainments.

in graceful, pleasing ways. Falstaff is skilled in such manoeuvres. Part of his great appeal as a comic character comes from the confidence with which he puts his foot in his mouth and the aplomb with which he removes it when he too realizes it is there. In *2 Henry IV* he operates in this way quite consciously; just as he would use his 'good wit' to 'turn diseases to commodity'[3] at the outset, so in the last scene, as he prepares to meet the new king, he would by that same wit turn impropriety to advancement, his own and that of his friends.

But Falstaff and company must address themselves to a serious problem on this occasion: their shoddy appearance constitutes a noticeable breach of decorum – more noticeable because the colourful, orderly procession of the royal party contrasts sharply with the disorderly parade that immediately follows (that of Falstaff, Pistol, Bardolph, Shallow, and the Boy). Falstaff himself draws attention to their attire and its impropriety when he boasts about how they might have appeared had he had the time to spend Shallow's thousand pounds on liveries. Falstaff's extravagant boast may have impressed – indeed, it may well have shocked – the pecunious Justice Shallow, but it has a rather different effect upon an audience: it heightens the awareness of Falstaff's failure to put on attire appropriate to the coronation. Falstaff simply fails to produce the display that *might* have been. Of course, sartorial pretensions and problems are not new for Falstaff, who is trying in vain to arrange for new clothes when he first appears in *2 Henry IV*. It is easy to understand then why Mr Smooth the silkman might have invited Falstaff to dine: a wardrobe for a man of his girth, when an ounce of silk cost two shillings, represented a sizeable sale.[4] By the same token Mr Dummelton's request for security is understandable: extending credit to Falstaff for twenty-two yards of satin would have been a big – and, as Hostess Quickly knows and Justice Shallow is to learn, a bad – risk. Because Falstaff's first problem recurs in the last scene, he remains the improvi-

3 *The Second Part of Henry IV* ed A.R. Humphreys, London 1966, I.ii.249-50; subsequent quotations are from this edition.

4 See Lawrence M. Clopper, ed, *Chester* (Records of Early English Drama, Toronto and Buffalo 1979, p 188), for the payment by the Innkeepers in 1597-8 'for silke ij ownsses for our frynge and sÿlke to sett it one with all, iiis vii d .' S. Schoenbaum, *William Shakespeare: A Documentary Life* (New York 1975, plate 158), reproduces the document granting Shakespeare four marks' worth of scarlet cloth for the coronation entry of James I in 1604.

dent, somewhat pitiable, failed gentleman who has never quite managed to produce the gentlemanly show he deems suitable for himself.

The problem of Falstaff's attire is especially serious in the context of the coronation celebrations. Arraying the civic party which received the monarch, dressing up the nobility which attended upon him, and decking out the city itself with tapestries, new gilt, fresh gravel, and new rushes (as the energetic activity of the strewers at the beginning of V.v reminds us) were important parts of the preparation for a royal entry, and they remain the most commonly noted aspects in records of Tudor instances. The records of the Guild of St George of Norwich provide a different measure of the seriousness of proper attire for these occasions. The guild ordained that certain citizens have their English gowns 'not furred but with some descrit lynyng'[5] prepared and ready for inspection by the Lord Mayor eight days prior to the planned arrival of the queen in 1578. Those who failed to do so faced prison or a fine of five pounds – a substantial incentive indeed! Falstaff is certainly not prepared or ready for the coronation entry: his attendants are unliveried and his attire is everyday stuff, sweaty and stained with travel. Despite the seriousness of his problem, Falstaff remains excited and optimistic, for by his good wit he would turn his breach of decorum into a pageantic emblem of zeal:

> O, if I had had time to have made new liveries, I would have bestowed the thousand pound I borrowed of you. But 'tis no matter, this poor show doth better, this doth infer the zeal I had to see him ... It shows my earnestness of affection ... My devotion ... (V.v.11-18)

Such allegorizing is not exclusively Tudor (it can be found in the pageants London prepared for Henry VI in 1432 and in those Edinburgh produced for Charles I two hundred years later), but turning impropriety to art, and possibly to account, is at least typical of Tudor times.

This is precisely the principle of design of the entertainment of Elizabeth by Lord Burleigh at Theobalds in 1591. The Lord Treasurer's manor house and his past entertainments of the queen there bespoke his eminence and her delight, both in the manor and in the company of its lord. Personal misfortune,

5 Jon Craig Moynes 'The Reception of Elizabeth I at Norwich' PhD dissertation, University of Toronto 1978, II, 726

however, made all this of little consequence: Lord Burleigh lost his mother in 1587; two years later his wife died, and in 1591 his daughter. Grieved by these losses, particularly that of his wife, Burleigh secluded himself; his visits to court grew briefer and less frequent. The character who received Elizabeth in 1591 explained this situation in order to account for his own unexpected, awkward presence:

> I am a hermitt yt this x yeares space
> haue led a sollytarye & retyred lyfe
> hear in my cell not past 3 furlonng*es* hence
> tyll by my fownder he that buyllt this howse
> forgettfull of his wryghttynge & his woord
> full sore agaynst my wyll I was remoued
> for he oretaken wt excessyue greefe
> betooke hym to my sylly hermytage
> and ther hathe lyued two years & som few monethes
> by reason of these most bitter accidents ... [6]

The absence of Lord Burleigh from the welcoming party at Theobalds was an even more striking impropriety than Falstaff's 'poor show.' Incapable of being hidden, the loss of Lord Burleigh was turned to the show's gain. His failure to observe the rubrics of hospitality provided the basis for the fiction by which the Hermit justified his presence and his petition. Quite clever despite avowed clumsiness, he complained about the expropriation of his hermitage, apologized for his ineptitude as the host of the great estate, ushered the queen into the manor house while pointing out distinctive amenities of Theobalds, praised her to the skies (of course), and, in conclusion, asked that she restore him to his cottage and Lord Burleigh to his manor house. Elizabeth, aware that gracious responsiveness was essential to the success of such shows, brought the entertainment to a satisfying close by solving the problems from which the show proceeded: she drafted a mock writ, issued under the great seal, ordering the Hermit to his cell and the Lord Treasurer to his home.[7] As a whole, the entertainment at Theobalds

6 BL ms Egerton 2623, f 15r, which has been printed by J.P. Collier, *History of English Dramatic Poetry* (1931; reprinted New York 1970) I, 283-8. Concerning his text, see W.W. Greg 'A Collier Mystification' *RES* I (1925) 452-4.

7 See J. Nichols *The Progresses and Public Processions of Queen Elizabeth* 2nd edn, London 1823, III, 75; or, for a reproduction (reduced) of the document,

in 1591 turned real grief and impropriety to art – the engaging fiction of a happy reception – and to advancement, for Robert Cecil, who may have written the Hermit's speech of welcome and who later played the part of the Hermit when Elizabeth visited Theobalds in 1594, was knighted before she departed in 1591.

This principle of design – turning problems of impropriety to account – may have had its origin in the need to solve real political problems. Street pageants could help ease the tension between a rebellious city and the monarch because with the 'language of pageantic display ... a city could create a privileged meeting place between itself and its king and define the real relationship between them in ways that transcended both the neutrality of convention and the tact of silence.'[8] This was certainly the case for York and Worcester at the time of the first Tudor progress in 1486. Both cities used civic pageantry to ingratiate themselves with Henry VII because both had jeopardized their good standing by openly supporting Richard III and his allies; in fact, Worcester still stood under indictment for treason at the time of Henry's visit.

By Shakespeare's time, this principle of design was well established in entertainments. Two examples will suffice: one from the well-known *Gesta Grayorum* and another from the virtually unknown 'goodwill's parte,' a little show of welcome, suggest more playful ways it found expression. In the latter case, Goodwill, played by one of the bigger boys of the Chapel Royal, appeared before the queen as she entered Greenwich Park. Bareheaded, he had a lance in one hand, a shovel in the other, a chain of gold on his chest, an anchor across his back, a post-boy's boot on one foot, winged heels on the other. The ridiculous costume was designed to provoke some questions (especially in an audience capable of reading the visual shorthand of emblematic attire), and the speech responded to those questions:

> This spade declares ye com*m*ons rich & poore,
> in equall sort ay ready at yo*u*r need
> nought but yo*u*r weale they do expect therfore,

Sotheby's *Catalogue of Valuable Autograph Letters, Literary Manuscripts, and Historical Documents* 15-16 Dec 1980, lot 299.

8 John C. Meagher 'The First Progress of Henry VII' *Renaissance Drama* ns 1 (1968) 48

> & thats ye guerdon y*at* y*ei* craue for meed.
> This booted legg approues *goodwills* intent,
> to ryde, to run to trauell farr & neare
> with anker heauede at sea *goodwill* is bent
> to make ye forrayn foe yo*ur* fame to feare.[9]

And so on. When decoded, each property attested to the goodwill (in various forms) of the people (in its various groupings); in short, goodwill was 'all in every part' (V.v.29).

Closer to Shakespeare's experience and to the writing of *2 Henry IV* was Gray's Inn's famous 'night of errors' – so called partly because of the performance of *A Comedy of Errors* and partly because of the great crush of people that prevented the Prince of Purpoole from properly receiving his friends from Lincoln's Inn and from entertaining them with the planned shows. The errors of this night were subsequently made part of a larger festive structure, however, when they became the basis both for an amusing trial in which the students of law 'preferred Judgments thick and threefold, which were read publickly by the Clerk of the Crown, being against a Sorcerer or Conjurer that was supposed to be the Cause of the Confused Inconvenience,'[10] and for the climactic masque of amity in which Graius and Templarius joined the ranks of Achilles and Patrocles, Pilades and Orestes, Scipio and Lelius. Thus the Christmas celebrations, upset by impropriety, were brought to a happy, harmonious ending. A similar situation developed three or four years later at the Middle Temple when the Prince d'Amour failed to receive the Lincolnians 'according to their worthiness, nor his own desire.'[11] Again the disruption of prescribed ceremonies occasioned a delightful fiction suggestive of the political intrigues of 'the dark Raign of the bright Prince of burning Love,'[12] a mock trial of the discontented lover who had 'practised factiously against the Prince, and earnestly stirred enmity betwixt him and the Lincolnians,'[13] and a banquet for the embassy from Lincoln's Inn at which their league was renewed. In both Christmas festivities, impropriety served as the starting point for several days' sport which culminated in a

9 *Records of Early English Drama Newsletter* 2 (1980) 5
10 *Gesta Grayorum* ed W.W. Greg, Malone Society, Oxford 1914, p 23
11 Sir Benjamin Rudyerd *Le Prince d'Amour* London 1660, p 88
12 Ibid, p 78
13 Ibid, p 88

comic resolution of earlier problems.

An audience attuned to this way of proceeding in entertainments may have been well pleased with the wit and irrepressible optimism of Falstaff as he portrays himself – zealous, devoted, and earnest in affection. He *is* delightful on this occasion, clever though not profound, and he may have reminded a regular theatre-goer of the witty old knight who in the twinkling of an eye turned base cowardice into an instinctive defence of the heir apparent. The fun Falstaff initiates is deepened by Pistol's assurances that despite their inappropriate attire, all shall be well – assurances directed primarily at Justice Shallow (a character more respectful of things past than Falstaff) but encouraging to the audience as well.[14] While giving Falstaff this last chance to jest, however, Shakespeare sets him up for his fall, and the rejection of Falstaff by Hal is as harsh as the old knight's demonstration of wit is charming.

Of course, the new king had little choice but to seem harsh on the occasion of his coronation entry, for the Tudor royal entry and progress, especially as choreographed by Elizabeth, dramatized and confirmed the ideals of the regime. To this end, what was most important was not the pageantry prepared by civic officials or lords of manor houses but the encounters between sovereign and subjects. This is the aspect of Tudor royal entries with the greatest dramatic potential; from it Shakespeare builds act V, scene v, of *2 Henry IV;* and as a result, Falstaff's little show of zeal – perhaps the 'fool-born jest' (V.v.55) which Hal refuses to entertain – gives way to the meeting of the old knight and the new king.

The coronation of Queen Elizabeth provides a clear indication of the significance of such encounters, for her entry, like that of Henry V in Shakespeare's play, was also marked by meetings of the queen and her people. In imagery indicative of the dramatic potential of an entry, Richard Mulcaster summed up the entire affair, saying that, 'if a man shoulde say well, he could not better tearme the Citie of London that time, than a stage wherein was shewed the wonderfull spectacle, of a noble hearted Princesse toward her most loving People, and the People's exceding comfort in beholding so worthy a Soveraigne ...'[15] Elizabeth not only smiled graciously in response to the 'prayers,

14 In this, I prefer the reading of the Folio, which attributes 'It doth' to Pistol.

15 Nichols *Progresses* I, 39

wishes, welcomminges, cryes, tender woordes, and all other signes'[16] of the crowd but also stayed her chariot to receive the gifts and listen to petitions of 'baser personages' who appealed to her. The prudence with which Elizabeth comported herself on this occasion informed her use of progresses throughout her reign, so that when her rule was only *a memory*, it was a fond one. Such a memory of Elizabeth heightened the disaffection for James:

> It is said, that your majestie, of an ingenious and riall nature, not delighting in our popular salutations, doe passe by great tropes of your commons with a kind of kinglie negligence, neither speaking nor looking upon them. The poore sort of people are bolde with your majestie; they prate of the manner of there late queene, whoe when she was publicly abroad, would often stay and speake kindlie to the multitud, discovering her riall accepture of their joyfull acclamations; and manie tymes alsoe saying, that her subjects hungrie eies might have there fyll in beholding there soveraigne. Your majestie must needs therefore in some sort satisfie there jealous affections. The poore rascales, soe farr as they dare, will be angry with you.[17]

The political importance of Elizabeth's openness to encounters with her people became most clear a decade after her death, when Sir John Hayward compiled his *Annals* (1612) for the education of Prince Henry in the ways of kingship. What Hayward judged instructive was not the pageantry, despite its traditional political wisdom and counsel, but the responses of the queen: her smiles, her solicitude, her readiness to accept gifts, such as the branch of rosemary 'geven to her Grace with a supplication by a poore woman' which 'was seen in her chariot til her Grace came to Westminster, not without the marveylous wondring of such as knew the presenter ...'[18] Such encounters were rich in lessons for the Stuart heir apparent, lessons not to be learned from his father. While expressing the values by which the queen would rule, these encounters confirmed those bonds of affection and of respect between sovereign and subjects that James unfortunately neglected.

16 Ibid, 38

17 This anonymous document has been printed from BL ms Cotton Faustina C II 12, f 61, by J. Somers, *A Collection of Scarce and Valuable Tracts* 2nd edn, rev and ed Sir Walter Scott, Edinburgh 1809, II, 147.

18 Nichols *Progresses* I, 59

The last detail from the account of the coronation entry of Elizabeth is especially interesting in relation to *2 Henry IV* because it contains a meeting like that of Hal and Falstaff between Elizabeth and a person known to those watching the entry. Because the woman who offered the rosemary was but a 'poor personage,' the queen's acceptance was a more impressive sign of her love for her people. Falstaff is also a character well known to the audience of Henry V's coronation entry – known to be self-indulgent, vain, riotous, disrespectful of law and order. His past associations with Hal have helped to make the prince appear to others 'a most princely hypocrite' (II.ii.54) and stirred fear for the commonwealth in the hearts of those close to the Crown. The reputation of Falstaff makes his meeting with the new king during the coronation entry problematic: unlike Elizabeth in 1558, Henry cannot smile graciously upon his disreputable vassal without dramatizing his acceptance of all that Falstaff stands for: licence rather than law, cowardice rather than fortitude, intemperance rather than temperance, partiality rather than indifferent justice. It is difficult to imagine that Henry V would not be sensitive to the importance of this encounter because, like his father, he knows the power of calculating the effects of public appearances. On this occasion, moreover, the king manages his public rejection of Falstaff so that there is no mention of the possibility of a renewal of association with his former companions when 'their conversations / Appear more wise and modest *to the world*' (V.v.100-1; italics mine).

Falstaff realizes too late that he and Hal, on the occasion of the coronation entry, are the 'observed of all observers' – players in a drama of moral and political import for the edification of the audience of the entry. There is some truth to the excuse Falstaff makes to Shallow to account for his public set-back, his claim that the king 'must seem thus to the world' (V.v.78), but he fails to see that such severity on the part of the king is not necessary, not even desirable. Had the old knight come properly attired to the coronation, had he adopted a position of love and dread before the new king, had he bowed down (as the city fathers of Worcester did before Henry VII in 1486 for their complicity in rebellion, as those of York did before Henry VIII in 1541 for the same reason, as Arthur Throckmorten hoped to do in an antimasque before Elizabeth in 1595), Henry V might have been able to respond less harshly. But Falstaff's leer and his too-familiar cry, 'God save thee, my sweet boy!' (V.v.43) do not give the king the chance to be gracious, yet just, in meeting him.

With the little show of zeal in which impropriety is turned to art (though not to advancement or account) and with the climactic encounter of sovereign and subject in which the moral and political values of the new regime are dramatized to the world, the dreadful passage of Henry V is a characteristic Tudor royal entry. At the same time, this last Tudor royal entry reflects important changes from those of earlier times. The first Tudor progress occurred after years of civil upheaval and in the midst of rumours of rebellion, but Henry VII treated York generously, pardoned Worcester, inquired into Bristol's obvious poverty, hearkened to the pageants of all, and thereby cultivated the love of his people. The coronation entry of Elizabeth occurred after years of religious strife and in the midst of political instability, yet the queen comported herself so that 'the people, to whom no musicke is soe sweete as the affability of ther Prince, were so strongly stirred to love and joye, that all men contended how they might most effectually testify to the same ...'[19] These royal entries confirmed the ideal love of subjects for their sovereigns, but the meeting of Falstaff and King Henry V confirms the ideal dread of subjects for the monarch and his justice.

As we might have expected, given the anachronisms in Shakespeare's other history plays, *2 Henry IV,* in the harsh lesson of its royal entry, is made from the world of the author rather than that of his characters – a world in which the multitude was a 'blunt monster with uncounted heads' (induction, line 17), in which great battles were won by broken promises, in which every area of life appeared diseased, in which the old queen, even after some forty-four years on the throne, could not – like the retrojected Henry V – enter the capital city for fear of 'some dangerous attempt.'

University of St Jerome's College
University of Waterloo

19 Sir John Hayward *Annals* ed John Bruce, London 1840, p 18

EUGENE M. WAITH

The Ceremonies of *Titus Andronicus*

Burley-on-the-Hill, where James I was to be so delighted by the masque of *The Gypsies Metamorphosed*, was the scene of Christmas holiday festivities in 1595-6 which included a performance of *Titus Andronicus* on 1 January. The choice of this play for such an occasion now seems very odd, to say the least, but perhaps less so when we notice that in the one known account of the occasion, the tragedy is valued mainly as a 'show.' Jaques Petit, the Gascon servant of Anthony Bacon, writes to his master: 'on a aussi ioué la tragedie de Titus Andronicus mais la monstre a plus valeu que le suiect.'[1] To some critics the word 'monstre' may seem to have an unintended appropriateness, but even those who do not consider the play merely monstrous will agree that spectacles of one sort or another constitute an unusually important element of its stage presentation. It is tempting to suppose that the performance at Burley-on-the-Hill inspired Henry Peacham's famous drawing of *Titus Andronicus*, if the date on the manuscript is 1595,[2] though we have no proof that Peacham was there. In any case, whenever and wherever it was executed, it suggests, in the variety of costume and gesture,

1 Lambeth Palace ms 654, no 167, as quoted in Gustav Ungerer 'An Unrecorded Elizabethan Performance of *Titus Andronicus*' *ShS* 14 (1961) 108 (contractions expanded)

2 The decipherment of the date is a puzzle to which 1594 or 1595 are the accepted solutions; see E.K. Chambers 'The First Illustration to "Shakespeare"' *Library* 4th ser, 5 (1925) 326-30.

something of the visual impact the play had. Many of the most striking appeals to the eye are made by ceremonies – the election of an emperor, a triumphal procession, prayers, a sacrifice, and burial rites, to go less than half-way through the opening scene. I believe that these ceremonies and other closely related visual effects make a vital contribution to the meaning of the play. 'La monstre' may be more directly related to 'le suiect' than Petit realized.[3]

The play opens with a flourish of trumpets followed by the arrival at opposite doors of the rival candidates for the office of emperor, accompanied by drummers, trumpeters, and flag-bearers, while senators and tribunes enter 'aloft.' The contenders, Saturninus and Bassianus, with their friends and soldiers, face each other across the stage as do opposing armies in some history plays, clearly presenting the threat of violence. But the tribune Marcus Andronicus, holding in his hands a crown, the emblem of rule, persuades them to 'plead [their] deserts'[4] peacefully. He also announces that the people's candidate is his brother Titus, who has saved Rome from the Goths. The forms of a democratic election are thus preserved and are dramatized by the spectacle of an incipient brawl turning into a political ceremony. G.K. Hunter has shown the remarkable similarity of this opening to that of *Romeo and Juliet,* where Montagues and Capulets enter at opposite doors and begin a fight which the prince ends, standing above, like Marcus, as an embodiment of civil order.[5] In *Titus Andronicus* ceremonies which order or partly conceal discordant energies are of special importance.

When most of the first group of characters has left the stage to continue the process of election, a second ceremony, more spectacular than the first, supervenes – the triumphal return of Titus. Heralded by more drums and trumpets and preceded by four of his sons, as pallbearers with one or more coffins,[6] the victorious general is drawn on stage in a chariot,

3 A.C. Hamilton calls attention to the 'formal ceremonies' of *Titus Andronicus* in his *The Early Shakespeare* (San Marino Calif 1967, p 73), relating them to myths and rituals which he believes to lie behind them. See also Nicholas Brooke's chapter on the play in *Shakespeare's Early Tragedies* (1968; reprinted London 1973), esp pp 19, 20, 22; and Ann Haaker '*Non sine causa*: The Use of Emblematic Method and Iconology in the Thematic Structure of *Titus Andronicus*' RORD 13-14 (1979-81) 143-68.

4 All quotations are from J.C. Maxwell's third edition (London 1961).

5 'Shakespeare's Earliest Tragedies' *ShS* 27 (1974) 3-4

6 Stage directions are inconsistent about the number of coffins; the use of a

behind which march the most distinguished of his prisoners, Tamora, the queen of the Goths, her three sons, and Aaron the Moor. For this is both a triumph and a funeral: the bodies of Titus's sons, who have died *pro patria*, are being taken to the tomb of the Andronici, a structure set up at the centre of the back wall of the stage. After a solemn march around the stage Titus alights from his chariot near the entrance of the tomb with his living sons on one side of him and his prisoners on the other.[7] The stage picture powerfully asserts his centrality as the chief support of Rome, while the combined ceremony of victory and burial shows how aptly he is 'surnamed Pius' (I.i.23), like Aeneas. The tomb becomes an emblem of devotion to family, fatherland, and the gods.

In the context of the feelings generated by this pageantry the demand of Titus's son Lucius that 'the proudest prisoner of the Goths' be sacrificed '*Ad manes fratrum*' (lines 96-8) has an appropriateness which at first inhibits the reaction of shock at the idea of human sacrifice. Are we (and were Elizabethans) being asked to give imaginative assent to the customs of another time and place? Before such a question can be answered, it is greatly complicated by the plea of Tamora for her son Alarbus, whom Titus has immediately handed over to Lucius. On her knees the queen puts her feelings as a mother against the demands of Roman piety and further reminds Titus that by being merciful he might rise to an even higher religious standard. The Peacham drawing is evidence that her prayer was, not only verbally but visually, an arresting moment.

When Titus dismisses it with a reassertion of piety – 'Religiously they ask a sacrifice' (line 124) – and Tamora says, 'O cruel, irreligious piety!' (130), the play presents the first of many double visions of its hero. His self-dedication to certain principles has produced a shocking loss of humanity, and yet this is no clear-cut case of the good man going wrong. We see a collision of two sets of values, neither of which should necessarily prevail in all circumstances. Of such conflicts the rhetorical *controversiae* were made, and *Titus Andronicus* often reminds one of

chariot is implied by Titus's reference to it at line 249; see Joseph E. Kramer 'The Revengeful City: A Study of *Titus Andronicus*' PhD dissertation, Princeton 1965, p 82.

7 The stage arrangements are, of course, guesswork. We know that property tombs were used, and the text clearly calls for some such representation here.

those cases, where arguments of almost equal force can be brought to support opposing judgments.

In the main the ceremony of triumph and burial tells in favour of Titus's view of the situation, and so does much of the language of the scene. The death of Alarbus is described by Lucius as 'Our Roman rites,' and the 'sacrificing fire' to which his body has been consigned is said to produce smoke which 'like incense doth perfume the sky' (lines 143-5). In the midst of this speech, however, is the disturbing clause, 'Alarbus' limbs are lopp'd' (Lawrence Danson thinks it may be Shakespeare's worst half-line),[8] which plays the brutal facts against the ceremonial way of interpreting them. And even the stage picture is not unambiguously pro-ritual, for as the rites are being described and as the bodies of Titus's sons are being laid in the tomb, the queen of the Goths and her sons are still there as reminders of the rejected plea for mercy, and with them the silent but surely (for an Elizabethan audience) ominous figure of Aaron the Moor.

The solemn words with which Titus now commits the bodies of his dead sons to the tomb gain an extraordinary power from the cross-currents of feeling inspired by the immediately preceding actions and dialogue. Rapt in contemplation of death, where one is 'Secure from worldly chances and mishaps' (line 152), Titus projects an admirable serenity, which we already see to be resting on shaky foundations. Shakespeare makes us aware of an unspoken counterpoint to this moving speech.

Violence again threatens ceremonial order when Marcus, as spokesman for the Roman people, asks Titus to be a candidate and assures him of election to the 'empery.' Saturninus, the eldest son of the dead emperor, immediately asks his followers to support his claim with their swords. Now Titus assumes the role of peacemaker and judge, and once again the ceremony, in which he plays the central part, shows him in a mainly favourable light, while at the same time it is obvious that he is making a foolish mistake. Bassianus, Saturninus's younger brother, making no threat of force, asks with perfect civility for Titus's support, but Titus hardly seems to hear him. As if there could be but one proper solution, he asks the people to choose Saturninus, who, a moment later, is acclaimed emperor. Declining the honour for himself, upholding the forms of election, and speak-

8 *Tragic Alphabet: Shakespeare's Drama of Language* New Haven 1974, p 8

ing reasonably in favour of the eldest son, Titus cannot seem entirely misguided (Shakespeare could count on widespread acceptance of the right of primogeniture), and yet Saturninus has already been established as wilful and violent in contrast to his law-abiding brother. When Titus instantly assents to Saturninus's proposal to marry Lavinia, with whom we know that Bassianus is in love, Titus's readiness to sacrifice everything to principle is painfully clear. Folly and self-righteousness are the obverse of his piety.

The ceremony of electing a new emperor is barely concluded before violence disrupts the established order as Bassianus, pointedly ignored in the preceding action, seizes his brother's bride. In the ensuing mêlée Titus is the only one of the Andronici to condemn Bassianus. To the others he is taking what belongs to him, but Titus's loyalty to the new emperor and to his own promise carry him to the point of killing his son Mutius for covering the escape of Bassianus. So completely does he identify himself with the course of action he has chosen that when Lucius tells him he has slain his son 'in wrongful quarrel,' he replies, 'Nor thou, nor he, are any sons of mine' (lines 293-4). Like Tamburlaine, he kills his son for being unworthy of him, but where Marlowe partly justifies his hero by making a comical coward of the son and discrediting Tamburlaine's enemies, Shakespeare creates a starker contrast. Only Titus can see the murder as an assertion of family honour. To everyone else it is a piece of wilful violence based on a hideous error of judgment. For the first time Titus is clearly wrong. Less clearly we may see a parallel between this sacrifice and that of Alarbus. When Titus is brutally spurned a few minutes later by Saturninus, sympathy for the hero is inevitably qualified. As in a *controversia,* the emperor's ingratitude must be weighed against Titus's self-deluded brutality.

The ceremony which immediately follows presents Titus's brother and remaining sons on their knees, begging him to allow the burial of Mutius in the family tomb. His initial angry rejection of his entire family is followed by reconciliation. The petitioners rise from their knees, place the body in the tomb, and kneel to say, 'He lives in fame that died in virtue's cause' (line 390). The ritual at least partially revalidates the piety of the Andronici.

It has been noted that the fifty-line episode of the burial of Mutius, like the equally brief one of the sacrifice of Alarbus, seems to have been added to a pre-existing text.[9] Both introduce visually striking ceremonies in which petitioners kneel to Titus. On one occasion he refuses; on the other he reluctantly accedes. Both complicate our understanding of the hero. These bits of evidence seem to show us an author increasing his use of what he sees as an effective device.

At the end of this long first movement the stage is again crowded with all the major characters, and Shakespeare gives us what could be seen as mockery of the preceding intercession followed by reconciliation. Here Tamora pretends to intercede with the emperor on behalf of Titus and his family; the Andronici kneel, and Saturninus feigns renewed friendship with them. That this spectacle is mere show we know from a long aside in which Tamora tells of her hopes for revenge and from Aaron's soliloquy, which follows when everyone else has left the stage. When the ominous black figure speaks at last, he adds a dimension to the political reality which some of the ceremonies have partially concealed. He may even act out a metaphor of revealing an unsuspected reality by discarding the drab clothing of a prisoner and putting on more brilliant attire as he says,

> Away with slavish weeds and servile thoughts!
> I will be bright, and shine in pearl and gold. (lines 18-19)

His speech ends with a prophecy of the 'shipwrack' of the Roman commonweal.

The 'solemn hunting' of the panther and the hart, which occupies much of act II, is not presented on stage in a spectacular way, though we hear horns and may see the dogs (in the second scene). The main stage action is the hunting of Bassianus, Lavinia, and the sons of Titus,[10] in the presentation of which Shakespeare introduces another kind of picture – the formal description which conjures up an imagined scene. The first instance is Tamora's attractive description of the woods (II. iii.10-29), which John Monck Mason considered the only speech in Shakespeare's style in the entire play.[11] This might be taken

9 See J. Dover Wilson's introduction to his edition (Cambridge 1948), pp xxxv-vi.

10 Joseph Kramer uses Tamora's phrase 'a double hunt' to stand for the double meaning of the hunt in his analysis of this important motif. See 'The Revengeful City,' pp 144ff.

11 *Comments on the Last Edition of Shakespeare's Plays* Dublin 1785, p 306

as a standard instance of verbal scene-painting if it did not contradict descriptions of the same woods that precede and follow it. Aaron has assured Chiron and Demetrius that 'the woods are ruthless, dreadful, deaf, and dull' (II.i.128). Tamora herself is to call them 'A barren detested vale' (II.iii.93), and later Titus will identify them with the 'ruthless, vast, and gloomy woods' where Philomela was forced (IV.i.53). To Tamora, in her anticipation of Aaron's embraces, all animate and inanimate nature 'doth make a gleeful boast' (II. iii.11). The subjectivity of these views can hardly escape notice.

Much more striking is the contrast between the mutilated Lavinia who appears on stage and Marcus's Ovidian description of what he sees as he stands looking at her, comparing her missing hands to branches cut from a tree, the blood flowing from her mouth to a bubbling fountain, and her cheeks to the sun (II. iv.16-51). The inappropriateness of such a response to Lavinia's situation poses a staggering problem for the director. Lyric and dramatic modes seem to collide; 'the action,' I once said, 'frustrates, rather than re-enforces, the operation of the poetry.'[12] The solution of some directors is to cut most or all of the Ovidian poetry,[13] but a rejection of the contradiction is not inevitable. Another way of interpreting the scene is to take the discrepancy between what we see on the stage and what Marcus says as a kind of double vision, analogous to those ritual gestures in the first act which make piety of human sacrifice or honour of the murder of a son. The strange images which Marcus substitutes for the mangled body of his niece provide a way of holding the experience off rather than expressing the emotions it arouses. He longs to rail at the unknown perpetrator of this horror to ease his mind, and he knows that 'Sorrow concealed, like an oven stopp'd, / Doth burn the heart to cinders where it is' (lines 34-7), but this sanative release is denied him. The fanciful picture he creates offers a temporary refuge even though the frustration of a more natural response threatens to intensify the repressed emotion. The double vision provided by this elaborate picture is neither rationalization nor wishful thinking but may be a desperate effort to come to terms with unbearable pain.

In the central scene of the play, where, after meeting Lavi-

12 'The Metamorphosis of Violence in *Titus Andronicus*' *ShS* 10 (1957) 48

13 Peter Brook and Trevor Nunn did so at Stratford in 1955 and 1972 respectively.

nia, Titus tries to save the lives of his sons by allowing his hand to be chopped off, only to have the hand returned to him with the heads of his sons, stage ceremonies and the analogous operation of pictorial poetry more and more transform reality into fantasy. A brief procession opens the scene, *'the Judges and Senators, with Titus' two sons, bound, passing on the stage to the place of execution, and* TITUS *going before pleading'* (III.i first stage direction). The victorious general and king-maker prostrates himself before officials who totally ignore him. The pantomime is complemented by Titus's conceit that the stones to which he has addressed his plea 'are better than the tribunes,' more sympathetic and softer-hearted (lines 37-47). When he thus explains his talking to the stones after the judges and senators have walked off, he is doing something stranger than justifying cruel behaviour as adherence to lofty ideals, but not altogether different.

His bitter outburst,

> dost thou not perceive
> That Rome is but a wilderness of tigers?
> Tigers must prey, and Rome affords no prey
> But me and mine (lines 53-6),

is a shrewd appraisal of the actual situation,[14] but also one of a series of vivid images which tend to push the action into an imaginary space – to offer a metaphorical reality which competes with what we see. The image of the hunting-down of the Andronici has been prepared for by the cynical references to Lavinia as the 'dainty doe' that Chiron and Demetrius seek to 'pluck to ground' (II.i.117; II.ii.26). Soon Titus is comparing himself to 'one upon a rock / Environ'd with a wilderness of sea' (III.i.93-4). These self-comparisons are, of course, examples of a kind of heightening often used by the poetic dramatist and need not be attributed to the speaker. In this play, however, where the difference between the hero's view and that of others is frequently an issue, these pictorial representations of Titus may be taken, at least in part, as his own. Like Marcus's description of Lavinia, they may constitute a way of dealing with a reality too horrible to face directly, and they also suggest powerfully the

14 For an excellent discussion of the thematic centrality of this metaphor see Alan Sommers '"Wilderness of Tigers": Structure and Symbolism in *Titus Andronicus*' EC 10 (1960) 275-89.

process by which Titus is being transformed from a victim into a revenger. As the prey of tigers, as one about to be swept away by the sea, he is the helpless object of powerful forces, though already his grief, like the Nile, 'disdaineth bounds' (line 71). In his fantasy of the Andronici sitting around a fountain, their tears will make a 'brine-pit' of it (129): sheer quantity can have its effect. Soon he imagines that 'with our sighs we'll breathe the welkin dim' (211), to which Marcus replies, 'O brother, speak with possibility, / And do not break into these deep extremes' (214-15). But Titus's passions have no bottom. No longer a man who is simply at the mercy of tigers or the sea, he is now the sea or the earth, responding to the wind and rain of Lavinia's sighs and tears:

> When heaven doth weep, doth not the earth o'erflow?
> If the winds rage, doth not the sea wax mad,
> Threat'ning the welkin with his big-swol'n face? (221-3)

In these images of himself the responsive and dangerous power of the revenger begins to appear. When the final blow falls with the delivery of his sons' heads, his memorable question, 'When will this fearful slumber have an end?' (252) and his chilling laughter show us that he will now live mainly in the alternative world of his fantasies.

The next scene (III.ii) presents us with a banquet, one of the standard forms of Elizabethan stage ceremony. The scene appears only in the Folio text and was probably a late addition,[15] made to provide an effective instance of Titus's fantasizing. It is not a state occasion like the banquet in *Macbeth* or the one to which Titus later invites the emperor and empress. Nevertheless, a certain formality is inevitable with the bringing in of a table and benches and the seating of the four Andronici, Titus, Marcus, Lavinia, and the young son of Lucius. Titus grieves; the boy comforts him, and then comes the one action of the brief scene: Marcus kills a fly with his knife. Titus at first protests this 'deed of death done on the innocent' (56), but when Marcus explains that it was a 'black ill-favoured fly, / Like to the empress' Moor' (66-7), Titus suddenly borrows the knife so that he can 'insult on' the fly's corpse, 'as if it were the Moor' (71-2).

15 For arguments that it was added see Joseph Kramer '*Titus Andronicus:* The Fly-Killing Incident' *ShS* 5 (1969) 9-19. I do not share Kramer's doubts of Shakespeare's authorship.

The killing of the fly becomes a ritual of revenge:

> Alas, poor man! grief has so wrought on him,
> He takes false shadows for true substances. (79-80)

The episode not only anticipates the final banquet but also prepares for the enactment of other fantasies such as the sending of Titus's messages. Young Lucius delivers to Chiron and Demetrius a bundle of weapons wrapped in a scroll with a famous quotation from Horace (IV.ii). Titus dispatches kinsmen to find Astraea and to deliver a petition to Pluto; he gives the Clown an 'oration' to present to the emperor (IV.iii). Visually more impressive is the mad ceremony which takes place in the middle of this scene of message-sending: at Titus's command Marcus, young Lucius, and the other kinsmen shoot arrows into the palace grounds 'with letters on the ends of them' addressed to various gods.

The initial ceremonies of act I, whether political, military, or religious, are all genuine ceremonies with traditional forms embodying the ideals to which the hero subscribes. Even when their validity, appropriateness, and applicability are questioned, the forms continue to sustain one side of the dialectic by reminding us of the hero's essentially noble nature. The ceremonies of the middle of the play serve a different, but related, function. Prayers to the paving stones, the ritual murder of a fly, and the dispatch of messages to the gods are form without substance. They express, not ideals with a questionable relationship to the situation at hand, but fantasies, clearly separated from external reality. All of them reflect the hero's obsession with redress of some sort; some show his abiding concern with justice; one specifically adumbrates his revenge. At this point in the play, when Titus's failings have come to seem less important than the horrible way in which his enemies have taken advantage of him, it is appropriate to focus attention not on moral dialectic but on the traumatic consequences of his experience. The mad games in which Titus engages his kinsmen have the additional function of preparing for yet another kind of ceremony – the purely deceptive one by means of which he carries out his revenge.

For the final ceremony Shakespeare reassembles all the surviving major characters and, as befits the author of a revenge play, kills off a large proportion of them. The Thyestean banquet, however, is preceded by a ceremony devised by Tamora to complete the ruin of the Andronici. It is brilliant not only in its staging (it must have contributed significantly to the 'monstre' noted by Petit) but also in its multiple perspectives on character and theme.

When Tamora, disguised as Revenge and accompanied by her two sons as Rape and Murder, visits Titus, she apparently has herself drawn in a chariot (V.ii.47ff), as such allegorical personages often are in a masque. The spectacle recalls the triumphal procession of the opening scene, when Titus rode in the chariot while Tamora and her sons walked behind as prisoners of war. The situations are not precisely reversed, however, for now Titus appears above, as at the door of his study, and Tamora entreats him to come down: she is again the petitioner. Her plan for persuading him to invite Lucius to his house is as mad as any of his, though Tamora is repeatedly described as unusually clever. So she obviously considers herself, taking great pride in this invention, which 'fits his lunacy' (line 70). Only her sublime self-confidence blinds her to the plain fact that Titus instantly knows who she is. In a play which repeatedly shows how 'pride goeth before destruction, and a haughty spirit before a fall,' she proves to be, if anything, a more egregious example than the hero. When she rides away in triumph, leaving her sons with Titus, she gives him his second victory over her and hers. Throughout the brief episode this spectacle is not merely form without substance but a sign that means the exact opposite of what it seems to signify.

The banquet, which is conclusive in so many ways, is an exceedingly grand affair. Trumpets not only announce the arrival of Saturninus, Tamora, and their train but, a moment later, the entrance of Titus,[16] dressed as a cook and bearing one of the fatal 'pasties' in his hand. He then places the dishes on the table, perhaps with such assistance as Lavinia can give. His welcome is ceremonious, and he explains his unusual costume by his wish 'to have all well' (V.iii.31) to entertain the emperor and empress. The guests are seated in their appointed places, and the banquet begins. The contrast beween these ceremonial gestures and the ensuing carnage fits perfectly in a play where every ceremony is in some way at odds with the situation which it solemnizes. The first death – Lavinia's at the hand of

16 The Folio omission of trumpets at this point and the addition of 'hoboyes's surely reduced the effect of this entrance.

her father – is presented by Titus as a re-enactment of the killing of Virginia to wipe out her shame. Here Saturninus is ironically cast in the role of shocked spectator and spokesman for propriety (lines 35-48). Next comes Titus's revelation of the true nature of the banquet, and then in rapid sucession the stabbings of Tamora, Titus, and Saturninus, leading to 'a great tumult' (in the appropriate words of Capell's stage direction). It subsides as the stage picture recalls the opening of the play.[17] Marcus and Lucius, standing above the assembled crowd, where Marcus stood once before, calm them with an explanation of what has happened and call for the reintegration of the Roman body politic. When Lucius is acclaimed emperor, the ceremonial order again prevails.

One of the most satisfying (and occasionally puzzling) characteristics of Shakespeare's mature writing is his extraordinary even-handedness with his characters, bringing out a great man's folly or blindness and a villain's moments of appealing humanity. When these antithetical qualities appear in a good actor's interpretation, they demand a corresponding complexity in the response of the spectator. In Chapman's words, 'Oh of what contraries consists a man! / Of what impossible mixtures!'[18] In its most impressive moments *Titus Andronicus* anticipates these later developments by offering simultaneously two contrary views of the hero, his family, and his enemies. Spectacular ceremonies and the closely related images of a pictorial poetry are the most conspicuous means of stimulating an awareness of these contradictions.

Yale University

17 The staging is highly controversial. See J.C. Maxwell's note on V.ii.69, p 138.

18 *Byron's Tragedy* V.iii.189-90

G.K. HUNTER

Sources and Meanings in *Titus Andronicus*

The belief that Shakespeare preferred to 'borrow' his plots instead of 'inventing' them (both words are highly culture-determined) might seem difficult to sustain today in the face of the complex picture of adaptation and refashioning we find, for example, in Kenneth Muir's *Shakespeare's Sources* or in more detailed studies of the kind of C.T. Prouty's *The Sources of 'Much Ado about Nothing.'* But mere details have little power to deflect our necessary myths; and the myth of Shakespeare the 'all-natural' bard, through unfashionable in its explicit form, clearly continues to sustain a preference for a Shakespeare with a passive relationship to the cultural context in which he worked.

Titus Andronicus is something of a special case inside this general situation. The play has no indisputable source, and most scholars, it seems, would be happy to learn that it was not by Shakespeare at all; it is the mark of their professionalism that they are not content just to register taste but seek to prove it. One way of exonerating Shakespeare from the exercise of personal responsibility that is implied by his 'invention' of the story of *Titus Andronicus* is to discover a source that the young author could be thought to have followed with the simple fidelity of an immature mind (Shakespeare was probably about thirty at the time). It is an additional advantage of this explanation that it allows the gruesome events of the *Titus* story to be incorporated inside another well-loved myth – that of the barbarism of Elizabethan popular taste, force-fed by decadent Italian *novelle.* H.D. Fuller, writing in 1901, remarked that 'though no novel of Titus Andronicus appears to have existed prior to the play, yet when we recall the origin of most dramas of that time, it is natural to suppose that the main outlines of the plot were not invented by the author of the extant text.'[1] No novella of Titus Andronicus has ever appeared, but R.M. Sargent is not far from the limits of the genre when he declares, having quoted Fuller, 'just such a "novel of Titus Andronicus" is known to be still in existence, in the form of a short, simple prose history.'[2] The so-called 'prose history' of Titus Andronicus (extant in the form of an eighteenth-century chap-book)[3] thus appears as a kind of Messiah, the answer to a mythic need.[4] It behoves the rational mind to examine such fulfilments of prophecy with the utmost scepticism.

Sargent's article arguing for the prose history as the source of *Titus Andronicus* has, however, been received (as Marco Mincoff remarks) 'with excessive credulity.' Mincoff's reply[5] somewhat overstates the opposite case, but the world of scholarship is much indebted to Professor Mincoff for pointing out the flimsiness of the received argument, however fulfilling it may be.[6] Sargent's argument is indeed grossly faulty both in its identification of 'facts' and in the logic of its process. Mincoff has demolished it substantially; my own notes multiply the instances of error, but there seems little point in pounding a building already in ruins. In what follows I take it for granted that there is no hard evidence that requires us to believe that the eighteenth-century prose history reflects an earlier (now lost) version which provided source for both the play of Titus and the ballad on the same subject.[7] Mincoff's alternative order (play reported by ballad; ballad reported by prose history) has at

1 H.D. Fuller 'The Sources of *Titus Andronicus*' PMLA 16 (1901) 8-9
2 R.M. Sargent 'The Source of *Titus Andronicus*' SP 46 (1949) 167 2
3 Reprinted in Geoffrey Bullough *Narrative and Dramatic Sources of Shakespeare* VI (1966) 34-44
4 The pressure to find such evidence shows itself again, but even earlier, in George Steeven's statement that Painter's *Palace of Pleasure* (the principal collection of *novelle*) speaks of the *Titus Andronicus* story as well known. Painter is in fact entirely innocent of any such report.
5 Marco Mincoff 'The Source of *Titus Andronicus*' N&Q 216 (1971) 131-4
6 G. Harold Metz, 'The History of *Titus Andronicus* and Shakespeare's Play' N&Q 220 (1975) 163-6, has sought (unsuccessfully, I believe) to reinstate the earlier view. My own comment on Metz: 'The "Sources" of *Titus Andronicus* – Once Again' N&Q April 1983.
7 Reprinted in Bullough *Narrative and Dramatic Sources* 44-8

least as much probability, even if less mythic resonance. My argument therefore aims to explore the literary consequences of assuming Mincoff's order, always taking into account the generic requirements of each literary document and remembering that each was written to make its own unique effect, not simply to create a link in a chain or provide fodder for source analysts.

The publication of ballads based on stories made popular by plays is a recurrent feature of Elizabethan printing,[8] and the assumption that the ballad on the story of Titus Andronicus was written to cash in on the play fits with the prevailing evidence more clearly than it defies it. But it is hard to take the argument any further than this, for none of the texts of the ballad entries I cite in note 8 has survived. The ballad on Titus Andronicus seems only to be extant today because it was reprinted in 1620 in Richard Johnson's anthology *The Golden Garland of Princely Pleasures*, along with an unentered ballad on King Lear,[9] clearly derivative from Shakespeare's play. The presence of this twin might seem to increase the likelihood that the Titus ballad is also derivative.

It is not the business of the broadside ballad writer to be inventive (in the modern sense) but to catch up whatever is

8 Most Elizabethan broadside ballads have not survived. The texts of such as have survived are usually undated and undateable (except within very wide limits). One is therefore obliged to rely on the entries in the Stationers' registers. In this investigation I have depended largely on Hyder Rollins, *An Analytical Index to the Ballad Entries in the Stationers' Registers 1557-1709* reprinted 1967 from SP 21 (1924) 1-324, but I have checked the material used in the relevant authorities – Greg's *Bibliography*, Chambers's *Elizabethan Stage*, the Harbage-Schoenbaum *Annals*, the *Short-Title Catalogue*. The following list gives the most obviously relevant entries of the period before the entry of *Titus Andronicus* (together with 'the ballad thereof') on 6 Feb 1594:

1 *The story of Tamburlayne the Greate* was entered on 6 Nov 1594. The play had been printed in 1590.

2 *The murtherous life and terrible death of the riche Jewe of Malta* was entered on 16 May 1594. The play is usually dated 1589/90, but it was not printed till 1633. It is probably worth noticing that Marlowe's play was entered in the register one day after the ballad (on 17 May 1594), though not to the same stationers.

3 *The Terannye of Judge Apyus* was entered 1569/70. The play of *Apius and Virginia* (by R.B.) was entered in 1567/68. It was not printed till 1575.

4 *A newe ballad of Romeo and Juliett* was entered on 5 Aug 1596. Shakespeare's play was not entered. It is usually dated 1595. It was printed in 1597.

currently notorious in the public mind. But the balladeer has another and more creative aspect to his trade in that he is expected to render the complex issues of local scandals and popular narratives into the generalizing oral style that characterizes the broadside no less than the traditional ballad. The main features of that rendering are well shown in the ballad of Titus Andronicus (as in that of King Lear), and the omissions and transpositions that we can see differentiating the play and the ballad of Titus Andronicus are clearly connected to the requirements of the different genres. The ballad has a tendency to address itself to an audience that accepts conservative military values; and so the Titus Andronicus ballad begins, 'You noble minds and famous martial wights,' and tells its story exclusively from the point of view of a military hero of old who (like the heroes of *The Mirror for Magistrates*) speaks from the grave and recounts the events leading to it from his own exclusive angle of vision[10]: 'I conquest home did bring [Tamora, Aaron, et cetera]'; but they 'consented ... against myself, my kin and all my friends ... My Lavinia was betrothed then to ... He being slain ... my three sons ... But now ... My daughter ravished ... My brother Marcus found her ... But when I found her ... I tore the milk-white hairs ...' Inevitably, this single-focus narrative reduces the other characters in the story to cartoon-like simplicity. The separate motives that Shakespeare provides for Tamora, Saturninus, Aaron, and others are not present. We hear now that they are 'proud' (line 23), 'adulterous' (27), 'murderous' (29); but these are the flat characteristics of a two-dimensional world of action which inhibits any attempt on our part to 'understand' them. They are the nightmare that Titus sees (and tells), but they occupy no space of their own and can only mean what his perspective allows them to mean. The lack of connection between events and lack of motivation are, of course, among the most remarked of ballad characteristics (see, for example, G.H. Gerould *The Ballad of Tradition* 1932) and cannot be used to point to a particular position in a chain of sources. Gerould speaks of

5 *A ballad wherein is shewed a knacke how to knowe an honest man from a knave* was entered on 5 Nov 1594. The anonymous play of *A Knack to Knowe an Honest Man* was acted in Oct 1594. It was entered on 26 Nov 1595 and printed in 1597.

9 Reprinted in Percy's *Reliques* ed Wheatley, 1876, I.231ff

10 A quick glimpse into the popularity of this mode is provided by Rollins's *Index* sv 'Lamentation.'

the ballad's events as 'flashes ... directed on what is essential to our imaginative and emotional grasp' (page 89). What is essential in the ballad of Titus Andronicus is our grasp on Titus's emotional state; and to sustain the genre everything else must be subordinated to that.

If one is to tell the same story in a different genre (and do so effectively), one must make connections between the parts that ballad technique has kept asunder. The prose history of Titus Andronicus is clearly enough organizing the focus to procure a different kind of unity, but the nature of the genre which defines the unity is not at all clear. J.Q. Adams, in the introduction to his facsimile text of the play,[11] quotes a set of 'history' titles from the catalogue of Cluer Dicey, the publisher of the eighteenth-century chap-book which contains the prose history of Titus, with the implication that the Titus history belongs with these others – and certainly many of these were tried favourites since the sixteenth century: *Thomas of Reading, Patient Grissil, Mother Shipton, Long Meg of Westminster, Groatsworth of Wit, Reynard the Fox.* But these works are radically different from the prose history of Titus Andronicus and do not give us normative standards by which we can judge what its author was trying to do. They show genuinely 'popular' features, which are absent from the prose history. They display a mixture of bourgeois realism and chivalric romance which allows strange or comic events to disrupt and transform the tenor of ordinary life. The Titus Andronicus history, on the other hand, has as little taste for the domestic as for the chivalric. Its handling of characters and events reflects an interest in political explanation which takes it far outside the normal definition of 'popular.' The generic focus that seems most relevant is that of history in the narrow or scholarly sense. And the author seems to be a man with an unusual grasp of later Roman history; an analysis of what is additional to the ballad story gives us a consistent image of his intention and achievement and justifies us in thinking, once again, that this is a work with its own rationale, not simply a link in the chain of versions.

'Give ear to me that Ten Years fought for Rome ... / In Rome I lived in Fame, full threescore years ... / When Rome's foes ... my sons and I were sent; / Against the Goths full ten Years weary War / We spent' – thus runs the ballad's wholly

11 *Shakespeare's Titus Andronicus, The First Quarto, 1594* 1930, p 8

traditional method of establishing place and time. The numbers are precise, but their function is not to establish precise historical data but to present traditional signals for *old* ('full three-score') and *long* ('ten Years weary War'). Note the contrast in the opening scene of the prose history:

> When the Roman Empire was grown to its Height, and the greatest Part of the World was subjected to its imperial Throne, in the Time of Theodosius, a barbarous Northern People out of Swedeland, Denmark, and Gothland, came into Italy ... under the leading of Tottilius, their King.

This author is trying to place his action inside a chronology which can be believed to be 'true.' He knows a number of relevant, and fairly obscure, names, by whose power he can give an appearance of historical accuracy to processes that are only evocative in the ballad telling. I am not, of course, claiming that the author of the prose history is a historian in the same sense as Mommsen or Gibbon. I can speak only of an appearance of accuracy, for the historical development he sets out is derived from different periods and is not an accurate depiction of any one. But the names he gives to the largely fictional or anonymous figures in the ballad are sufficiently the real names of Romans who were caught up, at one time or another, in the wars of the crumbling empire against the Goths. In the prose history the sons of the Gothic king are called Alaricus and Abonus. Alaric was of course the Gothic leader who sacked Rome in 410. His brother [in law] and successor was, however, called Adolphus, not Abonus.[12] Their father is called Tottilius, and Totila is another effectively placed historical figure. He was the king of the Goths who sacked Rome in 546, one hundred and thirty-six years after Alaric. But the situations of the two Goths were close enough to make the conflation true enough about either. Geoffrey Bullough quotes Gibbon's account of the horror in Rome when Alaric beseiged it (*Narrative and Dramatic Sources of Shakespeare* VI.9), but Gibbon's account of the siege by Totila is much closer to what is said in the prose history. Gibbon says that by

> the progress of the famine ... the poor ... were gradually reduced to feed on dead horses, dogs, cats, and mice ... A crowd of spectres, pale and emaciated ... surrounded the palace of the governor ... and humbly requested that he

12 Another possibility is that 'Abonus' is some reminiscence or distortion of Alboinus (or Albovinus), king of the Lombards in the reign of Justinian.

> would ... provide for their subsistence, permit their flight, or command their immediate execution. [The governor said he could not do this because] it was impossible to feed, unsafe to dismiss, and unlawful to kill, the subjects of the emperor. (chapter 43)

Compare with this the first chapter of the prose history:

> The Siege lasting ten Months, such a Famine arose, that no unclean Thing was left uneaten, Dogs, Cats, Horses, Rats and Mice, were curious Dainties ... most of those that were alive, looked more like Glass than living Creatures; so that ... the vulgar Sort came about the Emperor's Palace, and with piteous Cries implored him either to find some means to get them Food, to stay their fleeting Lives, or to make the best Terms he could, and open the Gates to the Enemy. This greatly perplexed him; the former he could not do and the latter he knew would only uncrown him.

I do not quote these parallel passages to argue that the prose historian must have read Gibbon. But there is a strong suggestion, in these and other matters, that he had an unusual knowledge of historical details that only became common property after Gibbon had published. Thus the opening sentence ('When the Roman Empire was grown to its Height, and the greatest Part of the World was subjected to its imperial Throne, in the Time of Theodosius ...') seems to offer us carelessly the knowledge that Theodosius was the last emperor to rule a combined empire. Theodosius the Great was in fact dead before Alaric besieged Rome; but as the story is one of imperial breakdown it seems just enough to allow him to preside over the reigns of his sons. The role of Titus in the story is parallel to that of Theodosius's great general, Stilicho the Vandal, whose campaigns seem to be remembered in the account given of Titus in the first two chapters of the prose history. The seige of Florence by Radagaisus in 406 was ended in much the same way as appears in the chap-book. Stilicho collected an army by purchase and persuasion, broke the siege, and killed the king, appearing suddenly before the walls of the city and astonishing the citizens by giving news of their salvation. In 403 Stilicho had defeated Alaric at Pollentia and captured the wife of the overthrown Gothic leader. He forced his enemy to flee through the mountains, and near Verona he defeated him again and comprehensively. In the prose history Titus defeats his Gothic enemy

('Tottilius'); 'he fled in great Confusion, and left the rich Spoils of his Camp, the Wealth of many plunder'd Nations, to Andronicus and his Soldiers.' (Compare Gibbon on Pollentia: 'The spoils of Corinth and Argos enriched the veterans of the West.') Titus and the Romans pursue the Goths through the mountains and defeat them comprehensively, killing Tottilius and capturing his queen. Only much later in both histories do the Goths recover power, and then by court intrigue, when the Roman hero, Titus or Stilicho, is overthrown by the hostility of a weak emperor, Saturninus or Honorius.

Detailed knowledge of such events in the history of the later Roman Empire was a rather rare commodity in the Elizabethan period, and the odds seem to me to lie against a chap-book writer having access to them in the years before the publication of *Titus Andronicus.* Pedro Mexia's *Historia Imperial y Cesarea* had been partly rendered into English (without acknowledgment) in Richard Reynolde's 1571 *A Chronicle of All the Noble Emperors of the Romans* (as has been pointed out to me by Professor A.R. Braunmuller). But Reynoldes, though he talks about Theodosius, 'Stilicon,' and 'Totile,' does not supply the detail, parallel to that in the prose history, which I derive above from Gibbon. These details come from a great variety of ancient sources, very few of which were available in English before 1594. One must assume either that the chap-book author was a learned man or that a learned intermediary (learned, perhaps, in 'the Italian copy printed at Rome' cited in the heading) had already digested the sources into a form which could be applied to the Titus Andronicus story.

But it is not the author's *knowledge* as a historian that gives us our principal insight into his aims in telling the story of Titus. We must, even more intently, observe his historical *attitude* as he substitutes for the impressive bareness of the ballad a system of explanations, a set of political and prudential motives, and a careful sequential ordering. The ballad simply tells us, 'When wars were done I conquest home did bring.' The historian knows that the invasions (after the Goths had seen Italy) did not end so easily. Even after the victory, the war goes on for ten years, and politics has to patch up what conquest cannot achieve. Thus the marriage of the emperor to the Gothic queen becomes what it is not in either the play or the ballad – a political act. The play makes the marriage an act of pique directed against the Andronici; the ballad simply says, 'The Emperor did make the Queen his Wife,' but in the prose history the marriage only ends the Gothic wars at the cost of promising a Gothic succession, to the scandal of the patriotic party represented by Andronicus. The hostility between Andronicus, striving to preserve Roman rule, and the queen, seeking to place Goths in all positions of authority, thus becomes a political hostility. In the ballad, the queen's hostility exists simply because her 'thoughts to murder were inclined' and the Andronici happened to be in the way. So with the murder of Bassianus:

> My Lavinia was betrothed then
> To Caesar's Son, a young and noble Man,
> Who in a Hunting, by the Emperor's Wife,
> And her two Sons, bereaved was of Life.

Once again the prose historian substitutes for ballad inconsequence (and for the play's personal relations) a wholly political motivation. Lavinia is here betrothed to the emperor's only son by a former marriage; 'The Queen of Goths hearing this, was much enraged, because from such a Marriage might spring Princes that might frustrate her ambitious Designs, which was to make her Sons Emperors.' It is only when political pressure fails that she turns to murder. And this political end seems to be sufficient satisfaction in itself, at least up to the point where the Andronicus boys, persuaded by Lavinia to look for her betrothed, 'unluckily coming in the Way where the Pit was digged, they both fell in.' It seems to be only at this point that the queen, her sons, and the Moor see the advantage of false accusations against the Andronici. And it is at this point that the prose history shows the most radical difference from the sequence of events in the ballad. The ballad is like the play in that the death of 'Caesar's son,' the accusation against the Andronici, and the rape of Lavinia form a confusedly interrelated but powerfully incremental set of events, only completed when the three heads and the amputated hand are returned to Titus and the mutilated Lavinia. This allows the play to take off into its arias of madness and despair. It is typical of the prose history that it separates out these elements and rationalizes the relationship between them. The author uses his chapter four to deal with the matter of Titus and his sons. We hear the detail of the false legal process, of the emperor's grief for his son, of the promise to spare the sons if Titus cuts off his own hand, and of the cruel hoax that returns the hand with the heads. 'Yet this was not all,' the chapter ends, 'for soon after another to be deplored Affliction followed, as shall in the next Chapter be shewn.' Chapter five is thus clear to deal separately with the matter of Lavinia. Her rape is again something that may begin by accident, but this also is given a separate and consecutive explanation. Her grief at the loss of her betrothed and her brothers leads her to frequent the lonely woods 'to utter her piteous Complaints and Cries to the sensless Trees.' This undefended loneliness is noted by the Moor and exploited by the queen's sons. And this it is (in the prose history) that is the immediate cause of Titus's madness, which affliction appears in the ballad (as in the play) after the hand and heads episode (visually powerful but less effective in telling).

In the ballad, the queen's appearance as Revenge is given a picturesque but mysterious relationship to Titus's madness:

> The Empress thinking then that I was mad,
> Like Furies she and both her Sons were glad,
> So nam'd Revenge, and Rape, and Murder, they
> To undermine and hear what I would say.

This is, as Bullough's meiotic expression has it, 'obscure.' If one does not know the play, it is difficult even to guess at what is going on. In the prose history, however, all mystery has gone; the motives behind the action have once again been rendered as explicit and political. The queen has neutered the Andronicus opposition, and now she becomes generally oppressive and impatient of *all* insubordination. No political function can be served by the bizarre visit to Andronicus, disguised as Revenge; and so this episode disappears. The plot against the sons has a straightforward basis. The 'friends' (relatives?) of Andronicus, 'finding they were in a bad Case, and that in all Probability their Lives would be the next, they conspired together to prevent that Mischief.' And so, 'lying in Ambush in the Forest when the two Sons went a hunting, they surprized them.' Then follows the cannibal banquet as in all three versions. But even at this point the prose historian manages to see the actions as part of a calculated political reality. In Shakespeare, Titus is killed by Saturninus; in the ballad, 'I stabbed ... myself, even so did Titus die.' In the prose history, however, we are given a rational explanation, as usual: 'After this, to prevent the Torments he expected, when these Things came to be known, at his Daughter's Request, he killed her; and so, rejoicing he had revenged himself on his Enemies to the full, fell on his own Sword and died.' The punctuation here raises some problems, but I think we can see what the author expects us to understand: Titus foresaw that his action against the royal family would expose his own family to judicial torture, and so he forestalled that by killing himself and Lavinia. It is entirely characteristic of this version of the story that its final action should be made a rational and self-conscious calculation. The prose historian joins other more professional historians in his effort to show that the bizarre story in the ballad is as capable of explanation as other bizarre episodes that historians (such as Gibbon) deal with, rendering the crazy actions of the present as the natural consequence of rational intentions and political understanding.

To explain both the ballad and the prose history as committed to change what they received because of the generic assumptions within which they were working avoids some rather naîve questioning of the kind of 'Why shouldn't B be more like A if it was in fact derived from it?' A more important consequence remains behind. If we see the ballad and the prose history committed to *their* generic versions, what are we to say of the version that appears in the play? If there is no reason to suppose that the play simply followed what it found in the history (no one has yet proposed the ballad as a source), we should complete this survey by considering the genre of the play seen as an independent invention, to investigate what relation can be established between that genre and the various alternative sources available to Shakespeare.

To call *Titus Andronicus* a 'Roman play' (and therefore comparable to *Julius Caesar, Coriolanus,* and *Antony and Cleopatra*) might seem to be bringing it into a league where it cannot hope to survive. If it is a Roman play it is certainly a very different kind of Roman play from these Plutarchan models. Its 'history' is impossible to locate in time, and its actions demand an extreme range of contradictory responses. This point has been wittily made by the late T.J.B. Spencer:

> Titus is a devoted adherent (not to say a maniacal one) of the hereditary monarchical principle, in a commonwealth that only partly takes it into account ... [the play] passing

> to a world of Byzantine intrigue in which the Barbarians (Southern and Northern, Moors and Goths) both by personalities and arms exert their baneful or beneficent influence. And finally, by popular acclaim, Lucius is elected Emperor ... Now all these elements of the political situation can be found in Roman history, but not combined in this way. *Titus* ... includes *all* the political institutions that Rome ever had. The author seems anxious not to get it all right, but to get it all in.[13]

As long as one can think of *Titus Andronicus* as a radically incoherent, juvenile, patched-up, or semi-revised play, or one produced by some other equally debilitating method, so long can this comic and slightly condescending view of its materials seem the right one. But if *Titus*'s manifestly 'unhistorical' Romanness is found a powerful or affecting vision of the world (as thousands found it in the great Brook-Olivier production of 1955), then Spencer's treatment seems inadequate. But the positive side of the question remains: how can the treatment of Rome in *Titus Andronicus* be described in ways that match with that theatrical experience? The second part of this paper is an effort to answer that question.

It is a commonplace of Roman history that its most admired historians presented an image of a bifurcated culture. On the one side we have an evocation of austere republican virtue, presented either in process by Livy or in retrospect by Tacitus and endlessly brought to the attention of later ages in the gallery of great ethical heroes, Scipio, Regulus, Brutus, and so on, who appeared as standard motifs in tapestries, engravings, illuminations, paintings. On the other hand we have the picture of the Roman emperors in Tacitus and Suetonius and later chroniclers ... decadent, corrupt, tyrannical, and lip-smackingly sensational (the *I Claudius* world). The problem for the inheritors of Roman Europe was to keep these two images inside a single frame, to connect Camillus with Caligula, Horatius with Heliogabalus, Cato with Commodus. This is not a problem that keeps many persons awake at night in the twentieth century, but the pressures on Renaissance writers to fulfil the promise of the Roman inheritance must have made it inescapable in the age of Shakespeare.[14] It must have been a complex business to evade

13 'Shakespeare and the Elizabethan Romans' *Shakespeare Survey* 10 (1957) 32

14 See G.K. Hunter 'A Roman Thought: Renaissance Attitudes to History

the simple perception that Henry VIII and Elizabeth (not to mention Henri IV and Charles V) were more like Tiberius or Theodoric in function than like Scipio or Brutus, their courtiers more like Petronius than Cicero; and to incorporate that political reality into the rhetoric of the republican ethos must have strained all the powers of *inventio* the Elizabethan authors possessed. It is my contention that *Titus Andronicus* shows this compacting of primitive republican virtue and decadent imperial miscegenation in a particularly obvious form, and I propose to use this perspective as a means of explicating what I take to be the purpose and shape of Shakespeare's invention.

The basic pattern of *Titus Andronicus* is supplied by material which lay close to Shakespeare's hand and has always been visible,[15] though not used (perhaps for reasons I have touched on at the beginning of this paper). If *Titus Andronicus* was written for first production in 1594 (a highly plausible proposition), it was written close in time to a much better-documented Roman work – *Lucrece*, published in 1594. The main source of Shakespeare's poem is, of course, Ovid's *Fasti;* but students of the poem point out that he also drew on Livy's account of the Lucrece story. The genre of Shakespeare's poem naturally emphasizes connection with the brilliant rhetoric of the Roman poet; but it is reasonable to suppose that the political context in Livy remained somewhere inside his mind. For Livy the rape is less a personal tragedy than a political exemplum; punishment of the royal rapist and expulsion of his family are absorbed into the larger story of unruly despotism being replaced by the rational forces of democracy and order.

The extent to which these political themes could find expression in an Elizabethan theatrical structure is made clear to us by a play based squarely on Livy's story – Thomas Heywood's *The Rape of Lucrece* (1607). Heywood begins his play with the rape's political causes. The wicked Queen Tullia is presented as a driving force behind the usurpation and parricide of Tarquinius Superbus. Her sons, the violent Sextus and Aruns (reduced from Livy's three to a more effective binary model), are

Exemplified in Shakespeare and Jonson' *An English Miscellany Presented to W.S. Mackie* ed Brian Lee, 1977, pp 93-118.

15 See (for example) J.C. Maxwell's introduction to his New Arden edition of the play (1953), p xxiv: 'it is linked in subject with *Lucrece*'; and p xxx: ' ... the story of Lucrece, which Shakespeare clearly had in mind while writing the play.'

younger versions of the same attitude to society, insanely competitive, posturing, and lustful. Opposite to these royal monsters are placed the noble families of Rome, kept by duty from tyrannicide but driven to divergent forms of passive resistance, lunacy, silence, or even song. Lucrece, as the daughter of one such nobleman (Lucretius) and the wife of another (Collatinus), is an integral member of this political group. The sexual attack on her is an attack on the whole aristocratic ethos and breaks down its *noblesse oblige* passivity, promotes the political revolution, and so establishes the great and good republic. Seen in this light the Lucrece story and the Titus Andronicus story look like alternative versions of the same archetype. In both cases we see an ambitious queen (Tullia / Tamora) with violent and ambitious sons (Sextus and Aruns / Chiron and Demetrius) encouraging a not-too-reluctant husband (Tarquinius Superbus / Saturninus) to exercise tyranny. The tyranny drives the traditional nobility (Collatinus, Lucretius, Brutus, Publicola / the Andronici) into distracted and even lunatic opposition, but which yet stops short of tyrannicide. The royal son(s)' rape of the young wife (Lucrece / Lavinia) whose husband and father belong to the opposition group is then the key event that turns opposition into bloody insurrection, ending with the establishment of a juster society.

The hypothesis that Shakespeare had the early books of Livy in his mind while writing *Titus Andronicus* seems to be borne out by some further details. In act I the sons of Andronicus demand 'the proudest prisoner of the Goths' as a religious sacrifice whose blood needs to be shed if they are to appease the spirits of their twenty-two dead brothers. For no obvious reason they drop into Latin to describe what they want:

> Give us the proudest prisoner of the Goths,
> That we may hew his limbs, and on a pile
> Ad manes fratrum sacrifice his flesh. (lines 96-8)

The Latin phrase may just be part of Shakespeare's creativity, but it sounds like a quotation, and if so it would be interesting to know where it comes from. The nearest I have found appears in Livy's book I, in the famous story of the three Horatii and three Curiatii, who fought for the precedence of Rome or Alba Longa. At the end of the combat only one Curiatius is alive. Horatius stands over him, ' ... exultans "Duos" inquit "fratrum manibus dedi: tertium causae belli huiusce ... dabo."' (Leaping up ... he said, 'I have given [or dedicated] two men to the shades of my brothers; the third I will dedicate to the cause this war is being fought for.') The grimness of the Horatius story and the grimness of the Andronicus religion certainly belong together. And other key moments in the Andronicus story seem to point to other key instances of the early Roman ethos. Titus kills his daughter to expunge her dishonour not simply on the model of Lucrece but with a direct reference to Virginius, who killed his daughter to save her from the lustful possession of Appius Claudius. He asks the emperor,

> Was it well done of rash Virginius
> To slay his daugher with his own right hand,
> Because she was enforc'd, stain'd, and deflower'd?
>
> (V.iii.36-8)

and being told that the precedent is good, he follows it. Likewise we find in Livy's story of Titus Manlius Torquatus a precedent for Andronicus's killing of his disobedient son, Mutius. The model is indeed even more extreme. Torquatus killed his son for successfully engaging in combat with the enemy after the order had been given that the army should not break ranks.

If these sources and allusions have the cumulative force I have suggested, one must allow that Shakespeare was presenting the Andronici as shaped to the model of the granitic founders of the republic, with their dedication to military discipline, to a harsh family ethic, and a contempt for individualism. But this primitive virtue is only part of the play. In the Lucrece story the disordered violence of the Tarquins is every bit as local and primitive as the ferocity for order that appears among their opponents. Shakespeare makes his picture of tyranny more colourful and yet equally authentic by feeding into it the cosmopolitan decadence of the later empire. A suggestion of the source for these effects is offered to us by the names he uses. And again we seem to find evidence of a careful attention to actual Roman history retailed by the best authorities. The name Bassianus is the most obvious clue. Many commentators have noted that Bassianus was the given name of the emperor better known as Caracalla, who reigned 211-17 AD. As long as Shakespeare is supposed to be following the chap-book, no sense of creative intent can be attached to the name; but if we think of him creating a structure out of opposed images of republican austerity and imperial decadence, then the history of the real Bassianus becomes obviously significant. Bassianus was the elder of the two sons of Septimius Severus, the younger being called Geta. The situation may have come to Shakespeare's attention in one of his favourite sources – Holinshed's Chronicles – for Severus died in Britain and the conflict between his two sons began at that point. The two sons seem to have been left with some degree of joint power (a recurrent problem in the later empire), and each, naturally enough, sought to improve his individual position by appealing to a separate constituency. Gibbon sums up their positions in a characteristic antithesis: 'The fierce Caracalla asserted the right of primogeniture, and the milder Geta courted the affections of the people' (chapter 6). It will be noticed that this is precisely the conflict that Shakespeare sets up in act I between the elder son (now called Saturninus) and the younger son (now called Bassianus). The introduction of the new name Saturninus and the switch of the name Bassianus from the fierce to the mild side, the elder to the younger son, may be due to the association of the word 'saturnine' with the planet or god Saturn, who signifies, Aaron tells us in this very play, 'a deadly standing eye ... cloudy melancholy ... fatal execution' (II.iii.30-6). In that case the appearance together of the two names Bassianus and Saturninus in the best account of the period is an extraordinary coincidence; and it may be easier to suppose that Shakespeare looked beyond Holinshed into Herodian's *History* (translated into English about 1550).[16] Herodian tells us (folio xli ff in the translation) the story of a tribune Saturninus who was sent to assassinate Bassianus and his father Severus. Instead of fulfilling the plot, he revealed it. Nevertheless Bassianus had him killed early in his reign, just about the time he killed his younger brother, in a fashion spectacular enough to justify an academic Latin play, written in the early seventeenth century.[17] It is not at all difficult to imagine a conflation of the two killings and a switch of names as a part of Shakespeare's creative process. But in the end creativity can only be

16 *Herodian of Alexandria, his History of 20 Roman Caesars* trans N. Smyth (1550?)

17 *Antoninus Bassianus Caracalla* extant in Bodleian ms Rawlinson C 590 and Harvard University ms Thr 10 1, ed W.E. Mahaney and W.K. Skinner, Salzburg Studies 52, 1976

measured by conjecture. The evidence may be plausible, but it cannot be coercive.

If I am right in my overall conjecture that Shakespeare took his image of the severe virtue of the Andronici from Livy (particularly from book I) and his picture of decadent imperial family disputes from Herodian, then one gets a good general sense of the ethico-historical structure he has set up for *Titus Andronicus.* Into the mould of the more unified Roman world of *Lucrece* he has poured much of the humanist's natural fascination with imperial wickedness, under which oppression was not merely political but insidiously anti-moral. As the well-documented case of Tiberius makes clear, the representatives of the old order were then not simply deprived of power; they had to be degraded, betrayed by their trusted associates, revealed as no better than those in charge. Flatterers, pandars, catamites, and eunuchs (even barbers) were given access to the power that was denied to a traditional aristocracy, which was compelled to praise flagrant decadence as if it represented traditional values. Shakespeare is not, of course, writing anything like Jonson's *Sejanus,* which documents the collapse of order before decadence with painstaking historical accuracy. Shakespeare invents a fable which will allow the expression of this theme by means of the popular techniques of the theatre (*Sejanus* was a theatrical failure). A set of simple opposites is used to keep the tension clear in outline though complex in detail: patriotic war against barbarians is set in opposition to miscegenation and weak acceptance of infiltration by lesser breeds; unbroken family loyalties are put against mutilating lust; political self-abnegation faces ruthless self-aggrandizement; the pieties of traditional religion are met by atheistic naturalism. And these thematic oppositions are presented here by groupings of persons with clear and differentiated natures and expectations, visible in their human and symbolic meaning to eye no less than ear.[18] Marcus is set against Saturninus, Saturninus against Titus, Titus against Bassianus and Mutius, the whole Gothic clan against the Andronicus family, Aaron and Tamora against Bassianus and Lavinia, Lavinia against Tamora with Chiron and Demetrius, Aaron

18 For an exploration of some of the ways in which stage space is used for this purpose see G.K. Hunter 'Flatcaps and Bluecoats: Visual Signals on the Elizabethan Stage' *Essays and Studies by Members of the English Association 1980* ed I.S. Ewbank, pp 16-47.

against Titus, et cetera. The loss of actuality in historical connections is compensated for by the insight we are given into recurrent meanings in Roman history. The context, in other words, is sacrificed to the basic conflict and to the violently theatrical emotions that project the conflict. The mode of the play is undoubtedly spectacular; and the Brook-Olivier *Titus* (if I may return to that touchstone) did not make its effect by denying the spectacle. My argument is that the play reveals a mind not simply seeking spectacle but everywhere using the spectacular to indicate the general lesson of Roman history and, even further, the relationship of primitive and decadent, whenever and wherever they occur. That this was a task whose achievement was entirely worthy of Shakespeare's inventive powers seems to me not to be open to doubt.

Yale University

ALEXANDER LEGGATT

Macbeth and the Last Plays

Each of Shakespeare's major tragedies takes its own distinctive risk with the genre. *Hamlet*'s central problem is not an action of the hero but his failure to act; *Othello* depends to a dangerous extent on the machinery of farce – eavesdropping, crossed wires, a missing handkerchief; *Lear* uses plot devices from Shakespeare's early comedies – the interrupted ceremony, the journey from the court to the world of nature, the convention of inpenetrable disguise.[1] *Antony and Cleopatra* takes so many risks we may wonder if it can be called a tragedy at all. In *Macbeth* there are two notable risks, and I will try to show that they are connected; the hero comes closer than any other tragic hero in Shakespeare (unless we count *Richard III*) to being a figure of pure evil; and the theatrical dimension of the play depends to a surprising degree on spectacle and supernatural machinery.

I would like to explore the distinctive achievement of *Macbeth* by what may look like a circuitous route, through the final romances (in which group I will include *Henry VIII*). If we could demonstrate that *Macbeth* was written in, say, 1613, it might well strike us as a parody of those plays, just as *Lear* seems at some points to be a grim parody of *As You Like It*. There are

All references to Shakespeare's plays are to *The Complete Works of Shakespeare* ed David Bevington, Glenview Ill 1980.

1 For an excellent discussion of *King Lear* from this point of view, see Susan Snyder *The Comic Matrix of Shakespeare's Tragedies* Princeton 1979, pp 137-79.

many tantalizing parallels. In the romances, children survive against terrible odds, beginning with Marina, born in a storm at sea at the cost of her mother's apparent death:

> A terrible childbed hast thou had, my dear;
> No light, no fire. Th'unfriendly elements
> Forgot thee utterly ... (III.i.56-8)

Posthumus is virtually born without a family: his mother dies in childbirth; his father and brothers are already dead – his very name stamps this fact on him. Perdita is born in prison and survives a tempest and a bear. The odds against Princess Elizabeth being born at all are great: in order to bring her to life England is thrown in turmoil and Christendom is split apart. The play dwells for a while on the suffering all this produces; but its final business is to celebrate the miracle. Macduff was also born against odds; but the language in which he himself describes his birth suggests not a miracle but a horrible perversion of nature: 'Macduff was from his mother's womb / Untimely ripp'd' (V.viii.15-16). When he deserts his family, his wife declares, 'He wants the natural touch' (IV.ii.9) – as though from his birth there were something not quite human about him.

The final romances are full of family reunions and miraculous returns from the dead. In *Macbeth* we see a family slaughtered – on-stage, in some productions – and in the figure of Banquo a return from the dead that suggests, like Macduff's birth, not a fulfilment of nature but a violation of it:

> The time has been
> That, when the brains were out, the man would die,
> And there an end; but now they rise again
> With twenty mortal murders on their crowns,
> And push us from our stools. (III.iv.79-83)

The wrinkles on Hermione's statue make the miracle of resurrection something natural, 'an art / Lawful as eating' (V.iii.110-11). Banquo too – but more disturbingly – returns not as a spirit but as a mortal body, bearing in his wounds the signs of his mortality. He seems not so much a ghost as a blood-stained corpse that won't lie down.

Sleep is another recurring motif. Pericles, Posthumus, and

Katharine sleep, and have benevolent visions promising future happiness. Macbeth cannot sleep – but the visions come anyway, visions of bloody daggers and clutching hands. Lady Macbeth can sleep, after a fashion; but not stay in bed or close her eyes. Her dreams are not reassuring visions of the future but broken, helpless memories of the past that still entangles her – with, for one quick moment, a glimpse of another world: 'Hell is murky' (V.i.35). In *Pericles* there is a magic doctor, Cerimon, who can bring the dead to life; Lady Macbeth's doctor is helpless and admits it. In short, motifs that will be used in the final romances to produce a sense of order and reassurance are used in *Macbeth* for an atmosphere of violation and fear.

All this may look like an application of Fluellen's critical method: there is a river in Macedon, and there is a river in Monmouth, and there is salmons in both. For all its rich variety Shakespeare's work is in the last analysis an integrated whole, and certain themes can be traced through his career – the importance of the family, the 'natural touch' and what it means, the imagination's resistance to death. It is not surprising to find that *Macbeth* shares these interests with the romances that lie – not so far, after all – in the future. For the parallels to be of special significance a stronger connection needs to be sought.

There are moments in the last plays when we seem to hear the voice not of this character or that but of the story itself. A firm narrative pattern – loss, wandering, final restoration – dominates these plays, and the characters' role in this pattern is at times more important than their psychology as individuals.[2] Thaisa's 'did you not name a tempest, / A birth, and death?' (V.iii.33-4) or the Old Shepherd's 'thou mett'st with things dying, I with things new-born' (III.iii.110-11) reduce the complex actions to a few simple principles: birth and death, loss and renewal. It is like hearing the beat behind the music. And at times we hear a different style in the writing that puts us in touch with a different level of reality – short, regular lines of rhymed verse that form a striking contrast with the free, irregular, and sometimes convoluted blank verse more usual in Shakespeare's last period. Gower, the chorus-narrator of *Pericles*, speaks this way:

2 Anne Barton has discussed speeches in the last plays that serve the dramatic situation at some expense to the consistency of the characters: see 'Leontes and the Spider: Language and Speaker in Shakespeare's Last Plays' *Shakespeare's Styles: Essays in Honour of Kenneth Muir* ed Philip Edwards, Inga-Stina Ewbank, and G.K. Hunter, Cambridge 1980, pp 131-50.

To sing a song that old was sung,
From ashes ancient Gower is come,
Assuming man's infirmities,
To glad your ear and please your eyes.
It hath been sung at festivals,
On ember-eves and holy-ales;
And lords and ladies in their lives
Have read it for restoratives. (I.chorus 1-8)

In the voice of Gower we hear, quite literally, the voice of the story, and its rhythm has the simplicity and regularity of a metronome.[3] Some of Ariel's speeches, and Prospero's epilogue to *The Tempest,* are written in a similar vein. It is a manner we have already heard in *Measure for Measure* as the duke tries to reduce the moral complexity of the action to a narrative design, a puzzle with a solution:

Craft against vice I must apply.
With Angelo tonight shall lie
His old betrothed but despised;
So disguise shall, by th' disguised,
Pay with falsehood false exacting,
And perform an old contracting. (III.i.270-5)

In *Measure for Measure,* however, the style may seem a little jarring. We are not so prepared as in the final romances for the story *as story* to assert itself so strongly.

In *The Winter's Tale* the effect comes not so much through a change of metre as through a sudden, stunning clarity when the oracle speaks out. The play is full of slow, difficult, involved writing – but the voice of the oracle is plain, terse, and direct: 'Hermione is chaste, Polixenes blameless, Camillo a true subject, Leontes a jealous tyrant, his innocent babe truly begotten, and the King shall live without an heir, if that which is lost be not found' (III.i.132-6). It may be the most un-Delphic pronouncement ever attributed to that oracle. We hear, once again, a different voice, the voice of the story itself, the beat behind the music. We hear that beat again later in the play, in the rhymed couplets of old father Time, who once more reduces the story to

3 If Shakespeare did not write Gower's early speeches, he may at least take the responsibility for leaving them as he found them; and the distinctive Gower style is found in the later scenes commonly attributed to him.

a few simple principles: 'I, that please some, try all, both joy and terror / Of good and bad, that makes and unfolds error' (IV. i.1-2).

The inner workings of the story are also revealed in the great ceremonial vision scenes in which we are given the sense of a higher power at work. Just as the characters fall into the pattern of a story, so they seem at times to be counters in a great game played by the gods themselves. These visions are usually presented as the characters' dreams; but they are also given to the audience as stage spectacle. Pericles sleeps and is visited by Diana, who tells him to go to the temple at Ephesus where he will find his lost wife. Here the vision itself is simple, and the spectacle is reserved (presumably) for the temple scene that follows. Elsewhere the connection between vision and spectacle is tighter. In *Henry VIII* Katharine falls asleep in her last illness and sees white-robed figures dancing around her and presenting her with a heavenly garland. Her spiritual reward is a compensation for her earthly loss, and her visionary triumph is contrasted with the very worldly triumph of Anne Bullen's coronation. But in the easy-going (possibly Fletcherian?) world of this play the contrast is surprisingly uncritical; each spectacle, each set of rewards, is valid on its own terms. The most elaborate of these vision scenes occurs in *Cymbeline*. There is a striking contrast between the laments of Posthumus's dead family – some of whom, like Banquo, still bear their mortal wounds – and the descent of Jupiter on his eagle from a world of light.[4] The thunderbolt that brings the ghosts to their knees dramatizes in a startling way the invasion of the mortal world by a divine power. There is a certain tension in this confrontation, unlike the smooth linking of the human and divine in *Henry VIII*. Jupiter is if anything rather testy at being called on to justify his actions. He tells the ghosts to stop complaining: he has everything in hand, and Posthumus's sufferings will lead him to happiness. He leaves with Posthumus a tablet containing a riddling prophecy that will be fulfilled and explained at the end of the play. There is a special style in the writing, heavily rhymed short lines; and again we are allowed to see the inner workings of the story. But with this revelation comes a surprise: the

4 The contrast was particularly telling in William Gaskill's 1962 production for the Royal Shakespeare Company: the ghosts were all in dark grey, with ashen faces; Jupiter and his eagle were all in gold, and his entrance was preceded by a shaft of golden light.

vision bestows on Posthumus a central importance that is not so evident in the play proper, where Imogen seems the central figure. There is a sense of dislocation, a disparity between the inner clockwork of the story as revealed in the moment of vision and the way the drama as a whole actually affects us; and this is something I will return to in *Macbeth.*

Other visions present us with a sense of ideal order in more earthly terms. The vision that Prospero stages for the betrothal of Ferdinand and Miranda gives us a world in harmony: water-nymphs dancing with harvesters suggest a harmony of the elements; the rainbow of Iris recalls God's promise to Noah; Juno descends (like Jupiter in *Cymbeline),* and she and Ceres bless the fertility of the land and of the lovers. The vision breaks up in disorder when Prospero recalls Caliban and his confederates; but for a moment we have glimpsed an ideal world in which heaven and earth, land and water, are brought together in a harmonious and fertile union. Perhaps the most engaging vision of order is presented at the end of *Henry VIII.* This is possibly Shakespeare's most spectacular play, but apart from Katharine's vision the spectacle involves not gods and spirits but the ceremonies of the court. The last ceremony is the christening of the infant Elizabeth, and after the stage spectacle of an elaborate procession Cranmer, suddenly inspired, gives us a vision of the future that makes the whole play fall into shape. As the elaborate action of *Cymbeline* is revealed as the working of Jupiter's will for Posthumus, so the recent history of England is shown to have an inner purpose: it produces the golden age of Elizabeth. Cranmer's vision of this age sums up many of Shakespeare's major concerns in the final plays and elsewhere. We have here a vision of the good social life under an ideal prince, a vision of order and harmony. And in the succession of James I – conventionally referred to as the Phoenix – we see a triumph over death as he revives the spirit of Elizabeth:

> All princely graces,
> That mold up such a mighty piece as this is,
> With all the virtues that attend the good,
> Shall still be doubled on her. Truth shall nurse her,
> Holy and heavenly thoughts still counsel her.
> She shall be lov'd and fear'd. Her own shall bless her;
> Her foes shake like a field of beaten corn,
> And hang their heads with sorrow. Good grows with her.

> In her days, every man shall eat in safety
> Under his own vine what he plants, and sing
> The merry songs of peace to all his neighbors.
> God shall be truly known, and those about her
> From her shall read the perfect ways of honor,
> And by those claim their greatness, not by blood.
> Nor shall this peace sleep with her; but as when
> The bird of wonder dies, the maiden phoenix,
> Her ashes new create another heir,
> As great in admiration as herself,
> So shall she leave her blessedness to one,
> When heaven shall call her from this cloud of darkness,
> Who from the sacred ashes of her honor
> Shall star-like rise, as great in fame as she was,
> And so stand fix'd. Peace, plenty, love, truth, terror,
> That were the servants to this chosen infant,
> Shall then be his, and like a vine grow to him.
> Wherever the bright sun of heaven shall shine,
> His honor, and the greatness of his name
> Shall be, and make new nations. (V.v.26-53)

Here the play comes close to the vision and methods of a Jacobean court masque, in which an ideal order is celebrated through poetry, music, dance, and spectacle, and all this is centred on the king himself, whose presence in the audience is the focus of the whole occasion. And perhaps in the last part of the speech in particular, with its suggestion of the immortality of true kingship, we recognize an affinity with the vision of the line of Banquo in the cauldron scene of *Macbeth.*

To some extent vision and spectacle in *Macbeth* are used, as we would expect, to create a sense of the larger social order that the hero violates by his crimes. For the Jacobean court the banquet was an occasion as significant as the masque; indeed, the two often went together. Clearly in *Pericles,* and with the effect of parody in *The Tempest,* the banquet is an important ceremony, an image of social order and celebration. Shortly after Duncan's arrival at Inverness there is a procession of servants across the stage, bearing a banquet for the king. In modern productions this is sometimes a perfunctory affair, but the opening stage direction of act I, scene vii, suggests that Shakespeare wants something dignified and impressive: '*Hautboys. Torches. Enter a Sewer, and divers Servants with dishes and service,* [and pass] *over the stage'*. The spectacle dramatizes the order that will be violated that night when the host murders his guest. The effect is clearer when Macbeth himself gives a banquet, with a forced bonhomie that shows him lacking in the true sense of occasion:

> MACBETH You know your own degrees; sit down. At first
> And last the hearty welcome. *[They sit.]*
> LORDS Thanks to your Majesty.
> MACBETH Ourself will mingle with society,
> And play the humble host.
> Our hostess keeps her state, but in best time
> We will require her welcome. (III.iv.1-6)

There is worse to come, of course: the guest of honour turns up dead; the host goes berserk, and finally the other guests are told, 'Stand not upon the order of your going, / But go at once' (III. iv.120-1).

But if the banquets suggest the social order that Macbeth violates, the effect of the spectacle in the cauldron scene is more complex and mysterious. In a way this scene corresponds to the visions of Jupiter and Diana, and the trip to the oracle in *The Winter's Tale.* Amid music and ceremony punctuated by thunder, we are given visions that put us in touch with the supernatural world and the inner workings of the story. There is also a special style, short, heavily rhymed lines, as in those moments of the final romances when we hear the beat behind the music. But this is a perverted vision scene. Instead of descending from a higher world the apparitions rise, as from a lower one. Apart from the straight warning about Macduff, they give, not a clear account of the character's destiny, but riddling hints. Like Diana and Jupiter, the last two apparitions promise happiness and security, but the promises are empty.

As so often in Shakespeare, the elements of ceremony, vision, and spectacle suggest the larger impersonal rhythms of life by which the individual characters are swept along. And the personal tragedy of Macbeth himself is contained within a larger story that, like the stories of the romances, is a comic structure – comic in the broad sense of leading to a happy ending of harmony, restoration, and order. One of the play's most intricate ironies lies in the fact that the witches are aware of this larger story; they know not only Macbeth's part in it but the parts played by Macduff and – even more important – Banquo. They admit this larger knowledge with palpable reluctance.

At their meeting with the generals, Banquo on two occasions addresses them at some length and is met with stubborn silence, whereas a short line from Macbeth is enough to set them going. When they do tell Banquo's fortune, their routine is less neat rhythmically, less well *rehearsed*, than their greeting to Macbeth:

> FIRST WITCH Lesser than Macbeth, and greater.
> SECOND WITCH Not so happy, yet much happier.
> THIRD WITCH Thou shalt get kings, though thou be none.
> So all hail, Macbeth and Banquo!
> FIRST WITCH Banquo and Macbeth, all hail! (I.iii.65-9)

This is not a part of the story they like, and they seem happy only at the end of the sequence when they can couple the names of Macbeth and Banquo in a neat ironic pattern. In the cauldron scene, when Macbeth asks about Banquo's issue, the first reply he gets is 'Seek to know no more' (IV.i.103). And yet, despite the witches' reluctance to tell the larger story, they will reveal it when compelled to do so.

The story of Macbeth is like an arc cut from a full circle; and at certain moments we get a glimpse of what the rest of the circle looks like. The most important of these is the procession of kings, the unbroken line of Banquo, that comes at the end of the cauldron scene. Macbeth recoils from it in horror:

> Thou art too like the spirit of Banquo. Down!
> Thy crown does sear mine eyeballs. And thy hair,
> Thou other gold-bound brow, is like the first.
> A third is like the former. Filthy hags,
> Why do you show me this? A fourth? Start, eyes!
> What, will the line stretch out to th'crack of doom?
> Another yet? A seventh? I'll see no more.
> And yet the eighth appears, who bears a glass
> Which shows me many more; and some I see
> That twofold balls and treble scepters carry.
> Horrible sight! Now, I see, 'tis true,
> For the blood-bolter'd Banquo smiles upon me,
> And points at them for his. (IV.i.112-24)

What Macbeth perceives is a terrifying relentlessness. (I think that is what the audience perceives as well, and this is a point I want to return to later.) But from the point of view of the larger story this is a vision of order. Though directors usually shy away from it (as they do from the processional entry of Duncan's banquet), it should have a stately, ceremonial quality. It reflects the permanence of kingship embodied in the words, 'The King is dead, long live the King.' In one sense the king never dies, though different individuals may embody him. The words of Henry V reassuring his brothers suggest this mystery, while giving it a local habitation and a (reassuringly English) name:

> This is the English, not the Turkish Court;
> Not Amurath an Amurath succeeds,
> But Harry Harry. (*2 Henry IV* V.ii.47-9)

In the presence of Banquo, still blood-stained but smiling at his posterity, there is the suggestion, as in the last plays, of a triumph over death. There is also a suggestion of fertility, as there is again later in the play when Macbeth is menaced by a green wood that comes after him. Appropriately, we have heard him complain about his fruitless crown and barren sceptre. All of this is connected with the idea of the immortality of true kingship. There is also, as in the court masques and in Cranmer's visionary speech in *Henry VIII*, a specific compliment to James I, for this is his line being shown, and the twofold balls and treble sceptres suggest the union of kingdoms under the new king. The description in act IV, scene iii, of the good king of England touching for 'the king's evil' has a similar effect; James himself, we know, performed this ceremony. And the speech of the English doctor has the same occasional, detachable quality as the speech on the imperial votaress in *A Midsummer Night's Dream*, with its obvious reference to Queen Elizabeth. It has a special value if the monarch is in the audience: 'this good king' (IV.iii.147) who cures his subjects is not just Edward the Confessor. Much has been written about the way in which *Macbeth* appeals to the interests of King James, and there is more than incidental flattery here. Shakespeare, like Ben Jonson in his court masques, uses the actual king as the focus for a vision of benevolent order not unlike the final vision of *Henry VIII*.

Affinities with the court masque and with the vision of ideal order in the romances may also help to make sense of that very difficult scene in England between Malcolm and Macduff – difficult, that is, if one approaches it as ordinary psychological realism. There are passages in the scene that, like Cranmer's vision of Elizabethan England, reflect a vision of an ideal monarch and an ideal land – but they reflect it upside-down. Malcolm lists the kingly virtues that he lacks:

> The King-becoming graces,
> As justice, verity, temp'rance, stableness,
> Bounty, perseverance, mercy, lowliness,
> Devotion, patience, courage, fortitude,
> I have no relish of them, but abound
> In the division of each several crime,
> Acting in many ways. (IV.iii.91-7)

Even when he reveals the truth about himself, he does so negatively, listing the vices he is innocent of:

> I am yet
> Unknown to woman, never was forsworn,
> Scarcely have coveted what was mine own,
> At no time broke my faith, would not betray
> The devil to his fellow, and delight
> No less in truth than life. My first false speaking
> Was this upon myself. (lines 125-31)

The psychological awkwardness of the sequence is the price Shakespeare pays for introducing an abstract vision of the ideal king; indeed, the awkwardness may be deliberate, for it suits the play to have this vision presented in a broken and refracted manner. The image of the ideal kingdom is similarly inverted in Ross's description of the nightmare that is Scotland:

> Alas, poor country,
> Almost afraid to know itself. It cannot
> Be call'd our mother, but our grave; where nothing,
> But who knows nothing, is once seen to smile;
> Where sighs and groans and shrieks that rend the air
> Are made, not mark'd; where violent sorrow seems
> A modern ecstasy. The dead man's knell
> Is there scarce ask'd for who, and good men's lives
> Expire before the flowers in their caps,
> Dying or ere they sicken. (164-73)

Fertility and security have become barrenness and death. This has the stylized exaggeration of Cranmer's speech, but it turns his vision upside-down.

In theory, the scene in England ought to be the centre of the play's positive moral vision. It is our fullest view of Malcolm, who will restore the kingdom to health; it shows the marshalling of the forces that will bring down the tyrant. Yet it is an odd, awkward, disjointed scene, full of suspicion and pain, as though Shakespeare did not want the vision of good to be too compelling. And in the sequence of quickly alternating scenes in which the invading army gathers and Macbeth prepares his defence, Macbeth is vivid and human while his enemies are oddly faceless. There is a similar effect early in the play: our strongest sense of Duncan's virtues comes not directly from anything he says or does, but in a broken, refracted way through Macbeth's horror at what it means to kill the king:

> Besides, this Duncan
> Hath borne his faculties so meek, hath been
> So clear in his great office, that his virtues
> Will plead like angels, trumpet-tongu'd, against
> The deep damnation of his taking-off ... (I.vii.16-20)

All of this alerts us to the crucial difference between *Macbeth* and the last plays: both present, through vision and ceremony, the sense of an ideal order. But while in the last plays that order is firm and clear, and confirming it is the main business of the play, in *Macbeth* the order is violated not just by the hero but, in a way, by the playwright as well: it comes to us through broken, twisted images; visions that should be reassuring are alarming; and the main business is not to save Scotland but to experience for ourselves the agony of Macbeth. In the larger story Macbeth is the villain, to be disposed of like Antiochus in *Pericles* or the Queen and Cloten in *Cymbeline* in order to produce the happy ending for the whole community. But how untrue that reading is to our actual response to the play. When in his final victory Malcolm speaks of 'this dead butcher and his fiend-like Queen' (V.viii.70), we recognize that in a narrow moral sense the description is just; and yet we resent it. It is not that we have seen virtues in Macbeth that Malcolm overlooks; it is rather that we have been too close to him, have seen his mind too clearly to be content with such an easy summary.

In the romances the rhythms of the story may seem, finally, more important than the experiences of any one character; but in the tragedies the experiences of the hero are the paramount experience of the play. The ordering of England and the dispensing of rewards and punishments are 'but a trifle' (V. iii.300) as we contemplate the final agony of Lear. At the end of *Othello*, seemingly important plot strands are tied up: Brabantio is dead, Cassio is the new governor of Cyprus – and the information seems to come to us faintly, from a great distance. In *Coriolanus* Rome itself, so solid, complex, and vitally important for most of the play, simply disappears as the hero dies alone in a strange city. So it is in *Macbeth*: though the tragic hero is a figure of practically unqualified evil, our concern is with him, and the restoration of order and decent humanity in Scotland leaves us curiously unmoved. It is not so much that we see hidden virtue in Macbeth, rather that Shakespeare forces us, to an alarming extent, to see the action through Macbeth's eyes. One simple technical sign of this is that we see the ghost of Banquo as he does; nobody else sees it, not even Lady Macbeth. I do not mean that the audience *becomes* Macbeth. There is still the detachment that drama cannot help creating; we watch him watching the ghost. But we share knowledge with him. We see into his mind as nobody else in the play does. And the procession of eight kings has an odd double effect. We recognize the image of order and stability; but Macbeth's horrified reaction also affects us, and we feel something of his panic at the relentless march of kings across the stage; against the stately tread of the procession, we feel the jagged rhythm of Macbeth's words. We know that the vision should be reassuring; but the primary effect is of alarm. Similarly, the appearance of Banquo's ghost at the banquet ought to be morally satisfying, like the appearance of Ariel as a harpy in the vision of the disappearing banquet in *The Tempest*, when the villains are given a fright and a lecture. But the scene is written to a large extent from Macbeth's point of view, and again his horror communicates itself to us. The march of Birnam wood ought to be a miraculous triumph of the green world over the wasteland, in which the followers of the new year, bearing lovely green boughs, drive out the dying god of the old year.[5] Instead, the moving grove is partly a gimmick (in the scene in which Malcolm gives the orders for camouflage)

5 For a reading of this type see John Holloway *The Story of the Night* London 1961, p 66.

and partly a nightmare (when the news is brought to Macbeth that the wood is on the march). Christopher Plummer, in the 1962 production at Stratford, Ontario, caught the latter quality exactly: anxious to confirm the messenger's report, he ran up a flight of stairs, looked out over the countryside, and then turned his face to the wall as though he had seen some unimaginable horror.

As we remain disturbingly close to Macbeth and his point of view, so we remain strangely remote from the larger story – and from the main instruments of that story, the three witches. While figures like Diana and Jupiter make a clear, strong, simple impression, there is a curiously blurred effect to the witches.[6] At the opening of their second scene, when they are off duty and sharing gossip, they seem almost human in their own repulsive way. But for the most part they are stylized, chanting figures bound by a ceremonial role. Like Gower in *Pericles* they speak a special, heavily rhymed verse and like him put us in touch, through this verse, with the inner workings of the story, the beat behind the music. Yet their ultimate role in the play is elusive: they are too closely involved with action to be simply chorus figures; and yet the nature of their involvement is surprisingly enigmatic. Whose side are they on, and what is their purpose? One would think the answers to those questions were simple enough – they are on the side of evil, and they are out to damn Macbeth. Yet if we compare them to the Vice figures of a morality play or to Mephistophilis in *Doctor Faustus,* we see that they do not have the same clearly announced motives or the same concentration of purpose. Even the prophecies in the cauldron scene are puzzling. There are two riddling pronouncements, misleading and ambiguous as we might expect; yet there is one straight, simple, and perfectly valid warning: 'Beware Macduff' (IV.i.71). And the witches are also responsible for presenting the play's strongest theatrical image of order, the show of eight kings. In a recent university production the play ended with the witches running off, giggling happily, with Macbeth's severed head. That gave them a clear motive: they collected heads. But in Shakespeare's play there is no final sense that they have a will or a purpose. They

6 As Anthony Harris has shown, the witches are not simply a dramatization of Elizabethan beliefs about witchcraft but more ambiguous figures, partly human and partly supernatural. See *Night's Black Agents: Witchcraft and Magic in Seventeenth-Century English Drama* Manchester 1980, pp 43-4.

are riddling messengers who put Macbeth in touch with his destiny and leave him to work out the consequences himself.

The remoteness of the witches from any human experience we can grasp and recognize is aided by the simplicity – the narrowness, in fact – of their language. That first scene has been much praised for the striking way in which it sets the play's atmosphere; but we should also notice the way it works together with the second scene. The witches may be elusive to us, but in their own nasty little world everything is clear and straightforward:

> FIRST WITCH When shall we three meet again?
> In thunder, lightning, or in rain?
> SECOND WITCH When the hurlyburly's done,
> When the battle's lost and won.
> THIRD WITCH That will be ere the set of sun.
> FIRST WITCH Where the place?
> SECOND WITCH Upon the heath.
> THIRD WITCH There to meet with Macbeth.
> FIRST WITCH I come, Graymalkin!
> SECOND WITCH Paddock calls.
> THIRD WITCH Anon.
> ALL Fair is foul, and foul is fair.
> Hover through the fog and filthy air. (I.i.1-12)

Beneath the atmospherics is the efficiency of a group of officers synchronizing watches. Questions are answered quickly and decisively; it is as though they have only one mind among them. (To paraphrase the gaoler in *Cymbeline* [V.iv.203-4], they are of one mind, and one mind bad.) And the scene ends with a simple inversion of language: 'Fair is foul, and foul is fair.' We may at first think of Satan's 'Evil, be thou my good.' But in Satan's attempt at inversion there is a feeling of strain, a recognition that he is trying to make language do what it cannot do, struggling with a moral universe that is to him finally intractable. The moral inversion of the witches is glib by comparison. For them, the rules are clear. In contrast, the next scene, in which Duncan receives reports of the battle, shows people getting information in a slow, confused, and contradictory way that we recognize as very human.

But most important is the contrast between the language of evil used by the witches and the language of evil used by Macbeth. Their language is simple and reductive. The ritual or ceremonial effects in the final romances suggest a heightened imagination; the rituals of the witches show an imagination not just perverted but diminished. The recipe for the witches' brew is gruesome enough, but (like many horror movies) it is picturesque rather than genuinely shocking. The language of Macbeth himself is another matter:

> How is't with me, when every noise appalls me?
> What hands are here? Ha! They pluck out mine eyes.
> Will all great Neptune's ocean wash this blood
> Clean from my hand? No, this my hand will rather
> The multitudinous seas incarnadine,
> Making the green one red. (II.ii.56-61)

After that, lines like 'Eye of newt and toe of frog, / Wool of bat and tongue of dog' (IV.i.14-15) sound tame.

When Macbeth listens to the prophecies of the witches on the blasted heath, he is like a figure in a folk-tale in which the hero is allowed three wishes. The effect is simple, stylized, and familiar. And his story is misleadingly reduced to a simple pattern: thane of Glamis, thane of Cawdor, king hereafter. But when Macbeth tries to deal with the feelings the prophecies arouse, we leave folk-tale behind. The soliloquy 'Two truths are told, / As happy prologues to the swelling act / Of the imperial theme' (I.iii.127-9) is full of uncontrollable feelings and impulses, very different from the simple idiom in which the witches set up the sequence. And we leave the folk-tale image still farther behind in the scenes between Macbeth and his lady. Lady Macbeth's brilliant combination of emotional blackmail with redefinition of value and even of language – 'When you durst do it, then you were a man' (I.vii.50) – makes this one of the great temptation scenes in literature. We see two human personalities working together in a complex and exciting way; it is a far cry from the simple image of Macbeth addressed by three witches.

When it comes to the clockwork of the story, the witches know more than Macbeth; but when it comes to the moral apprehension of evil, Macbeth knows far more than the witches. They give us a patterned and formal expression of evil, largely in externalized images – fog and filthy air, eye of newt and toe of frog. They are reductive, limited, and finally remote. But Macbeth records for us the effect of evil on a fully human mind, a mind that is aware of pity, kindness, and decency, that can see evil not as a self-contained system but as a terrible violation of a greater order. This suggests that, for all the supernatural machinery of the play, evil matters to Shakespeare most of all as a human phenomenon. And when we compare this play with the more old-fashioned plays of Shakespeare's age, we can see that his supernatural machinery is in fact quite carefully restrained. In the miracle plays, some moralities, and in *Doctor Faustus,* devils appear, complete with fireworks. Sometimes Satan himself is a character. Satan is represented in *Macbeth* only by oblique references to 'the common enemy of man' (III.i.68). In older plays we get a clear view of hell; the mouth of hell was a standard piece of scenery. In *Macbeth,* as in *Paradise Lost,* hell is murky.

There is even a sense in which Macbeth has more effect on the unseen world than the witches do. The most powerful supernatural images are not the stage effects produced on cue by the witches but the images that rise, bidden or unbidden, into Macbeth's mind. In the early scenes he calls on darkness to engulf the world, and for him it does. As he murders Duncan, the air is filled with visions and voices; we learn the morning after that even ordinary people, uninvolved in the murder, have seen strange sights. He cannot control the results of the attempted murder of Banquo and Fleance; but he can, it seems, control the atmosphere in which it takes place. Just before the murder, there is a speech in which night actually seems to come at Macbeth's command:

> Come, seeling night,
> Scarf up the tender eye of pitiful day,
> And with thy bloody and invisible hand
> Cancel and tear to pieces that great bond
> Which keeps me pale! Light thickens, and the crow
> Makes wing to th' rooky wood;
> Good things of day begin to droop and drowse,
> Whiles night's black agents to their preys do rouse.
> (III.ii.49-56)

The witches can riddle and prophesy; but Macbeth can unleash evil on the world.

Characters in the last plays find happiness through trusting the supernatural powers and doing their wills. By contrast, Macbeth's least impressive moments are when he submits to the witches, especially in the last few scenes when he clutches his prophecies as a desperate assurance of mere survival. He is most impressive when he explores, with terrible honesty, the desolation of his own mind. In the last act he alternates between the grim but authentic vision of 'Tomorrow, and tomorrow, and tomorrow' (V.v.19-28) and the empty jingling optimism of 'But swords I smile at, weapons laugh to scorn, / Brandish'd by man that's of a woman born' (V.vii.12-13). When he repeats the prophecies, he sees himself as a figure in a story, a folk-tale hero with a charmed life. But he ceases to be a free man. At the end of the play, he seizes his freedom, and it is as though he has broken loose from the story in which he had allowed the witches to trap him:

> Though Birnam wood be come to Dunsinane,
> And thou oppos'd, being of no woman born,
> Yet I will try the last. (V.viii.30-2)

He will die; but he will die on his own terms, in his own way. In the romances the final emphasis is on the integrity of the community: the group that gathers at Hermione's statue, the golden age of Elizabeth, when every man will 'sing / The merry songs of peace to all his neighbors' (V.v.35-6). But here, as in the other tragedies, the focus is on the solitary figure who wins at the last an integrity of his own.

To sum up roughly, I think we have in *Macbeth* two kinds of drama. One is a simple and in a way satisfying tale of a villain punished and a suffering kingdom restored to health and order. This tale is told through theatrical means that belong to the traditions of masque, romance, and folk-tale, the tradition of Shakespeare's last plays. Spectacle and ceremony, processions and banquets, riddles and prophecies, idealized visions of a golden world under a perfect king – these are the methods of this kind of drama. But throughout the play this tradition is introduced only to be broken, parodied, and perverted so that Shakespeare can make way for the other kind of drama, the one that really interests him in *Macbeth* – the trip inside the mind of the character who is technically the villain of the story but cannot be reduced to that alone. Chronology prevents us from calling *Macbeth* a parody of the final romances; but when Shakespeare wrote it, his imagination was, it seems, already alert to the possibilities that that kind of drama presents, possibilities that would have been suggested to him by earlier romance drama and by the court masque; and he was already starting to explore, exploit, and challenge those possibilities – as though he could not work within the form until he had broken it first.

University College
University of Toronto

JAMES M. NOSWORTHY

Macbeth, Doctor Faustus, and the Juggling Fiends

Macbeth has been called a play about damnation, and this raises the question of Shakespeare's obligations to *Doctor Faustus,* the great seminal play upon that theme. If, for many years, Shakespeare critics failed to shed much light on this matter, it was for the good reason that many of the significances of Marlowe's play had passed unrecognized. It was not until the middle of the present century that the late Sir Walter Greg, in a monumental act of scholarship, resolved the play's formidable textual problems and thereby opened up the way for a number of revelations that have a direct bearing on *Macbeth.* To say that Shakespeare went to Holinshed for the history of Macbeth but to Marlowe for the tragedy of *Macbeth* would be to exaggerate, but such a claim is not wholly without justification.

At the outset, Faustus, like Macbeth, is presented as a man of virtue whose achievements and potentialities are alike enormous. Yet his lust for knowledge, like Tamburlaine's lust for glory or Barabas's for riches, makes him vulnerable; and he is shown at a point when it is opportune for the powers of evil to launch their attack. He resolves to dedicate himself to the study of divinity, but when he turns to Jerome's Bible, he is immediately confronted with several contradictions in the scriptures. These contradictions appeal to his scepticism, to his ambition to discover what God forbids, and straightaway he rejects divinity in favour of necromancy. It is through supernatural trickery, however, that he has been led to draw a false conclusion, as

Mephistophilis reveals to him at the end of the play:

> 'Twas I, that when thou were i'the way to heaven,
> Damned up thy passage. When thou took'st the book
> To view the Scriptures, then I turned the leaves
> And led thine eye. (V.ii.90-3)[1]

If Macbeth is likewise possessed and enkindled to a crime which is alien to his heroically virtuous character – a character to which the Bleeding Captain, Duncan, and Lady Macbeth all attest – the way in which this is brought about calls for consideration. The methods employed by the Weird Sisters, though subtle to a degree, are not unfamiliar. Their initial salutation is something of a confidence trick. The First Witch's greeting is a mere statement of fact, since the thanedom of Glamis has passed in due succession from father to son. That of the Second Witch, who also employs the present tense, is likewise factual, for already in the preceding scene Duncan has condemned the treacherous thane of Cawdor and conferred his title on Macbeth. Hence the third prediction, with its very indefinite 'hereafter,' is not necessarily any more than the kind of encouraging message that fortune-tellers extract from tea-leaves. It is instructive to compare Shakespeare's presentation, which is susceptible of misinterpretation, with the forthright account given by Thomas Heywood in *The Hierarchie of the blessed Angells* (1635):

> The first of them did curtsie low, her vaile
> Vnpinn'd, and with obeisance said, All haile
> *Mackbeth Thane Glanius.* The next said,
> All haile *Caldarius Thane.* The third Maid,
> Not the least honor vnto thee I bring,
> *Mackbeth* all haile, that shortly must be King.[2]

To this Heywood adds a marginal note that Glanius and Caldarius 'were Names of Honor which *Mackbeth* had afore receiued,' thus making his version of the threefold acclamation consist of two statements of fact and one prophecy whose fulfilment is both imminent and ineluctable. Shakespeare, too, makes it clear to his audience that the Glamis and Cawdor titles already

1 *The Complete Plays of Christopher Marlowe* ed Irving Ribner, New York 1963

2 Thomas Heywood *The Hierarchie of the blessed Angells. their names, orders and offices. The fall of Lucifer and his angells* London 1635, p 508

belong to Macbeth, but, like Holinshed and unlike Heywood, he is content to assign to the Third Witch something that is a forecast rather than a prophecy. What the Weird Sisters have, in fact, set before Macbeth are two pieces of stale news and an attractive but remote prospect. He, unfortunately, does not see things in that way, nor do they intend that he should, for their acclamations are so framed as to allow ample scope for erroneous judgment. It is not only that the interpretation of any one of the salutations is largely, if not wholly, dependent upon that of the others but also that whatever conclusion is reached may be further affected by temporal ambiguity. Thus 'hail to thee, Thane of Cawdor!' (I.iii.49)[3] can be taken, thanks to omission of the actual verb, to refer to either a present or a future state, while in 'that shalt be King hereafter' (line 50), the adverb can cover anything from Heywood's 'shortly' to the distant future. It may be added that the promise held out to Banquo, 'Thou shalt get kings, though thou be none' (67-8), similarly lacks definition and thereby leads Macbeth to further error.

It is surely no coincidence that *Macbeth* and *Doctor Faustus,* two plays concerned with the destruction of the human soul, should begin with the seduction of a virtuous character through a simple trick, supernaturally operated, that relies on verbal ambiguity to promote misunderstanding which, in its turn, serves to enkindle what have hitherto been controllable, however strong, ambitions. One may of course argue that Faustus wants reason to tempt him away from faith or that Macbeth wants his wife to prick the sides of his intent (she even hints later that he has once spoken to her of murdering Duncan when neither time nor place adhered); but to make much of these possibilities would be to consider too curiously. At the outset, Faustus and Macbeth are presented as nobly ambitious men who are gulled by guileful agents of the supernatural.

There is a marked correspondence between the tempters in both plays. Valdes and Cornelius, as Greg has shown, are not themselves famous or potent necromancers; but they operate effectively as the Devil's decoys and, by playing upon Faustus's gathering ambitions, entice him to the compact with Mephistophilis. Their Shakespearian counterparts are similarly of strictly limited ability. Minsheu in his *Guide into the tongues* (1617) pro-

3 All references are to the New Arden *Macbeth* ed Kenneth Muir, London 1953.

vides a convenient summary of the status and powers of conjurers and witches:

> *the* Coniurer *seemeth by praiers and inuocation of* Gods *powerfull names, to compell the* Diuell *to say or doe what he commandeth him: The* Witch *dealeth rather by a friendly and voluntarie conference or agreement betweene him or her and the* Diuell *or* Familiar, *to haue his or her turne serued in* lieu *or stead of blood, or other gift offered vnto him, especially of his or her soule: So that a* Coniurer *compacts for curiositie to know secrets, and worke maruels; and the* Witch *of meere malice to doe mischiefe: And both these differ from* Inchanters *or* Sorcerers, *because the former two haue personall conference with the* Diuell, *and the other meddles but with* Medicines *and ceremoniall formes of words called* Charmes, *without apparation.*[4]

This seems, inter alia, to accommodate Shakespeare's witches. They are, like Major Bagstock, 'devilish tough and sly' and wonderfully colourful. They can raise winds and sail in sieves, are adept at stealing chestnuts, and can play havoc with sailors, though it seems that actual shipwreck is beyond their capabilities. Their cookery is remarkable, though the recipe is one that anyone so inclined could follow. The apparitions which rise from the cauldron and which they acknowledge as 'our master' materialize only through the vastly superior powers of Hecate:

> Upon the corner of the moon
> There hangs a vap'rous drop profound;
> I'll catch it ere it come to ground:
> And that, distill'd by magic sleights,
> Shall raise such artificial sprites,
> As, by the strength of their illusion,
> Shall draw him on to his confusion. (III.v.23-9)

All in all, the three witches have a repertoire of music-hall tricks which, when set beside the magic of Prospero, expose them as the merest of amateurs.

Lady Macbeth's role as temptress is, of course, a decisive one, but she, too, lacks authority. At base an ordinary woman, she has no vision, sees no ghosts, meets no witches, and, in the end, floats away on a stream of disconnected memories that reg-

4 John Minsheu *The Guide into the tongues* London 1617, p 90, col 2, 'Coniuration bb'

ister guilt but not remorse. She does not interest the powers of darkness, and one outstanding piece of irony in a play fraught with irony is that her impassioned pleas to the spirits that tend on mortal thoughts receive no answer. The Devil's purpose, in this play, is to corrupt the virtuous. He has neither time nor tricks to spare for someone who is very well able to proceed to hell under her own momentum.

Thus far, in both *Doctor Faustus* and *Macbeth,* the central characters have been wrought upon by internal and external forces of similar weight and character. Both now reach the major turning point at the same stage – that is, at the quarter-way mark – and with like consequences. The parallel may now seem to be about to break down, but this is not really so. The signing of a covenant and the murder of a king are, admittedly, two very different things, but both are infallible recipes for damnation. It is with Duncan's blood that the compact between Macbeth and Satan is signed. This is something that Macbeth acknowledges, both before the deed, when he speaks of the 'deep damnation of his taking-off' (I.vii.20), and after it, in accepting that he has given his eternal jewel to 'the common Enemy of man' (III.i.68). The explicit personal contact between man and devil, which is essential to *Doctor Faustus,* is not appropriate to Shakespeare's purpose, but he accommodates the unseen satanic presence in his own resourceful way by raising a storm that is remarkable even by his memorable standards:

> where we lay,
> Our chimneys were blown down; and, as they say,
> Lamentings heard i'th'air; strange screams of death,
> And, prophesying with accents terrible
> Of dire combustion, and confus'd events,
> New hatch'd to th'woeful time, the obscure bird
> Clamour'd the livelong night: some say, the earth
> Was feverous, and did shake. (II.iii.55-62)

The cataclysm is one that has no parallel either in Lennox's young remembrance or the threescore and ten years of the Old Man, who, with Ross, reveals that there had also been monstrous portents. The sheer intensity of this cosmic disorder immediately reminds us of *Julius Caesar,* but there it is occasioned by the stature of the mightiest Julius himself. The heavens themselves may blaze forth the death of princes, but there are limits which do not extend to unworldly nonentities such as Duncan. It is the satanic character of Macbeth's crime that disturbs the natural order: I do not think that derangement of this magnitude could possibly have been organized by either a nagging wife or three melodramatic witches.

The fatuous consequences of Faustus's bargain are emphasized by a dramatic ineptitude that evidently attaches far less to Marlowe than to his collaborator. The observation, in a student essay, that '*Doctor Faustus* has a beginning, a muddle, and an end' is nearer to the truth than its perpetrator, perhaps, realized. In *Macbeth* there is no muddle, and, although the tension is often relaxed, the variety of action and quality of presentation ensure that our interest is permanently engaged. This, perhaps, obscures the fact that Macbeth's inheritance of Dead Sea fruit is even more worthless than Faustus's. For him, all that ensues is futility and despair. He obtains a fruitless crown and with it a power that he no longer has the will or the ability to exercise.

Macbeth degenerates spiritually as well as mentally, and this raises the difficult question of whether, like Faustus, he takes on the infernal nature while retaining his human soul. In Marlowe's tragedy the abstruse transition is straightforwardly presented as a consequence of the bond, which has, as its first condition, *'that Faustus may be a spirit in form and substance'* (II.i.95). Though we may nowadays hesitate to accept that Shakespeare intended Macbeth to undergo a similar transformation, we must concede that Elizabethan excursions into the supernatural often disable latter-day scepticism; and this is, after all, a play lavish in its use of witches, ghosts, and infernal paraphernalia in general. There is, too, a moral in the fact that criticism has not infrequently likened Macbeth to the Satan of *Paradise Lost*. It is clear that, immediately after the murder of Duncan, something peculiar happens:

> One cried, 'God bless us!' and, 'Amen,' the other,
> As they had seen me with these hangman's hands.
> List'ning their fear, I could not say, 'Amen,'
> When they did say, 'God bless us' ...
> But wherefore could not I pronounce 'Amen'?
> I had most needs of blessing, and 'Amen'
> Stuck in my throat. (II.ii.26-32)

We recall that Claudius in *Hamlet* and Angelo in *Measure for Measure* attempt prayer vainly, but neither is deprived of the power of utterance. Macbeth, by contrast, is denied access to God, as Faustus is:

> O, he stays my tongue! I would lift up my hands, but see,
> they hold 'em; they hold 'em. (V.ii.56-7)

The implication for Macbeth is that he is now at one with Satan, that he is excluded from grace and repentance, that he is, quite simply, a damned spirit.

In the final part of the play Macbeth's demonic essence is revealed from time to time in several ways. Kittredge has remarked on the way in which he identifies himself with the lying spirits by himself continuing their oracle in rhyme. His former associates now season their habitual references to the 'tyrant' with more sinister names and, by the middle of the fourth act, the epithets are beginning to come thick and fast. He is variously designated 'a devil ... damn'd in evils,' 'devilish Macbeth,' 'Hell-kite,' 'this fiend of Scotland,' and 'Hell-hound.' To young Siward he is Satan's peer: 'The devil himself could not pronounce a title / More hateful to mine ear' (V.vii.8-9). Macduff has no illusions about the nature of his compact with the divinities of hell:

> Despair thy charm;
> And let the Angel, whom thou still hast serv'd,
> Tell thee, Macduff was from his mother's womb
> Untimely ripp'd. (V.viii.13-16)

In the end he serves that angel by pronouncing damnation upon himself and others:

> Infected be the air whereon they ride;
> And damn'd all those that trust them! (IV.i.138-9)

> The devil damn thee black, thou cream-fac'd loon!
> (V.iii.11)

> Accursed be that tongue that tells me so. (V.viii.17)

When we come to the last of these imprecations –

before my body
I throw my warlike shield: Lay on, Macduff;
And damn'd be him that first cries, 'Hold,
enough!' (V.viii.32-4)

– it is permissible, however hazardous, to wonder whether a fine demonic significance has not been lost through a printer's error. Was Shakespeare really responsible for the insignificant adjective 'warlike,' or did he, as has been plausibly suggested, write 'warlock'? The deepest damnation is of life itself. In denying that it has any meaning, he is embracing the satanic principle of universal negation which is crystallized by Goethe's Mephistopheles in the line: 'Ich bin der Geist der stets verneint.' Macbeth, too, has become the spirit that eternally denies.

This notion of a spiritually transformed protagonist may be held to rely upon evidence that is suggestive rather than conclusive. It is nevertheless well supported by Shakespeare's use of a device, that of double location, for which, once again, he was indebted to Marlowe. It is in a solitary grove near Wittenberg that Mephistophilis, when Faustus asks, 'how comes it then that thou art out of Hell?' replies, 'Why this is Hell, nor am I out of it' (I.iii.75-6). Later, in Faustus's study, he amplifies this assurance:

Hell hath no limits, nor is circumscribed
In one self place, but where we are is hell,
And where hell is, there must we ever be. (II.i.119-21)

Shakespeare, with his penchant for all kinds of double dimension, does not hesitate to thrust hell into Scotland when the occasion serves. Whether this applies to the brief, impalpable opening scene of the play is, perhaps, a moot point; but in Macbeth's first encounter with the witches, the setting, a 'blasted heath,' seems unearthly even for Caledonia, especially as Holinshed locates the meeting 'in the middest of a laund,' set amidst woods and fields. The later encounter, in act IV, is altogether more definite. It takes place, according to all editors, in a cavern or dark cave, but this merely perpetuates the dubious surmise of Nicholas Rowe. The location is obviously somewhere in Scotland, not far from Inverness and accessible for Lennox.

At the same time, it is also the pit Acheron, as Hecate has already indicated:

> get you gone,
> And at the pit of Acheron
> Meet me i'th'morning: thither he
> Will come to know his destiny. (III.v.14-17)

The duality attaching to the second meeting can surely apply also to the first one.

There has already been ambiguity of location immediately following the murder of Duncan. The tranquillity of Dunsinane turns to pandemonium in its popular and, quite probably, in its literal sense, for one can readily credit the invisible presence of thcordant character who proclaims himself to be the Porter of hell-gate. Like the grave-diggers in *Hamlet,* he is comic in manner but not in matter, and just as they gloat on the harsh realities of death, so he makes merry with the still harsher ones of damnation. It is only in the exchanges with Macduff that he is revealed as a common janitor. What his initial soliloquy seems to convey is that this is hell, nor is he out of it. His admonition comprehends the Mephistophelean fusion of servility and menace: 'I pray you, remember the porter.' We do.

The other main instance of hell's intrusion is, I think, more sinister. It is also, unfortunately, more controversial. At the end, Macbeth, in his 'valiant madness,' is left with just one follower, whose name is Seyton. The suggestion that Shakespeare intended a quibble on Satan has been ridiculed by commentators who point out that the Setons of Touch were hereditary armour-bearers to the kings of Scotland. But Shakespeare was not the man to let slip an opportunity, and there are several relevant considerations. The two names are almost, if not wholly, identical in pronunciation, and the pun is consistent with the sombre puns that occur elsewhere in the play. The dovetailing of mortal and immortal is a device that Shakespeare occasionally employs in other plays – as witness Marcade (corrupted from Mercury) in *Love's Labour's Lost,* Autolycus in *The Winter's Tale,* Eros in *Antony and Cleopatra,* and even Antony himself inasmuch as he is to be accounted a reincarnation of Hercules. There is, furthermore, the fact that Seyton's name bears a strange emphasis. It is spoken, or rather shouted, four times within the space of thirty lines; and this is odd considering that the dialogue of the play never once admits the names of Lennox, Angus, Menteith, Caithness, young Siward, Lady Macduff, or even Lady Macbeth. I suggest, then, that Shakespeare, availing himself of what was really a ready-made quibble, transformed Seyton into a dual-purpose figure who, like the Porter, goes about his modest task at one level but brings with him blasts from hell at the other.

Elsewhere there are glimpses of hell such as Lady Macbeth's recognition, as she stares into the darkness, that 'Hell is murky.' Most of these are momentary, but the long scene at the English court yields a notable synthesis. It is here that Macbeth's demonic nature is first proclaimed, but the further implication is that he is the regent of hell. In the graphic and cleverly spaced reports of both Macduff and Ross, Scotland, 'almost afraid to know itself,' is depicted as an inferno of Macbeth's making. Its horror and desolation are tellingly emphasized by reference to the miraculous offices of England's divinely ordained and divinely inspired monarch. The charge that has sometimes been brought against this whole scene, that it is tedious and in parts superfluous, is unjustified. What it affords, among other things, is a full and detached view of hell as seen from some Elysian vantage-point. It also reveals that Macbeth has advanced from particular to universal crime and that he has further degenerated from usurping tyrant to fiend incarnate. It reinstates virtue and declares war on the Devil.

Thus far I have considered those features common to *Macbeth* and *Doctor Faustus* for which Shakespeare may have been in some measure indebted to Marlowe. General comparison of the two plays shows that Shakespeare's infinitely greater skills yielded infinitely greater results. What he added were various trappings, usually satanic in orientation, which serve to enrich the texture of the play. One of these adjuncts is sustained equivocation. It goes far beyond the ambiguous assurances of the juggling fiends, covering all manner of reversals, contradictions, and oppositions, notably of fair and foul, and even extending to such sporadic intruders as the Porter, the Old Man, and the Bleeding Sergeant, who says 'Yes' when he means 'No':

DUNCAN Dismay'd not this
Our captains, Macbeth and Banquo?

SERGEANT Yes;
As sparrows eagles, or the hare the lion. (I.ii.33-5)

Another important form of augmentation is to be found in Macbeth's sequence of visions, beginning with the momentary 'horrid image' that

doth unfix my hair,
And make my seated heart knock at my ribs,
Against the use of nature (I.iii.135-7)

and moving on to the naked babe and heaven's cherubim, the air-drawn dagger, the voice that cried 'Sleep no more,' and the ghost of Banquo. It is, I suspect, mainly on the strength of these visions that certain critics have claimed that Macbeth is a poet. It is true that these passages display to perfection those transports of the imagination that are proper to poets, and also, as Shakespeare elsewhere observes, to lunatics and lovers, but Macbeth is none of these. He is, however, a man inextricably entangled with the forces of evil, and such men also have their visions or delusions, imposed from without either to entice or to torment.

The last of these satanic embellishments that I wish to consider concerns Shakespeare's use of triads. This is a topic which seems to have received comparatively little attention and has to be approached with caution, like so much that bears upon the occult. There are no grounds for supposing that Shakespeare was an ardent numerologist like, for instance, J.S. Bach; but like most Elizabethans, he would have had a working knowledge of the so-called science that dealt with the meaning of numbers. In particular he would have been fully responsive to the significance of the number three, together with its multiples, and especially its square, which Christian neo-Platonism, fortified by the doctrine of the Trinity, had systematically imposed upon practically the whole of creation, with the result that three came to be regarded as *the* mystical number. He would have known too that, despite its supernal authority, three was an essential component in various satanic practices which were impious parodies of sacred rites. There are elsewhere in Shakespeare's plays occasions when these trines figure in magical or demonic contexts, but *Macbeth* is unique in its profusion.

What the received accounts provided were three Weird Sisters who greeted Macbeth with three predictions, and there the matter ended. Shakespeare begins by adding their familiars, Graymalkin, Paddock, and Harpier, whose name is withheld until later in the play, but the fact that these number three is hardly surprising. They may, however, be regarded as a declaration of intent, for in the third scene of act I there is more ambitious supplementation. The First Witch, who is the most vocal of the three, shows a predilection for treble repetition:

> A sailor's wife had chestnuts in her lap,
> And mounch'd, and mounch'd, and mounch'd. (lines 4-5)

She too introduces the multiple – 'Weary sev'nights nine time nine' (22) – and then proceeds to use three words, 'dwindle, peak, and pine' (23), all of which mean the same thing. All three witches then wind up the charm with:

> Thrice to thine, and thrice to mine,
> And thrice again, to make up nine. (35-6)

For the meeting with Macbeth Shakespeare adjusts Holinshed's shapeless predictions so that, in the case of the First and Second witches, they accord exactly with this three times three formula:

> All hail, Macbeth! / hail to thee, / Thane of Glamis!
> All hail, Macbeth! / hail to thee, / Thane of Caw-
> dor! (48-9)

It is tempting therefore to surmise that, in the Third Witch's salutation, 'All hail, Macbeth! that shalt be King hereafter' (50), Shakespeare wrote 'hereafter' as two words, which would have been etymologically justifiable.

The later witch scenes employ similar devices. Hecate, the triple goddess, predicts with near-Euphuistic symmetry:

> He shall spurn fate, scorn death, and bear
> His hopes 'bove wisdom, grace, and fear (III.v.30-1)

and the major scene that follows begins with:

> 1 WITCH Thrice the brinded cat hath mew'd.
> 2 WITCH Thrice, and once the hedge-pig whin'd.

(IV.i.1-2)

The incantation, 'Double, double, toil and trouble: / Fire burn and cauldron bubble' (lines 10-11), is thrice repeated. There are three apparitions, two of whom use the triple formula, 'Macbeth! Macbeth! Macbeth!' and provoke the rejoinder: 'Had I three ears, I'd hear thee' (78). Macbeth's final request elicits the thrice-repeated 'Show!' and leads to the pageant of eight kings whose failure to fit into the exact pattern of Scottish history has raised problems for editors. I think that Shakespeare's concern may have been more with the cabalistic number than with historical accuracy, so that the show of eight kings plus Banquo produced the requisite nine phantasms. The vexed problem of the mysterious Third Murderer in III.iii admits of a similar resolution. It was necessary that, in a context of evil, the triadic principle should be observed. The shadowy third accomplice has a satanic aura that renders the various speculations about his identity quite unnecessary.

For the rest, triads are conspicuous in the Porter scene, where three imaginary malefactors – farmer, equivocator, and tailor – are admitted to hell, and where the Porter regales Macduff and Lennox with his exposition of the three things that drink especially provokes and the nine ways in which it equivocates with lechery before it leaves him. Significant here is his assurance that 'we were carousing till the second cock' (II.iii.25), that is, until three o'clock, since that presumably was the time of Duncan's murder. Lady Macbeth, in the sleep-walking, which occurs on the third night of watching, counts the strokes of one and two, and it is evidently on the third stroke that she concludes, 'why then 'tis time to do't.' Macbeth's meditation on the futility of life begins with the triple formula 'To-morrow, and to-morrow, and to-morrow' (V.v.19) and is expressed in terms of yesterday, today, tomorrow and fools, players, idiots. Earlier in the play, when he fails in his attempt to become a third supplicant to the Almighty, he hears the voice that cries:

> Glamis hath murther'd Sleep, and therefore Cawdor
> Shall sleep no more, Macbeth shall sleep no more!

(II.ii.41-2)

Here, as Bradley perceptively remarked, the voice 'denounced on him, as if his three names gave him three personalities to suffer in, the doom of sleeplessness.'[5] The point that must be stressed is that these triads invariably occur in contexts that are evil, and usually satanic. They attach to Macbeth, the Porter, and the murderers; to Hecate, the witches, and the apparitions, but never to the guiltless, such as Banquo, Malcolm, or Macduff.

Macbeth, then, is a fabric of Satanism unique in its complexity and intensity. Its preoccupation is with a man's appropriation by the Devil and with the fate of his immortal soul. It examines exhaustively those abuses which, according to the inflexible beliefs of its time, pre-empt damnation and shows that on the primrose way to the everlasting bonfire there are few things as innocent as primroses. Ultimately it is the most problematic of all the tragedies simply because the issues of redemption and damnation are contingent on what Milton calls 'the unsearchable dispose of Highest Wisdom,' so that we should not, even in our thoughts, dispatch Macbeth to hell unless we are completely satisfied that such is also God's intention. Though we have supped full of all the horrors that have gone to the making of 'this dead butcher,' we may not allow this to obliterate the memory of a time before those horrors began – the memory of a pre-eminent warrior who, in his innocence and integrity, was the least flawed of Shakespeare's tragic heroes. Marlowe, in his epilogue to *Doctor Faustus,* reminds us:

> Cut is the branch that might have grown full straight,
> And burnèd is Apollo's laurel bough
> That sometime grew within this learnèd man, (lines 1-3)

and this, *mutatis mutandis,* applies equally to Macbeth, whose downfall is rendered the more disturbing because at no point is he offered that grace which is available to Faustus and which he constantly rejects. In *Macbeth* the presence of Satan, with his franchise for unrestricted and, eventually, irresistible malignity, is made all the more terrible by the unbroken silence of God. If a man of heroic character is to be destroyed both body and soul through a venial fault, an astute piece of timing, a cheap trick, and an unchallenged program of malevolence, life is indeed a tale told by an idiot but signifying something worse than nothing. We may reasonably ask whether Shakespeare believed it to be God's will that the Devil should score such easy victories, or

5 A.C. Bradley *Shakespearean Tragedy* 1904; reprinted New York 1955, p 288

that a man possessed of devils should be damned for actions alien to his true nature which he has no power to resist.

Late of University College of Wales
Aberystwyth

ANNE LANCASHIRE

The Emblematic Castle in Shakespeare and Middleton

The castle – a major physical fact of life for medieval man – was also one of the most important emblematic figures in English moral literature of the medieval period.[1] Moreover, as in reality a stronghold to be defended against enemies and within which to imprison captured opponents, within a moral frame of reference it naturally had acquired a number of emblematic meanings, above all those of a / the castle of virtue (or of a virtue) or of mansoul (the soul as contained within man's body) or of the world assaulted – especially through the five senses – by vice; b / the castle of female chastity or specifically of the Virgin Mary harbouring Christ within; and c / the castle of hell, or of pride, lechery, or other vices: a castle sometimes obviously hellish, sometimes with a deceptively pleasant appearance, either forcing or enticing man to enter to imprisonment.[2] Emblematic castles good and bad – such as the Castle of Care, Tower of Truth, and Castle of Kynde in *Piers Plowman* – were ubiquitous in medieval moral and religious allegory; and the moral tradition of the castle was not confined to literature but existed as well in medieval pageantry and drama.[3] A castle apparently of

1 See eg Roberta D. Cornelius *The Figurative Castle* published dissertation, Bryn Mawr 1930, passim, and G.B. Owst *Literature and Pulpit in Medieval England* Cambridge 1933, pp 77-87.

2 Ibid

3 The castle in general was, in fact, one of the major scenic devices of English medieval art and pageantry: see G.R. Kernodle *From Art to Theatre*

virtue or of heaven, for example, with four virgins, was featured in London celebrations of 1377 at the coronation of Richard II[4]; and in the drama proper, moral use of the castle appears to have been widespread. A castle of mansoul is the thematic centrepiece of the elaborate fifteenth-century moral play *The Castle of Perseverance* – and not simply as a metaphor in the dialogue but also as an actual, major theatrical property dominating the playing area. An emblematic castle of worldliness and of female chastity is important at the start of the Digby saint's play of *Mary Magdalene* (circa 1480-1520)[5] and here too is arguably present as a physical property throughout the dramatic action. In the cycle drama of the late fourteenth to sixteenth centuries, both heaven and hell were apparently sometimes physically represented as emblematic castles,[6] as was possibly also Noah's ark (a castle of virtue-salvation).[7] Other castles which were at least partially moral emblems also appeared in the cycles; Emmaus, for example, seems regularly to have been represented as a castle.[8] Sometimes stationary and sometimes moving on wheels, the property castle, constructed basically of wood and of canvas, would have served both as a spectacular scenic reality and as a familiar moral emblem in the dramatic action.

As an emblem of virtue or of vice, or of mansoul caught

Chicago 1944, pp 76-7, and Glynne Wickham *Early English Stages, 1300-1600* vol 1, London and New York 1959, p 91.

4 See Wickham EES I, pp 54-5.

5 Here and below, play dates are from Alfred Harbage's *Annals of English Drama, 975-1700* rev S. Schoenbaum, Philadelphia 1964.

6 In the Wakefield and York cycles, for example, hell (see the Harrowing of Hell plays) clearly has both gates and walls, and can be besieged; and for hell-castle as a cycle-play norm, see the scholarship cited below in n 14. In the N-Town cycle, heaven is a high tower with gates (see Alan H. Nelson 'Some Configurations of Staging in Medieval English Drama' in *Medieval English Drama* ed Jerome Taylor and Alan H. Nelson, Chicago and London 1972, p 133; and see also Kernodle *From Art to Theatre* pp 81-2, for pageant heaven-castles).

7 Kernodle provides (fig 7, p 25) an illustration, from the Caedmon ms of ca 1000 AD, of Noah's ark as a castle.

8 See eg the York, N-Town, and Chester cycles. Also the York Entry into Jerusalem both begins (as do also the N-Town and Chester entries) and ends, as Kernodle has pointed out (p 83), with an apparent scenic castle; and the N-Town cycle also includes a castle for Herod, in its Adoration of the Magi play. This kind of castle may of course have been in large part simply an artistic convention – a way of representing a city or town (see Kernodle, p 36); but given the religious subject matter of cycle drama, it seems likely to have been a significant moral emblem as well.

between the two, the morally metaphoric castle continued into the Renaissance period in moral non-dramatic works such as Spenser's *Faerie Queene*. In the area of dramatic entertainment, by the late sixteenth and early seventeenth centuries the morally emblematic castle continued to be an important thematic and staging device in courtly and civic pageantry,[9] in part through the tradition of the tournament castle, itself sometimes emblematic from at least 1501.[10] We find, for example, a Castle or Fortress of Beauty besieged by 'Children of Desire' in a court entertainment of 1581[11]; the allegory is of course partly secular but is also in the moral tradition of the castle of female virtue or chastity. A Castle of Envy with 'hell-borne defendants' is featured in a fireworks display of 1613 to celebrate a royal marriage[12]; and, in the streets of London, a number of emblematic castles occur in Lord Mayor's shows of the early seventeenth century – for example, a Castle of Envy in Thomas Dekker's 1612 *Troia-Nova Triumphans* and a Castle of Fame and Honour as the chief device in Thomas Middleton's 1617 *The Triumphs of Honour and Industry*. As in at least some medieval drama and pageantry, these castles in courtly entertainments and in London civic shows were actual, physical structures – large stage properties visually expressing moral meaning.[13]

Castles abound in the dialogue of stage plays, especially history plays, of the late sixteenth and early seventeenth centuries; but only one of them has hitherto commonly been treated as emblematic, and then not in staging terms but only in thematic ones. Since the 1960s and the work of John Harcourt, Glynne Wickham, and others, the dialogue-established castle at Inverness in which Shakespeare's Macbeth murders King Dun-

9 See eg Wickham *EES* I, pp 225-6, though he maintains (pp 91-2) that the castle is much less used in Renaissance pageantry than in medieval.

10 For the tournament castle itself, see Wickham *EES* I, p 43, and for its sometimes emblematic nature, see below, n 13.

11 See John Nichols *The Progresses and Public Processions of Queen Elizabeth* vol 2, London 1823, pp 312-29; and see also John R. Elliott, Jr, 'Medieval Rounds and Wooden O's: The Medieval Heritage of Elizabethan Theatre,' in *Medieval Drama* ed Neville Denny, Stratford-upon-Avon Studies 16, London 1973, pp 233-6.

12 John Nichols *The Progresses, Processions, and Magnificent Festivities, of King James the First* vol 2, London 1828, p 535

13 For an extremely useful listing of a large number of castles, both realistic and emblematic, in medieval and Renaissance drama and pageantry to 1558, see the index to Ian Lancashire's *Dramatic Texts and Records of Britain: A Chronological Topography to 1558* University of Toronto Press 1983.

can has been universally recognized as a traditional hell-castle, indebted to the hell-castle of the medieval cycle drama and drawing above all on the traditional features of the cycle plays dealing with the Harrowing of Hell.[14] Wickham and John Doebler have also pointed out that the play's castle of Dunsinane, before which Macbeth is ultimately (in the play, though not historically) killed by Macduff, participates too in hell-castle tradition when Macduff, as a saviour figure, enters it and subsequently defeats the fiend-like Macbeth.[15] They have suggested that the dialogue-established castles – also including Macbeth's court at Forres – thematically merge into one[16]; and certainly Shakespeare in *Macbeth* does not seem to have been particularly concerned with realistic geography – witness, for example, the difficulties experienced by editors attempting precisely to locate I.ii and V.ix.[17] *Macbeth,* like medieval cycle drama, is simultaneously historical and universal, specific and general. Indeed, we should probably go even further in interpreting Macbeth's castle(s) as emblematic. The traditional hell-castle of Inverness, Forres, and Dunsinane doubtless incorporates too the castle in which Macduff's wife and children are slaughtered[18] as all Scotland becomes a hell under Macbeth's rule; and it also, in moral-

14 John B. Harcourt '"I Pray You, Remember the Porter"' *Shakespeare Quarterly* 12 (1961) 393-402; Glynne Wickham 'Hell-Castle and its Door-Keeper' *Shakespeare Survey* 19 (1966) 68-74, reprinted in his *Shakespeare's Dramatic Heritage* London 1969, pp 214-24; John Doebler *Shakespeare's Speaking Pictures* Albuquerque 1974, pp 132-7; Paul A. Jorgensen *Our Naked Frailties* Berkeley, Los Angeles, and London 1971, passim; etc

15 Wickham 'Hell-Castle' pp 70, 74; Doebler *Shakespeare's Speaking Pictures* pp 132-3

16 Wickham 'Hell-Castle' pp 70, 74 (implied only); Doebler *Shakespeare's Speaking Pictures* p 132. The castles merge, of course, not only through Harrowing of Hell tradition but also through techniques such as the sleep-walking scene at Dunsinane carrying us back to the murder at Inverness.

17 Editorial stage directions for I.ii, eg, sometimes place the action at the court at Forres, sometimes locate it at an army camp (whose geographical position in Scotland is also a matter of dispute). Some scholars solve the problem, deliberately or incidentally, by denying Shakespeare's authorship of the scene. See eg H.H. Furness's Variorum edition of *Macbeth* Philadelphia 1873, I.ii, textual n to modern scene heading, p 7, and appendix, p 391; and Kenneth Muir's Arden edition, London 1962, n to I. ii, p 5. J.L. Styan, *Shakespeare's Stagecraft* (Cambridge 1967), persuasively argues (like Muir) that the place of Shakespearian stage action is in general 'an irrelevance for which Shakespeare cared nothing' (p 29). For the problematic V.ix, see the nn in Muir's edn (pp 167-8) to the modern scene

ity-play tradition, becomes the castle of mansoul, or of conscience (Macbeth's), conquered by sin. The play thus metaphorically demonstrates that, as Doebler puts it, 'Macbeth ... is a resident of hell wherever he may be on earth.'[19] The final scenes of *Macbeth,* with Christian forces assaulting a non-Christian stronghold, may also owe something to the tradition of the mock battle, which sometimes featured Christian and non-Christian forces warring at a castle.[20] Shakespeare works with historical reality and with various emblematic meanings of the castle, drawing all together.

Scholars dealing with the emblematic castle in *Macbeth* have dealt with thematic interpretation only, though G.R. Kernodle has suggested in another context that the tiring-house wall at the back of Shakespeare's stage served as a castle façade in *Macbeth* V.v.[21] Given, however, the appearance of property castles both in the medieval religious drama upon which *Macbeth* is in part based and in contemporary Renaissance pageantry, we should ask whether the emblematic castle in Shakespeare's play might not also have been a major physical reality on the stage, certainly in V.v and perhaps elsewhere, too – even perhaps as metaphoric background throughout the dramatic action. The text provides no answer, nor does the lack of any castle-staging information in Simon Forman's account of a 1611 *Macbeth* performance he attended at the Globe theatre, Forman being suspect as a reliable eyewitness.[22] We are forced into pure

heading, and also the Variorum edn, explanatory nn, p 295.

18 Wickham (*Shakespeare's Dramatic Heritage* pp 224-31) points out an influence here of the cycle plays of the Massacre of the Innocents.

19 Doebler *Shakespeare's Speaking Pictures* p 135; see also Jorgensen *Our Naked Frailtie* p 139 and passim. Edmund Creeth, *Mankynde in Shakespeare* (Athens Ga 1976), argues at length (pp 40-72) that *Macbeth* is in the tradition of medieval temptation plays headed by *The Castle of Perseverance,* though he does not mention Macbeth's castles. William A. Armstrong, *Shakespeare's Typology: Miracle and Morality Motifs in 'Macbeth'* (published Westfield College [London] lecture of 2 May 1968), interprets *Macbeth* in part similarly, in pointing out (pp 11-15, 21-2) connections in *Macbeth* between hell-castle tradition and Judgment Day tradition, with Macbeth as in part a damned soul.

20 See below and n 58.

21 Kernodle *From Art to Theatre* p 138. Doebler (*Shakespeare's Speaking Pictures* p 116) speaks of Inverness castle 'insofar as it is made to exist on stage,' but does not become more specific.

22 For Forman's account, which reads more like a plot narrative than like a performance description, see the transcription by J.M. Nosworthy (pp 115-16) in '*Macbeth* at the Globe' *The Library* ser 5, 2 (1947-8) 108-18.

speculation: that a play drawing so heavily on emblematic tradition for its moral themes might well have drawn, in at least some stagings, on medieval and Renaissance emblematic stagecraft as well. Moreover, use of a formal, emblematic castle as a set background for the playing out of the dramatic action would certainly have made sense of the flow of action through the otherwise somewhat puzzlingly and discontinuously located V.v-ix.[23]

The castle of the main plot of Thomas Middleton's and William Rowley's *The Changeling* (a play often likened, as a 'tragedy of damnation,' to *Macbeth*) has for some time been recognized as not merely a (dialogue-established) location for the action but the 'dominating ... image' of the play[24] – a citadel set against the madhouse of the sub-plot, standing in part (as Vermandero's castle) for Beatrice-Joanna (Vermandero's daughter) and her innocence or chastity (in part his own virtue) and terribly revealed by the play's end as a hell of sin and damnation.[25] 'We are all ... [in hell], it circumscribes here,' comments the newly wise Vermandero in his castle (V.iii.164),[26] finally aware of his daughter's (and by implication of his own) sinfulness. The castle has been linked with the Petrarchan tradition of the castle of the beloved[27]; and it has been very generally discussed simply

Leah Scragg, 'Macbeth on Horseback' *Shakespeare Survey* 26 (1973) 81-8, argues against Forman's reliability for performance details.

23 See Muir's edn, V.v-ix and nn (pp 165 and 167-8) on the modern scene headings to viii and ix, and also the Variorum edn's textual nn at the headings to v-ix and commentary at the heading to ix (the Variorum treats viii and ix as one scene, viii, so the relevant nn and comments for ix come part way through the Variorum viii, on pp 294-5).

24 T.B. Tomlinson 'Poetic Naturalism – *The Changeling' Journal of English and Germanic Philology* 63 (1964) 648-59, esp 650; see also Tomlinson's *A Study of Elizabethan and Jacobean Tragedy* Cambridge and Melbourne 1964, pp 192-208; J. Chesley Taylor 'Metaphors of the Moral World: Structure in *The Changeling' Tulane Studies in English* 20 (1972) 41-56; and Barbara Joan Baines *The Lust Motif in the Plays of Thomas Middleton* Jacobean Drama Studies 29, Salzburg 1973, pp 99-102. Note too that the source story of *The Changeling*'s main plot (see N.W. Bawcutt's edn, Revels Plays, London 1961, pp 113-27) does *not* take place wholly at Vermandero's castle; but Middleton, except in I.i, has limited the main-plot action to the castle.

25 The castle – of seeming virtue turned to vice – is thus yet another of the play's changelings, and resembles in this respect the hell-castle of *Macbeth* (see eg Doebler *Shakespeare's Speaking Pictures* pp 114-6, 126, 132, on the fair appearance of Inverness Castle).

26 Here and below, *Changeling* quotations are from the edn by N.W. Bawcutt.

27 Thomas L. Berger 'The Petrarchan Fortress of *The Changeling' Renaissance Papers* (1969) 37-46. For a general discussion of the play's Petrarchanism,

as a seeming stronghold defeated from within.[28] *The Changeling*'s castle is, however, even more clearly the traditional emblematic castle of moral literature and drama[29] – simultaneously here the castle of female chastity (Beatrice-Joanna's)[30] and of mansoul (Vermandero's – and perhaps also Alsemero's), or of human virtue assaulted by internal enemies (man's inherent, original sins) represented above all by Beatrice-Joanna ('that broken rib of mankind' V.iii.146) and her wilfulness. In moral tradition, will is often the chief danger to the castle of virtue.[31] As the characters fall into sin, the castle becomes a hell; and *The Changeling* thus presents to us an entirely personal (or domestic) version of the political and personal hell-castle of *Macbeth*. Middleton, of course, in part through the civic pageantry that he himself wrote (including seven Lord Mayor's shows from 1613), was especially used to working with emblematic traditions, as in his Lord Mayor's show of 1617 (see above), which featured a castle. An emblematic castle is also found in his 1613 Lord Mayor's show, *The Triumphs of Truth*, and a castle variant, a battlemented Tower of Virtue, in his 1621 Lord Mayor's show, *The Sun in Aries*.[32] Middleton's pageant castles were actual structures – constructed, visual emblems. Could *The Changeling*'s castle have been so as well? – an emblematic device in front of which the strongly moral action was played out?

Other castles of English Renaissance drama doubtless also

see Robert Ornstein *The Moral Vision of Jacobean Tragedy* Madison 1960, pp 179-90.

28 Eg Tomlinson 'Poetic Naturalism' passim, and *Study* pp 192-208

29 For *The Changeling* in general as a symbolic moral play rooted in orthodox Christianity, see Penelope B.R. Doob, 'A Reading of *The Changeling*' *English Literary Renaissance* 3 (1973) 183-206, though she does not deal with the moral tradition of the emblematic castle.

30 Baines has associated Beatrice-Joanna with the castle (*The Lust Motif* pp 99-102), and has pointed out in a footnote (n 8, p 101), to support the association, the emblematic tradition of the castle as outlined by Owst (see above, n 1). Many of Berger's points (see above, n 27) about Beatrice-Joanna as a Petrarchan fortress apply equally well to Beatrice-Joanna in the moral-castle tradition.

31 See Cornelius *Figurative Castle* p 7 and chap 3, espec pp 27-8; also Owst *Literature and Pulpit* pp 80-1.

32 For all of these Middleton pageants, see Thomas Middleton *Works* ed A.H. Bullen, vol 7, New York 1964. The 1613 *Truth* castle has been thought to have been an allusion to the forts of the East India Company (see William Herbert *The History of the Twelve Great Livery Companies of London* vol 1, London 1834; reprinted New York and Newton Abbot 1968, p 200), but a moral meaning is also (and even more) likely.

have emblematic significance. John Doebler, for example, has recently suggested that Flint Castle in Shakespeare's *Richard II*, from the walls of which the defeated Richard descends, is a traditional emblematic Castle of Fortune; and John R. Elliott, Jr, has independently suggested that Flint Castle was actualized as a property on stage.[33] Moreover, at the play's end Richard is murdered in a hell-castle prison. (Compare Marlowe's *Edward II*, with its torture-murder of the king, in a castle prison, by Lightborn – that is, Lucifer.[34]) we should look more closely at other castles in Renaissance history plays. Note, for example, in relation to Shakespeare's *Henry IV* plays, that hell-tavern in moral tradition can be a 'devil's castle,' a physical location set in opposition to the castle of virtue (as, in part, in the Digby *Mary Magdalene*).[35] Court and tavern are the two chief locations of the *Henry IV* plays.

For the present, however, I want to look at the tradition of the emblematic castle in only two other Renaissance plays. Both were written by Thomas Middleton during the period of his Lord Mayor's shows with castles (1613 and 1617): *The Witch* (of circa 1609-16) and *Hengist, King of Kent* (of 1615-20).[36]

The *Witch* castle is extremely minor but shows how Middleton's mind (like the minds of at least some of his fellow dramatists) tended to function in emblematic ways. Nowhere throughout the play is a castle mentioned until, in the final scene, we are told that 'the Devill, in a Sheepe-skyn' (line 17), Antonio, has died falling through a trapdoor 'into a depth / exceeds a Temples height: Which takes into it / part of the doongeon, that falls threescore ffaddom / vnder the Castle' (2063-6). The castle reference is a narrative surprise: it has no background, no follow-up in the script. We have not been thinking of the play's action as involving castles. Clearly, for the death of his human-devil figure, Middleton has used the image of the traditional castle of hell with its battlements above

33 Doebler *Shakespeare's Speaking Pictures* pp 79-80; Elliott 'Medieval Rounds and Wooden O's' pp 245-6

34 Ironically, Edward seems at Lightborn's entrance first to expect a harrowing of hell – but the light he sees is that not of Christ but of the Devil.

35 Owst *Literature and Pulpit* p 438

36 Quotations below are from Thomas Middleton's *The Witch* ed W.W. Greg and F.P. Wilson, Malone Society Reprint, 1950 for 1948; and Thomas Middleton's *Hengist, King of Kent: or The Mayor of Queenborough* ed R.C. Bald, New York and London 1938. In quotations from *Hengist*, Bald's raised letters have here been lowered.

and dungeon below,[37] or of a tower of heaven or virtue with a hell pit beneath. Moreover, in the dungeon of the traditional hell-castle stands a boiling cauldron for the torture of damned souls[38]; and the witch scenes of Middleton's play – like those of *Macbeth* – use a cauldron, into which the sub-plot figure Almachildes – equivalent in lust to the main plot's Antonio – almost falls (385-6). (Compare the association of witches' cauldron and Macbeth's castle[s], as images of hell, in Shakespeare's play.[39]) The unprepared-for castle reference may thus surprise a modern reader, but it is in fact Jacobean dramatic shorthand and emphasizes the strongly moral and emblematic nature of the drama. Like *The Changeling* with its emblematic castle, *The Witch,* as I have pointed out elsewhere, is a work in large part about the self-destructiveness of lust, and its title refers not only to Hecate, chief character of the literal 'witch scenes,' but also to the various characters of the two main plots who, by fair means or foul, sexually 'enchant' one another.[40] Like *Macbeth,* too, it is probably a play with allusive moral and political significance.[41] Stage properties for the play must have included a cauldron (for V.iii); but presumably the unexpected 'castle' is merely an emblematic dialogue reference.

In *Hengist, King of Kent,* unlike *The Witch,* we see Middleton working out his emblematic-castle preoccupation (as in the later *Changeling*) throughout the action. Like *Macbeth,* to which it has been compared in other ways and with which it shares chronicle history as a principal source,[42] *Hengist* contains two major castles: Thong Castle, built by the ambitious,

37 See eg Wickham 'Hell-Castle' pp 70-1.

38 See eg plates I.A and II, accompanying Wickham's 'Hell-Castle' article, between pp 64 and 65, and Doebler *Shakespeare's Speaking Pictures* pp 132-3 and plate 28.

39 See eg Doebler *Shakespeare's Speaking Pictures* pp 126, 132-3; and for the cauldron as a traditional image of hell, see G.K. Hunter 'The Theology of Marlowe's *The Jew of Malta*' *Journal of the Warburg and Courtauld Institutes* 27 (1964) 234-5.

40 For both of the preceding points, see this author's '*The Witch*: Stage Flop or Political Mistake?' in '*Accompaninge the players*': *Essays Celebrating Thomas Middleton, 1581-1980* ed Kenneth Friedenreich, AMS Press 1983.

41 See my '*The Witch*.'

42 For the comparisons see eg Irving Ribner *The English History Play in the Age of Shakespeare* London 1965, pp 259-60; David L. Frost *The School of Shakespeare* Cambridge 1968, pp 56-63 (though I find his views largely unacceptable); and R.C. Bald's *Hengist* edn, pp xlvi-viii. For *Hengist*'s chronicle sources, see Bald's edn, pp xxxvii-ix.

worldly, pagan Hengist after a clever trick in acquiring land from the native King Vortiger, and Vortiger's castle in Wales, in which Vortiger, the Saxon (that is, pagan) Horsus, and Vortiger's Saxon wife Roxena all die in flames at the play's end. In *Hengist* the second castle has obvious emblematic meaning. Like Malcolm and Macduff advancing against Macbeth in Dunsinane, the virtuous Aurelius and Uther, Christian brothers of the King Constantius earlier murdered by Vortiger, advance at the play's climax against the evil Vortiger (power-hungry, lustful, and the discarder of his Christian wife Castiza for a pagan bride) in his castle; and the dialogue explicitly refers to the Day of Judgment with its destruction of the world by fire.

> VTHER My Lord the Castle is so fortifide
> AURELIUS So fortifide – lett wilde fire ruin it
> That his destruction may appeare to him
> Ith figure of heauens wrath at ye Last day;
> That murderer of our Brother ... (V.ii.2-5)

Other references to Judgment Day events also occur: to whirlwinds, to 'noise yt starts ye world,' and to hell's trumpet (V. ii.124-40)[43]; and the pagan Roxena, a 'trivmphant whore,' begins to suffer fire's torment (V. ii.162-202). Margot Heinemann has recently pointed out the probable topical connection of Roxena with the Whore of Babylon, figuring the Roman Catholic Church (opposed to the true Church of England, Castiza)[44]; and the connection should be seen as part of, and strengthening, the play's Judgment Day motif.[45] Vortiger's castle with its sinful inhabitants (Vortiger, Horsus, Roxena) thus becomes at the play's end an image of the sinful, irreligious world doomed to apocalyptic burning – just as Macbeth's castle becomes in V.v-ix of Shakespeare's play an image of hell harrowed – while the virtuous Christian characters (Aurelius, Uther, Vortiger's cast-off wife Castiza), like *Macbeth*'s Malcolm and Macduff, redeem the times and begin a new world. *Hengist*, like *Macbeth*, at its climax thus becomes an emblematic play about the self-inflicted damnation-destruction of worldliness and false religion (or of those with entirely worldly concerns) and about salvation through Christian virtue.[46]

43 For Judgment Day prophecies and signs, see eg the Chester cycle play of The Prophets of Antichrist and the Bible's book of Revelation.

44 Margot Heinemann *Puritanism and Theatre* Cambridge 1980, pp 140-1

45 Roxena, eg, like the Whore, carries a cup of gold (cf Rev 17:4) and commits fornication with (one of the) 'kings of the earth' (Rev 18:3).

Like Macbeth's castle at Dunsinane, *Hengist*'s V.ii castle of worldly power (including false religion) – and also of mansoul (Vortiger's, Horsus's, and Roxena's) damned and of seeming chastity (Roxena's) turned to whoredom – links emblematically with earlier castle(s) in the play. As in *The Changeling*, Middleton in *Hengist* is working (as was common in contemporary pageantry[47]) with two contrasting general main-plot physical and moral locations: in *Changeling*, with temple (I.i) and castle (I.ii-v), chastity-virtue in love (love 'to the holy purpose' I.i.6) is set against wilful sensuality (physical or entirely worldly love); in *Hengist*, with monastery (I.i) and castle, general spiritual and eternal concerns are set against worldly, temporal ones. And, as in *Changeling*, Middleton in *Hengist* focuses mainly upon the castle, upon human worldliness or sin. The first scene of *Hengist* brilliantly contrasts – with its procession of monks set against Vortiger and the crown he forces upon Constantius – monastery and court (that is, castle), spiritual life and worldly rule[48]; and the Thong Castle built by Hengist later in the play is the epitome of political calculation, good fortune (the pagan Saxons are all 'sons of fortune,' II.ii.39-40), and earthly ambition; it is the base upon which Hengist, the play's main-plot titular

46 Baines (*The Lust Motif* p 94) points out that *Hengist* – in spite of modern critical attention largely to Middleton's psychological insight into the sexual motivations of his characters – is a play 'characteristically medieval and not modern.' She, however, sees the play (pp 94-5) as focusing simply upon the destructive power of lust: a reading which necessitates (pp 96-7) viewing both titular heroes, Hengist and Simon (the mayor of Queenborough), as outside the main concerns of the drama. Judith Doolin Spikes, 'The Jacobean History Play and the Myth of the Elect Nation' *Renaissance Drama* 8 (1977) 117-49, does not deal with *Hengist* but interestingly suggests that Jacobean history plays in general are secular versions of older religious drama, showing history as a process of continuing warfare between good and evil, Christ and Antichrist, with the English as God's elect nation.

Armstrong's persuasive argument (see above, n 19) for a connection in *Macbeth* between hell castle and Judgment Day traditions would suggest an even closer, specific link, in this respect, between *Hengist* and *Macbeth*.

47 See eg David Bergeron *English Civic Pageantry 1558-1642* Columbia SC 1971, pp 19, 50.

48 Samuel Schoenbaum in *Middleton's Tragedies* (New York 1955, pp 75-6) and in his earlier '*Hengist, King of Kent* and Sexual Preoccupation in Jacobean Drama' (*Philological Quarterly* 29 [1950] 185) in part makes this point. We should also remember that in medieval tradition the monastery was sometimes associated with the spiritual (emblematic) castle, usually as a

hero, builds his power. It is also the image of his daughter Roxena and her supposed chastity, through whom (in her calculated marriage to Vortiger) Hengist gains political strength. When at the play's end, before Vortiger's fired castle, the dialogue refers not to a specific, real geographical location but to a universal, moral setting, the Day of Judgment, the effect is, as with the castles in *Macbeth,* that Vortiger's V.ii castle of worldly rule (including false religion and sexual sin) blends with the earlier court scenes and especially with Hengist's Thong Castle, the latter having been also linked explicitly in earlier dialogue with worldliness and the Judgment Day.

> Methinks it [Thong Castle] looks as if it mockt all ruin
> Save that greate Mrpeece of Consumation,
> The end of time, wch must Consume even ruin
> And eate that into Cinders (IV.ii.7-10).

The sinful worldliness of the play in general – including Roxena, herself a castle of whoredom rather than of chastity – is thus consumed by the Judgment Day wildfire of V.ii, as the world of fortune is defeated by godly Christian virtue. As in *Macbeth,* the personal and the political come together.

The play's double title and comic sub-plot reinforce Middleton's main-plot emblematic emphasis on the castle: on public and private worldliness, on power-hunger, false religion, and sexual appetite. The title, *Hengist, King of Kent, or The Mayor of Queenborough,* focuses our attention in the main plot(s) on Hengist, not in narrative terms the play's most important character but the play's ambitious, worldly ruler par excellence, the fortunate builder and owner of Thong Castle and the father – the literal and symbolic begetter – of the sexual enchantress Roxena, whom he uses to achieve power. In the sub-plot Simon the tanner, who, also through fortune, becomes the mayor of Queenborough, is the opportunistic and irreligious Hengist's equivalent in the everyday world of middle-class (early seventeenth-century) England,[49] with his political ambitions, his

place of virtue, set against worldly vice (see Cornelius *Figurative Castle* pp 49-57).

49 The sub-plot is clearly not set in the chronicle-history past but in contemporary England; and Heinemann (*Puritanism and Theatre* pp 144-8) suggests it deliberately parallels specific political events of the early seventeenth century. She also persuasively argues (pp 136-44) that the main plot com-

disregard of religion (see, for example, V. i.55-60), his joking about the Seven Deadly Sins (III. iii.207-37), and his ascent to wealth and office in part through using sexual appetite (see II. iii.68-70 and III.iii.142-5, 168-73). The two men – calculating and power-hungry – are associated first in the acquisition by Hengist of the land for Thong Castle, Simon readily providing Hengist with the thong; and thereafter Hengist takes a special interest in Simon. And as Hengist's ambition and irreligion lead to his ultimate destruction by his Christian enemies, so Simon's ambitious folly and foolish pride lead to his being temporarily blinded and cheated in front of his own rival and enemy, the Puritan Oliver.

Unlike the most arresting and memorable characters of the main plot – Constantius, Castiza, Horsus, Roxena, Vortiger, all (except in part Constantius) black and white moral exempla – both Hengist and Simon are above all men of worldly ambition and sexual politics, and are believably non-extreme.[50] Simon especially (with the other characters from his plot line) is from the real world, not the main-plot world of moral emblems, though through Hengist he too is associated with the emblematic Thong Castle. His worldly ambition and manoeuvring are limited by his everyday circumstances; and his ultimate fall is partial only, as he finds himself deceived by travelling players. Simon, as an everyday parallel to Hengist (who is himself more 'ordinary' than his main-plot fellows), helps to relate the main-plot emblems and characters to the personal, religious, and political world of Middleton's audiences.[51] Simon is real, comic – and disquieting, as we see in him a wholly believable example from the middle classes of the ambition, irreligion, and folly which in the main plot lead inevitably to tragedy in a final moral Judgment.

The castle(s) of *Hengist* raise an important question about the staging of the play – and, by extension, about the staging of other Renaissance plays, such as *Macbeth*, with emblematic castles. Clearly some sort of castle is physically realized on stage at

ments on early seventeenth-century political-religious controversy.

50 Baines points out (*The Lust Motif* pp 96-7), eg, that the stories of Hengist and of Simon are 'dull' in comparison with those of the other main-plot characters. Moreover, in the main plot, we never see Hengist (unlike Vortiger, Horsus, and Roxena) going to dark extremes, except for his treachery in IV.iii.

51 See also above, n 49.

the end of *Hengist*, for the sinful characters appear above on its walls and are there burned.[52] The castle could have been simply the playhouse gallery (permanent, or a temporary structure erected for *Hengist* only); and the fiery finale could have been symbolically staged with, for example, streamers of red cloth or with one or more actors appropriately costumed.

> ROXENA Oh for succor
> Whose neere me, help me, saue me, ye flame
> Itts ye figure of poore Vortiner ye Prince
> Whose life I tooke by poyson (V.ii.146-49).

But medieval cycle pageants of the world's end and the judgment of souls featured, at least in Coventry – where the plays continued to be staged until 1579 – an apparently spectacular, staged destruction of the world by literal fire.[53] And just as *Macbeth* is linked above all not only in dialogue and in plot to Harrowing of Hell tradition but also in stage effects – knocking, comic porter figure, castle entrances by Macduff, references to sounds, and so forth – to the Harrowing of Hell plays (and others) of the medieval mystery cycles, so *Hengist* is probably linked with Judgment Day tradition not only through explicit dialogue references but also, as far as possible, through staging. We have already noted the general use of scenic castle devices in the medieval cycle drama; and John R. Elliott, Jr, has recently suggested that the Renaissance history play (to which genre *Hengist*, despite its additional fictional material, belongs) developed from the spectacular staging of medieval religious drama and routinely made use of its large stage properties, such as castles.[54] David Bergeron has also argued for a general influence of

52 Certainly Roxena is burned; presumably, in the end, Vortiger and Horsus must be too, since the entire castle is being destroyed by wildfire.

53 Records of the Coventry Drapers, who were responsible for the Coventry cycle's Judgment pageant, include payments for setting the worlds on fire and for a link (torch) to set the worlds on fire (in 1563, 1565, 1567, 1568, 1569, 1571); and the same conflagration is doubtless also included in other years in general payments for keeping hell-mouth and/or fire (in 1561, 1562, 1566, 1570, 1572, 1573). I am grateful to Prof R.W. Ingram and to the Records of Early English Drama project for allowing me to consult the REED *Coventry* records volume (University of Toronto Press 1981) at the copy-editing stage. (Appendix 2 to the volume contains further mid-sixteenth-century references to setting the world on fire, from an antiquarian transcription of a Drapers' account book.)

54 Elliott 'Medieval Rounds and Wooden O's' pp 223-46. Wickham also

Renaissance pageantry on the public-theatre drama of the period[55]; and fireworks and spectacular staged burnings of castles took place in at least three major pageant entertainments of 1610-13 in London,[56] while Middleton himself included in his first Lord Mayor's show, the 1613 *Triumphs of Truth*, a grand climax of a conflagration: Truth's companion, Zeal, burning with flames shot from his head the chariot of Error and its accompanying beasts. (A castle apparently stands present throughout this scene.) Such effects, too, may not even have been unusual in the theatre proper of the late sixteenth and early seventeenth centuries. In the late 1580s and early 1590s, for example, Christopher Marlowe, a dramatist heavily influenced by earlier dramatic traditions, called for various kinds of fire effects in four of his plays (*Dido, Jew of Malta, Doctor Faustus,* and most notably *2 Tamburlaine,* with its burning town [III.ii] and apparent on-stage burning of two bodies [III.iv]); and R.C. Bald cites in his 1938 edition of *Hengist* (page 124) two seventeenth-century stage plays with fire/firework effects. We must certainly consider the possible original use in *Hengist* of a large castle property or structure which was at least in part fired for a spectacular climax to the play. Perhaps hence, in part – as Bald long ago suggested about the fireworks only – the play's extraordinary seventeenth-century popularity.[57] And perhaps also, through this staging, a reinforcement of what Heinemann has recently found to be the political and religious topicality – involving Protestant-Catholic conflict – of *Hengist*: for in at least three entertainments for royalty in 1610-13 the grand finale consisted of the destruction – in two cases involving fireworks – of a Turkish (that is, non-Christian) castle by Christian forces: a visual exhibition of Christianity (true religion) triumphant over paganism (false religion).[58] A major impulse behind the creation of *Hengist*

argues the second point, about Renaissance drama in general, in eg *Early English Stages, 1300-1660* vol 2, pt 1, London 1963, pp 280-323.

55 Bergeron *English Civic Pageantry* p 1

56 See Nichols *King James* II, 322-3 (a water battle and fireworks involving the blowing up of a castle, 6 June 1610, at the Creation of Prince Henry); II, 532-5 and 538 (fireworks involving castles fired, 11 Feb 1613, at the marriage of James I's daughter Elizabeth); and Thomas Dekker's 1612 London Lord Mayor's show, *Troia-Nova Triumphans* (which includes a Castle of Envy with fireworks).

57 See Bald's edn, pp xiv-xv.

58 See Nichols *King James* II, 323 (mock battle, merchants – presumably Christian – against Turks: Creation of Prince Henry, 1610); II, 528-9 and

may thus even have been the emblematic mock-battle castle – rooted in tournament tradition – with its associations of political-religious warfare.

If a large castle structure was used for the last scene of *Hengist*, would it have been brought on stage only for that scene (doubtless on wheels, like castles in the London Lord Mayor's shows of the period), or would it have been brought on earlier to represent Thong Castle as well or perhaps to remain emblematically on stage throughout the action, an ever-present symbol of the play's moral concerns? Kernodle, Wickham, and others have suggested that the English Renaissance stage may have been richly emblematic, with stage façade or large properties used to achieve almost the effect of medieval simultaneous staging[59]; but John Elliott has suggested more recently that large wood and canvas castle properties were wheeled on and off stage as required.[60] Different kinds of staging may have been used in different theatres, by different acting troupes, and for different plays; and in *Hengist* the specifics of castle staging are perhaps irrelevant. A large castle property for *Hengist*, however managed – either on stage throughout the play or moved in and out – would have effectively emphasized the symbolic nature of the drama. *Hengist*, like *Macbeth*, is a drama obviously both historical and moral, specific and universal, and more significantly emblematic than realistic.

A stage castle for *Hengist*, 1615-20, would strongly suggest the use of an emblematic castle property also for the earlier *Macbeth* (1606?), which *Hengist* in part imitates in other ways, and the later *Changeling* (1622). (Middleton was a playwright

539-41 (mock battle, Christians against Turks: marriage of the Princess Elizabeth to the Protestant Elector Palatine, 1613); II, 538 (fireworks display, Christians against Turks: marriage of the Princess Elizabeth, 1613). Religious warfare in pageantry was traditional: eg, the London Midsummer Watch of 1521 included a castle with defenders against a Turkish horseman in pursuit; a royal pageant of 1518 at Greenwich included a castle and knights who fought against Turks; and in 1581 at Leith in Scotland a Pope's castle on boats on the river was assaulted and fired. See *Calendar of State Papers* (Venetian) vol 3: 1520-1526, London 1869, no 244, pp 136-7; *Calendar of State Papers* (Venetian) vol 2: 1509-1519, London 1867, no 1088, pp 466-7; Anna Jean Mill *Mediaeval Plays in Scotland* St Andrews University Publications 24, Edinburgh and London 1927, p 55 and n 3.

59 See eg Wickham *Shakespeare's Dramatic Heritage* chap 8, esp pp 139-45 (properties); Kernodle *From Art to Theatre* esp pp 130-53 and 217-19 (façade); J.L. Styan *Shakespeare's Stagecraft* pp 30-1.

60 Elliott 'Medieval Rounds and Wooden O's' passim

prone to self-imitation.) We can perhaps never know what was originally done; but we should at least consider the possibility that emblematic staging was used for all three of these plays concerned, like so much of medieval religious drama (staged emblematically and simultaneously), with the damnation and salvation of man's soul. Moreover, given the round central structure of *The Castle of Perseverance* staging plan, and similar round castles in some medieval and Renaissance art,[61] it is also interesting to contemplate the possibility of some *round* emblematic castles on the Renaissance stage. The circle, after all, is a central image in *The Changeling*: from the circle of perfection, which Alsemero initially uses to figure his intended marriage to Beatrice-Joanna, to the circle of the game of barley-brake and of earthly hell, in which all the characters find themselves by the play's end, and including the ring imagery discussed in detail by a number of scholars.[62] *Hengist*, too, is a play with significant circle imagery, linked with the play's emphasis upon fortune (emblematically associated with a wheel), from the prologue's reference to the audience itself circling the stage to (immediately) the crown Vortiger forces upon Constantius (a round 'mark of fortune' I.i.66), to the figure of Fortune in dumb show, between I.i and ii, holding a 'golden round,' to the historical detail of the acquisition by Hengist of land for the building of Thong Castle: as much land as could be encompassed by a thong of leather. And Vortiger, besieged finally in his castle by Uther and Aure, speaks of his enemies and/or deserts which 'in a dangerous ring Circle my safetye' (V. ii.50). A final ring restores order to the world of the play: Aurelius's ring sent to free Castiza and her father and uncle (V. ii.206-8). No such imagery looms large in *Macbeth*: but a round, emblematic hell-

61 See eg Samuel C. Chew *The Pilgrimage of Life* New Haven and London 1962, fig 57 (a 1556 rounded Castle of Knowledge); and Doebler *Shakespeare's Speaking Pictures* p 80 and plate 14 (a sixteenth-century round Italian Castle of Fortune). Merle Fifield, 'The Arena Theatres in Vienna Codices 2535 and 2536' *Comparative Drama* 2 (1972) 259-82, prints six miniatures of what she believes to be arena theatres with a central round-castle structure; and the N-Town Play of the Adoration of the Magi also speaks, perhaps literally, of a round castle of Herod – as Nelson points out, 'Some Configurations of Staging' p 141.

62 See eg Normand Berlin 'The "Finger" Image and Relationship of Character in *The Changeling*' *English Studies in Africa* 12 (1969) 162-6; Dorothea Kehler 'Rings and Jewels in *The Changeling*' *English Language Notes* 5 (1967-8) 15-17; and J. Chesley Taylor 'Metaphors of the Moral World' pp 43-6.

castle would nicely parallel the round hell-cauldron of the witch scenes.[63] And, of course, a round on-stage castle would also reflect both the ring of the audience circling the playing area (see the *Hengist* prologue, lines 5-6) and the essentially round, castle-like structure of the public playhouse itself – a visual detail helping to extend the thematic impact of the play into the real world of its audience.[64]

Even without a round castle structure on stage, of course, the playhouse itself would in part become, for *The Changeling* and less obviously for *Hengist*, the hell of the sinful world circumscribing us, the audience, here. Shakespeare's *Richard II* finally, offers a related round castle: not merely Flint Castle itself (possibly staged as appropriately round, as – like Thong Castle – the Castle of Fortune Doebler suggests[65]) but a metaphoric round castle standing for temporal, fallible man himself.

> ... for within the hollow crown
> That rounds the mortal temples of a king
> Keeps Death his court ... ;
> Infusing him [the king] with self and vain conceit,
> As if this flesh which walls about our life
> Were brass impregnable; and, humour'd thus,
> Comes at the last, and with a little pin
> Bores thorough his castle wall, and farewell king!
> (III.ii.160-70)[66]

This kind of castle may even be suggested also in the *Hengist* prologue (lines 5-6). In the postlapsarian world, all men exist

63 See above, n 39.

64 This effect of hell-within-hell-within-hell is paralleled in medieval and Renaissance art: see Doebler *Shakespeare's Speaking Pictures* plate 28, and pp 132-3.

65 Though, however, Doebler interprets Flint Castle (pp 79-80) as an emblematic Castle of Fortune and provides an illustration (plate 14) of a round Castle of Fortune in a sixteenth-century Italian woodblock, he does not suggest a round, on-stage property in *Richard II* but states that the play's castle walls would be 'represented by the upper stage of the public playhouse' (p 79).

66 Quoted from Peter Ure's edn, New Arden Shakespeare, London 1961

precariously within round castles, mocked by fortune and ultimately by death, until 'that great masterpiece of consummation' finally arrives to change the temporal to the eternal.

University College
University of Toronto

JAMES C. BULMAN

Coriolanus and the Matter of Troy

I

Shakespeare lived in an age that still had access to heroic traditions. The codes of chivalry were not long dead – still lived, in fact, in men such as Philip Sidney; and schoolboys were versed in Homer and Virgil, Ovid and Seneca. Historians could therefore draw ready correspondences between history and myth. Holinshed could characterize figures of the recent past as epic conquerors; Daniel could write of English paladins out of whose deeds 'new immortal *Iliads* might proceed'[1]; and North could employ a Homeric idiom, even quote the great heroic poets directly, to define the natures of Plutarch's noble Greeks and Romans. History, for the English, existed on a continuum with classical mythology; the popular legend of Brute's founding of Troynovant attests to that. But perhaps Heywood, in *An Apology for Actors,* accounts for the genesis and transmission of heroism most succinctly. The process, he suggests, is one of emulation: one learns to pattern one's behaviour on the admirable performance of heroes past. The 'bold English man' of 'our domesticke hystories' patterned his great deeds on those of ancient heroes such as Alexander, just as Alexander was inspired by even more

1 Samuel Daniel *The First Fowre Bookes of the Civile Wars Between the Two Houses of Lancaster and Yorke* London 1595, IV, p 42; cited in *Narrative and Dramatic Sources of Shakespeare* ed Geoffrey Bullough, London 1962, IV, p 421

ancient models: 'had Achilles never lived, *Alexander* had never conquered the whole world.'[2] Elizabethans thus honoured the conventions of epic mythology in their histories and created a heroic reality firmly predicated upon fiction. Myth and history merged to make legend, and historical figures acquired the patina of their bronze-age prototypes. In the Elizabethan imagination, Henry V *was* an Alexander; Talbot *was* a Hector; Essex, at least for Chapman, *was* an Achilles.

The dramatist's problem of how to depict a hero is different from the historian's, however. His art is more mimetic than narrative: if he attempts to create a hero of real flesh and blood – even stage blood – some of the mythic patina is bound to be sullied. How, then, is he to dramatize heroism? If he resorts to a series of conventions and stock scenes to define the hero, as many of Shakespeare's predecessors did, he risks caricature and destroys mimetic credibility. But without reference to those conventions, his risk is just as great; for he must find new criteria unrelated to stage tradition by which an audience can appraise heroism. The hero must virtually create himself, without the benefit of stage heroes past; and in two hours' traffic, that feat is well-nigh impossible – even for a hero.

The verisimilitude of Shakespeare's tragic heroes thus depends inevitably on their relationship to heroic tradition. Shakespeare could not, like Swift's spider, spin new forms of heroism out of the web of his imagination without recourse to the ancient matter that had shaped his audience's expectations. Indeed, he relied heavily on those expectations; in each of his heroic plays he incorporated allusions to and conventions from his literary and dramatic heritage to serve as models from which to evolve a more authentic representation of heroism. From the play's formal relationship to tradition emerges its reality; in the hero's personal response to it resides his.

The representational power of any work of art springs only indirectly from its truth to life, more directly from its struggle to embrace and at the same time transcend the literary models that once served to represent life. As Howard Felperin has recently argued, 'The notion that poetry imitates "life" leads

2 This passage from Thomas Heywood, *An Apology for Actors* (1612), is quoted more fully in two recent works that deal with the literary and dramatic background of Elizabethan heroic drama: David Riggs *Shakespeare's Heroical Histories* Cambridge Mass 1972, pp 7-9, and Eugene Waith *Ideas of Greatness* London 1971, p 83.

nowhere, in so far as we have no way of conceiving of, much less comprehending, life except through the mediation of sign systems ... that is to say, through the necessary aid of art.'[3] Each new work must incorporate models that provide mimetic points of reference; by discarding them, it may achieve a greater illusion of reality. A credible representation of heroism, therefore, would require a 'restless dialectic between convention and the repudiation of convention' and expose as inadequate, however necessary, 'the established and stable forms of prior art and the life they can but stiffly gesture toward' (Felperin, pages 9-10).

Shakespeare, near the end of his career, found a precise dramatic analogue for the way in which we, as audience, perceive a work of art in the 'restless dialectic' with which characters in *Coriolanus* respond to the conventions of heroism. Volumnia, gloating that the wounds her son brings home from war will amply persuade the citizens to elect him consul, defends the legitimacy of convention to define his heroism.

> O, he is wounded, I thank the gods for't ... I'th'shoulder and i'th'left arm. There will be large cicatrices to show the people, when he shall stand for his place. (II.i.116, 141-3)[4]

Outward shows of honour reflect intrinsic merit, she seems to say; and Rome had codified this assumption in a ceremonial peep-show wherein the warrior donned a gown of humility, showed his wounds to the citizens, and thereby won their voices. The citizens require the mediation of such 'established and stable forms' to affirm the reality of the hero, whereas he, who declares that such forms have become meaningless, repudiates them and attempts simply to play 'the man I am' (III.ii.16) as if the reality of his manhood were theatrically unprecedented. The patricians accept these forms as necessary signs of an intrinsic merit and reward them with a leap of faith: Coriolanus is their god. The tribunes, however, regard them as shams, glorified by the patricians in order to keep the citizenry in awe but

3 *Shakespearean Representation: Mimesis and Modernity in Elizabethan Tragedy* Princeton 1977, p 39. Felperin owes something to the studies by Walter Jackson Bate and, more psychoanalytically, Harold Bloom, of the writer's struggle to overcome the 'anxiety of influence' of previous writers; but Felperin's concern, like mine, is not so much with the psyche of the writer as with the ways in which the works themselves incorporate and reshape previous works.

4 All quotations are from the New Penguin edition, ed George Hibbard, Harmondsworth 1967.

inadequate to represent a man's true nature – especially Coriolanus's. We, as audience, may choose to respond to the heroic conventions with simple assent, like the citizens, or simple dissent, like Coriolanus; or we may choose, like the patricians and the tribunes, to respond in a more complex fashion. The fact that the play dramatizes all those options would seem to suggest that the most fitting response would embrace and and transcend them all; in other words, it would require a continuous 'restless dialectic' within us between assent and dissent, faith and scepticism. Our choice – and ultimately our attitude towards the hero and all he does – depends on our ability to pick up the dramatic cues Shakespeare offers us; and that ability presuppposes a familiarity with heroic tradition.

II

A brief look at *Coriolanus*'s allusion to the matter of Troy will reveal how complex Shakespeare's use of heroic tradition could be. It was not unusual for heroic plays to allude to the Trojan War: the legend had, after all, been passed to the Renaissance through various medieval redactions and was a staple of any schoolboy's curriculum or any reader's list of fovourite romances. Thus, when Volumnia casts herself as Hecuba to her son's Hector –

> The breasts of Hecuba,
> When she did suckle Hector, looked not lovelier
> Than Hector's forehead when it spit forth blood
> At Grecian sword, contemning (I.iii.41-4)

- an audience would at once have understood her to mean that Coriolanus embodied the virtues of valour, constancy, and fortitude belonging to the noblest Trojan of them all. With customary pro-Trojan bias, medieval English writers transformed Homer's Hector into a paragon of chivalric virtue. Chaucer considered such virtue to be above might in his 'parfit knight':

> Of Ector nedeth it namore for to telle:
> In all this world ther nys a bettre knyght
> Than he, that is of worthynesse welle;
> And he wel moore vertu hath than myght.
> (*Troilus and Criseyde* II.176-80)[5]

Lydgate more classically emphasized Hector's prowess; but his imagery of light, redolent of Christian texts, tempered such prowess with virtue:

> This Priamus hadde childre many on,
> Worthi pryncis, & off ful gret myht;
> But Ector was among hem euerichon
> Callid off prowesse the lanterne & the lyht;
> For ther was neuer born a bettir knyht.
>
> (*Fall of Princes* I.5930-4)

This tradition enabled Shakespeare to invoke Hector in his earliest plays as an exemplary blend of manly strength and Christian courtesy. The Countess of Auvergne taunts Talbot with a diminutive comparison:

> I thought I should have seen some Hercules,
> A second Hector, for his grim aspect
> And large proportion of his strong-knit limbs.
>
> (*1 Henry VI.* II.iii.19-21).[7]

The comparison succeeds in raising Talbot to a plateau of legendary heroism; and it also puts Hector in the company of a demigod and elevates his heroism to mythic proportions. King Henry imagines Hector as the supreme defender as he apotheosizes a departing Warwick: 'Farewell, my Hector, and my Troy's true hope' (*3 Henry VI* IV.viii.25); and it is as a city's champion, too, that Marcus conceives of Titus Andronicus as 'the Roman Hector' (IV.i.88).[8] So secure was Hector's reputation, in fact, that Shakespeare could easily afford to parody his achievements in

5 In *Chaucer's Major Poetry* ed Albert C. Baugh, New York 1963

6 John Lydgate *Fall of Princes* ed Henry Bergen, Washington DC 1924-7. See also a comparable passage in Lydgate's *Troy Book,* a work to which Shakespeare had frequent recourse. Lydgate and Caxton, the other source for most of Shakespeare's 'siege' material, based their accounts indirectly on the spurious eye-witness accounts of Dictys (fourth century, pro-Greek) and Dares (sixth century, pro-Trojan), literary impostors who supplanted Homer during the Middle Ages and who, in their conflicting biases, helped to create ambiguities in later attitudes towards Homeric heroes.

7 All quotations from the *Henry VI* plays are taken from the New Arden editions, ed Andrew S. Cairncross, London 1957, 1962, 1964.

8 See the Signet Classic edition of *Titus Andronicus* ed Sylvan Barnet, New York 1964.

the pageant of the Nine Worthies in *Love's Labour's Lost*, where, as played by the braggart Armado in wretched rhyme, Hector –

> the heir of Ilion;
> A man so breathed, that certain he would fight, yea
> From morn till night, out of his pavilion (V.ii.650-2)[9]

- challenges Costard-Pompey to a duel, ostensibly to defend the honour of his lady, the pregnant Jaquenetta, but in fact to defend himself from the charge of having gotten her with child. The burlesque of chivalry implicit here demonstrates to what extent Hector had been transformed into a medieval knight.

To understand the conception of Hector that informed Shakespeare's allusions to him in *Coriolanus*, however, one must turn to *Troilus and Cressida*. In that play, Shakespeare assumes that the audience will bring traditional expectations to the matter of Troy; and on that assumption he creates a tension between those expectations and actual performance, between conventional heroic evaluations, which he carefully preserves, and a context that explodes those evaluations.

It is usually assumed that in *Troilus* Shakespeare treats Hector no more seriously than the other heroes: not as an epic warrior whose death is tragic in any real sense but as parody of those blindly heroic knights who trod the boards in earlier, popular plays. Hector, after all, keeps company with fools on both sides: with other Trojans such as Paris, whose knightly mount only Helen can appreciate, and Troilus, who swaggers himself out on's own eyes; and with Greeks such as Ajax the dolt, Achilles the vain, and a host of generals in whose mouths epic diction becomes mere fustian. In Hector, it would follow, Shakespeare ridicules chivalric excess, as though he were little changed from Armado's lampoon. The chief evidence for this interpretation lies in the contradictory stand Hector takes during the Trojan council scene. To Troilus's claim that 'particular will' determines value, that simply a commitment to Helen makes her worth defending, Hector rejoins, ' 'Tis mad idolatry / To make the service greater than the god' (II.ii.56-7)[10] and refers instead to the 'moral laws / Of nature and of nations' (lines 184-5) to fix a more absolute value. Helen, he argues,

9 See the Signet Classic edition, ed John Arthos, New York 1965.
10 All quotations are from the Signet Classic edition, ed Daniel Seltzer, New York 1963.

must be returned: reason refutes the romantic claim that a commitment alone can make a worthless object worthy.

Yet the truth of such reasoning is something to which Hector cannot subscribe. In a sudden and, to some critics, a satirically devastating about-face, he forsakes reason to embrace Troilus's subjective idealism:

> Hector's opinion
> Is this in way of truth. Yet ne'ertheless,
> My spritely brethren, I propend to you
> In resolution to keep Helen still;
> For 'tis a cause that hath no mean dependence
> Upon our joint and several dignities. (II.ii.188-93)

Hector in fact admits to having already sent 'a roisting challenge' among the Greeks in the name of his lady (Andromache this time, not Jaquenetta), a challenge that undermines the basis of his argument that Helen is not worth fighting for. Fighting in the name of woman is exactly what Hector commits himself to, and in the most chivalric of terms (compare I.iii.264ff). His choice of particular will is deliberately wrong-headed; we search in vain for a credible motive. Some critics have levelled against him a serious charge of dissembling, of playing devil's advocate; others have found in him a consistent love of sport, as much in intellectual as in physical combat.[11] Neither motive satisfactorily explains his behaviour. If we expect psychological verisimilitude and weigh his actions in light of the 'reason' he has acknowledged to be 'truth,' we are stymied. It is easy, then, to resort to the explanation that Hector is another butt, a caricature of errant chivlary.

Shakespeare may have had something else in mind. Hector may defy our conventional expectations because he acts not according to the logic of the individual psyche, which we are accustomed to applying to Shakespeare's heroes, but according to the symbolic logic of the play's broader concerns. Douglas

11 Mark Sacharoff, in 'Tragic vs. Satiric: Hector's Conduct in II.ii of Shakespeare's "Troilus and Cressida"' SP 67 (1970) 517-31, attempts to clear Hector of the imputation that his having issued a challenge to the Greeks undermines his argument against Troilus. The challenge, he argues, was issued in sport during a truce; it was not intended to result in the decisive encounter that Caxton and Lydgate make of it. Sacharoff's is perhaps the most ingenious way of getting Hector off the hook that critics have yet devised.

Cole vigorously defends Hector's reversal as 'not without purpose. On a dialectical level, it confirms the impotence of ethical truth in the face of a seductive and destructive myth of honour and dignity.'[12] Alan Dessen, identifying a morality-like structure in the council scene, suggests that Hector's reversal represents reason's inability to 'stand up against the siren call of Honour,' its psychological motivation subordinated to its function in the Trojan psychomachia.[13] Both critics understand Hector as a figure drawn from a more allegorical than representational mode of drama. In the fashion of earlier dramatists, Shakespeare externalizes Hector's character. Hector has no inner life: he is insensible to contradiction, suffers no internal warfare, fails to engage in reflective soliloquy as Shakespeare's thinking heroes do. The mimetic mode Shakespeare employs to convey his heroism is far simpler and more conventional than that he employs for, say, Troilus; and if we understand the requirements of that mode, our expectation of psychological verisimilitude fades.

Hector becomes the emblem for constancy to an ideal that Troilus longs to be. Going off to battle despite the prophetic dreams and warnings of his family, he embraces Troilus's romantic creed –

> Life every man holds dear; but the dear man
> Holds honor far more precious-dear than life (V.iii.27-8)

- and takes a vow to fight that is as sacred to him as Troilus's vow to love Cressida: 'The gods have heard me swear' (line 15); 'I must not break my faith' (71). It is revealing that Hector manifests his constancy in devotion not to another character, for that would have required some psychological development, but

12 'Myth and Anti-Myth: The Case of "Troilus and Cressida"' SQ 31 (1980) 81

13 The quotation is from a paper Dessen submitted to a seminar on Shakespeare's characterization at the meeting of the Shakespeare Association of America in San Francisco in April 1979. 'Hector's about-face is crucial for the scene and for the play as the major demonstration of the mentality behind the keeping of Helen and a series of later choices about Cressida, "fair play," and honour,' he writes. 'Our logic of psychological realism and "consistency" may be inadequate to deal with a larger theatrical logic based upon surprise and upon an ensemble display of a Trojan mind rather than the mind of a single "character."' Dessen develops the idea that this scene adopts the technique of the 'stage psychomachia' in *Elizabethan Drama and the Viewer's Eye* Chapel Hill 1977, pp 152-4.

to a code of behaviour inherent in knighthood-courtesy.

Hector tends to project his ideal courtesy on to others and to assume they will abide by its rules. Realizing that he is to be pitted against his own cousin Ajax, son to Hesione, he declares that theirs will be only a 'maiden' battle and refuses to shed familial blood. Unlike Caxton, who harshly concludes that Hector's courtesy to Ajax cost Troy the war, Shakespeare does not suggest that this encounter is decisive. In fact, he treats Hector's courtesy with delicacy and admiration. Even the Greeks, who scorn chivalry, praise Hector's courtesy. Ajax transcends his own boorishness to say, 'Thou art too gentle and too free a man' (IV.v.138); and if there is a tinge of criticism here, there is none in Nestor's apotheosis of Hector as a 'Jupiter' who deals life, not death, in battle (line 190): 'I wish my arms could match thee in contention, / As they contend with thee in courtesy' (204-5).

The context of the Trojan War, to be sure, makes such courtesy a bit preposterous. In act V a disillusioned Troilus, even while admiring Hector's clemency in the abstract, condemns it as 'fool's play' in practice (iii.43). Troilus takes his cue from Caxton who, echoing Virgil, inveighs against Hector's offer to do Ajax's pleasure: 'Non est misericordia in bello That is to say ther is no mercy in bataill.'[14] Troilus finds finds in Hector's courtesy a kind of hamartia: 'Brother, you have a vice of mercy in you, / Which better fits a lion than a man' (lines 37-8), an analogy that ennobles Hector's character even as it disparages his wisdom. When, in the alliterative language of an antique revenger that Troilus will shortly become, he urges Hector to 'leave the hermit pity' and to let 'The venomed vengeance ride upon our swords, / Spur them to ruthful work, rein them from ruth' (45, 47-8), Hector calls him 'savage.' Troilus defends himself with the realist's answer – an answer that Hector, whose reality extends no farther than his emblematic function permits, of course cannot understand: 'Hector, then 'tis wars' (49).

Our response to Hector's courtesy, then, is ambivalent. Although it is shown to be a foolish way to deal with Greek faith, it nevertheless is a valiant attempt to create constant value. Achilles, in his discourteous vaunting, has given Hector fair warning that he will not subscribe to the chivalric code; yet Hector, true to the code, allows Achilles to escape when he has

14 Caxton *Recuyell of the Historyes of Troye* ed H. Oskar Sommer, London 1894, II.589-90

him down. Achilles insults him: 'I do disdain thy courtesy, proud Troyan' (V.vi.15). Hector's naîveté thus appears all the more wilful when he assumes shortly thereafter that Achilles will offer him a courtesy in kind: 'I am unarmed; forego this vantage, Greek' (viii.9). This assumption epitomizes Hector's faith that the world will conform to his standard of conduct, a faith more naîve than Troilus's faith that Cressida will be true. Yet the faith is a part of chivalric intention; there is dignity in its formal simplicity; and when Shakespeare gives us no reason to expect that Hector should move beyond the bounds of that convention, we would be wrong to ridicule him for staying within it.

By the time Troilus accuses Hector of having a 'vice of mercy,' Hector has assumed the mantle of idealism that Troilus in despair has cast off:

> No, faith, young Troilus; doff thy harness, youth.
> I am today i'th'vein of chivalry.
> Let grow thy sinews till their knots be strong,
> And tempt not yet the brushes of the war.
> Unarm thee; go, and doubt thou not, brave boy,
> I'll stand today for thee and me and Troy. (V.iii.31-6)

The language could not be clearer. Hector is moving further and further into the realm of allegory, carrying the significance of both Troy and Troilus on his shoulders. He is their prince, their champion, who in defying augury for the sake of worldly honour is ripe for a fall in the *de casibus* tradition of Lydgate's *Fall of Princes.*

The context of Hector's death reinforces that tradition. It places him in the antique world of the early chronicle plays, in which the hero could die simply by falling from his high place without having to suffer any psychological dilemma. Hector's death had served as a model for the death of York narrated in *3 Henry VI*:

> Environed he was with many foes,
> And stood against them, as the hope of Troy
> Against the Greeks that would have enter'd Troy.
> (II.i.50-51)

Rhyming couplets give a formality to Hector's death that underscores its function as an emblem, like Talbot's and Hotspur's, for the fall of chivalry; and this formality parodies the mode of tragic expression Shakespeare had used in his early histories.[15] In a more comic context, Hector's lines might have been spoken by Bottom's Pyramus:

> Now is my day's work done; I'll take my breath.
> Rest, sword; thou hast thy fill of blood and death.
> (V.viii.3-4)

The context here, however, is not comic; and if the antique style tends to detach us from the substance, it does not make us ridicule the substance any more than it would in a chronicle play. Achilles adds to the formality by personifying Troy as the corpse of her fallen hero:

> So, Ilion, fall thou next! Come, Troy, sink down!
> Here lies thy heart, thy sinews, and thy bone.
> (V.viii.11-12)

We may recall Talbot who, in defining his heroic identity as an emblem for England's might, invokes the army as 'his substance, sinews, arms, and strength' (II.iii.62). In both cases, the representative of chivalry is swept up in the grip of forces greater, if less courteous, than himself.

In Hector's death Shakespeare creates an enclave of medievalism that requires us to confront heroic conventions head-on. It is tempting, of course, to try to smooth out the play's troublesome tonal shifts by applying uniform, satirical criteria to all the heroes: such a view necessarily assumes that Shakespeare exaggerated and deformed conventions to make Hector a butt of ridicule and his death, heroic burlesque. An alertness to Shakespeare's employment of conventions in context, however, suggests that Hector's chivalry, though insufficient to hold its

15 In *Shakespeare's Problem Plays* (Toronto 1949, p 85) E.M.W. Tillyard marks the chronicle-play style of the play's last scenes. 'It is natural enough for Shakespeare to be compressed and staccato or stylised' when dealing with such a mass of 'antique matter,' he writes; and citing Achilles' last lines to Hector, he observes that 'Achilles's brutality reminds Shakespeare of the Wars of the Roses, where the decencies of chivalric warfare had been forgotten.'

place in modern warfare, may not be as ridiculous as contemporary opinion has judged it to be. Those conventions are an acceptable dramatic means of representing a legendary heroism that, even if displaced by more complex modes of mimesis, still could function legitimately on the Elizabethan stage. Hector's death is tragic according to values that its morality-like formalism of presentation permits us to accept. It does not contradict but rather complicates the play's assessment of those values as inadequate to define a tragic heroism such as we look to find in a more psychologically developed character.

III

When Volumnia brags that Coriolanus is her Hector, she raises problems; for Coriolanus is far from a medieval knight, and his isolation, pride, and wrath – the manifold descriptions of his metallic hardness, his inhuman, almost godlike strength to run reeking o'er the lives of men – have prompted one critic to identify him instead with Homer's Achilles.[16] But there is no evidence, in any of his previous plays, that Shakespeare derived his *Iliad* matter from sources other than Caxton, Lydgate, and their ilk. He even ignored Chapman's recently published *Seauen Bookes*, though he may have read them, when writing *Troilus and Cressida*. Thus there is little reason to think that he would suddenly, at the end of his career, have traded a medieval for a more classical conception of Homer's heroes. On the contrary, I find evidence that he distinctly recalled scenes from his own

16 Reuben Brower, in *Hero and Saint: Shakespeare and the Graeco-Roman Heroic Tradition* Oxford 1971, pp 359-75. Coriolanus's choler and impatience, his bloodiness and aloneness, the link between his heroic energy and love for his mother, and his shifting from rage to sorrow all bring Homer's Achilles to Brower's mind. The analogies are strong, but they remain analogies; Brower provides no substantial evidence that Shakespeare's imagination totally displaced its earlier conception of Achilles for a purer Homeric Achilles. And the fact remains, of course, that Shakespeare calls Coriolanus a Hector more than once – never Achilles. Brower shifts his ground and admits to seeing a strain of Homer's Hector in Coriolanus as well. In the climactic scene of his capitulation, Coriolanus 'like Hector ... sees his son as the reincarnation of his own heroism' (p 368). 'In the play, where the bond with the mother is so central to the hero's character, the son is the first to kneel, and in the wholly new passages between Coriolanus and his son, the parallel to Hector suggests that in a domestic and "natural" moment Coriolanus becomes less Achillean' (p 379).

Troilus when writing *Coriolanus* and an examination of these recollections may help to clarify the way in which Shakespeare created Coriolanus's heroic authenticity.

Though his stoic fortitude puts him in a world apart from chivalry, Coriolanus shares Hector's concept of honour as an absolute commitment to one's purpose. His trust in a bond of friendship with his fellow warriors, and in particular in his fraternal vows with Cominius, owes something to the courtesy that knights honoured in one another:

> I do beseech you
> By all the battles wherein we have fought,
> By th'blood we have shed together, by th'vows
> We have made to endure friends, that you directly
> Set me against Aufidius ... (I.vi.55-9)

Coriolanus may not talk of pavilions and entering the lists, but his desire to fight only the bravest man is analogous to Hector's challenge, broadcast among the Greeks to rouse Achilles from his torpor, and to his blunter request to Achilles:

> I pray you, let us see you in the field.
> We have had pelting wars since you refused
> The Grecians' cause. (*Troilus and Cressida* IV.v.265-7)

Coriolanus, of course, does not fight in the name of his lady, unless that lady be his mother. But he does look on Aufidius, as Hector looks on Achilles, as someone with whom he shares a community of heroic values that transcend party lines. He sins in envying Aufidius's nobility: 'And were I anything but what I am, / I would wish me only he' (I.i.229-30). Coriolanus's praise of his enemy grows more hyperbolic, perhaps more chivalric, when he thinks, as Hector does, of war as a sport:

> Were half to half the world by th'ears and he
> Upon my party, I'd revolt, to make
> Only my wars with him. He is a lion
> That I am proud to hunt. (lines 231-4)

It is natural, then, that when banished from Rome, Coriolanus seek his world elsewhere in a union with Aufidius and, out of courtesy, offer him either his throat or his service. Aufidius responds with a courtesy that would have warmed the cockles of a Trojan heart:

> Let me twine
> Mine arms about that body, whereagainst
> My grainèd ash an hundred times hath broke
> And scarred the moon with splinters. Here I clip
> The anvil of my sword, and do contest
> As hotly and as nobly with thy love
> As ever in ambitious strength I did
> Contend against thy valour. (IV.v.109-16)

In time, Aufidius will fail to honour the love he here professes – a breach of courtesy much like Achilles' that will dissever bonds of heroism that Coriolanus thought had wedded them forever. Echoes of *Troilus and Cressida* point up Coriolanus's inability to come to terms with such inconstancy in a fellow warrior. Aufidius himself, when they fight, casts him in an antique role – and, by implication, casts himself as Achilles –

> Wert thou the Hector
> That was the whip of your bragged progeny,
> Thou shouldst not scape me here. (I.viii.11-13)

Herein lies the importance of our knowing not just Homer but Shakespeare's own revision of the Troy legend; for he patterns Coriolanus's relationship with Aufidius after his own, not Homer's, conception of Hector's relationship with Achilles, the death of Coriolanus after his own conception of the death of Hector.

In the selfsame moment that he calls Coriolanus a Hector, Aufidius identifies in himself a motivation that makes him kin to Achilles. 'Not Afric owns a serpent I abhor / More than thy fame and envy' (I.viii.3-4), he confesses; and we recall Achilles' similar concern for his suffering reputation, 'My fame is shrewdly gored' (III.iii.228). Each one is motivated less by a faith in intrinsic value than by a desire to win fortune in men's eyes, for which the tangible signs of success, whether or not they represent true heroic achievement, are a *sine qua non.*

It takes just this one additional defeat at Coriolanus's hands to convince Aufidius that an *appearance* of honour counts for more than the thing itself. Weighing the Achillean option – wrath or craft – he marks his own fall to policy:

> Mine emulation
> Hath not that honour in 't it had; for where
> I thought to crush him in an equal force,
> True sword to sword, I'll potch at him some way
> Or wrath or craft may get him. (I.x.12-16)

Even this early in the play, he warns us that, like Achilles, he will disdain courtesy – in this case, the laws of hospitality, decidedly medieval laws for a Volscian – to indulge a private revenge:

> Where I find him, were it
> At home upon my brother's guard, even there,
> Against the hospitable canon, would I
> Wash my fierce hand in's heart. (I.x.24-7)

We must look on with suspicion, then, when he embraces Coriolanus like a bride on his threshold. He may recognize in Coriolanus an absolute merit, a 'sovereignty of nature' (IV.vii.35) that remains constant despite the whims of popular judgment; but he recognizes, too, that such sovereignty is worth little if the people elect not to honour it. His questioning why Rome refused to acknowledge Coriolanus's merit is similar to Achilles' questioning why the generals passed by him without deference; and his answer echoes Ulysses' observation that all value is relative, all reputation subject to envious and calumniating time:

> So our virtues
> Lie in th'interpretation of the time;
> And power, unto itself most commendable,
> Hath not a tomb so evident as a chair
> T'extol what it hath done. (IV.vii.49-53)

Praise for deeds past, as Ulysses warns Achilles, will not keep honour bright. Aufidius applies this wisdom to his envy of Coriolanus: just as the tribunes have done, so will he twist the interpretation of Coriolanus's virtues in the public eye, divorce his heroic achievements from their conventional significance, in order to sully his reputation. Thus, the paradox that 'most absolute' Coriolanus could never understand: 'When, Caius, Rome is thine, / Thou art poor'st of all' (IV.vii.56-7). What ought to signify most clearly his heroic worth instead will signify nothing.

Achilles stops at nothing to win Hector's honours from him. Even the act of feasting, which traditionally signifies a community of heroism, will be turned to advantage:

> I'll heat his blood with Greekish wine tonight,
> Which with my scimitar I'll cool tomorrow.
> Patroclus, let us feast him to the height.
> (*Troilus and Cressida* V.i.1-3)

Shakespeare marks the disjunction between reputation and performance most jarringly when Achilles arms to do battle with Hector. Ulysses voices the traditional expectation of Achilles in conventional hyperbole: 'O, courage, courage, princes! Great Achilles / Is arming, weeping, cursing, vowing vengeance!' (V.v.30-1). But Achilles meets that expectation in the least chivalric way possible. He calls his Myrmidons about him, as Al Capone might have called his hit men, to instruct them in the art of a gangland slaying:

> when I have the bloody Hector found,
> Empale him with your weapons round about;
> In fellest manner execute your arms.
> Follow me, sirs, and my proceedings eye;
> It is decreed Hector the great must die. (V.vii.4-8)

Once they perpetrate this bit of mayhem, taking Hector most discourteously, his helmet and shield off, Achilles instructs them to report the deed falsely and thereby to maintain his legendary fame: 'On, Myrmidons, and cry you all amain, / "Achilles hath the mighty Hector slain!"' (V.viii.13-14); next, to satisfy Homeric tradition, he determines to tie Hector's 'body to my horse's tail; / Along the field I will the Troyan trail' (lines 21-2). By thus displaying 'proof' of a deed he has never done, Achilles attempts to reconstitute the myth of his own heroic virtue.

Just so, Aufidius attempts to 'work / Myself a former fortune' out of Coriolanus's death (V.iii.202-3). Calling his conspirators together much as Achilles has called his Myrmidons, he first demonstrates how he will argue that the people ought to withdraw their confirmation of Coriolanus's heroic value by making the Roman compromise appear to be an instance of Coriolanus's treachery; second, how he will argue that such treachery must be paid for with death; third, how Coriolanus's death will result in the rebirth of his own fame:

> At a few drops of women's rheum, which are
> As cheap as lies, he sold the blood and labour
> Of our great action. Therefore shall he die,
> And I'll renew me in his fall. (V.vi.46-9)

Public recognition, Aufidius agrees with Achilles, can make the man.

Coriolanus enters the scene like Hector, innocent in his heroic certainty – 'Hail, Lords! I am returned your soldier' (V.vi.71) – and thus unsuspecting, he is provoked to rage when Aufidius taunts him with 'Breaking his oath and resolution' (line 95), anathema to a hero. His rage is all the pretext Aufidius needs to set his conspirators upon Coriolanus for what looks like an unpremeditated murder. The strategy works: one lord judges that Coriolanus's 'own impatience / Takes from Aufidius a great part of blame' (146-7); and as he delivers an epitaph on Coriolanus's 'noble memory' (155), an act of magnanimity that recalls his earlier embrace of Coriolanus, Aufidius is once again securely the heroic idol of his tribe. By manipulating conventions in order to win a fame that fact will not support, he, like Achilles, cheapens the significance that customarily accrues to heroic tradition. The death of Coriolanus, therefore, like the death of Hector, raises the question of how to evaluate convention's role in heroic mimesis: whether the outward and visible signs may be trusted to represent an inward and spiritual strength.

If *Coriolanus* refers so pervasively to *Troilus,* to what end? Shakespeare's purpose, we may assume, was subtler than my catalogue of echoes suggests. One answer may lie in the mimetic distinctions Auerbach draws between history and legend. History achieves its reality by recreating a sense of the past with a richness of context and fullness of detail that legend does not require. When Shakespeare turned to Plutarch for his source and, in particular, drew from that source a figure about whom Elizabethans knew little, he had no choice but to strive for historical verisimilitude. Coriolanus was not the stuff of legend because unknown heroes never are. He was, on the contrary, a real Roman; and Shakespeare painstakingly recreated the cultural traditions and political situations in which Plutarch placed him.[17] Those details that make act I seem needlessly complicated to an audience – the political haggling between senators and tribunes over the corn laws, the republican tensions between patricians and citizens, Coriolanus's intolerance of the political turn of events – all reinforce the impression of historical authenticity; and Coriolanus's relationship with others, especially with his mother, is developed with a psychological complexity that compels us to apply naturalistic criteria to the play.

Legend, however, makes no such demands on us. Our criteria for judging it are far more elementary. We do not expect from it the historical details, cross-currents, and uncertainties that contaminate the purity of action and confuse the simple orientation of characters. What Auerbach writes of Homer's method may be applied to Shakespeare's treatment of Hector and Achilles, if not to the whole of *Troilus*:

> Legend arranges its material in a simple and straightforward way; it detaches it from its contemporary historical context, so that the latter will not confuse it; it knows only clearly outlined men who act from few and simple motives and the continuity of whose feelings and actions remains uninterrupted.[18]

Whereas Coriolanus's isolation results from a psychological and political struggle, Hector's isolation is symbolic. His relationship with his wife and mother matters little; for Coriolanus, it matters a great deal. Troy, for Hector, exists as but a spur to glorious deeds; Rome, for Coriolanus, is a city of mortal consequence. Similarly, whereas Achilles may in bold, metaphoric strokes fell Hector in order to preserve his own reputation, Aufidius, to achieve the same goal, must justify a public motive for slaying Coriolanus, frame a scene for appearance's sake to provoke Coriolanus, and then consider the political consequences of his

17 For Shakespeare's debt to Plutarch, see Bullough *Narrative and Dramatic Sources* V; Brower *Hero and Saint* pp 205ff, who discusses how Plutarch modified epic heroism in the context of Roman republicanism; and two more recent studies that deal with Shakespeare's concept of Rome as shaped by Plutarch and others: J.L. Simmons *Shakespeare's Pagan World* Charlottesville 1973; and Paul A. Cantor *Shakespeare's Rome* Ithaca 1976.

18 Erich Auerbach *Mimesis: The Representation of Reality in Western Literature* trans Willard R. Trask, Princeton 1953, p 19

action. Legend is unencumbered by such considerations.

When Shakespeare alludes in *Coriolanus* to the matter of Troy as he had dramatized it in *Troilus,* he establishes mimetic points of reference that ally history with legend to create a dramatic counterpoint. The death of Hector in particular provides a legendary model on which the death of Coriolanus may be constructed so as to test convention against historical verisimilitude. Such a model – while establishing by contrast the relative realism of Coriolanus's tragedy – also clarifies the conflicting forces that cause his tragedy, imbues them with legendary significance, and, ultimately, raises the action almost to mythic status. Shakespeare in this way does for a little-known history what already had been done for him in sources for his English history plays and others such as *Julius Caesar, King Lear,* and *Antony and Cleopatra*: review history through the clarifying lens of legend.

Like the other tragedies of Shakespeare's maturity, *Coriolanus* presumes in its audience a familiarity with heroic tradition that can be tapped to create a rich network of associations. But in studies of Shakespeare's reworking of sources, perhaps not enough has been made of how his reference to his own earlier work contributes to the mimetic sophistication of his later plays. Just as a proper understanding of Hector and Achilles in *Troilus* may depend more on our knowledge of Shakespeare's early chronicle plays than of Homer or his medieval redactors, so our understanding of *Coriolanus* may be enhanced if we realize that Shakespeare modelled the relationship between Coriolanus and Aufidius at least in part on the relationship between Hector and Achilles as he had developed it in *Troilus.* It is not necessary to assume that Shakespeare's audience was aware of his allusions to his own earlier work: even a modern audience with less access to heroic tradition will perceive shifts of idiom and tensions between history and legend in a given play without reference to other plays in the canon. Nor is it necessary to assume that Shakespeare himself was fully conscious of the extent of his self-reference. Echoes and transformations of his earlier work may play an important part in Shakespeare's mimetic art without his conscious intent. Such self-reference does, however, allow us insight into the creative process, conscious or unconscious, by which Shakespeare chiselled heroic tragedy out of the intractable stuff of history.

Allegheny College

R.B. PARKER

Coriolanus and 'th'interpretation of the time'

I

At the end of act IV in Shakespeare's play, Coriolanus's great enemy, the Volscian leader Tullus Aufidius, comments on the self-defeating nature of Coriolanus's character and the slippery impermanence of political judgments and of human values in general:

> So our virtues
> Lie in th'interpretation of the time;
> And power, unto itself most commendable,
> Hath not a tomb so evident as a chair
> T'extol what it hath done.
> One fire drives out one fire; one nail one nail;
> Rights by rights fuller, strengths by strengths do fail.
> (IV.vii.49-55)[1]

The precise meaning of the lines about the 'tomb' and 'chair' is notoriously difficult (the old Variorum edition has some twenty pages discussing it), but the context makes their general tenor clear. Aufidius believes not only that political authority depends on power and that this is always temporary,

1 References to the play are to George Hibbard's edition of *Coriolanus* (London 1967). Most editors read the 1623 Folio's 'fouler' (1 55) as 'falter,' not 'fuller.'

ousted sooner or later by newer power, but also – as the pun on 'virtues' indicates – that time renders the value of political action wholly relative: 'rights by rights ... do fail.' No standard of public behaviour can be reliable because none is permanent.

This is one of Shakespeare's bleakest comments on human history. It is more chilling than Ulysses' similar warning that 'Time hath, my lord, a wallet at his back, / Wherein he puts alms for oblivion' (*Troilus and Cressida* III.iii.145ff), or Duke Vincentio's disparagement of life's vanity (*Measure for Measure* III.i.5ff), since both of those are speeches of negative persuasion, meant to have a positive moral effect on Achilles and Claudio respectively; and its implications go beyond the accidie of Macbeth's 'Tomorrow and tomorrow and tomorrow' (*Macbeth* V.v.19ff) because the latter so clearly arises out of a particular, personal guilt and foreshadows self-destruction. Aufidius, however, coldly accepts that only might is right and that right itself is therefore temporary; and the play then shows him acting on this cynicism successfully.

The dramatic power of *Coriolanus* depends, in fact, on the steadiness with which it confronts the bitter element of truth in Aufidius's analysis without succumbing to it. The contradictory values held by patricians and plebeians, Romans and Volscians, are so evenly balanced in the play that they seem to cancel each other out. No party is wholly true to its principles; each is opportunistic; and the breakdown in communication that characterizes the language of the play exists not only between the rival power groups but also, more tellingly, within each faction itself.[2] The result is brilliantly complex, and *Coriolanus* has

2 Madelaine Doran, for instance, points out in *Shakespeare's Dramatic Language* (Madison 1976, pp 182ff) that the characteristic rhetoric of *Coriolanus* is one of dilemma, antithesis, and paradox – ie of unresolved contradiction – which is accompanied by frequent stage requirements for *noise* – of battles, triumphs, and the rejoicing or blood-hunting mob. A recent adaptation of the play which exploits this element is John Osborne's *A Place Calling Itself Rome* (London 1973). Osborne transposes *Coriolanus* to Britain in the seventies, where meetings and departures take place at airports, labour confronts management over bargaining tables, demonstrations block the London squares, and the Volscian war takes place in the war-torn streets of some Irish town like Derry. The adaptation is not a particularly good one, but it does conjure up vividly the sense of fragmented reality – of flashing lights, crowds chanting contradictory slogans, and especially, floods of grammatically meaningless demagoguery – that characterizes political violence without principles and a society which lacks coherent goals.

accordingly been interpreted in widely different ways: as a tragedy, as a comedy, as satire; as a vindication of traditional hierarchy; as an assertion of the common people's rights; and as a deeply pessimistic play which sees no value on either side of the class struggle. As Aufidius implies, every generation has felt itself free to reinterpret the play according to its own political bias.[3]

To grasp the deeper coherence of the play and to understand what Shakespeare finds to oppose historical relativism, it is necessary to go beyond Aufidius and to consider more deeply the term 'political' itself. And to get at this the play must first be placed within the contexts of Shakespeare's developing, and darkening, concept of political life and the political situation at the time the play was written.

II

Like all intelligent people of his time (or any time), Shakespeare was passionately interested in politics; and, though only ten of his plays are officially classed as 'Histories' in the 1623 Folio, in fact well over half of the canon has politics as its central or strong secondary interest. And following these plays through chronologically, one can discern a distinct pattern of development, whose key is a progressive questioning of current political orthodoxy, as Shakespeare tests it by application to actual persons in particular circumstances – what the jargon now calls 'situational politics.' Yet this progressive disillusion is accompanied by an unfalteringly tough-minded recognition that there can be no shirking of politics, no evasion of social responsibility. Mankind is necessarily and inevitably a political animal, as Aristotle pointed out in book I of his *Politics*, because he must learn to live in communities – in the 'polis.'

The development of Shakespeare's political thought, then, goes something like this. The early history plays – the three parts of *Henry VI* and *Richard III* – are very orthodox. They cover a period of national breakdown, but they interpret it against the

3 This relativism is even more evident in the stage history of the play (and its adaptations), where interpretation swings regularly between glorification of strong leadership at the one extreme and adulation of the proletariat at the other. Recent discussions of the stage history can be found in Philip Brockbank, ed *Coriolanus* London 1976; and Ruby Cohn *Modern Shakespeare Offshoots* Princeton 1976.

secure medieval doctrine that, because of the Fall of man, the state must limit original sin by imposing a fixed, hierarchical order under the king's unquestioned authority, rebellion against which is heinous sin. This doctrine assumes that religious, ethical, and political values all run neatly in parallel – though already, even this early, there is a disconcerting ability in Shakespeare to see the human vulnerability of his titular villains: Joan La Pucelle or Richard of Gloucester. And it is to this view of society that the analogy of the body politic to the physical body, which Menenius misuses at the beginning of *Coriolanus*, also belongs.

Shakespeare does not stop at this point, however. A crucial change of direction occurs with the writing of *King John* in 1594 – between the two tetralogies on the struggles of the houses of York and Lancaster. In *King John* Shakespeare was confronted with the problem of combining diametrically opposed traditions: a protestant tradition which saw John as England's champion against interference by Rome and the Catholic powers of Europe; and an older, no less powerful tradition which saw him as a usurper who had his nephew Arthur murdered to secure his throne. Shakespeare does not really manage to combine these polarities, and the exercise they afforded him in exploring contradictory motives seems to have deepened his awareness of the complexity of political decision, of the possible antagonism between politics and ethics as rival systems of value, and of what Kantarowitz has documented as the 'King's two bodies' – the split between the central office of power and the fallible man who holds it.

Thus, as we continue further into 'York and Lancaster's long jars,' from the first tetralogy into the second, though we move from the weakest king, Henry VI, to the strongest, Henry V, two realizations progressively darken the political assurance of the earlier plays. There is, first, an increasing scepticism about kingship itself and the price even a good king must pay for political efficiency. The early plays about unsuitable kings are followed by plays in which suitable – that is, successful – kings are seen with an irony that dips close to tragedy in Henry V's speeches before Harfleur and on the eve of battle of Agincourt. There is a growing sense that power corrupts, brutalizes, isolates, and dehumanizes. Moreover, this is accompanied by a dismal feeling that the process may be historically unending, cyclical, a Möbius strip: after Henry V, as the epilogue reminds us, we get back to Henry VI once more. So Jan Kott and others have argued that Shakespeare came to see politics as an absurd 'Great Machine,' an endless conveyor belt which raises new rulers to power only to destroy each of them in his turn.

However, this is not the end either. Shakespeare digs further in *Troilus and Cressida, Julius Caesar,* and the great tragedies. The classical plays remove the issues from the religiously loaded (and politically dangerous) question of kingship. There can be few more scathing indictments of false patriotism than *Troilus and Cressida,* and the ethical-political dilemma of the high-minded assassin Brutus in *Julius Caesar* leads straight into the problems of the tragedies, culminating in the huge excavation of *King Lear.* And in *King Lear* Shakespeare arrives at a dialectical concept of values, in which ethics and politics interact rather than merely run parallel and where both stem from the relationship between parent and child, the basic unit of society.

By the time he reaches *Coriolanus,* then, Shakespeare understands 'political' in a much wider sense than he did in his early plays or as we normally use the term today. He includes the narrower meaning, of course – the struggle for power and the question this raises of which are the best institutions for authority – but he sees these as interacting with what we may call more broadly 'culture' (in the anthropological sense): that is, he shows a triple interaction between the individual, his institutions – including the family, which is the basic institution – and society as a whole, which is at the same time the product and the cause of the other two; hence the knot between mother and country which Coriolanus cannot untie and of which Volumnia, typical Roman matron that she is, is as much the victim as the agent.

III

There are thus two main political issues in Shakespeare's *Coriolanus.* The obvious one is the class conflict between patricians and plebeians, which is complicated by external war against the Volscians and which raises questions of right government. But there is also the more basic question of patriotism. What is it shapes the link between an individual and his society before class conflict even appears?

Two key alterations from Shakespeare's main source (North's translation of Plutarch) can guide us on the first issue.

Shakespeare makes the main plebeian grievance the dearth of corn, the Senate's lack of action to remedy this situation, and Coriolanus's personal opposition to free corn doles. Actually, in Plutarch the main grievance was about usury, and the corn issue was only raised *after* the Volscian campaign (which helped to create it) and *after* Coriolanus had already been refused the consulship. Secondly, there is the question of tribunes – the principle of popular representation and its possible misuse. In Plutarch the right to tribunes had been granted before the corn riots, and these tribunes played no part in Coriolanus's failure to become consul, though they did play a part in his later banishment (according to Livy) by insisting on a popular vote by tribes instead of the existing system, which unduly favoured the patricians. Now, both of these changes – the emphasis on corn riots and the focus on the tribunes – reflect events in England during the first years of James I's reign, which would have been evident to the play's original audience and may well have attracted Shakespeare to the story in the first place.

The beginning of James's reign was also a time of exceptionally bad harvests and soaring food prices, and in 1607 (the play is dated 1608-9) this resulted in outbreaks of rioting in several northern and midland counties, including Warwickshire – where Shakespeare, of course, was born and where he owned land to which he was soon to retire. Unlike previous revolts these were purely peasant uprisings, not led by the gentry; they were ill organized and pathetically ill equipped, and were put down savagely by the gentry themselves because, beyond the engrossing of corn, their ultimate target was the enclosure system, the amassing of large estates by driving peasant smallholders off the land. Because Shakespeare was a land speculator and one of the chief storers of malt in Stratford, it has been argued that he must have sided with the gentry in this struggle; but this seems at least questionable. His basic sympathies can be more clearly gauged from Lear and Gloucester's hard lesson that it is necessary to share the 'superflux, so each man have enough,' the phrasing of which is closely echoed in the first scene of *Coriolanus.* I can find no suggestion in the play that Shakespeare did not sympathize with the First Citizen's cry that 'the gods know I speak this in hunger for bread, not in thirst for revenge,' nor with the desperation of the choice he offers his fellows: 'You are all resolved rather to die than to famish?' (which is, after all, merely a choice of deaths).

The arrogance of the gentry, so obvious in the 1607 uprisings and in the characterization of Coriolanus, was also a matter of contemporary concern. As Lawrence Stone has documented exhaustively, the social mobility of the late Elizabethan and early Stuart period threw the whole definition of class into question; and the aristocracy, many of them newly created, reacted with fierce self-assertion. There were plenty of young noblemen in the courts of Elizabeth or James who could have served as a model for Coriolanus, but two in particular stand out. Elizabeth's shamed favourite, the second Earl of Essex, who had been cheered on his way to Ireland in 1599, was execrated by the same London mob at his execution three years later for having tried to seize the government; and in a sermon from Paul's Cross in 1601, Bishop William Barlow instanced Coriolanus as 'a gallant young, but a discontented Romane, who might make a fit parallel for the late Earle, if you read his life.' An even closer model was Sir Walter Raleigh, another favourite of the old queen and Essex's successful rival, who was notorious for his warmongering, for his pride, and for holding monopolies on several basic commodities, including cloth and wine, which kept their prices high. When Raleigh was put in charge of mobilizing the Cornish miners at the time of the Armada, Lord Treasurer Burleigh was warned they would not follow such a man; the London mob attacked him when King James had him arrested in 1604; and while Shakespeare was writing his play, Raleigh was actually in the Tower on charges of conspiracy to treason, after a travesty of a trial.

Yet Raleigh was unquestionably a very great man, and ironically, though the Londoners could not be expected to understand this, his concept of government was much more democratic than the king's. James had set forth his idea of monarchy above the law in a book called *The Trew Law of Free Monarchs* in 1598; and when he came to the throne of England five years later, this brought him into immediate confrontation with the English House of Commons. One particularly relevant area of conflict was the king's right of 'purveyance' – the commandeering of supplies for the royal household – which the Commons refused to ratify for James in 1606, raising the same question of responsible stewardship as the plebeians raise about corn supplies in Rome. Two details of this tussle are particularly interesting. The two parliamentary leaders, Hare and Hyde, were continually disparaged by James as 'tribunes of the people,' and he warned that 'if any such plebeian tribunes should incur any offense ... Commons would correct them for it.' Secondly, the moderates in the argument, aware of its potential for civil war, constantly argued for 'mildness,' for the discussion to be conducted 'mildly' – the same word that is urged on Coriolanus when he is forced back to face the voters who have repudiated him, and to which Laurence Olivier always gave a particularly snapping emphasis on his exit in the Old Vic production of 1938: 'Well, mildly be it then – mildly' (III.ii.145).

Besides being in the line of Shakespeare's developing concept of politics, then, *Coriolanus* also touched certain sensitive issues of the early 1600s, issues which eventually resulted in the parliamentary-Puritan revolution of 1639. What was basically in question was the concept of the state as a fixed hierarchy, with authority as unquestionable: a traditional position presented in the equally traditional parable of the belly and the members with which Menenius quietens the rioters in the first scene. Now, one of the recurrent critical errors in interpreting *Coriolanus* is to take this parable, and Menenius himself, too seriously and to assume that they represent Shakespeare's own opinion. The allegory is clearly shown to be at variance with the facts of Roman life; but even beyond this, I think it is meant to be questionable as an ideal. For a seventeenth-century audience, accustomed to hearing the image used as justification for kingship (it was an especial favourite with King James), it would seem odd in the first place to apply it to a non-monarchical state; and this is pointed by the fact that, though the Second Citizen brings up the 'Kingly crowned head' (I.i.113), Menenius's parable has no head, just members, and the smiling sovereign belly. Moreover, the static, inflexible reality behind this apparently benign ideal of the state had already been exposed in an earlier image of Menenius, when he tells the rioters:

> ... you may as well
> Strike at the heavens with your staves as lift them
> Against the Roman state, whose course will on
> The way it takes, cracking ten thousand curbs
> Of more strong link asunder than can ever
> Appear in your impediment. (I.i.65-70)

Later, the same juggernaut image of a resistless, impersonal machine will be applied several times to Coriolanus, the creature of this dehumanizing state.

Besides these limitations of the body-politic ideal itself, there is also the fact that anyway it is clearly lip-service, ignored in practice by the patricians as much as by the plebeians. Menenius himself uses it as a way of quieting and delaying the rioters. As soon as Coriolanus shows up, his tune changes to 'Rome and her rats are at the point of battle.' Menenius is a dangerous character (dramaturgically) because he makes the audience laugh; but it must be recognized that he is a voluptuary, revelling in feasts while he sympathizes with the starving poor; a wily clown, like Falstaff, who uses laughter for selfish ends; with a touch of the black-mouthing Thersites railer too, when his personal interests are crossed Politically he is pure opportunist, not a true conservative at all: a sail-trimmer, who backs up Volumnia when she tells Coriolanus that there is no need to be sincere in wooing plebeian votes, yet grows 'most kind' to the tribunes when they in turn are in power; who separates Rome from her 'rats' when all is well but wriggles from responsibility by calling it 'your doing' when Rome is attacked I cannot see how this combination of Ulysses, Falstaff, and Polonius can possibly be accepted as the wise and moderate statesman that some critics (misled perhaps by his favourable presentation in Plutarch and Livy) have described. And the rest of the patricians are no better. They even let Coriolanus be hooted out of Rome by the mob, which explains his anger against patricians and plebeians alike (a change, this, from Plutarch), and provides the burden of the one important soliloquy Shakespeare permits him, as he goes to join Aufidius:

> O world, thy slippery turns! Friends now fast sworn,
> Whose double bosoms seem to bear one heart,
> Whose hours, whose bed, whose meal and exercise
> Are still together, who twin, as 'twere, in love
> Unseparable, shall within this hour,
> On a dissension of a doit, break out
> To bitterest enmity. (IV.iv.12-18)

Coriolanus has now learned the same lesson of instability as Aufidius expresses in the speech which provided our subtitle.

Yet the plebeians on their side are seen to be no better.

Shakespeare sympathizes with their desperation; he shows them individually as nice, touchingly self-critical, and requiring only that their votes be asked for 'kindly' – which puns, of course, on 'kind,' meaning naturally 'kin.' En masse, however, they are the usual Shakespeare mob: irrational, unstable, savage, and at the mercy of every whim and demagogue. They are also, for the most part, bad soldiers, reluctant to fight, ready to run, and eager to loot. And their tribunes manipulate them as cynically as the patricians. Yet the tribunes are not villains either. The balance is held so very evenly. Their cause is basically just, and Shakespeare gives us an attractive if slightly ludicrous vignette of their satisfaction with the Roman populace after Coriolanus has gone and before news comes of the Volscians' renewed attack. However, the cynical explanation they find for Coriolanus's agreeing to be second in command to Cominius – that this will let him take the credit for a victory but leave Cominius to bear responsibility for a defeat (I.i.261-70) – gives us their measure immediately. The tribunes are clever but mean-minded men, without much imagination or any breadth of political experience, clever at internal politics but ignorant of foreign affairs, and with much too much self-importance. On the other hand, they do learn quickly: it is they who persuade Volumnia to plead with her son to spare Rome (instead of Virgilia, as in Plutarch), and at the end Sicinius politically (in both senses) hurries off to join in Volumnia's victory triumph. (She has lost a son, we might say, and gained a tribune.)

Thus, the facts of Roman life on both sides, including his own character, give Menenius's parable the lie. What we see is no organic body politic but a Rome torn by factional strife, Machiavelli's politics of the power struggle. Characteristically, however, the only person who states openly what all confess to privately is Coriolanus himself, in his attack on the tribunate. His grasp that

> ... when two authorities are up,
> Neither supreme, how soon confusion
> May enter 'twixt the gap of both and take
> The one by th'other (III.i.109-12)

is essentially correct; but his way of dealing with it is all wrong. Like his mother he is willing to see politics as no different from war; but unlike her, he sees war romantically in terms of single combat and solo heroism: a very different vision from the facts of dry blood on the face, the tears of widows, espionage, and the arbitrary decrees of an army of occupation, of which Shakespeare carefully reminds us in the play.

But if Coriolanus has no sense of the body politic – merely of the realities of power, what then is his link to the state? It is, of course, the link of personal loyalty, working only through his mother, Volumnia. Besides testing the cliché of the body politic – the cliché of Menenius's famous speech – Shakespeare's play also tests the cliché of the mother country – 'our dear nurse,' as Volumnia puts it (V.iii.120). The central image of the play is Coriolanus against the rest.[4] He lacks almost any developed sense of comradeship, even with his equals. He prefers to do things *alone* – the word re-echoes through his speeches ('alone I did it'). He is only at home on the battlefield, and then only fully when he is in single combat. He refuses praise less from modesty than to keep his comrades at a distance; and (differing here from Plutarch) he forgets the name of his Corioli host, shrugs, and makes no further effort to save him. The plebeians are mere raw material for his battles; or 'rats'; or disembodied 'voices.' And even Aufidius, whom he sees idealistically as his one chivalric equal, is rapidly pushed into second place when Coriolanus joins him, taking over his command as earlier he had Cominius's.

Such a lack of relationship is awe-inspiring. 'He that is incapable of living in society,' says Aristotle in book I of the *Politics*, 'is a god or a beast.' And, as has often been remarked, the patricians constantly call Coriolanus godlike, and even the tribune Brutus complains that he speaks to the people

> As if you were a god to punish, not
> A man of their infirmity. (II.i.81-2)

But the Coriolanus who is welcomed back to Rome like a god is driven out again like an animal, 'a lonely dragon' (IV.i.30); and there are other images to balance the god image too. He is several times described as a killing machine, a monstrous blood-covered juggernaut; and these images are used not by his enemies but by his friends, Cominius and Menenius, recalling Menenius's similar image for the impersonal Roman state which

4 Cf Hibbard, pp 8-9.

helped create Coriolanus. Another recurrent image of perverted relationship is the preference of fighting to the marriage bed – used by Coriolanus, by Volumnia, by Cominius, by Aufidius, and by one of Aufidius's servants – which has even led some modern producers to hint at a homosexual attraction between the two leaders[5] – quite wrongly. The repetition is important, but the comparison itself is a Renaissance commonplace. Most crucial of all, however, is the 'boy of tears' (V.vi.101) – the image of the damaged adolescent agonizingly dependent on his mother, with which Aufidius breaks down Coriolanus's self-control in Antium and betrays him to his death.

That term 'boy' is both the psychological and the political heart of Shakespeare's play, because clearly Coriolanus is Volumnia's creation as Volumnia is Rome's. The invented scene of young Marcius ripping apart a butterfly to his grandmother's delight ('One of his father's moods') shows just how Coriolanus was raised and is recalled later when Menenius says the Volscians follow Coriolanus against Rome 'with no less confidence / Than boys pursuing summer butterflies / Or butchers killing flies' (IV.vi.94-6). We hear the echo here of Gloucester's cry in *King Lear*: 'As flies to wanton boys are we to the gods, / They kill us for their sport.'

For Volumnia, Coriolanus is a husband-surrogate, her means to vicarious fame[6]: she shows almost no feeling for him as a separate person. She exults grotesquely with Menenius over

5 Brian Bedford's 1981 production at Stratford, Ontario, is the latest to take this line, following earlier interpretations by Tyrone Guthrie and Michael Langham.

6 This insight into the plight of talented women in a male-dominated society, and the mischief it can cause, is interestingly developed in another adaptation of the play, Charlotte Brontë's novel *Shirley* (1849), chapter 6 of which is titled 'Coriolanus.' The Roman class struggle is here transposed to the Luddite machine-wrecking riots of 1812, with Yorkshire mill-owners representing the novel's patricians, their workers the plebeians, dissenting ministers the hypocritical tribunes, and war against Napoleon the Volscian campaigns, bankrupting the mill country by an embargo on trade with France. The interest (and ambiguity) of the novel centres particularly on the title character, Shirley Keeldar, a strong-minded young aristocrat who, in contrast to the Virgilia-like heroine, Caroline Helstone, is determined to play a man's role in society. She whistles in an unladylike way, rides her horse hell-for-leather, and, armed with two pistols to repel mutinous mill-hands, is humorously called 'Captain Keeldar.' To the extent that she is is a land-owning Tory to whom the Whig hero has reluctantly to turn for help to save his mill, she stands in the same relationship to him as Aufidius does to Coriolanus, and the hero's subsequent

the number of wounds he is bringing back, their glee deliberately contrasted to Virgilia's distress, and whereas Plutarch says her fault was over-leniency, Shakespeare, with brilliant insight, makes her rather over-severe: one of the 'taboo-on-tenderness' school of child-raising (to quote Professor L.C. Knights[7]). Her method of dominating her son is demonstrated in the scene where she cajoles and emotionally bullies him to return to the plebeian electors who have rejected him,[8] a scene which Shakespeare added and which looks forward to the climactic persuasion scene before Rome. Her method is to demand that love be earned, and her final tactic, which always works, is icy withdrawal: 'At thy choice then' ... 'Do your will.' And what is fascinating is that Coriolanus treats the plebeians just as his mother treats him: as inferiors to be disciplined, their gentler side ignored, mere means to his own glory who must *earn* the patricians' care by risking themselves in war, as he does, who must be threatened into unpalatable action, as his mother threatens him. He even tries the same tactic of abandonment – 'I banish *you* ... thus I turn my back. / There is a world elsewhere' (III.iii.122, 134-5) – and trails off into exile with the classic little boy's comment, 'I shall be loved when I am lacked' (IV.i.15). Beneath the politics of state obviously lie the politics of the family: we are watching the indictment of a way of life, the perverting Roman emphasis on *virtus*, where 'valour is the chiefest virtue' (II.ii.84), not just one man's weakness.

Hence the tensions of the climactic persuasion scene before Rome, in which Volumnia denies the distinction her son is des-

proposal to her can therefore be seen as a literalization of the sexual terms in which Aufidius and Coriolanus talk of their relationship. She turns him down, however, for the interesting reason that they are too alike; her efforts to help repel the workmen's attack are snubbed by him; the only responsibility she is finally given for the mill her money has saved is to be allowed to teach in the village school; and she ends by making a very strained marriage to the hero's brother because, as her tutor, he can literally be considered her 'master' ('"My pupil," he said. "My Master," was the low answer.') As a novel *Shirley* has notable defects, but its presentation of the worker-industrialist disputes of 1812 as extensions and metaphors of the clash of sexes in a society where direct expressions of a woman's ability and energy are denied throws into fascinating relief an element also implicit in Shakespeare's analysis of Rome.

7 L.C. Knights *Some Shakespearean Themes* London 1959, p 152. Knights takes the phrase from chap 6 of Ian V. Suttie *The Origins of Love and Hate* New York 1952.

8 Hibbard, p 39, considers this 'the real crisis of the play.'

perately trying to make between 'mother' and 'country.' If the class struggle were the only level of political interest in the play, this scene would not work as a climax. What is on trial is the Roman way of life itself. The scene is a virtual replay of the previous browbeating scene. Volumnia pleads, cajoles, threatens, instructs the other pleaders, moves them about, then uses her ultimate weapon, withdrawal. And Coriolanus crumbles. On one level it is a scene of bitter irony, because Volumnia has no real sense of what she is doing: she insists on treating as political heroism what is clearly psychological dependence and seems to have no idea of the damage she has done her son. Menenius's image from the earlier scene returns to haunt us:

> Now the good gods forbid
> That our renowned Rome ...
> ... like an unnatural dam
> Should now eat up her own! (III.i.289-92)[9]

Yet the surrender is also very moving, less because it is heroic than because it is a genuinely loving act on Coriolanus's part, made not as a Roman but as a son; and though this is undercut by Volumnia's imperviousness as she goes off for her first personal triumph and by Coriolanus's own apparent relapse into arrogance on his return to Antium, still, for one moment, he does realize fully what has happened to him and the price he is paying for it and will have to pay.

The phrasing of this *anagnorisis* is interesting. After he has reached out and, weeping, held his mother 'silent' by the hand (a brilliant dramaturgical stroke whose devastating effect can be lost in just the reading), he bursts out with:

> O mother, mother!
> What have you done? Behold, the heavens do ope,
> The gods look down, and this unnatural scene
> They laugh at. O my mother, mother! O! (V.iii.183-6)

That word 'unnatural' cuts two ways. It is bad in so far as it can be interpreted as Coriolanus's ultimate surrender to his social and familial conditioning, since, as R.D. Laing explains in his Massey Lectures, *The Politics of the Family*:

9 Cf Volumnia's own angry comment to Menenius: 'I sup upon myself, / And so shall starve with feeding' (IV.ii.50-1).

> The 'deeper' social laws are implanted in us, the more 'hard-programmed,' the more 'pickled' into us, the more like 'natural' laws they come to appear to us to be. Indeed, if someone breaks such a 'deeply' planted social law, we are inclined to say that he is 'unnatural.'[10]

Coriolanus had tried to live 'As if a man were author of himself, and knew no other kin' (V. iii.6-7); but confronted with his mother's cold obduracy and his own unassuaged need for her, he has to accept her definition of him again, knowing it will destroy him. As Laing would put it, he is playing out a scenario written generations before he was born. Yet the cry must be taken at its face value, too. The situation *is* unnatural. The mutual kneeling of parent and child recalls the similar scene in *King Lear,* and Coriolanus's decision to put his feelings for his mother above all else – despite their warping and despite her own cold lack of reciprocity – is an affirmation at the same level of relationship that Lear too finally comes to rest on.

And so the play achieves genuine tragedy. Not because in Coriolanus we have a sacrificial victim for our own repressed class hatred and desire to curse (as Kenneth Burke ingeniously argues[11]); nor even because Coriolanus's political success (the survival of Rome) offsets his private defeat, in an inversion of the usual tragic formula (though this is closer to the truth). It is tragic because though – as in *King Lear* – it will not last, and nothing can be built upon it, Coriolanus's decision is an affirmation of the familial link on which a healthy society has to be built and which Shakespeare had come to see as the truly *political* core of human society set against the constant flux of history. It is an insight which, I have argued, he worked out for himself in many plays, but – as Ernst Cassirer shows in his *Myth of the State*[12] – it aligns him with the Renaissance neo-Platonists, who also set against the static body-politic ideal on the one side and Machiavelli's endless power struggle on the other their own belief that man's instinct for society was a good thing, rationally dynamic, not static, and based not on endless competition but on an extension of the reciprocities of family life. It is *this* ideal, not the decapitated body politic, that Shakespeare sets against

10 R.D. Laing *The Politics of the Family: Massey Lectures 1968* Toronto: CBC 1969, p 22

11 Kenneth Burke '*Coriolanus* and the Delights of Faction' *Hudson Review* 19 (1966-7) p 201

12 New Haven 1946, chap 6

his largely pessimistic vision of 'th'interpretation of the time' and a Rome where *pietas* has been sacrificed to *virtus.* And it is this ideal, not his battles, that gives Coriolanus his ultimate victory over Aufidius's pragmatic cynicism.

Trinity College
University of Toronto

R.W. INGRAM

'Their noise be our instruction': Listening to *Titus Andronicus* and *Coriolanus*

Asked if Aufidius is in their city, the senators of Corioli defy Coriolanus (as I prematurely call him):

> No, nor a man that fears you less than he:
> That's lesser than a little. (*Drum afar off*) Hark, our drums
> Are bringing forth our youth ...
> ...
> (*Alarum far off*) Hark you, far off!
> There is Aufidius. List what work he makes
> Amongst your cloven army.
> MARTIUS Oh, they are at it!
> LARTIUS Their noise be our instruction. Ladders, ho!
> (I.iv.14-22)[1]

Stage directions for music, and their interpretation, are not always so clear.[2]

Coriolanus was not printed until the First Folio: the text is unusually rich in stage directions. Many of these are for music or include music; others are for the sounds of voices, so used that I count them among the complex of musical sound effects

1 Quotations are from the New Penguin Shakespeare *Coriolanus* ed G.R. Hibbard, Harmondsworth 1967.

2 I read the line: 'The sound of that alarum is enough; we attack. Get the scaling ladders up.' However, the Arden footnote suggests slightly wider possibilities.

in the play. My main concern here is with the way in which these sounds, whether heard on-stage or off-stage, affect what is seen on stage. Indeed, they are rarely merely 'heard' but are an important element in the play's physical movement and spectacle; we are intended, in fact, to look at them with our ears. In the strictest sense of the word, the 'music' in *Coriolanus* is almost entirely that of flourishes, alarums, and ceremonial calls. The larger music in the play includes the voices of soldiers and citizens, often massed in choruses ranging from the fierce to the jubilant. The most dramatic moments come when those forces fuse in one outburst – and this is one reason why the play's most dramatic moment is one of complete silence.

These sounds are carefully ordered in a pattern of music and sound that rests on interpretation of stage directions and, occasionally, of the text alone, where looked-for directions do not exist. Some of the problems of such interpretation and looking must be taken up before turning to *Coriolanus.*

One of Peter Brook's earliest successes was the Stratford-upon-Avon Memorial Theatre production of *Titus Andronicus* in 1955.[3] I use the musical directions of the first act of *Titus* as examples of problems of interpretation germane to my general argument. *Titus* is in several ways convenient for this purpose. It is the first, as *Coriolanus* is the last of the tragedies (and both are Roman), allowing a comparison of early and mature writing, a comparison which is sharpened because there are connections in situations and words between *Titus* and *Coriolanus.* In addition, *Titus* exists in three quartos – 1594, 1600, and 1611 – before the First Folio printing, and there are interesting differences in musical directions among them.

The musical effects in *Titus* are energetic and melodramatic. Each makes a strong impact; the contrasts between them within the act are theatrical but not always dramatic – that is, they are not convincingly shaped into a pattern over the whole act (nor, indeed, are all the effects over the whole play). The young artist scatters fine ideas without making the most of them.

The opening is of a formality reminiscent of the earlier histories: *Richard II, 1* and *2 Henry VI,* and not to be approached again until *The Two Noble Kinsmen* (and there gorgeously

3 For a detailed descripton of this production (and its curiously unnerving music composed by Brook himself) see Daniel Scuro '*Titus Andronicus*: a crimson-flushed stage!' *Theatre Collection Bulletin* no 17, Ohio State University 1970, pp 40-8.

expanded): '*Flourish. Enter the Tribunes and Senators aloft; and then enter Saturninus and his followers at one door, and Bassianus and his followers at the other, with drums and trumpets*' (I.i.1).[4] The brothers are rivals for the Roman crown. Their brief, ritualistic exchange is seemingly settled by Marcus Andronicus, Titus's brother, who enters with the crown to announce that 'the people of Rome ... by common voice' (lines 20-1), have chosen Titus. The brothers accept this decision and 'go up into the Senate-house' (63), preceded by a flourish (found only in the Folio). However, this grandly formal opening proves to be but prologue to the swelling act of Titus's own victorious return. A Captain whets the audience's appetite for the expected spectacle, announcing that:

> ... Rome's best champion,
> Successful in the battles that he fights,
> With honour and with fortune is return'd
> From where he circumscribed with his sword,
> And brought to yoke, the enemies of Rome. (65-9)

One of Shakespeare's greatest skills was winning theatrical effect by expectation startlingly deceived. Here, loud and shining triumph such as greets Coriolanus on his return to Rome in the glory of his new name is expected (II. i.155-65). Instead, the expectant audience is surprised to quiet awe by the darker pomp of a funeral procession: '*Sound drums and trumpets, and then enter two of Titus' sons, and then two Men bearing a coffin covered with black; then two other sons; then Titus Andronicus; and then Tamora, the Queen of the Goths, and her two sons, Chiron and Demetrius, with Aaron the Moor,* and others as many as can be ... ' (line 69).

With youthful bravado, Shakespeare changes the mood by having Titus's sons drag Alarbus off to summary execution. They quickly return, presumably bloodied – 'See, lord and father, how we have perform'd / Our Roman rites' (lines 142-3) – and all is ready for the interment. 'With loud 'larums welcome them to Rome,' says Titus's oldest son: '*Sound trumpets, and lay the coffin in the tomb*' (147, 149). The sacrifice allows the change of mood from sombre to louder ceremonial.

Problems of what are and are not directions, and how they

4 Quotations are taken from the New Arden Shakespeare *Titus Andronicus* ed J.C. Maxwell, London 1953.

should be understood, are nicely posed by this sequence. The entry of Titus, his sons, and their prisoners is not specifically called a 'dead march.' A customarily resounding victory-entry offset by the appearance of the mourning men and the coffin(s?) would be, of itself, a theatrical effect, but, to my mind, it would chime against the mood of the speeches that follow. The more forceful contrast is with the ferocity of the sacrifice of Alarbus and the more sonorous interment of the appeased sons of Titus. In the First Folio this moment is heightened past the quartos' direction which I have quoted, and becomes: *'Flourish. Then sound trumpets, and lay the Coffins in the tomb.'* Only the Folio calls for 'Coffins,' whereas it agrees with the quartos in calling for only one at the entry of the funerary-victory procession.

Lavinia now appears to render her 'tributary tears' (line 159), and a new action begins – the election of the emperor. Marcus Andronicus and tribunes, Saturninus, Bassianus, and vague 'others' reappear on the upper stage from the Senate-house, whence they had presumably been forced to retire in order to provide bodies for the entry of Titus (similarly, most members of that procession must have even more silently – certainly without any direction – have left to reappear above).[5] In place of the black 'funeral pomp' (176), Titus is offered 'This palliament of white and spotless hue' (182) as candidate for election as emperor. Riding with sure authority over the uneasy private murmuring of Saturninus and Bassianus, Titus asks:

> People of Rome, and people's tribunes here,
> I ask your voices and your suffrages:
> Will ye bestow them friendly on Andronicus? (217-19)

The tribunes reply that 'The people will accept whom he admits' (line 222). They do so, it seems, without the loud applause and noise we might expect to hear. However, Shakespeare withholds that acclaim for only a few lines, until Titus

5 William A. Ringler, Jr ('The Number of Actors in Shakespeare's Early Plays' *The Seventeenth-Century Stage* ed G.E. Bentley, Chicago and London 1968, pp 110-34), suggests that more actors than usual were available when the play was first performed in June 1594 because 'it was written in the uncertain and difficult period during which the Elizabethan acting companies were being re-formed, when some of them went bankrupt and others temporarily joined together' – this being reflected in the text (123-4). The later quartos and the Folio ignore the temporary 1594 luxury of 'extra' actors and make no change in their requirements.

chooses Saturnine as emperor; Marcus cries:

> With voices and applause of every sort,
> Patricians and plebeians, we create
> Lord Saturninus Rome's great emperor,
> And say 'Long live our emperor Saturnine!' (230-3)

Here the text is forceful in its implicit direction. It is hard to imagine the crowded stage remaining silent at this moment, but the three quartos print no direction here. The Folio, however, prints after Marcus's cry: 'A long Flourish till they come downe.' This is the only indication that Saturninus, Bassianus, and their attendants had entered, on the upper stage, at line 169: loud acclamation would most naturally accompany the 'long flourish.' Were we to assume that the Folio records only a post-1611 staging, the silence of the three quartos is still unlikely to have been matched by that of the crowded stage.[6]

Saturninus welcomes his new additions, honours Titus by taking the victor's daughter, Lavinia, as his empress, and gives the signal to leave in triumphant processional.

> Romans, let us go:
> Ransomless here we set our prisoners free:
> Proclaim our honours, lords, with trump and drum.
> (lines 273-5)

The quartos and Folio print no direction supporting this firm order. Once again the audience is denied the sight and sound of celebratory processional, possibly by Bassianus, who dangerously interrupts to urge his claims to Lavinia. Notwithstanding, I think it as likely and as theatrically effective that the sounds do ring out as the procession begin to leave, and that this ceremonial departure is abruptly halted by Bassianus's claim.

Saturninus's order, whether carried out or not, is quickly

6 Other formal acts are also only partially annotated, eg Titus's kneeling before the emperor (389-459). Maxwell's note to line 457 points out: 'The kneeling and rising in this scene are somewhat complicated, as Professor Ellis-Fermor points out to me. There never are any stage directions to say when the characters rise, and here there is none for Titus's kneeling either. I suppose he kneels again as soon as the Emperor enters. It would seem dramatically more effective for him to be in the same posture right from l. 415, when he is first mentioned, up to l. 459.' See also Hibbard note to I.iv.29, p 198.

lost amid the fray that breaks out. Titus's son, Mutius, killed by his father for taking Bassianus's side, is, when Saturninus has settled the quarrel by scorning Lavinia and taking Tamora for his bride, buried by his brothers' side in the tomb. No trumpets are asked to sound for him. Hardly is this done when the opening tableau is strongly recalled as Saturninus enters with 'Tamora and her two sons with the Moor at one door. Enter at the other door Bassianus and Lavinia with others' (line 398). The Folio accords Saturninus his emperor's dignity of a flourish at this entry. However, when he first enters 'aloft' to announce his choice of Tamora, no edition prints any such direction although this might seem a sufficiently formal entry to merit one (298). When he leads his party off, he declares:

> Lords, accompany
> Your noble emperor, and his lovely bride,
> Sent by the heavens for Prince Saturnine,
> Whose wisdom hath her fortune conquered.
> There shall we consummate our spousal rites. (333-7)

It would be odd if this rhetorical flourish had no musical flourish to round it off. A loud exit in state would also give Titus's brief following soliloquy sharper impact. With a politic peace made between Saturninus and Titus and his sons, the act ends to the sound of trumpets with a formal exit of all but the Moor.

This bold array of effects illustrates many of the problems posed by directions, or lack of them, for music (or, indeed, other effects) in Shakespeare (or his fellows). The text, as we have seen, can ask directly for music without there being any direction for it. On other occasions, the situation may 'demand' music because of dramatic convention or social habit (often the same thing) with neither stage direction nor indication in the spoken word. Here the danger is to look for what 'the eye of man hath not heard, the ear of man hath not seen.' Generally, I believe it is reasonable to assume that social convention ruled even where its edicts are not explicitly asked for in directions, where an audience would be disconcerted if no music were heard (as at the formal exeunt of Saturninus and his court above). Entries and departures of rulers, returns of victorious generals, triumphant or solemn processions were always musical in real life. Loud alarums were signals that guided battles; courtly ceremony had its special music; everyone's daily life had occasions for music. None the less, there remain the awkward situations when one cannot be sure if music was intended to be heard or not. Custom called for it, but 'what custom wills, in all things should we do't'; opportunities for theatrical *coups de théâtre* would be lost, and Shakespeare was not one to 'fool it so.'

The door opens to conjecture, but the interpretation of stage directions, explicit or implicit, must use conjecture. There is no absolute and final text with absolute and final directions. A putative author of the canon wrote: 'If a man shall begin with certainties, he shall end in doubts: but if he will be content to begin with doubts, he shall end in certainties.'[7] A double-edged warning as the instruction in noise is sought.

Texts change, stage business varies. Shakespeare may never have blotted a line, but that seems to have been because he often did not blot out a first version before writing a second. In a sense, he edited as he wrote, and it is hard for anyone with theatrical experience to imagine that what he wrote was held inviolate, either by himself or by the company. Music might be used in one place one year but not in that place another. Hotson may be right: when *Twelfth Night* was played at court, a place had to be found for Hales to sing, whereas in public performances further rearrangement had to be made.[8] I think it probable that more music was heard in the plays than is directly asked for in text or in directions. These indications would have gone into the prompt-book, and the printed texts that have come down to us do not include all of these. Even where printed texts do have prompt-book directions – as, for instance, those in the Folio *Titus* additional to those in the 1611 quarto – it is arguable that not all of them have been printed. J.C. Maxwell's Arden edition of *Titus* is based on the First quarto of 1594; the additional directions found in the Folio, he suggests, 'reflect the increased use of music in the early seventeenth century' (page xviii). As they consist (in the first act) of six additions of the word 'flourish' (I.i.1, 3, 149, 233, 398, 495, the last actually misplaced to the beginning of act II), three of them added to existing directions for music (lines 1, 149, 495) and the other three for a state exit (63), acclaim of the new emperor (233), and a state entry (398), when such music would be expected at any period, they more likely reflect a reliance upon a prompt-book,

7 Francis Bacon *The Advancement of Learning* 1605, I.v.8. The lure of the second half of Bacon's saying must also be guarded against.

8 Leslie Hotson *The First Night of Twelfth Night* London 1954, pp 142-3

recording practices prior to the 'early seventeenth century.' Other formal exits and entrances in the first act have been noticed where no directions were added in 1623, though 'custom' would have sanctioned them. Perhaps they were overlooked in the rough collation of the prompt-book with the Third Quarto made by the Folio's printer.[9]

Custom is flouted several times elsewhere. The presence of cornets is sometimes taken to indicate that the play was meant for an indoor theatre, the trumpet's sharp tones being suited to a public theatre: *Coriolanus* uses both. In the battle at Corioli the opposing armies are apparently differentiated by distinctive drum calls; trumpets, however, are associated only with the Romans. They ring out when Coriolanus is saluted with his new name (I.ix.65); almost immediately Aufidius enters to the sound of '*A flourish. Cornets*' (I.x.1). In Rome the distinction is lost. Trumpets herald Coriolanus's triumphant entry, but, after pausing to greet his family and Menenius, he moves off to the Senate to a flourish of cornets (II.i.160, 197).

The full and narrative stage directions for *Coriolanus* suggest that Shakespeare was trying to make up for his absence during performance preparations. Minor details are left to be settled in the theatre ('*Enter seven or eight Citizens*' II.iii.1; '*Enter three or four Conspirators of Aufidius's faction*' V.vi.8), but enough is firmly written in to suggest that this is one play that Shakespeare did know how he wanted performed. The features of its musical score can be heard even when not seen: 'from the early shouts, the drums and trumpets of battle and ovation, through the incantatory chants of "it shall be so," the routine street cries of Rome at peace, fresh panic and commotion, quiet and tension, to the "sackbuts, psalteries and fifes" and the Romans unshouting the cries that banished Martius; and, alone of the plays, it calls specifically at the end for the sounding of "A dead march."'[10] When heard and seen more closely, however, the

9 See Maxwell, n I.i.1.

10 *Coriolanus* ed Philip Brockbank, New Arden Shakespeare, London 1976, p 74. His comment on the dead march is contradicted by *King Lear*, which ends 'Exeunt, with a dead march.' The exact term is not used at the end of *Hamlet* but is not a dead march asked for by: 'Exeunt marching; after the which a peal of ordnance are shot off'? A silent close to *Richard II*, which ends with King Henry saying,

March sadly after. Grace my mournings here
In weeping this untimely bier. *Exeunt*

would be unlikely (Henry had entered to a flourish fifty lines earlier). A score may be as variously performed as any other.

Not to overplay musical analogy, *Coriolanus* might be described as a symphonic work in three movements: a prelude introducing the main themes of the work leads into the first movement proper, the battle at Corioli; the second movement is 'Coriolanus in Rome'; and the last, 'Coriolanus in exile' (Hibbard's 'overture' and *tres partes* [page 17] are, harmoniously, the same.) The prelude opens furiously: '*Enter a company of mutinous Citizens, with staves, clubs, and other weapons*' (I.i.1). Coriolanus announces his abrasive character but is quickly called away to war with the Volscians, whose leaders are briefly seen. Before the noisy battle that will fill the rest of the movement there is a quiet domestic interlude of Virgilia, Volumnia, and Valeria.

Coriolanus is the focus of action for the rest of act I. His violent bravery is orchestrated in mounting crescendos of the instruments of war and the shouts of the soldiers. '*Drum and colours*' (iv.1) bring on the Roman forces before the city of Corioli. That Aufidius's men are near pleases Coriolanus: 'Then shall we hear their 'larum, and they ours' (line 9). He orders the trumpeters: 'Come, blow thy blast' (12). They sound the parley which brings the defiant Senators to Corioli's walls; at once the noise of Aufidius's alarums from which Lartius takes 'instruction' is heard (13-22). Amid more alarums the fight begins; Coriolanus's incredible solitary exploit leads to the fall of the city. The alarums roll on even while the Roman looters scurry across the stage. Coriolanus is furious, especially as the battle is far from over:

> And hark, what noise the general makes! To him!
> There is the man of my soul's hate, Aufidius,
> Piercing our Romans. (I.v.9)[11]

There is no direction for Cominius's 'noise,' but the text is clear. There is a momentary lull in the visibly observed battle as we see Cominius in sensible withdrawal; then the battle surges into the audience's sight again as Aufidius is rescued from Coriolanus by some of his men (I.viii). In swift immediacy and unbro-

similar case could be made for *Antony and Cleopatra*.

11 The clash between the seen and the heard, involving music often, was a favourite varied theme, whether Richard II in his death-cell, Claudius's brash celebrations, or Coriolanus muffled before Aufidius's house (see below).

ken order, there follows: *'Flourish. Alarum. A retreat is sounded'* (I. ix.1), and the Romans are victorious.

Once more the volume of sound rises. Coriolanus's refusal of a tenth part of the spoils wins the sudden favour of the soldiers: *'A long flourish. They all cry "Martius! Martius!" cast up their caps and lances'* (I.ix.40). The instruments of war now play music of acclaim, and the raucous popular voice of protest that began the play and was heard among the soldiers scorning the wild sortie alone into Corioli now exuberantly applauds the new hero. Throughout the rest of the play the massed voices of the people will swing between these extremes of hooting fury and rapturous acclamation.

Coriolanus accepts their plaudits with his characteristic fusion of gritty courtesy and assertive modesty:

> May these same instruments, which you profane
> Never sound more! When drums and trumpets shall
> I'th'field prove flatterers, let courts and cities be
> Made all of false-fac'd soothing ...
> ...
>   No more, I say.
> ...
>   you shout me forth
> In acclamations hyperbolical,
> As if I loved my little should be dieted
> In praises sauced with lies. (I.ix.41-51)

Cominius accepts this only to dub him by his new name:

>   from this time,
> For what he did before Corioles, call him,
> With all th'applause and clamour of the host,
> Caius Martius Coriolanus.
> Bear th'addition nobly ever!
>   *Flourish. Trumpets sound, and drums.*
> ALL Caius Martius Coriolanus! (lines 61-6)

Thus Shakespeare has raised the volume: the music is louder and longer, and the generals join the men in a concerted crying-up of Coriolanus.

The sound falls away; weariness follows on the exhilaration of warfare; Coriolanus forgets the name of the poor man in Corioli who used him kindly: 'I am weary, yea, my memory is tired' (I.ix.90). As the Romans leave, *'Aufidius, bloody, with two or three soldiers'* (I.x.1) appears. The visual shift is balanced by the aural one from trumpets and drums to the less harsh sound: *'A flourish. Cornets.'* Such relatively subdued scenes mean much in an act of rushing noise: the cornets sound like a diminishment of the victorious trumpets of Coriolanus.

The quieter mood carries through the beginning of act II, the second movement of the 'symphony.' Menenius and the tribunes pick up the quarrels of the start of act I, but in less vehement a manner. When the ladies enter with their news of Coriolanus's return victorious, Menenius throws up his cap with an old man's, 'Hoo!' (II.i.100). It is an almost sad echo of the soldiers cheering Coriolanus and an ironic harbinger of the mob's hooting yet to come. The sounds of *'A shout and flourish'* (line 150) off-stage cut across Menenius's and Volumnia's excited but gruesome arithmetic of Coriolanus's wounds. The ugly mood of the citizens and their off-stage shouts of violence (I.i.45) that began the play change into the key of joyful welcome. The volume of sound and its sweep between hatred and near-idolatry not only help build Coriolanus's stature but just as powerfully create the turbulent background against which his life runs. Even at this triumphant moment the two tribunes are standing aside (II.i.90), and Volumnia voices a truth that has darker implications than she is aware of:

> These are the ushers of Martius. Before him
> he carries noise, and behind him he leaves tears.
> Death, that dark spirit, in's nervy arm doth lie,
> Which, being advanced, declines, and then men die.
> (lines 151-4)

He will do so until he is dead, but now he is at his apogee. A sennet sounds, a special and, to the audience, instantly recognizable series of notes used to welcome a person of distinction, a musical mark of Coriolanus's new rank. A herald reasserts the glory of his new name; again the trumpets sound, and the whole assembly roars: 'Welcome to Rome, renownèd Coriolanus!' (160) The clamour finely sets off the first of two memorable moments of quiet in the play when he first kneels to his mother and then turns to Virgilia: 'My gracious silence, hail!' (168) In all his military splendour and wearing the oaken garland of victory, he stands then, hand in hand with his wife and mother, a tableau to be recreated much later when, as victor over Rome, he spares that city at his mother's plea and at his own life's cost. Amid renewed noise the procession moves on to the Capitol, leaving the tribunes behind to mutter vituperatively.

They can do nothing for the time being but wait their chance to bring him down, while the ordinary people of Rome make 'A shower and thunder with their caps and shouts' (II. i.259).[12] The duet is carried on in the quietly sensible remarks of the officers laying out cushions in the Senate. Trumpets had cut off the quick duet of Menenius and Volumnia, announcing the great military parade in Coriolanus's honour. Now, to a sennet of cornets (presumably cornets as they sound for the end of the Senate [II. ii.154] and assuming no more switching of instruments), the first grand civic procession enters, and the long electoral debate begins that ends with Coriolanus's leaving Rome. Into this debate are woven mention of voices, tongues, cries, telling, and speaking; the sounds are also heard of all of these, rising and falling as the numbers engaged grow rapidly from small groups to larger, culminating in the savagery of the hooting mob. Time and again the 'voice' of the massed crowd makes its distinctive contribution to the bleak music of the play.

The themes of this music are clear, but often harsh. So, Coriolanus in the market-place, seeking 'if it may stand with the tune of your voices that I may be consul, I have here the customary gown' (II.iii.84-6), is, as it were, asking for a 'tune' which is out of harmony with his own music. Momentarily the tune does 'stand' for him, but it alters as these minnows, at the bidding of their degraded Triton – no longer blowing the seas to storm or calm with his conch-horn, 'being but / The horn and noise o'th'monster's' (III.i.94-5) – outrage him with their dissonant and peremptory 'shall.' The tune changes again until, in a last effort, using Hamlet's figure of the drab unpacking her heart mixed with echoes of Othello's farewell to the music of war, Coriolanus asks for the tune of Rome's changeable voices:

12 See G.K. Hunter 'Flatcaps and Bluecoats: Visual signals on the Elizabethan Stage' *Essays & Studies 1980* London 1980, pp 16-47. Also, Jean MacIntyre (University of Alberta), in 'Words, Acts, and Things: Visual Language in *Coriolanus*' *English Studies in Canada* (Winter 1983), takes up this matter in some detail.

Well, I must do't.
Away, my disposition, and possess me
Some harlot's spirit! My throat of war be turned,
Which choired with my drum, into a pipe
Small as an eunuch, or the virgin voice
That babies lull asleep! (III.ii.110-15)

His blunt military voice cannot 'pipe small'; it is a drum and trumpet that cannot, in any field, prove a flatterer. He tries to tune his own voice to 'mildly,' but the tribunes find it much easier to set the plebeians' more pliant voices to a reiterated 'din confus'd' of litanies of punishment for Coriolanus: 'To th'rock; to th'rock with him' (III.iii.75); 'It shall be so, it shall be so' (lines 106, 119); 'Our enemy is banished! He is gone! Hoo-oo! / *They all shout, and throw up their caps*' (137).

Coriolanus is a play of contrasted pairs of tableaux that use both sight and sound. Coriolanus, hand in hand with his mother and wife at two climactic moments of his life, has been glancingly noticed. Now Shakespeare offers two more. This scene of delirious citizens chanting wildly and throwing caps in the air recalls that similar one when lances and caps were thrown into the air amid cheering for the heroic fighter (I.ix.40). Now the demonstration is before an empty space, as it were; the elation is for a Coriolanus who is not there. Quickly, another tableau of contrasts is set up: the play began with '*a company of mutinous Citizens, with staves, clubs, and other weapons*' erupting on stage to say: 'First, you know Caius Martius is chief enemy to the people?' (I.i.7-8); this second movement of the play ends with the same citizens, still mutinous (might not some of them have weapons after the way in which they were lately 'beat in'? [III.i.227]), but now victorious over their 'enemy,' bustling off to see his ignominy:

Come, come, let's see him out at gates, come!
The gods preserve our noble Tribunes! Come!
(III.iii.142-3)

After the carefully patterned tumult and shouting of the first three acts, the play's last movement opens quietly with Coriolanus's farewell to his family and friends. The visual sign of his fall is made very clear when he appears 'in mean apparel, disguised and muffled' (IV.iv.1), before Aufidius's house in

Antium, from whence 'Music plays' (IV.v.1): 'A goodly house. The feast smells well, but I / Appear not like a guest' (lines 4-5). Coriolanus, lately the centre of worshipping crowds and then, perversely, of witch-hunting mobs, is now an unattached figure at the hearth. He stands muffled in a drab anonymous cloak who was used to be seen in a commanding soldier's armour, badged with blood. The festive 'music' that can be heard – it is actually the only time the word occurs in the play, which emphasizes the fact that it is 'melodious' music as against the starker rhythmic music that dominated the first three acts – signifies good cheer and fellowship. It works as much as the surly behaviour of the servants to mark Coriolanus's isolation.

After this musical pause, the action accelerates towards the final tragic action.[13] No noise of war now. The great struggles and clamorous Roman noise have made their effect. Attention now focuses on Coriolanus as victorious Volscian general and his reaction to Roman pleas for mercy; it is how Coriolanus acts as victor over his own people that matters, not how he won that victory. Briefly we see and hear the Romans about their daily affairs; Sicinius complacently notes, 'Our tradesmen singing in their shops' (IV.vi.8).[14] Scarcely has this cheerfulness broken in, however, than it is turned into cries of confusion by the fearful news of fresh Volscian attacks and of Coriolanus leading them. *'A troop of Citizens'* (line 130) scurry nervously on, trying to take back their cries of banishment (140-57). The massed choric voices have splintered into faint-hearted words; flourishing drums and trumpets are silenced; all moves to the one moment of absolute silence in the play. Volumnia bends her son's will to hers for the last time – she is aware only of that; he is aware of its far wider significance. He 'holds her by the hand silent' (V.iii.183). He tells his uncomprehending mother what she has done and asks Aufidius: 'would you have heard / A mother less? Or granted less?' (lines 93-4). With Aufidius's suave reply, 'I was mov'd withal' (194), the final action begins.

The short run to Coriolanus's death is punctuated by the two most tumultuous outbursts of instruments and voices in the

13 The manner in which this is a 'musical pause' I have discussed elsewhere: see 'Musical Pauses and the Vision Scenes' in *Shakespeare's Last Plays* ed Waldo F. McNeir and Thelma N. Greenfield, Eugene Ore 1966, pp 234-47.

14 I believe that Brockbank is correct when he takes Sicinius's words as an indication for a scene-setting of market stalls and a few tradesmen singing in them (n IV.vi.1, and p 73).

play, yet ends with the cheerless beat of a dead march. The outburst that once greeted Coriolanus as the victor over the Volscians bursts out afresh around his womenfolk to celebrate, in a curious way, Coriolanus's second withdrawal from Rome. Coriolanus is being acclaimed in his absence as the generous victor; but the plain fact that he is not there shades the Roman noise with something akin to hysteria.

This last Roman music is most carefully scored. 'Why, hark you!' (V.iv.47) cries a messenger:

> *Trumpets, hautboys, drums beat, all together*
> The trumpets, sackbuts, psalteries and fifes,
> Tabors and cymbals and the shouting Romans
> Make the sun dance. Hark you! (lines 48-50)

The messenger increases the size of the orchestra, whether from fervour of the moment or by Shakespeare's artistic licence cannot be said. He may even be speaking the truth, a truth not fully recorded in the stage direction. The sound of *'a shout within'* (50) is heard. Menenius hastens to meet the ladies:

> This morning for ten thousand of your throats
> I'd not have given a doit. Hark, how they joy!
> *Sound still with the shouts* (55-6)

This surging noise has carried through Menenius's speech. The ladies, with senators and other lords, cross the stage as the reverberant noise accompanies them. The First Senator, too hopeful, would have the noise be Rome's instruction:

> Unshout the noise that banished Martius,
> Repeal him with the welcome of his mother.
> Cry, 'Welcome, ladies, welcome!'
> ALL Welcome, ladies, welcome!
> *A flourish with drums and trumpets. Exeunt.* (V.v.4-7)

Essentially the 'welcome' is for Coriolanus, for his deed, but in stunning theatrical effect it turns out to be for Aufidius, who enters before its echoes have died away. The jubilant noise is backdrop for the downfall of Coriolanus. When, soon after the procession of welcome has left, there is heard *'Drums and trumpets sound, with great shouts of the people'* (V.vi.49), it is yet the noise of welcome, but now that of the Volscians, inspired, as always in the play, by Coriolanus: 'he returns / Splitting the air with noise' (lines 52-3). This bitter recognition by one of the conspirators for his death is answered at once by a fellow-conspirator:

> And patient fools,
> Whose children he hath slain, their base throats tear
> With giving him glory. (52-4)

It is Volumnia's remark before an earlier triumphal entry of her son's, that 'before him he carries noise, and behind him he leaves tears' (II.i.151-2), changed into another key. To the theatre audience it is, on the simplest level, the loud noise that always greets Coriolanus, whether it comes from Romans or Volscians; yet the simplest is perhaps properly the deepest level as well because, ultimately, there is nothing to choose between Roman and Volscian crowds: 'All tongues speak of him,' as Brutus said in another context (II.i.197). To both sides, Coriolanus can say:

> For your voices I have fought,
> Watched for your voices ...
> ...
> for your voices have
> Done many things, some less, some more. Your voices!
> (II.iii.125-9)

Thus, he returns to Corioli, the city of his name, *'marching with drum and colours; the Commoners being with him'* (V.vi.70). The Roman commoners cheered him in and hooted him out; those of Corioli change their cheers too: 'Kill, kill, kill, kill, kill him!' (line 131) It is akin to the sudden murder at the end of Richard Strauss's *Salome* as a nauseated Herod orders his soldiers to kill Salome; they rush to obey, and in a sudden orchestral clamour and two brutal chords she is crushed beneath their shields. Shakespeare, however, does not allow the barbaric howls to close his play. There is a coda in which the senseless calls for death subside into the recognition of a single high tragic death. The lords, as vainly as the Roman citizens, attempt to unshout the noise that killed Coriolanus: 'Hold, hold, hold, hold!' (131) Aufidius's provocation is admitted, but the deed grows upon him: 'My rage is gone, / And I am struck with sorrow' (148-9).

The final image is of Aufidius and 'three o'th'chiefest soldiers' taking up Coriolanus's body and bearing it out as the drums speak mournfully, sounding a '*dead march*' (150-6).

The dramatic poetry of *Coriolanus* tells the fortunes of its hero, and by its nature must 'avail itself to the full of those other forms of expression – spectacle, stage effects, and, above all, physical movement – which make it radically different from all other kinds of poetry ... A speech is, of course, a form of action ... The great problem that confronts the dramatic poet is that of gearing the words to those other two basic constituents of a play, the action and the characters.'[15] I have suggested how the 'music' of the play – and its connection with spectacle and action – helps this 'gearing.' Various instruments and voices differently combined make the music for *Coriolanus.* Occasionally they are heard as a powerful orchestral and choral *tutti;* at other times instruments and voices are played off against each other; sometimes single instruments answer each other singly in martial counterpoint. Late in the play the indistinguishable noise of the Romans and Volscians recapitulates the central public theme of the play's music before falling abruptly into the coda of the dead march. The voices and jubilant instruments are emblematic of the merging of the two societies into one body. It is in this single large society that Coriolanus pursues his tragic destiny.

If the play has sometimes been in danger of being silenced by the argued music, or the arguer's voice, it has not been for want of trying to envision – and hear – a performed play. My concern has been with what I construe as Shakespeare's demands for music, not the musician's satisfaction of what he thought those demands entailed. I have not stood with Granville:

> How was the Scene forlorn, and how despis'd
> When Tymon, without Musick, moraliz'd?
> Shakespears sublime in vain entic'd the Throng,
> Without the Charm of Purcel's Syren Song.[16]

Whatever the inestimable worth of Purcell's support, there

15 G.R. Hibbard 'The Forced Gait of a Shuffling Nag' *Shakespeare 1971: Proceedings of the World Shakespeare Congress Vancouver, August 1971* ed Clifford Leech and J.M.R. Margeson, Toronto 1972, pp 76-88

16 Epilogue for *The Jew of Venice,* quoted in Hazleton Spencer *Shakespeare Improved* 1927; reprinted New York 1963, p 98

remains 'Shakespeare's sublime.' Part of that sublimity is the uncommon art of marrying art to necessity in using music, sounds, noise. Thus, I end on a practical note, remarking vulgar necessity in words taken from a recent lively history of the American musical that touch upon the most received custom of all in Shakespeare's theatre:

> Most of the finest art has been made for a designated space, an occasion, a time, a place, a person, or a purpose. For centuries the best artists earned their livelihoods not by yearning, threatening suicide, or feigning epilepsy in an effort to obtain next to impossible materials, but by fulfilling precise assignments while utilizing readily available means.[17]

University of British Columbia

17 Lehman Engel *Words with Music* New York 1972, p 3

M.C. BRADBROOK

Publication and Performance in Early Stuart Drama: Jonson, Webster, Heywood

The permanence of printing may always be challenged by the penetrative force of performance. Jonson put printing first; Webster balanced performance and publication; Heywood constantly protested his reluctance to commit drama to cold print. The writer's aim will be modified by his relations with the crafts of printer and actor. Jonson had early acting experience, but was by nature a director; Webster, an exceptionally sympathetic but relatively independent citizen; Heywood, like Shakespeare, a fully professional actor and playwright who spent most of his very long working life with one company. At the court of Queen Elizabeth, small material reward came from print to Gascoigne, Spenser, or Lyly; and nobler writers who took a direct part in the social 'game' of courtly wooing, a Dyer or a Raleigh, went no further towards publication than to hang their verses on trees. As for print, they would as lief the town crier spoke their lines.

The printing of epigrams and characters, from the mock courts of Christmas Princes at the Inns of Court, came towards the turn of the century. In the reopened choristers' theatres of St Paul's and Blackfriars, verbal tilting became more lethal as the Christmas games of the lawyers were institutionalized. Law supplied playwrights, audience, and some finance. If Education might teach good manners by exposing Folly, satire became a duty and denunciation a proof of zeal. The lawyers had mainly satirized one another. Practice in whitewashing a client and blackening an opponent might be considered part of their training, and no ill feeling need remain out of court. But London was the centre of the printing trade (the Stationers' company were perfectly ruthless in destroying a university press that threatened their monopoly). The printing of plays started as a regular practice with the choristers' plays, the young lawyers' wish to display their own eloquence, the companies' need to advertise, and lack of the financial power to control their authors (as did Henslowe of the Bankside).

Until the middle of the sixteenth century, as Glynne Wickham has recently observed, plays were occasional events associated with particular festivals of the church year or with private festivities such as a wedding.[1] The 'device' for such entertainments gave a speech for the occasion to a symbolic figure whose garments and attributes 'deliver the nature of the person ... and the word the present office' (as Ben Jonson put it in describing the pageants for King James's entry to London). Commenting on this, Wickham observes:

> The concept is a difficult one to define precisely in words, largely because the visual element formed so crucial a part of it. Moreover, it incorporated a striking paradox; for while the visual component was designed to arrest attention and boldly to proclaim an idea, the form in which it was cast was often designed, like a riddle, to conceal a secret. (page 66)

The 'secret' was often some personal application; if it was in praise of the Chief Spectator, it could be a personal plea (as in some of Gascoigne's shows for Queen Elizabeth), or it could be an open secret which spectators were expected to share.

Peele's *Device of the Pageant born before Wolstan Dixi* (1585) opens the way for the pageant by a speech of homage from a Moor riding on a lynx – at once an heraldic beast of the Skinners' company and, in the imagery of the five senses, emblem of keen sight. Boys representing arts and trades, the city herself, assorted Virtues, and the River Thames extol the Lord Mayor and the queen, with additions from torch-bearing nymphs. No riddles here; but when in the Accession Day tilt a decade later Peele wrote on the familiar school theme of choosing a course of life, the characters representing Hermit, Secretary of State, and Soldier were covertly identified.[2] In Lyly's comedies, the queen

1 Glynne Wickham *Early English Stages* III, London 1981, p xvii

provided the only unambiguous figure.

Icons for public entertainments all over Europe remained extremely conservative.[3] The sophisticated for private sports sought devices – witty and new. In Ben Jonson's *The Case is Altered,* Antonio Balladino (Anthony Munday) protests, 'I do use as much stale stuff, though I say it myself, as any man does in this kind, I am sure.' He does not write to please gentlemen. Nor did Dekker, who protested at Jonson's making the genius of the City for King James's royal entry masculine, in the Roman fashion. Though played by Alleyn, this genius lacked the appeal of the maiden city, married to the hero of the day; cities, like ships, should be feminine. Ben Jonson moved into print as a dramatist when he moved from the public to the choristers' theatres. *Every Man out of his Humour* (1599), which had failed in public, was published with a dedication to the Inns of Court. Dedications were usually addressed to individuals in hope of reward; Jonson made his name in the theatres where the lawyers dominated, putting his general appeal to the kind of audience he wanted. In the 'Characters prefixed to the Action' he identified himself with their kinds of composition and instructed both readers and players in the mode of approach. Writing for boys, he could take the role of dominie, which was highly congenial to him; but in *Cynthia's Revels,* dedicated to the 'fountain of manners,' the court itself, and the most strictly verbal of his early comedies, Jonson plyed the tawse upon the great, in a manner not calculated to win their favour. Gentlemen are satirized in act I, ladies in act II; the games played include Substantive and Adjective, a Thing Done and Who Did It, a Challenge at Courtship (of the kind that Sir Toby Belch tried to teach Sir Andrew Aguecheek), and finally a Litany of Repentance. At the end, he probably used an effigy of Queen Elizabeth as a 'device' to transform the envious Macilente. A play of characters needs little action; it is a procession, a verbal parade, and therefore is as clear in print as in action.

In the opening scene, Sogliardo, 'an essential clown ... enamour'd of the name of gentleman,' is coached to be 'a Gentleman of the Time.' He must buy new clothes, swear fashion-

2 See *The Life and Minor Works of George Peele* ed David H. Horne, New Haven 1952, 178-81.

3 George R. Kernodle *From Art to Theatre* Chicago 1944, p 105. The *Ballet Comique de la Reyne* and Bruno's *Spaccie delle Bestie Triomphante,* both of 1582, supplied the bases for two Caroline masques of 1632 and 1634.

able oaths, be melancholy at meals and 'humourous' at plays; 'Ruffle your brow like a new boot, laugh at nothing but your own jests, or else as the noblemen laugh.' He should send letters of commendation to himself (a trick practised as late as 1700 by Witwoud in *The Way of the World*) and hire servants who can maintain themselves by petty theft.

Here was satiric introduction for ignorant country youths, who had been dependent on *The Book of Riddles* or *The Hundred Merry Tales* for conversation. The game of characters was played widely – Shakespeare shows Portia and Nerissa amusing themselves at the expense of the suitors in *The Merchant of Venice* (I. ii), while the 'device' of the caskets itself consists of the riddling outer objects and the 'word,' with accompanying image, each conceals. In Ben Jonson, the characters function as a group; a whole society was defined from a single point of view, that of a judicious spectator, summing up the evidence. The young lawyers were being rehearsed for a place on the bench. The little microcosm chosen, whether court, city, or lawyers' inn, reflected a moral judgment on a purely social situation.[4]

In performance, interaction of characters could be formal or minimal, which suited the choristers. Jonson uses social rituals like the drinking game in *Every Man out of his Humour* (V.iv).

His next play for the choristers, *Poetaster* (1601), antagonized the army , the law, and the stage: years later, Ben Jonson was to boast to Drummond of Hawthornden that he had written it against the lawyer-dramatist John Marston, though in his 'Apologetical Dialogue' his disclaimer was 'I named no names.' When Julia and Ovid play at being gods in order to satirize her father the emperor, Jonson comes near the dangerous heart of these private games; for the parting of these lovers, he turned however to the public stage for the popular 'device' of the second balcony scene in *Romeo and Juliet*. As a personal acknowledgment this play was dedicated to the Middle Temple's Christmas Prince, Richard Martin, who had interceded with Lord Chief Justice Popham on Jonson's behalf.

In their reply, *Satiromastix*, the players shrewdly exploited the inconsistency between Jonson's lofty contempt for 'Opinion' and his very obvious attempts to advertise himself. This same inconsistency is found among the lawyer-poets, especially in Marston's masterpiece *The Malcontent* (1604), which he offered to

4 The most famous of character books, John Earle's *Microcosmographie* (1628), was followed by, among others, Wye Saltonstall's *Picturae Loquantes* (1631).

his former opponent, Ben Jonson, proclaiming himself now both friend and admirer. Marston had begun to print very early, but had insured himself against scorn by dedicating his first play to Nobody. The two sides of the malcontent himself, the noble banished duke, Altofront, and his disguised self, the bitter fool, owe a great deal to Hamlet and his antic disposition, but they also resemble the two sides of a satirist. The character Malevole is given at the start as a 'monster' (I.iii.16-20). The part, played by boys, attracted Burbage, and the men's company took it over. The play was in print, and they were entitled to do so; Marston and Webster supplied some additions. The company led by Burbage and Shakespeare had learnt what Kenneth Muir termed 'Shakespeare's Open Secret.'[5] Performance itself had shown that the apparent inconsistencies, contradictions, unexplained changes could add depth and integrity to the actor's role; and from the leading part might extend to the whole play. Interplay between the 'delightful Proteus,' Burbage, and the rest grew out of a company where the playwright was also a supporting actor. The non-verbal aspects were drawn from a text rich in all the complicated energies it generated. The gaps allow the actor to 'breathe' inside his part; it is not possible to pluck out the heart of Hamlet's mystery. And in the dynamics of performance, as Melchiori has observed in translating the text, 'gestures, colours, the physical presence of the actors, sounds, music, noises (take a slap for example) all play their part.'[6] Recently the dynamics of contradiction have been traced in the philosophy of Shakespeare's time.[7]

These could be simplified in the 'perspective picture.' a device which showed an anamorphic image of death turning into love, mirth into grief; such might serve to suggest much deeper mysteries, as when Cleopatra sees Antony as one way like a Gorgon, the other way a Mars. The old opposition of image and 'word' had become fused; the malcontent as played by Burbage must have been in sharpest contrast to the successful choristers' version. Ironic play on this fact is essential to the induction which was among the earliest printed works of John

5 *Shakespeare Survey* 34, ed Stanley Wells, Cambridge 1981

6 Giorgio Melchiori 'Translating Shakespeare: An Italian View' *Shakespeare Translation* 5, Tokyo 1978, p 20

7 See Norman Rabkin *Shakespeare and the Common Understanding* Berkeley 1976; and Robert Grudin *Mighty Opposites: Shakespeare and Contrariety* Berkeley 1979.

Webster. The playgoers who sit in judgment are also 'characterized' – that is, satirized. It is notable that Shakespeare himself uses the definition of 'characterists' ironically – as when Iago satirizes the Good Housewife – in front of Emilia; or Cornwall draws the character of a blunt man to discredit Kent.[8] To understand such 'open' writing, what was printed had to be reconstructed as full performance by the reader, though implicitly given.

The Malcontent achieved three editions in the course of 1604. The fame of the London theatres had built up a market for plays so that even statesmen like the Earl of Devonshire could amass a good library for 'recreation.' Before the reign of Elizabeth, twenty-seven plays only had been printed; no less than 103 of the 168 printed in her reign had appeared after 1590.[9] Ben Jonson's new claim for the dignity of the form was being justified.

Shakespeare's gentle art of feeding his conception of the play in performance to the actor-reader through the implications of his language gave to the audience that kind of involvement usually generated by special occasions – such as the appeals in the choruses of *King Henry V*, and that which the Essex conspiracy tried to exploit by a command performance of *King Richard II*. Shakespeare sometimes seems to have authorized a 'witty' text, like *Titus Andronicus* (1594) or *Love's Labour's Lost* (1598), but most were retained by his company, unless some unscrupulous 'stolen and surreptitious copies' appeared.

Webster's second incursion into print in the year 1604 was the 'Ode' he contributed to Stephen Harrison's *The Arches of Triumph*, a set of fine engravings celebrating the seven arches built for the *Magnificent Entertainment* of King James's entry to London. Webster makes three significant points; whilst memories of joys are transient, memories of sorrow abide; the stone arches permanently commemorating cruel Roman wars are compared with Harrison's painted woodwork. Yet the common joys of that great national celebration, in which the city represented the whole kingdom's relief that civil war had been averted,[10] have

8 The 'Character of a Blunt Man' is one of Earle's most penetrating satires.

9 H.S. Bennett *English Books and Readers 1558-1603* Cambridge 1964, p 255

10 See M.C. Bradbrook 'The Politics of Pageantry' *Poetry and Drama: Essays in Honour of Harold Brooks* ed A. Coleman and A. Hammond, London 1981.

been captured, 'giving them new life when they were dead.' *Life,* the quality for which actors were praised, could be preserved even for those parts of the occasion which were not verbal; the work of his 'good countryman and friend' challenges that which Folly imputes only to strangers (London as Troynovant perhaps assisted in this bold claim).

> Perfection must be bold, with front upright,
> Though Envy gnash her teeth, whilst she would bite.

This final 'device' or icon of Webster's own creation was to be contradicted two years later when, in publishing the text of his court masque, *Hymenaei,* Jonson confessed that Envy could not be eliminated:

> Only the envy was that it lasted not still, or, now it is past, cannot by imagination, much less by description, be recovered to a part of that spirit it had in the gliding by.

Later he was to quarrel with his collaborator, Inigo Jones, whom he wished to demote to coadjutor. At the court, where the chief performers did not speak but royalty appeared in some divine epiphany to dance, there was little chance that the 'word,' spoken by their servants, would win priority, although the text was probably printed as a sort of program and given to the king – this certainly happened to the mayoral Triumphs, where the playwright employed for the 'device' now contracted with the Livery company for printing some five hundred copies.

The next of Shakespeare's tragedies to appear in print came from the press of a young man who was Webster's contemporary, friend, and fellow parishioner of St Sepulchre's, who might also be seen as the first craftsman from the printing house to collaborate with actor and playwright. Nicholas Okes, apprenticed at Christmas 1595 to Shakespeare's fellow townsman, Richard Field, who had just printed *The Rape of Lucrece* (Nicholas was to reprint it a dozen years later), set up business in 1606 at the sign of the Hand near Holborn Bridge with one press, two assistants, and a scanty supply of type. Through the close work of Peter Blayney, we now know that Okes specialized in the printing of single plays; more is known about the detailed working of his press during the first two years of his trading than of any other printer of the time.[11] It is too early to estimate the general bibliographical effect of Blayney's work; but Okes's quarto of *King Lear* (1608) was to leave a deep impress upon the mind of John Webster. The world of madmen, where identity is lost, touches the world of the 'characterist' only when Mad Tom describes his other 'self,' a 'serving man proud of heart.' In those scenes where Lear, his Fool, and Mad Tom achieve a unity of the outcasts, we reach a world that is also the obverse of the satirist and that of the royal masquers (who were all dressed alike, a band of supernatural unity). It supplied Webster with a new tragic vision, which was to combine with his training among the lawyers in a masterpiece that Okes published four years later, *The White Devil* (1612).

The year 1608, which saw the closing of the choristers' theatres and the publication of *King Lear*, saw also the first translation of Theophrastus, supposed model for the characterists. The ambitious Puritan cleric Joseph Hall, who had begun his career by a quarrel with Marston, added to this volume his own offering of incense at the shrine of James I, in his character of a Good Magistrate:

> He is the ground of good laws; the refuge of misery; the comet of the guilty; the paymaster of good deserts; the champion of justice; the patron of poets; the tutor of the church; the father of his country; and as it were another God upon earth.[12]

This voice, emerging among abrasive epithets, 'stabbing similes,' and sharp epigrams of a satirist, has the effect of a masquer appearing after a grotesque antimasque – strangely and perhaps unintentionally dramatic.

Another portrait of James had caused the closure of the choristers' theatres, and on the public stages the court masque had become the device for presenting depravity, *The Revenger's Tragedy* being a play of the king's own company.

The King's men also staged Jonson's *Volpone*; the alterna-

11 Peter W.M. Blayney *The Texts of 'King Lear' and Their Origin*; vol I *Nicholas Okes and the First Quarto* Cambridge 1982. Okes was the son of a horner (ie a man who pasted a sheet of paper with the alphabet and the Lord's Prayer on a board and covered it with sheeting of horn, as a child's first reader). He was possibly the grandson of Nicholas Okes, lute player, who in 1561 received payment for his part in a Lord Mayor's Triumph (*Malone Society Collections* III.41).

12 Quoted from T.F. Kinlock *The Life and Works of Joseph Hall* London 1951, p 202. Hall's *Vergidemiae*, which initiated the quarrel with Marston, appeared in 1597.

tion of godlike powers revealed in the court masque with city vice revealed in 'Venice' was later to be introduced into the masque itself by the new 'device' of the antimasque, first supplied by Jonson in 1609.

It is only recently that the 'clashing tones' and 'horrid laughter' of Webster's tragedies have been recognized as achieving a complex unity through performance.[13] The disjunctions and changes of tone and direction which critics found disruptive make these the most actable of Jacobean plays after Shakespeare's, and they are now freqently revived. Webster, though not an actor, was the first in publishing his text to praise the leading actor by name; later he was the first also to append the names of the actors to their role.[14] He had begun his career in collaboration with Heywood, Dekker, and other popular writers. (Dekker's account of the *Magnificent Entertainment* of 1604 includes sentiments in the commentary that are very close to Webster's 'Ode.') Later he was to work with the clown William Rowley, leader of the Queen's men (who also worked with Middleton and Heywood). Yet Webster had been entered at the Middle Temple and collaborated with Marston; as the son of a wealthy coachmaker he was poised uncertainly between citizen and legal 'wit.'

In the very carefully phrased note 'To the Reader' prefixed to *The White Devil* (1612), Webster recorded his good opinion of playwrights whom he distinguished for style, works, and composition (Chapman, Jonson, Beaumont and Fletcher) and the 'right happy and copious industry' of his friends 'Master Shakespeare, Master Dekker and Master Heywood.' *Industry* was the word for craftsmen; these were men writing for performance, whose works were to be met only in the theatre. Dekker had hopefully praised his friend's 'brave triumphs of industry and poetry' before *The White Devil* made its début upon the boards of the Red Bull Theatre.[15]

13 See Jacqueline Pearson *Tragedy and Tragicomedy in the Plays of John Webster* Manchester 1908; and Nicholas Brooke *Horrid Laughter* London 1979, chap 4, which is particularly concerned with production. Compare Michael Scott *The Plays of John Marston* London 1978.

14 Praise of Richard Perkins comes at the end of *The White Devil;* he played Flamineo. The actors' names precede *The Duchess of Malfi.*

15 In 1609 two of Shakespeare's fashionable works had been pirated – the Sonnets; and *Troilus and Cressida,* published by a pair of young stationers. W.R. Elton thinks Marston may have procured the copy from his inn. Dekker's praise comes in his dedication of *If it be Not Good ...*

Webster, heroically attempting to unite the sophisticated style of the Inns of court playwrights in their intimate roofed playhouses with the spectacle and dramatic range of the open stages, had worked slowly; he confessed: 'I do not write with a goosequill winged with two feathers' – as in the 'Apologetical Dialogue' appended to *Poetaster*. Jonson, charged that he will scarce bring forth a play a year, had replied 'Tis true! I would they could not say that I did that!' The pains of a writer for print did not chime with the quick extemporizing expected on the boards. In *Satiromastix* Jonson had been shown painfully beating out an ode to spontaneity; a detractor was later to characterize Webster scratching his head, twisting his mouth, like a figure from an antimasque at Blackfriars.[16]

Webster's own 'full and heightened style' is so burnished that every word sparkles, most of them, like Chapman's, being adapted and transformed from reading in modern writers. His story too, like Chapman's, is taken from modern history, an innovation in tragedy. The scene of railing between Ludovico and Flamineo (III.iii) is in the style of Marston his ally, like his 'stabbing similes' and his disjunctive leaps. On the other hand, he had not neglected spectacle. The six ambassadors who attend Vittoria's trial appear later at the election of the pope wearing the insignia of noble Orders – the Garter, the St Michel, the Saint Esprit, whose holy emblems might have drawn the rebuke that later Sir Henry Wotton was to administer on the copying of noble insignia in Shakespeare's *King Henry VIII* (1613) '... sufficient ... to make greatness very familiar if not ridiculous.' The gorgeous scene at the wedding tourney (with the Medici disguised as a Moor, his companions in religious habits) must have been very expensive to produce. Yet the ferocious and surrealist fable, the deep uncertainty of the very natures of Vittoria, Monticelso, or Florence, leave at the core of the play a Shakespearian mystery.

Webster blamed the weather and the audience for his play's failure, rather inconsequently comparing groundlings to those ignorant readers who go to bookshops in search of new books, not good ones. He himself, with the help of Nicholas Okes, sent it to those same bookshops, complaining that he

16 Henry Fitzjeffrey of Lincoln's Inn; printed in *Certain Elegies done by Sundry Excellent Wits* as 'Notes from Blackfriars' (1618). See M.C. Bradbrook *John Webster, Citizen and Dramatist* London 1980, chap 8, for Webster's quarrel with the lawyers about acting.

would really have preferred to write classical closet drama; but the public won't even consider *that.* Disappointment and proud self-justification give Webster a distinctly Jonsonian accent here. His next tragedy, *The Duchess of Malfi,* succeeded with the King's men, and was therefore withheld from publication.

His best-selling work was the anonymous thirty-two characters contributed to the sixth edition of Sir Thomas Overbury's *A Wife* (1615), which carried as subtitle, '... Many witty characters and conceited news written by himself and other learned Gentlemen his friends.' This best seller was to furnish the model for one of the most popular forms of the century. It was 'Overbury,' not Joseph Hall, who provided a definition of what a character was – squared out 'by our English level.' Not a hieroglyph, *imprese,* or emblem, but

> ... it is a picture (real or personal) quaintly drawn in various colours all of them heightened by one shadowing. It is a quick and soft touch of many strings, all shutting up in one musical close; it is wit's descant on any plainsong.

This has about as much resemblance to Theophrastus as Renaissance popular drama to classical plays.

When Webster and Overbury's other friends in the Middle Temple collectively built up his posthumous work, they were using the old confident form of surveying and judging the social scene to probe an infamous history of black magic and brutal murder, which all the plots of revenge plays could scarcely outgo. The net was already closing on those who in 1613 had poisoned Overbury, then a prisoner in the Tower of London. Suspicion pointed at the Lord Chamberlain, patron of all poets for court performance, and his wife – the Earl and Countess of Somerset. Next year they stood trial before the House of Lords[17] and were convicted of a crime which cast its shadow even upon the Crown itself.

A Wife had been reputedly given to the earl by Overbury as an ideal that would deter him from pursuing Frances Howard, then Countess of Essex; this had roused her murderous rage. Webster had also presented the king's favourite with his elegy for Prince Henry, *A Monumental Column,* as an example of

17 For the Overbury murder, see William McElwee *The Murder of Sir Thomas Overbury* London 1952; and Beatrice White *Cast of Ravens* London 1965. Sir Nicholas Overbury, Thomas's father, was a bencher of the Middle Temple. The fullest edition of *A Wife* is that by James E. Savage *The Conceited Newes of Sir Thomas Overbury and his Friends* Gainesville Fla 1968.

good life. *A Wife* was therefore an item in that court news which for three years buzzed round the earl and countess; and in editing this volume (or at all events contributing the biggest share to the enlarged edition), Webster was joining such famous contributors as Sir Henry Wotton, who wrote 'The Character of a Happy Life,' and John Donne, 'The Character of a Dunce.' His successful tragedy, *The Duchess of Malfi,* had not only opened with three character sketches of the main figures; it had continued in a dark atmosphere of rumour and hidden menace which reflects the atmosphere of the English court; it had incorporated and transformed some material from *A Monumental Column.* The duchess faces immolation as 'a loving wife' (IV.i.73-4), but her secret death in prison is stigmatized as 'murder.' The fourth act, with its unearthly rituals, its chorus of madmen, makes Shakespearian demands on audience and actors for which the 'characters' of the opening scene had served only as prologue. It may be that Webster felt when the truth was exposed that life had overtaken art; he wrote no more in this vein for the stage. Jonson, too, after 1616 retired from the public stages; he also published his collected *Works* in folio, carefully expunging from *Hymenaei,* written a decade earlier to celebrate her first nuptials, the name of Frances Howard.

Among his contributions to this prestigious volume of Overburian 'characters' Webster included the 'Character of an Excellent Actor' and the nostalgic 'Character of a Fair and Happy Milkmaid,' echoing the elegaic note of his tragedy.[18] It is the note of mourning; the milkmaid hopes to be buried in the spring.

Webster praises the 'life,' the energy of good actors; their 'full and significant action of the body' charms the audience, till a man of thought might apprehend 'the Ghosts of our ancient Heroes walked again,' whilst their speaking improves the art of the poet: 'for what in the poet is but ditty, in him is both ditty and music,'

> He is much affected to Painting, and 'tis question whether that make him an excellent Player, or his Playing an exquisite Painter.[19]

18 *The White Devil* V.iv.95-104; *The Duchess of Malfi* III.v.18-21; IV.ii.12-14. The character was further known from its use in Izaac Walton's *Compleat Angler.*

The pictures here given of the court include the game of Conceited Newes, which Jonson had satirized some years before in his epigram on 'The Court Pucelle,' whose chamber is 'the very pit / Where fight the prime cocks of the game for a wit'[20] – one set of news being contradicted by the next. Webster's own 'Character of a Courtier' observes, 'The substance of his discourse is news ... he is not, if he be out of court; but like a fish breathes destruction, if out of his element.' Among the 'News from Court' in Webster's edition of 'Overbury' is the daring affirmation:

> That men's loves are their affliction. That titles of honour are rattles to still ambition. That to be a King is Fame's butt, and fear's quiver. That the souls of women and lovers are wrapped in the portmanque of their senses.

Somerset had been given his earldom to make him a fit match for the Countess of Essex; 'Fame's butt ... fear's quiver,' quibbling on the damage inflicted on the king and his notorious fear of physical attack, offers the complete refutation to Joseph Hall's encomium. The next edition of 'Overbury' contained elegies on the now-acknowledged fact of his murder, a denunciation of 'the clean contrary wife,' and a salute to Overbury's marriage to immortality, through his poem.

The last work which Webster published through his friend Nicholas Okes was *Monuments of Honour*, a mayoral Triumph which contained more criticism of the Crown, in 'wits descant' on the traditional plainsong of the old devices.[21] In the year previous to this, 1623, the year of Shakespeare's First Folio, he had given Okes the text of *The Duchess of Malfi*, for which young John Ford of the Middle Temple wrote verses of commendation based on Jonson's tribute to Shakespeare. After placing Shakespeare above the Greeks and Romans, Jonson wrote:

19 The painters and limners of the period who congregated near Webster's home have recently been studied by Mary Edmond (The Walpole Society, vol 47, 1978-80). Many were rather what we should call decorative painters than picture makers; like Shakespeare and Burbage, devisers of *imprese* for tourneys, etc.

20 For this poem, see Herford and Simpson *The Works of Ben Jonson* VIII, Oxford 1952, p 222. Savage identifies the Pucelle with Cicely Bulstrode and the author of the 'Foreign News' with Sir Henry Wotton. Lady Southwell contributed to the ninth edition.

21 See the passages cited in nn 10 and 16 above.

Thou art a Moniment without a tomb
And art alive still, while thy book doth live,
And we have wits to read, and praise to give.

Ford wrote of Webster:

Crown him a poet whom nor Rome nor Greece
Transcend in all theirs, for a masterpiece:
In which, while words and matter change, and men
act one another, he, from whose clear pen
They all took life, to memory hath lent
A lasting fame, to raise his monument.

Middleton, the London pageant poet, Rowley, leader of the Queen's men and Webster's collaborator, also assured Webster the sort of 'monument' that he had offered the Lord Mayor, that his friends had offered Overbury – the monument of print.

Another member of the Queen's men succeeded Webster and Middleton in the devising of city triumphs; this was Thomas Heywood, longest-lived and most productive playwright of his time, who has now sunk into neglect. His plays have not been edited since 1874; his other works have not been edited at all. This, however, might not have disturbed him, for print was not his medium.

For thirty-nine years, from 1602 till his death in 1641, Heywood was an actor and sharer in the company successively under the patronage of the Earl of Worcester, Queen Anne, the queen of Bohemia, and Queen Henrietta; he must have given the kind of continuity that John Heminges gave to Shakespeare's company. Webster calls him 'beloved friend'; their elegies for Prince Henry had been bound up together with Tourneur's and printed, of course, by Nicholas Okes. Heywood's was dedicated to Worcester.

The son of a Lincolnshire parson, descended from minor gentry of Mottram, Cheshire, Heywood became as completely a Londoner as Peele, Munday, or Dekker. No stories clustered round him; he, however, could describe all the dramatists by their familiar names – Will, Ben, Kit, and the rest – and write a *General (though Summary) Description of all the Poets both foreign and modern,* with their 'portraits,' which was never printed. He repeatedly protested that he did not seek publication,[22] but if his plays were taken down in shorthand and wretchedly set out, he would print by agreement with his company. In his *Apology for Actors* (1613), where he speaks on behalf of his friends and is supported by their commendations, he thanks Nicholas Okes for being 'so careful and industrious, so serious and laborious to do the author all rights of the press' while castigating William Jaggard for unauthorized printing of two of his songs in an edition of *The Passionate Pilgrim* attributed entirely to William Shakespeare – with which, Heywood said, Shakespeare was 'much offended.' Elsewhere he complained of a schoolmaster in West Ham who had appropriated his Latin translations.[23]

In a prefatory note before *The English Traveller*, published in 1633 when he was nearly sixty, Heywood is more explicit than any other playwright of his day. He states that he had a hand 'or main finger' in 220 plays (the number surviving is now twenty). His plays 'are not exposed unto the world in volumes to bear the titles of works (as others)' for three reasons. First, some 'by shifting and change of companies' are lost; others are held by actors who want the exclusive right; lastly, Heywood has no ambition to be 'in this kind voluminously read.'

The English Traveller was for Heywood an exceptional play; as the prologue says, 'He only tries if once bare lines will bear it.' There is no spectacle, no combat, marriage, not so much as song, dance, or masque. It reworks a theme he had used all his life, the deceived husband or lover who forgives his erring spouse or mistress. From Matthew Shore in the early *King Edward IV*, through the heroes of *A Woman Killed with Kindness* (1604) to the delicate portraits of Geraldine and Old Wincot in *The English Traveller*, he was to proceed to the great triumph of *Love's Mistress* (1634), the story of Cupid and Psyche, which was the queen's birthday offering to the king, and staged for the court by Inigo Jones. This was far above the level to which Heywood usually aspired, but it is a misnomer to call his work

22 See the prologue to *If you Know not Me, you Know Nobody*, the preface to *The Rape of Lucrece*, the prologue to *A Challenge for Beauty*. The epilogue to *The Royal King and the Loyal Subject* repeats the apology of the preface to *The Four Prentices of London*: 'This play is old' ... but then,

What's now out of date, who is't can tell
But it may come in fashion and suit well?

23 See A.M. Clark *Thomas Heywood, Dramatist and Miscellanist* Oxford 1930, pp 80-2.

'bourgeois tragedy'; the family feels its corporate unity shattered by the lady's betrayal; in the plot, all the servants play a significant role; their loyalty is that of the country household. Among the swampy miscellanies which Heywood compiled in his later years, *The Hierarchy of the Blessed Angels,* dedicated to the Catholic queen, reduces the whole universe to a household centre.

In addition to these miscellanies, some of which were in folio, Heywood wrote four mayoral Triumphs during the 1630s for which his motto on the title page was *Redeunt Spectacula* (in this, he deputized for Ben Jonson who, as city chronologer, should have been writing them).

The basic reason for Heywood's not publishing his dramas was none of the three given in *An Apology for Actors* but rather that Heywood thought pictorially, in so far as he 'thought' at all. He enjoyed that instinctive sympathy and rapport with his audience and his fellow actors which is the theatre's especial gift. Modern critics like T.S. Eliot and L.C. Knights, who ignore the dimension given by performance, dismiss him.[24] For Heywood a play, though dynamic, had the dual components of the 'device.'

An Apology for Actors emphasizes the need to *see* a play:

> To see, as I have seen, Hercules in his own shape hunting the Boar, knocking down the Bull, taming the Hart, fighting with the Hydra, murdering Geryon, slaughtering Diomed, wounding the Stimphalides, killing the Centaurs, pashing the Lion, squeezing the Dragon, dragging Cerberus in chains, and lastly on his Pyramides writing *Nil Ultra,* O these were sights to make an Alexander.
>
> (pages 20-1)

The argument from example had been Philip Sidney's, but Heywood not only rejoiced in the effectiveness of 'inexplicable dumb shows and noise' which Sidney rejected; as dramatist of the Red Bull, he also rejoiced in the mixture of hornpipes and funerals. His printed texts are but as scores for orchestra, or scenarios – Lamb termed him a prose Shakespeare – but what he lacks is precisely the poet's power to integrate the 'activities' with the actual texture of the writing itself.

24 'The sensibility is merely that of ordinary persons in ordinary life ... of those of Heywood's plays which are worth reading, each is worth reading for itself.' T.S. Eliot *Elizabethan Essays* London 1934, p 107. Knights uses a Leavisite approach to Heywood in chap VIII of his *Drama and Society in the Age of Jonson* London 1937.

He does not argue the case for acting but presents the grand theatres of the ancient world, the careers of ancient actors, as a herald might blazon a noble ancestry. Webster says he has erected 'monumental theatres' from ancient ruins. In the theatre he intuitively adopts a structure that is absent from his other writing. *The Four Prentices of London,* his early and notorious romance (Beaumont was to parody it in *The Knight of the Burning Pestle*) does not work like a dream play of pure enchantment, such as Peele's *The Old Wives' Tale.* It is true that Godfrey of Bulloigne, one of the Nine Worthies, and his three brothers begin their adventures in exile as London prentices, that one shipwreck lands them as far apart as the very bounds of Europe – to meet as crowned kings and conquerors of Jerusalem. Yet the adventures are worked out with the logic of modern science fiction and in the same manner as the balanced plots and sub-plots of his later plays. There is not only a balance between the main story and the melodramatic sub-plot of *A Woman Killed with Kindness,* but both are perhaps meant to contrast with the exotic violence of the King's men's great success of the same year, *Othello.* In presenting a double bill at court before Queen Anne and the Prince of Wales in 1612, *The Rape of Lucrece* was combined with *The Silver Age* – that is, the story of Amphytrion, the innocent adultery that ensured the birth of Hercules, an implicit contrast with the story of the rape. In these matters Heywood acquired increasing skill, without forgoing his earlier theatrical material. In *Love's Mistress,* the clown purloins what he takes to be Psyche's Box of Beauty (it is a replica, substituted by Cupid) and paints his face, unconsciously, with black spots, recalling the spotted Conscience of Robert Wilson's *Three Lords and Three Ladies of London* (1588). As the leading men of Heywood's company were clowns, he had always to find them a part; but if this sometimes means that the plays read as if written for as well as by Bully Bottom, the stage effect can be different.

In Heywood the actor controlled the writer; structure evolved for performance. In the passage quoted from *An Apology for Actors,* the excitement of the actor remembering the adventures of Hercules as he had both written and played them in *The Silver Age* and *The Brazen Age* can be felt in the climactic build of the sentence. Although Heywood objected to thefts by printers, he himself had no scruples in borrowing from the plays he heard only in the theatre, more especially those of

Shakespeare, which evidently stuck in his memory.

The Rape of Lucrece (1607) makes the clashing tones of Webster sound positively harmonious by contrast. Nicholas Okes had reprinted Shakespeare's rhetorical poem that same year – perhaps it was used in the theatre for exercises, as the Sonnets are used today by the Royal Shakespeare Company.

The poem contains a bashful servant whom Lucrece sends to summon her husband after the rape. In Heywood, the clown, who is given the Shakespearian name of Pompey, is shown revealing in a three-man catch what he must not say; and this immediately precedes the tragic death scene of Lucrece.

VALERIUS Did he take fair Lucrece by the toe?
HORATIUS Toe, man?
VALERIUS Ay, man.
CLOWN Ha, ha, ha, ha, man.
HORATIUS And further did he strive to go?
CLOWN Go, man?
HORATIUS Ay, man.
CLOWN Ha, ha, ha, ha, man fa derry down, ha fa derry down.

This perhaps does not differ from the jig which followed *Julius Caesar* at the Globe; the crowd may not have distinguished it from the Clown in *Anthony and Cleopatra* or the Porter in *Macbeth.* When 'the stranger who acted Valerius' added new songs, Heywood printed them, including that Latin ditty, 'The Cries of Rome,' which advertised 'Salt, salt, white Worcestershire salt!' *The Rape of Lucrece* also contained Scevola thrusting his hand in the fire, Horatius at the bridge, and a final duel in which Tarquin and Brutus kill each other. Perhaps the most serious lines in the play are those in which three nobles discuss the misgovernment of the Tarquins, and Lucrece's husband advises 'harmless sports' as a protection in bad times. 'So shall we seem offenceless and live safe.' In *An Apology for Actors* (where this story is cited as a remedy against lust) Cicero is quoted as telling the ruler that plays kept the subject harmlessly employed, when otherwise they might be tempted into sedition. Tullia, who shows distinct traits of both Goneril and Lady Macbeth, at one point exclaims, 'There is no earth in me, I am all air and fire!' *The Four Ages*, a secular equivalent of the craft cycles which runs to five plays, starting with the birth of Jupiter, includes the reworking of material from earlier plays and more lines from the Globe. Saturn's wife, preparing to sacrifice the infant Jupiter at her husband's command, exclaims, 'I'll kiss thee ere I kill thee'; Medea invokes a

> Goddess of witchcraft and dark ceremony
> To whom the elves of hills, of brooks, of groves,
> Of standing lakes and caverns vaulted deep
> Are minister, three-headed Hecate ...

Neither *Othello* nor *The Tempest* were yet in print; Sinon's 'A horse, a horse!' capped by Pyrrhus's 'Ten kingdoms for a horse to enter Troy!' might be justified since the cry of Richard III had become common property. The conclusion of the series – which required the co-operation of the two companies, owing to the size of the cast – shows the death of all participants in the Trojan War except Ulysses and Aeneas, who is instructed (in another borrowing) by the Ghost of Hector –

> Heu, fuge, nata dea; teque his pater eripe flammis

– to set out for the founding of Rome and London, the New Troy. Heywood's reshaping of earlier theatrical devices may have been a reason for avoiding print, but it did not prevent his response to new styles. When in 1615 he published *The Four Prentices of London,* where, to the blare of drums and trumpets, the grand old circus parade moves in strict if gaudy symmetry, he apologized for 'my first practice ... as plays were then, some fifteen or sixteen years ago, it was then in the fashion.' Since those days he had progressed to Medea hanging in the heavens surrounded with 'strange fiery works,' and nearly twenty years later, in *Love's Mistress,* he was to provide a stage equivalent for Quarles's *Emblems,* the loves of Amor and Anima, published that same year.

The sub-plot of *The English Traveller* combines a Plautine story with a beast fable (Reynard the Fox fixes a coxcomb on the head of the Old Lion, subverting the Lion's whelp) and both with the popular theme of the London Prodigal, which he had treated before in *The Wise Woman of Hogsdon.* He can write a duel for two railers (Sinon and Thersites in *The Iron Age,* who greet each other as 'urchin' and 'toad'), but he was never in his life guilty of a witticism.[25] Saturn becomes only a king of Crete; Plutus comes not from Tartarus but Tartary, with a train of camels. In the four mayoral Triumphs of the thirties, Heywood put London always at the centre and was tacitly critical of the court simply by ignoring it. He could revive for the Puritan Haberdashers their patron St Katherine; he worked happily with Gerard Christmas, the king's painter for the navy, and collaborated with him in designing the figures and scroll-work for *The Sovereign of the Seas,* publishing in 1637 *A True Description of His Majesty's Royal Ship.* Christmas prepared the devices for the mayoral Triumphs; that of 1635 featured a big water show and parodied the royal masque of the previous year, *Coelum Britannicum.* The last Triumph, *London's Peaceable Estate* (1640), celebrated the city's overseas plantations in Ireland, Virginia, and the Bermudas; the River Nile provided almost Websterian fable; but there was also direct and poignant warning of the dangers ahead – which the court had recognized from another point of view in *Salmacida Spolia,* the last masque. Nicholas Okes was succeeded by John; they continued to print Heywood, who, fortunately for himself, was buried in his parish church of St James, Clerkenwell, before the king raised his standard at Nottingham and the Londoners closed the theatres. Nicholas was buried in St Bartholomew the Less 11 April 1645.

The range of Jonson's work demands to be seen as a whole; it is only as background that Webster's minor works (including *The Devil's Law Case*) deserve to be set beside his two masterpieces; but with Heywood there is a case for looking at what his age most applauded and which today presents the most difficult reading. For it is in his spectacular work rather than in *A Woman Killed with Kindness* and *The English Traveller* that the collaboration with Okes and Rowley, or with Webster, may with labour be reconstructed.[26] When a detractor taunted Webster as 'the playwright-cartwright,' he was demoting the member of the powerful Merchant Taylors' company, but it was a craftsman's fellowship who erected the monument of the First Folio 'only to keep the memory of so worthy a friend and fellow

25 Heywood is guiltless of the 'stabbing simile,' that favourite tool of the satirist, of Marston and Webster – which also survived as late as Witwoud in *The Way of the World.* Millamant is driven to cry, 'Truce to your similitudes!' (2.1)

26 See my article 'Thomas Heywood: Shakespeare's Shadow' *Essays in Theatre* I (University of Guelph, November 1982) 1.

alive, as was our Shakespeare.' Webster and Heywood shared the spirit that prompted this enterprise – which none the less, without the example of Ben Jonson's Folio, might not have appeared. (The only other folio of plays to appear was that of Beaumont and Fletcher in 1647; for the succeeding age, these made up English drama.) The collective origins that inhibited print in Shakespeare's case, but his alone, also eventually ensured publication.

Cambridge